OPPOSING VIEWPOINTS® SERIES

| Russia

Other Books of Related Interest:

Opposing Viewpoints Series
American Values

Civil Liberties

Cuba

North and South Korea

At Issue Series
Does the World Hate the United States?

Drones

Is China's Economic Growth a Threat to America?

WikiLeaks

Current Controversies Series
Espionage and Intelligence

Human Trafficking

Importing from China

Politics and Religion

"Congress shall make no law . . . abridging the freedom of speech, or of the press."

First Amendment to the US Constitution

The basic foundation of our democracy is the First Amendment guarantee of freedom of expression. The Opposing Viewpoints series is dedicated to the concept of this basic freedom and the idea that it is more important to practice it than to enshrine it.

OPPOSING VIEWPOINTS® SERIES

❙ Russia

David Haugen and Susan Musser, Book Editors

GREENHAVEN PRESS
A part of Gale, Cengage Learning

GALE
CENGAGE Learning·

Detroit • New York • San Francisco • New Haven, Conn • Waterville, Maine • London

Elizabeth Des Chenes, *Director, Content Strategy*
Cynthia Sanner, *Publisher*
Douglas Dentino, *Manager New Product*

© 2014 Greenhaven Press, a part of Gale, Cengage Learning.

Articles in Greenhaven Press anthologies are often edited for length to meet page requirements. In addition, original titles of these works are changed to clearly present the main thesis and to explicitly indicate the author's opinion. Every effort is made to ensure that Greenhaven Press accurately reflects the original intent of the authors. Every effort has been made to trace the owners of copyrighted material.

Cover Image copyright © photo.ua/Shutterstock.com.

LIBRARY OF CONGRESS CATALOGING-IN-PUBLICATION DATA

Russia / David Haugen and Susan Musser, book editors.
    pages ; cm. -- (Opposing viewpoints)
    Includes bibliographical references and index.
    ISBN 978-0-7377-6969-2 (hardcover) -- ISBN 978-0-7377-6970-8 (paperback)
    1. Russia (Federation)--Foreign relations--21st century. 2. Russia (Federation)--Politics and government--21st century. I. Haugen, David M., 1969-, editor. II. Musser, Susan, editor. III. Series: Opposing viewpoints series (Unnumbered)
    DK510.764.R828 2013
    947.086--dc23
                                                    2013000349

Printed in the United States of America
    1 2 3 4 5   17 16 15 14 13

Contents

Chapter 3: What Relationship Should the West Foster with Russia?

Why Consider Opposing Viewpoints?

> *"The only way in which a human being can make some approach to knowing the whole of a subject is by hearing what can be said about it by persons of every variety of opinion and studying all modes in which it can be looked at by every character of mind. No wise man ever acquired his wisdom in any mode but this."*
>
> *John Stuart Mill*

In our media-intensive culture it is not difficult to find differing opinions. Thousands of newspapers and magazines and dozens of radio and television talk shows resound with differing points of view. The difficulty lies in deciding which opinion to agree with and which "experts" seem the most credible. The more inundated we become with differing opinions and claims, the more essential it is to hone critical reading and thinking skills to evaluate these ideas. Opposing Viewpoints books address this problem directly by presenting stimulating debates that can be used to enhance and teach these skills. The varied opinions contained in each book examine many different aspects of a single issue. While examining these conveniently edited opposing views, readers can develop critical thinking skills such as the ability to compare and contrast authors' credibility, facts, argumentation styles, use of persuasive techniques, and other stylistic tools. In short, the Opposing Viewpoints Series is an ideal way to attain the higher-level thinking and reading skills so essential in a culture of diverse and contradictory opinions.

In addition to providing a tool for critical thinking, Opposing Viewpoints books challenge readers to question their own strongly held opinions and assumptions. Most people form their opinions on the basis of upbringing, peer pressure, and personal, cultural, or professional bias. By reading carefully balanced opposing views, readers must directly confront new ideas as well as the opinions of those with whom they disagree. This is not to argue simplistically that everyone who reads opposing views will—or should—change his or her opinion. Instead, the series enhances readers' understanding of their own views by encouraging confrontation with opposing ideas. Careful examination of others' views can lead to the readers' understanding of the logical inconsistencies in their own opinions, perspective on why they hold an opinion, and the consideration of the possibility that their opinion requires further evaluation.

Evaluating Other Opinions

To ensure that this type of examination occurs, Opposing Viewpoints books present all types of opinions. Prominent spokespeople on different sides of each issue as well as well-known professionals from many disciplines challenge the reader. An additional goal of the series is to provide a forum for other, less known, or even unpopular viewpoints. The opinion of an ordinary person who has had to make the decision to cut off life support from a terminally ill relative, for example, may be just as valuable and provide just as much insight as a medical ethicist's professional opinion. The editors have two additional purposes in including these less known views. One, the editors encourage readers to respect others' opinions—even when not enhanced by professional credibility. It is only by reading or listening to and objectively evaluating others' ideas that one can determine whether they are worthy of consideration. Two, the inclusion of such viewpoints encourages the important critical thinking skill of objectively evaluating an author's credentials and bias. This evaluation will illuminate an author's reasons for taking a particular stance on an issue and will aid in readers' evaluation of the author's ideas.

It is our hope that these books will give readers a deeper understanding of the issues debated and an appreciation of the complexity of even seemingly simple issues when good and honest people disagree. This awareness is particularly important in a democratic society such as ours in which people enter into public debate to determine the common good. Those with whom one disagrees should not be regarded as enemies but rather as people whose views deserve careful examination and may shed light on one's own.

Thomas Jefferson once said that "difference of opinion leads to inquiry, and inquiry to truth." Jefferson, a broadly educated man, argued that "if a nation expects to be ignorant and free . . . it expects what never was and never will be." As individuals and as a nation, it is imperative that we consider the opinions of others and examine them with skill and discernment. The Opposing Viewpoints series is intended to help readers achieve this goal.

David L. Bender and Bruno Leone,
Founders

Introduction

> "*The USSR collapsed due to the suppression of natural market forces in the economy and long-running disregard for the interests of the people. We cannot repeat the errors of the past.*"
>
> —*Vladimir Putin,*
> Foreign Policy, *February 21, 2012*

> "*[Vladimir Putin's] power is very much based on the apathy of the population, which is natural probably after tumultuous years followed the collapse of the Soviet Union and of course the lack of the reasonable alternative. . . . I think it's just a matter of time and most important, matter of price, because the social revolt in Russia is inevitable.*"
>
> —*Garry Kasparov,*
> Big Think, *December 20, 2010*

Russia is the world's largest nation, covering an area of more than seventeen million square miles that stretches westward from the Bering Sea across northern Asia and into Eastern Europe. Though ethnic Russians account for more than 80 percent of the population, the vast country is home to 165 other ethnic groups that speak one hundred different languages and live in twenty-one national republics and numerous autonomous regions. Russia is also diverse in climate and geography. Being much closer to the North Pole than to the equator, Russia's great northern expanse is covered by frigid tundra. Moving southward, the tundra gives way to taiga (coniferous forests) and eventually to dry treeless steppes on the borders with Ukraine, Kazakhstan, and Manchuria. In addition, a few large mountain chains—such as the Caucasus in the southwest and the Urals in the west—further divide the nation.

Uniting this large federation of republics under a strong central government has never been easy. The Kremlin did have some advantages when the new Russia came into being on December 31, 1991. After the demise of the Union of Soviet Socialist Republics (USSR), or the Soviet Union, on December 26, the Russian Federation retained more than 60 percent of the USSR's gross domestic product. It also preserved organizational and military power because ethnic Russians dominated both government offices and the former Soviet armed forces. Despite such vestiges of strength and order, Russia in the post-Soviet era struggled early on with stabilizing its economy. The administration of President Boris Yeltsin tried to correct an ongoing recession by liberalizing industries and markets, thus freeing them from former state control. The plan triggered rampant inflation and simply allowed wealthy conglomerates to buy up or at least buy into key industries—and the recession continued. However, market privatization led to the disappearance of government subsidies for certain products and resources, and coupled with slashed public assistance funds, these savings helped the nation balance its budget and begin growth in the late 1990s. In addition, while various regional governors had freer rein to assert local power in the years immediately following the collapse of the Soviet Union, the Kremlin began using its growing revenue strength to fiscally muscle the republics back into line.

When Vladimir Putin took over office from Yeltsin in 2000, the new headman was quick to centralize power. He let it be known that he was considering the introduction of regional governors general, leaders who could oversee a collection of provinces and enforce Moscow's rule. He also began cultivating support among political leaders within provinces who were rivals of the sitting governors, ensuring that a strong opposition force was on hand to check abuses of power. In a 2000 Program on New Approaches to Research and Security in Eurasia (PONARS Eurasia) memo, Steve Skolnik, head of the Ford Foundation's Moscow office, called it Putin's "Divide and Rule" strategy—one "that seeks to reassert central control over Russia's provinces without provoking a confrontation with all of Russia's regional leaders simultaneously." Four years later, Putin banned the public election of governors and assumed the right to appoint them. This multipronged consolidation strategy has been successful. In October 2012, as Putin resumed the presidency after a four-year hiatus, free elections were once again permitted in five gubernatorial races, as a test for future popular elections in other regions, and the votes instated to power candidates loyal to Putin's United Russia party. While opposition leaders argued that the elections were unfair, Putin told the public that the results of the limited elections were "yet another step that confirms voters' intention to support the current institutions of power and the development of the Russian state."

Though protests of Putin's return to power prove that his leadership is not favored by all, most Russians seem to favor a strong leader—especially in times of economic uncertainty. In a May 2012 Pew Research Center poll, 75 percent of those surveyed attested that a strong economy was better for Russia than a good democracy. A similar number of Russians claimed to have a "favorable" impression of Vladimir Putin. Thus, Russians support, or at least tolerate, their leader's opening of natural gas pipelines to the Pacific with the state-owned Gazprom investment, and they accept his purge of bureaucracy and its attendant corruption. In a May 2006 *Slate* article, Peter Savodnik, an editor at the *Moscow Times*, testified, "Whether it's single-handedly rerouting massive oil pipelines or reorganizing the federal bureaucracy, Putin has not so much resurrected a dead superstate as responded to Russians' long-festering desire for a 'strong hand.'" Savodnik maintains that the traditional linking of patriotism in Russia to a combined love of leader and state has less traction with young people, but he insists that many Russians still idolize strong rulers and see them "as extensions of themselves."

John Lloyd, director of journalism at Oxford University, believes the idolization will not last. He contends that Russian's economic spurts are creating winners and losers and that many of the underprivileged are disenchanted with a system that seems to reward wealth and personal connections. For example, in a December 31, 2011, blog post for Reuters news service, Lloyd writes that university students—more apt to express the rebelliousness of youth—are fed up with the corruption in academic institutes "where entrances and degrees are routinely bought by rich parents." In addition, Lloyd argues that because economic strength is wedded to government oversight, when economic crises occur, the problems of poor governance become more obvious to the Russian people. He flatly states, "Russia has stopped being a success," and he predicts Putin's control will erode if the old Soviet-style centralization of power continues to weigh on the economy and infringe on the rights of the people.

As Vladimir Putin enters his third term as president, Russia enters its third decade of post-Soviet liberalization. Increased global scrutiny was placed on Russia when temporary asylum was granted in July 2013 to US citizen Edward Snowden, who leaked details of a massive government surveillance program. In addition, human rights groups called for the boycott of the 2014 Winter Olympics to be held in Sochi, Russia, after the passage of sweeping anti-gay legislation by the Putin government. Though it is uncertain how the state, its leader, and its people will fare in the coming years, there is no shortage of commentators willing to make predictions. In *Opposing Viewpoints: Russia*, several observers and insiders offer their views on the strengths and weaknesses of the government and the economy, as well as on the ultimate stability of the country. These experts debate Russia's present policies and future prospects in chapters that ask What Is Russia's Role in International Politics?, Is Russia Moving Toward Democracy?, What Relationship Should the West Foster with Russia?, and How Is Russian Culture Changing? Taken together, these critics give shape to the paths open to Russia in the second decade of the twenty-first century and to the Western world that must contend with the once, and perhaps future, superpower.

OPPOSING
VIEWPOINTS®
SERIES

What Is Russia's Role in International Politics?

Chapter Preface

When the Soviet Union collapsed in 1991, observers in both the East and West hoped for the birth of a popular democracy in Russia and its allied republics. Indeed, in the following year, Freedom House, a democracy watchdog organization, ranked several former Soviet states and Communist-controlled countries as at least "partly free" in their governance. Over the next two decades, however, the prospects have dimmed. A few of the "partly free" nations—such as Ukraine and Armenia—have remained so, while many others have slipped in their rankings as authoritarian regimes took over.

In the new Russia, Vladimir Putin, a former officer in the KGB—the Soviet secret service—rose to the presidency in 2000 and reassumed leadership in 2012 after briefly serving as prime minister under Dmitry Medvedev's four-year presidential term that began in 2008. Putin's leadership style has been critiqued by outsiders as being dictatorial. Even as prime minister, he seemed to be a partner to Medvedev rather than a subordinate. Putin oversaw the quelling of the separatist movement in the republic of Chechnya, invaded Georgia in support of pro-Moscow enclaves, dismantled political opposition parties in Russia, and curtailed the power of nongovernmental organizations—strongly suggesting to critics that Putin brooks no dissent and simply disregards democratic virtues. In a 2011 report for Freedom House, Arch Puddington added that "Russia under Putin has functioned as an 'enabler' for despots in surrounding countries. Whatever Russia's differences with neighboring countries over energy policy, trade, or diplomacy, Putin has almost invariably supported authoritarian leaders when their democratic failings have been called to account by the international community."

Putin enjoys considerable public support in Russia, but some insiders and outsiders fear the president is returning the state to its Soviet roots. In February 2012, he wrote in a government-owned newspaper that Russia planned to invest $772 billion in updating and increasing its military to respond to global instabilities and the race for resources; Russia has a wealth of oil and natural gas. Putin predicted, "In a situation of global economic and other kinds of hardships, it may be very tempting for some to resolve their problems at others' expense, through pressure and coercion," and therefore he felt the country was acting wisely to protect itself. In addition to what some see as military posturing, Russia under Putin has tried to broker an energy deal with China, its old Communist ally, and has warned the West against taking armed action against Iran, a nation that has boasted of its attempts to build a nuclear weapon.

Putin's leadership signals to many a re-emergent Russia, not a nation still finding its way in the aftermath of the Soviet system's collapse. Critics have wondered why the United States remained inactive when Soviet tanks rolled into Chechnya and Georgia, and why it now tolerates Putin's admonitions about intervening in the Middle East. In a June 7, 2007, article for *Time*, Zbigniew Brzezinski, former national security advisor to President Jimmy Carter, argued that "Russia has gained impunity in part because of the effects of America's disastrous war in Iraq on U.S. foreign policy." In his view, the United States suffered a loss of credibility in the international community and narrowly focused its attention on the war against terrorism. Rather than ignite a new Cold War, Brzezinski insisted that the United States should "pursue a calm, strategic (and nontheatrical) policy" toward Russia in hopes of enticing more moderate Russian leadership to temper Putin's hard-line rhetoric and actions. In the following chapter, several contemporary analysts debate whether Russia's policies have altered in Putin's third term as president.

"Russia has used its influence both to reward its friends and punish its enemies, seeking to regain its influence over the region."

Oil, Carrots, and Sticks: Russia's Energy Resources as a Foreign Policy Tool

Randall Newnham

In the following viewpoint, Randall Newnham describes how Russia, after a period of declining energy fortunes in the late twentieth century, has emerged as a profitable producer and exporter of oil. Newnham argues that Russia's oil wealth has derived from new pipeline networks as well as energy relationships with its own member states, former Soviet republics, and foreign nations. Newnham maintains that Russia has built its energy empire by using carrot-and-stick methods that reward loyal allies with a continuous flow of oil and punish dissident satellites and states with higher priced fuel supplies. These policies have assured the dependence of some states on Russian oil and convinced others that to balk at Moscow's influence is to risk fuel shortages. Randall Newnham is an associate professor of political science at Penn State University.

Randall Newnham, "Oil, Carrots, and Sticks: Russia's Energy Resources as a Foreign Policy Tool," *Journal of Eurasian Studies*, vol. 2, no. 2, July 2011, pp. 134–143. Copyright © 2011 by Elsevier. All rights reserved. Reproduced by permission.

As you read, consider the following questions:

1. Under which Russian president does Newnham say Russia's energy influence reached unprecedented heights?

2. According to the author, what tiny "republic" in Moldova has been able to remain a viable enclave of pro-Russian support thanks in part to Moscow's willingness to subsidize the republic's gas bill?

3. Why does Newnham believe America should be concerned about Russia's growing oil power and wealth?

In the past decade, Russia has increasingly moved back onto the world stage as an important actor. After a noticeable decline under Gorbachev and Yeltsin, the Putin era saw a resurgence of Russian power. A key component of this power is Russia's ability to use its oil and gas reserves as foreign policy tools. If anything, the role of such policies has only increased under the new Russian president, Dmitry Medvedev. Before taking office he was the chair of the state gas monopoly, Gazprom, a key instrument of Moscow's 'petro-power.'

Recent examples of the role of this power have included both 'petro-carrots' (using oil and gas to reward allies) and 'petro-sticks' (using resources to punish states which defy the Kremlin). . . . States such as Georgia, the Ukraine and the Baltic states have been punished with supply interruptions and higher prices after their governments turned toward the West. Conversely, those who remained friendly to the Kremlin—such as Armenia, Belorussia, Ukraine before 2005, and the tiny statelets of Abkhazia, North Ossetia, and Trans-Dniestr—have been granted ample oil and gas at subsidized prices. . . .

The Growth of Russia's Energy Influence

The roots of today's Russian oil and gas influence date to the country's Soviet past. At that point, . . . the Kremlin consciously began an effort to make Russian energy indispensable throughout both Eastern and Western Europe. By the 1970s, Soviet energy influence was a major headache for the West (Klinghoffer, 1977). This energy influence declined temporarily in the late 1980s and 1990s, due to low oil prices, the dislocations of the collapse of the USSR, and the privatization of many oil companies. However, Russia's ample resources and extensive network of pipelines ensured that its 'petro-power' was ready to re-emerge under President Putin.

During the 1950s and 60s the Soviet Union deepened its efforts to link itself to its Warsaw Pact allies economically. Under the Council for Mutual Economic Assistance (CMEA or COMECON), economic cooperation of all sorts was designed to complement the Soviet Bloc's military and ideological ties. While the CMEA had begun under Stalin, in 1949, in those years the Bloc members felt economically exploited. Khrushchev, in contrast, hoped to build a 'socialist division of labor,' in which the USSR and its allies would all profit. At the same time, this web of mutual dependence would make it very difficult for any state to leave the group.

A key part of this emerging 'socialist division of labor' was the USSR's role as the dominant supplier of raw materials and energy to the rest of the Bloc (Kramer, 1985; Newnham, 1990). A pattern began then which continues today: Russia deliberately gave its allies oil and gas at highly subsidized prices—but only if they remained politically compliant (Marrese & Vanous, 1983). Loyal states which experienced political problems, such as Poland during the Solidarity period of 1980–81, were helped with even more generous subsidies. Meanwhile, critics of the Kremlin—such as Romania—were forced to rely on the much pricier world market for fuel.

The reliance of Eastern Europe (and the rest of the USSR) on Russian oil and gas was only increased by these subsidies. Huge energy-hungry industries were built up, many of which (such as petrochemical plants) relied totally on subsidized fuel. Average consumers, too, were accustomed to profligate energy use. For example, many apartments throughout the Soviet Bloc were built with no individual thermostats and no gas meters, encouraging waste.... This legacy of dependence remains a powerful source of leverage for the Kremlin today.

Soon another important part of today's Russian energy influence was formed: the idea that the new East European pipelines would also allow large amounts of Soviet oil and gas to be exported to the capitalist West (Jentleson, 1986). This would earn Russia valuable hard currency, and would also serve as an important political tool, perhaps allowing Moscow to pry Western Europe away from American influence. Even in the early 1960s, U.S. leaders feared that the Druzhba [Friendship] oil pipeline, then under construction from Russia to East Germany, would allow the Soviets to gain influence in the West. Accordingly, the U.S. pressed West Germany and other suppliers to halt shipments of large diameter pipe and other equipment to Russia (Newnham 2002: 132–136). The issue simmered for decades, with another major confrontation erupting under President Reagan, who pressed NATO to boycott the new natural gas pipelines which Russia was building to Western Europe (Jentleson, 1986). Nonetheless, the new links were completed, and have only deepened over the years.

The stage was set, then, for Russia to be able to use its energy power in two effective ways: first, by subsidizing its allies, and second, by selling to its enemies at full world market price, reaping rich profits. Either way, the Kremlin gained power....

Fortunately for the West, and for Russia's downtrodden East Bloc allies, the world market price for oil collapsed in 1986. Many experts, like the late economist and former Russian prime minister Yegor Gaidar, have argued that this played a major role in the rapid collapse of the USSR (Gaidar, 2007). Falling oil and gas revenue made it hard for Russia to afford the Cold War, helping to force a pullback from Afghanistan and other Third World ventures. The declining price of oil and gas forced Russia to prioritize its shipments to the wealthy West, cutting subsidized exports to Eastern Europe. This helped to destabilize the Soviet Bloc. Meanwhile, at home, falling oil and gas revenue hurt Russia's economy, putting another nail in the coffin of the Gorbachev government.

During the Yeltsin years, the slide in Russia's 'petro-power' continued. Several reasons can be cited for this. First, oil prices remained very low. Second, partly as a result, the overall Russian economy remained in free fall, increasing the government's desperation for hard currency exports. Third, these economic dislocations only helped to drive down oil and gas production, further reducing revenue. Finally, the privatization of Russian resources helped ensure that much of the limited 'petro-power' Russia retained would be exercised by businessmen, not politicians. . . .

The desperate need to close yawning budget gaps helped to force the Kremlin to privatize valuable state assets quickly, at fire sale prices—including oil and gas fields. As the Yeltsin years progressed, privatization steadily eroded state influence in the oil and gas sectors. Most oil resources were sold off, sometimes for pennies on the dollar. For example, Russian businessman Roman Abramovich was able to buy the oil firm Sibneft for about $100 million in 1995—and sell it for over 130 times more ($13.1 billion) ten years later (Kramer, 2005). By the late 1990s, oligarchs were able to gain control of oil fields without making any real payments; under the so-called 'loans for shares' program even short-term loans were enough to strip assets from the bankrupt Russian state. While foreign companies were not allowed to buy existing oil fields, they were permitted to secure majority control of potentially lucrative undeveloped fields.

By the end of the Yeltsin years the state retained control over only about ten percent of Russia's oil, hardly enough to control export policies. . . .

Russia Raises Natural Gas Prices ($/TCM) on Former Soviet Republics Unevenly

Country	2005	2006	2007	2008
Armenia	$56	$110	$110	$110
Belarus	$46	$ 46	$110	$125
Georgia	$63	$110	$235	$235
Moldova	$80	$110	$170	$190
Ukraine	$50	$ 95	$130	$160

These figures are measured in terms of dollars per thousand cubic meters, or TCM.

TAKEN FROM: Randall Newnham, "Oil, Carrots, and Sticks: Russia's Energy Resources as a Foreign Policy Tool," *Journal of Eurasian Studies,* July 2011.

In the gas sector the Kremlin's role was stronger, but still weakened. Most natural gas production remained under Gazprom, the state-owned energy giant created just before the fall of the USSR. However, large shares of the company had been sold to domestic and foreign buyers, reducing the state's stake to about 38%. While the state retained influence, Gazprom's decisions were increasingly based on economic, not political calculations. Its usefulness as a tool of state leverage was declining. In the last years of the Yeltsin era, speculation was rampant that even Gazprom would be fully privatized, which would have virtually eliminated the Kremlin's energy power.

In the latter years of Yeltsin's rule many analysts concluded that not only did the Kremlin not control the oil and gas industry—in many ways, the industry controlled it.... Fragmentation of the Kremlin's authority had reached a point where no clear decision-making procedure could be discerned at all. The contrast to today's forceful Russian state was stark.

Russia's 'Petro-Power' Returns

Under President Putin Russia's energy influence reached unprecedented heights. Several factors combined to produce this result. First, the world market for oil and gas greatly favored Russia and other producers in 2000–2008. These products became both valuable and rare, ideal preconditions for the use of any form of economic linkage. . . . While prices have moderated in the current worldwide recession, a return to the era of 'cheap oil' as in the 1990s is unlikely. Second, the Putin administration moved to take control of the country's oil and gas sector. This allowed Russia to harness its potential economic power for *state* purposes, a crucial condition which was largely lacking in the late Yeltsin years. Third, Russia moved aggressively to increase its control over oil and gas assets outside its borders, notably the pipelines which carry its products to the world. In sum, Russia is now much more free to use its oil and gas to either impose painful costs or offer lucrative benefits to states which it seeks to influence.

A key factor in the rise of Russia's 'energy power' was the state of the world market in oil and gas during Putin's reign. Supplies were tight worldwide, meaning that Russia's customers had few alternatives to buying from Moscow. States could not easily evade Moscow's energy sanctions or impose countersanctions. For example, the EU would have found it virtually impossible to boycott Russian oil or gas to express its distaste with Putin's foreign policy or his increasingly autocratic actions at home. Also, prices soared to record highs after Putin became president in 2000, with oil reaching almost $150 a barrel by mid-2008. This turnaround from the Yeltsin years allowed Russia to rake in massive profits from oil and gas sales. This in turn allowed the Kremlin to pay off Russia's foreign debts, which loomed so high under Yeltsin that they prevented Russia from fully using its petro-power, as was noted above. Today, while the recession has cut into Russia's financial reserves, it remains far more solvent than in the 1990s. If a country such as Belarus threatens to temporarily suspend Russian oil or gas shipments through its pipelines, Russia can shrug off the threat. It knows that it can afford a temporary drop in revenue, unlike in the Yeltsin years.

The tightness in world markets allowed Moscow to retain and expand its dominant market shares among its energy customers—and also to reel in new customers, such as China and Japan. For example, Belarus obtains essentially all of its natural gas from Russia—99%. The Baltic states depend on Moscow for about 89% of their gas supplies, Georgia for 88%, and Ukraine for 69%. Even some Western customers have similarly high levels of dependence, such as Austria (72%) and Greece (85%) (EIA, 2007c:6). . . .

To defend its 'petro-power,' Russia strives to keep as many of its partners as possible in a state of energy dependence, a dependence which can be manipulated as Russia chooses. A key component of this strategy is the control of pipelines and other energy facilities in neighboring countries. Russia aims to control pipelines in Poland, Belarus, Ukraine and the Baltic states which take Russian oil and gas to other countries. If it cannot control these transit routes, it will try to bypass them, for example with the new Nord [North] Stream pipeline through the Baltic Sea, running directly from Russia to Germany. At the same time Moscow controls pipelines through its own territory which carry oil and gas from the Caspian and central Asian countries, and works hard to ensure that these countries cannot find alternative export routes. . . .

'Petro-Carrots': Oil and Gas as Economic Incentives

As in the days of the Warsaw Pact, loyal allies are rewarded with ample amounts of subsidized energy, at great cost to Moscow. Today, of course, the recipients are different, since most of Central Europe has entered the EU and NATO and is no longer allied to the Kremlin. Thus, . . . major recipients of petro-carrots have recently included the Ukraine (under President Kuchma), Belarus, and several small secessionist enclaves in Moldova and Georgia. While this aid has not always succeeded (notably in Ukraine at the time of the Orange Revolution), it has helped to keep pro-Kremlin leaders in power in Belarus, Abkhazia, South Ossetia, and the Trans-Dniestr region. This influence in what Moscow tellingly calls the 'near-abroad' is highly important, since it sustains Russia's ambitions to remain a major power.

Russian generosity to the Ukraine under President Leonid Kuchma was a clear case of using oil and gas pricing to favor a client state. Kuchma, who led the Ukraine from 1994 to 2005, was quite friendly to Russia, signing a "Treaty on Friendship, Cooperation and Partnership" with Moscow, designating Russian as an official language, and siding with Russia on many foreign policy issues.

Not surprisingly, these policies were rewarded by the Kremlin with subsidized oil and gas sales. Throughout Kuchma's time in office, Moscow kept gas prices frozen at about $50 per thousand cubic meters (TCM). In fact Kiev paid far less than even that, because much of the supply was simply given to Ukraine as 'transit fees' for gas being sent on to Western Europe. Also, Ukraine was allowed to fall far behind on even the limited payments it did owe, piling up a large debt to Russia. The political nature of these subsidies became only too clear after the pro-Western 'Orange Revolution' of 2004, when Kuchma was succeeded by Viktor Yushchenko. . . . Oil and gas 'carrots' suddenly became 'sticks' in Moscow's fight against Yushchenko.

Another prime example of a country favored by Russian oil and gas incentives is Belarus. Clearly, Russia was not rewarding Belarus for political or economic reforms; under the dictatorial President Lukashenko, Belarus has remained a Soviet-era remnant in the region. Yet Lukashenko has consistently backed Moscow in foreign policy, to the extent of pursuing for years the hope of creating a new federation with Russia. Thus the Kremlin has ensured that Belarus would be favored with extremely cheap gas. In 2006, Belarus paid only $47 per TCM, at the same time Russia was demanding $230—almost five times more—from the new pro-Western Ukrainian government (Vinocur, 2006).

The country's feeble, still largely state-run economy even has difficulty paying for the extremely discounted gas it receives. Until recently, Russia has been willing to overlook this. During the Yeltsin era, for example, Belarus was able to 'pay' its debts by such measures as giving up its claims on joint Soviet-era assets in Russia (1993) and giving up claims for "damage caused by Soviet troops in Belarus" (1996) (Lane, 1999: 168). Both of these claims were rather far-fetched, since Belarus had seized Soviet facilities on its own territory and damage from the Soviet-era military was hardly Yeltsin's responsibility alone.

Putin gradually increased the pressure on Belarus to pay somewhat fairer prices for its energy, although the country is still subsidized. . . . Russia increased prices for its allies, such as Belarus and Armenia, but raised prices for more hostile states—such as Ukraine, Georgia and Moldova—by far more. Thus a 'price scissors' was created, which allows Moscow to benefit in two ways. First, it greatly increases its overall revenue, as all customers pay more. Second, the price differential allows it to punish its enemies and reward its friends at the same time. It is hard for Belarus to complain about having to pay $100 per TCM for its gas when Georgia is paying more than twice as much.

The massive price differentials and generous treatment of Belarusian debts have been instrumental in keeping the country afloat economically, and thus in keeping Lukashenko in power. The policy must therefore be scored as a significant success for Moscow. The West has long tried to sponsor opposition movements in Belarus, as in the 2006 presidential election when the 'Zubr' movement united behind the pro-Western candidate, Alexander Milinkevich. Yet Lukashenko's claim to have created "stability"—thanks in large part to low unemployment, subsidized food and energy—helped ensure that his opponent's support remained limited. He would likely have won reelection even without the paranoid police tactics and electoral cheating which he used to ensure overwhelming victory. Energy incentives helped to ensure that there would be no 'Orange Revolution' in Minsk.

In addition to the generous petro-subsidies offered to compliant neighbors like Belarus, Moscow has also cleverly used incentives to support several pro-Russian enclaves in less compliant states. Moldova, for example, has long been a thorn in Moscow's side, with its nationalistic policies alienating the Russian minority there. In response, Russia has supported the breakaway 'Trans-Dniestr Republic,' run by Russian speakers. Like Belarus, it has preserved the symbols and style of the old USSR. Also like Belarus, this tiny 'republic' has been unable to pay for even its subsidized gas—yet Moscow has remained tolerant. By March 2007 the 'republic' had accumulated $1.3 billion in debt to Gazprom, which it announced it simply would not pay (Solovyov, 2007). Yet the gas kept flowing.

Similarly, subsidized oil and gas has been provided to two breakaway regions of Georgia, a state which . . . has been a major target of Russian oil and gas sanctions. South Ossetia and Abkhazia, both backed by Russian 'peacekeeping troops,' have carved out de facto independence from Georgia, and their defiance allows Moscow to increase military and political pressure on the Georgian leadership (Maloney, 2007). Moscow has spent lavishly to support them. For example, Gazprom plans to spend about $600 million building new pipelines and gas infrastructure in South Ossetia (Lowe, 2007), a region with about 70,000 inhabitants. Clearly, this is a politically motivated investment. All of these enclaves—the Trans-Dniestr Republic, Abkhazia, and South Ossetia—are impoverished, backward areas which could not survive economically, without Moscow's help. The fact that all of them remain in existence,

16 years after the collapse of the USSR, must be credited in part to Moscow's 'petro-carrots.'

Another aspect of Russian oil and gas power is its potential use in 'bribing' individuals and corporations. By offering corporations shares in oil and gas fields, pipelines, and other projects, Russia can win influential allies abroad. In recent years Russia has been careful to keep majority control of such projects in its hands. Yet with energy prices sky-high, foreign firms seem willing to accept minority stakes. . . .

'Petro-Sticks': Oil and Gas as Economic Sanctions

In contrast to Russia's generous treatment of its political allies, those who oppose the Kremlin have faced economic punishment. This has included punitive price hikes and even oil and gas embargos. These tactics became obvious to the world at the start of 2006, when Russia cut off gas shipments to the Ukraine and Georgia. Ukraine faced another punitive gas cutoff at the start of 2009. The Baltic states have also been targeted. However, 'petro-sticks' have also been used in many more subtle ways, as we shall see, through measures such as punitive price increases and demands for debt payment. While these pressure tactics have not always brought immediate compliance with Moscow's wishes, they have had the dual effect of weakening Russia's opponents and setting an example *pour l'encouragement des autres.*

The Ukrainian case is one of the most well-known examples of Russian oil and gas sanctions. This is true not only because the Ukraine is an important state in its own right, but because cutting off Russian gas to that state can have a major impact on broader world markets. The main Russian gas pipeline to Western Europe runs through Ukraine, meaning that Kiev can easily react to any Russian supply cuts by reducing or stopping the flow to the rest of Europe. Under President Yeltsin this threat was enough to tie the Russians' hands, forcing them to compromise repeatedly with Kiev on gas supplies and pricing. As one author put it, voicing the common view in the late 1990s, any Russian threat to cut supplies was "not really credible," because Moscow needed the transit route as much as Kiev needed Russian gas (Rutland, 1999: 168). Under Putin, this relatively benign policy ended—to the consternation of both the Ukrainians and Western Europe.

In late 2004 the Ukraine was convulsed by the dramatic dispute between presidential candidates Viktor Yanukovych and Viktor Yushchenko. Yanukovych, the designated successor of the incumbent president, Leonid Kuchma, was considered friendly to Moscow, and the Kremlin made its support for him clear (Yasmann, 2006). When Yanukovych was proclaimed the winner in a fraud-tainted vote in November 2004, Moscow rushed to accept his victory. The subsequent "Orange Revolution" by supporters of the pro-Western Yushchenko, which eventually succeeded in forcing a new election, was roundly condemned by Moscow. Yushchenko's victory in the second contest in late December seemed to push the Ukraine out of the Russian orbit. Even worse, he succeeded due to a popular uprising backed by the West. Such a "color revolution" (first seen in Serbia with the overthrow of Milosevic, then later in Georgia, Kyrgyzstan and Lebanon) seemed to Moscow to be a possible model for an uprising against Putin himself. As such, it could not be tolerated.

Accordingly, during the tense electoral campaign the Kremlin and its surrogates openly brandished the 'gas weapon.' As the leader of one pro-Moscow Ukrainian organization said, "what else but gas could convince the people of Ukraine that it's better to be a friend of Russia than the EU and NATO?" (Yasmann, 2006). It was made clear that a vote for Yushchenko was a vote for winters with no heat, shuttered factories, and economic collapse. After Yushchenko's final victory at the end of 2004 these threats began to be put into action.

Ukraine's 2005 gas contract with Gazprom had already been signed. But it soon became clear that after that the country would face a harsh price increase. Gazprom claimed, unconvincingly, that this was simply part of a natural increase to reach world market prices (WMP)—i.e., the prices paid by Western European states. Somehow, though, this need to increase the gas price had never been noticed under Kuchma, when prices held steady at about $50 per TCM for many years. Now, suddenly, Moscow demanded an almost fivefold increase to West European levels—about $235 per TCM. In addition, Gazprom suddenly demanded payment of Ukraine's accumulated debt for gas service. If successful, Gazprom's demands would have bankrupted Ukraine.

Matters came to a head at the end of 2005, when the annual gas contract expired and the two sides could not reach a new agreement. To the world's surprise, at the start of 2006 Gazprom quickly began to shut off the gas flow to the Ukraine. Even some commentators on Russian state-owned television were quite open in stating that "the gas cutoff is retribution for the Orange Revolution" (Yasmann, 2006). Moscow ignored Kiev's threats to retaliate by cutting the flow on to Western Europe. That region's supplies, too, fell greatly in the next two days, before normal shipments were restored on January 3.

In the end, the Kremlin did not achieve a complete victory. It was, however, able to force the Ukraine to agree to double the price it paid for gas, to about $100 per TCM. This imposed a massive economic drain on the Yushchenko regime. The price also had the virtue of still being below the WMP, which would allow the Kremlin to easily justify future price increases. Yushchenko and the Ukraine were thus effectively held hostage, never knowing when the next economic blow would fall. And the price increase had a political effect; with rising economic discontent, President Yushchenko's party did less well than expected in the March 2006 parliamentary elections, stalling the progress of his Orange Revolution (Myers and Kramer, 2006).

Predictably, Russian meddling continued after 2006. Every action of President Yushchenko was met with more threats of gas supply cuts, price increases, or new debt repayment demands. The pattern was the same in the fall 2007 parliamentary elections in Ukraine, which brought Yushchenko's ally Yulia Tymoshenko into power as prime minister. Again, the Kremlin tried to induce voters to favor her opponent, Yanukovych, with thinly veiled economic threats. When that failed, Gazprom again stepped in, cutting Ukraine's gas supplies in early 2008 in yet another dispute over debt repayment—which was widely seen as punishment for Tymoshenko's victory (Harding, 2007). Finally, at the start of 2009 Gazprom again cut off gas shipments, again greatly reducing supplies sent to Western Europe for several days.

As the victories of Yushchenko and Tymoshenko show, the Kremlin's pressure tactics do not always appear to work immediately. However, when Moscow is defied there is a price to pay; the Ukrainian economy has suffered a real drain thanks to Gazprom. As David Baldwin notes in his classic work *Economic Statecraft*, the success of sanctions cannot be measured only by whether they immediately bring political victory. One must also count the costs imposed as a success, since they weaken the opponent (Baldwin, 1985: 132–133). Gazprom's price increases also have the added virtue of simultaneously strengthening the Kremlin—quite directly, since Gazprom is state owned. Additionally, the Ukraine's economic problems have imposed a political cost on Yushchenko and his pro-Western allies, weakening both political support and their ability to implement their campaign promises. Every Ukrainian hryvnia sent to Moscow for gas is one that cannot be spent on popular programs such as health, education or public works.

Furthermore, as noted above, the Kremlin successfully showed its resolve by ignoring Ukraine's efforts to disrupt gas flows to Western Europe. For years 'transit states' such as

Ukraine, Belarus, and Poland had felt immune from Russian sanctions, believing that they could live without Russian gas better than Russia could live without West European hard currency from gas sales. But now rising oil and gas prices had enabled Moscow to pay off its debts and build up huge currency reserves, freeing it to use its resource leverage more aggressively. This is an important lesson for the future: When push comes to shove, the Kremlin will cut Western Europe's energy artery to achieve its political goals. This lesson has struck home in Western Europe, with leaders throughout the EU now following every energy dispute between Russia and its neighbors with obvious concern. The EU has been pushing Russia to accept an "energy charter," pledging to forswear politically motivated embargoes, yet Moscow has steadfastly refused. In the future, Ukraine's limited leverage as a transit state looks likely to decline further, as Russia finds alternative ways to reach its wealthy Western customers. . . .

Conclusion

Russia's 'petro-power' has become an increasingly clear threat to all the states which buy Russian oil and gas. This is obviously especially true for the small, poor, highly dependent states of what Russians call the 'near-abroad'—the former Soviet states. As we have seen, Russia has used its influence both to reward its friends and punish its enemies, seeking to regain its influence over the region. It has shown it can be successful, and even when it is not it can impose high costs on those who dare to defy it.

Yet the impact of Russia's actions extends far beyond Russia's immediate neighbors. For example, Western Europe now has great cause for concern. Although it is less dependent on Russia than the former Soviet states, Moscow's willingness to ruthlessly use its 'petro-power' has led to much worry among EU states—and . . . to increasing efforts to persuade Russia to sign an energy charter restraining its influence. Other countries, such as the U.S., also have reason to be concerned about Russia's oil wealth. While the U.S. does not depend directly on Russian oil and gas, it has many allies that do. Russia also exerts some influence on global prices, especially in today's unsettled, nervous 'seller's market.' It has recently tried to enhance this leverage by creating an organization of natural gas exporters, modeled on OPEC. Any decision by Moscow to limit production would immediately cause world prices to jump.

Finally, the U.S. and others around the world are also concerned about another facet of Russia's 'petro-power': the huge war chest of oil and gas revenue that Moscow has accumulated. By early 2008 Russia held over $157 billion in its 'Stabilization Fund,' one of a number of 'sovereign wealth funds' which have emerged in recent years worldwide (Kramer, 2008). Disturbingly, these sovereign wealth funds are often held by countries which are undemocratic and have limited commitment to free markets. Also, more and more, countries with regional or worldwide geopolitical ambitions control large wealth funds. For example, Russia, Venezuela and Iran rank among the top wealth fund holders (Truman, 2007: 3). And this new wealth is clearly based on oil and gas; of the 19 top fund states in 2007, at least 13 had wealth based mainly on that source (Ibid., and author's calculations).

In short, the surging price of oil and gas has driven a fundamental reallocation of global wealth. This can be seen in the fact that oil exporting states had a collective balance of payments surplus of $88 billion in 2002 and $571 billion in 2006, an increase of almost five times in only four years (Andersen, Fick, & Hansen, 2007: 50). Despite the current decline in oil prices, projections for the longer term future are even more sobering. A recent report projected that sovereign wealth funds could expand from $2.5 trillion in 2007 to $27.7 trillion in 2022 (Sesit, 2007). Thus, as the world warily watches the rise of politically ambitious 'petro-states' like Russia, there is reason for concern.

References

1. Andersen, Thomas, Fick, Sofie, & Hansen, Frank (2007). Petrodollars, portfolio restructuring and long-term interest rates. *Monetary Review.* 49–59, No. 3.

2. Baldwin David (1985). *Economic statecraft.* Princeton, NJ: Princeton University Press.

3. Energy Information Administration (2007c). *Country analysis briefs: Ukraine.* www.eia.doe.gov/NewCabs/V6/Full.html, Accessed 09.08.07.

4. Gaidar, Yegor (2007). *Collapse of an empire: Lessons for modern Russia.* Washington, DC: Brookings Institution Press.

5. Harding, Luke (October 3, 2007). Russia issues gas ultimatum to Ukraine. *The Guardian.*

6. Jentleson, Bruce (1986). *Pipeline politics: The complex political economy of east-west energy trade.* Ithaca, NY: Cornell University Press.

7. Lane, David (Ed.) (1999). *The political economy of Russian oil.* Lanham, MD: Rowman & Littlefield.

8. Lowe, Christian (July 25, 2007). *Russia pours cash into Georgia rebel region.* Reuters.

9. Klinghoffer, Arthur (1977). *The Soviet Union and international oil politics.* New York: Columbia University Press.

10. Kramer, Andrew (February 8, 2008). Russia creates a $32 billion sovereign wealth fund. *New York Times.*

11. Kramer, Andrew (September 29, 2005). Russian gas giant to buy nation's no. 5 oil producer. *New York Times.*

12. Kramer, John (1985). Soviet-CEMA energy ties. *Problems of Communism,* 34(4), 32–47.

13. Maloney, Daniel, South Ossetia's Role in Russia's Buffer State Foreign Policy. Paper presented at annual meeting of the Northeastern Political Science Assn. and International Studies Assn.-Northeast, Philadelphia, November 2007.

14. Marrese, Michael, & Vanous, Jan (1983). *Soviet subsidization of trade with Eastern Europe: A Soviet perspective.* Berkeley: University of California.

15. Myers, Steven, & Kramer, Andrew (March 30, 2006). Gas deal roils Ukraine and may have cut leader's votes. *New York Times.*

16. Newnham, Randall (2002). *Deutsche mark diplomacy: Positive economic sanctions in German-Russian relations.* University Park, PA: Penn State Press.

17. Newnham, Randall, "Soviet Oil and Gas Trade with Eastern Europe: Developments in the 1980s," California Seminar on International Security and Foreign Policy Discussion Papers, 112 (1990).

18. Rutland, Peter (1999). Oil, politics, and foreign policy. In David Lane (Ed.), *The political economy of Russian oil* (pp. 163–188). Lanham, MD: Rowman & Littlefield.

19. Sesit, Michael (July 23, 2007). The limits of free market principles: sovereign wealth funds raise hackles in the west. *International Herald Tribune.*

20. Truman, Edwin (August 2007). *Sovereign wealth funds: The need for greater transparency and accountability.* Peterson Institute for International Economics. www.petersoninstitute.org Policy Brief, No. PB07-6.

21. Vinocur, John (January 3, 2006). For Schröder and Putin, linkup no coincidence. *New York Times.*

22. Vladimir, Solovyov (April 6, 2007). *Moscow's hand tired of giving: Transdniestrian leader abuses Russian generosity.* (Kommersant (Moscow)).

23. Yasmann, Victor (January 3, 2006) Russia: Moscow Uses Different Lever of Influence, Same Message. Radio Free Europe/Radio Liberty Newsline (www.rferl.org).

"*Unless the Russian government adopts a fundamentally different domestic [energy] pricing strategy that prompts further investment, triggers significant gains in domestic energy efficiency, and frees supply potentials for exports, Russia will barely be able to maintain its perceived status as an energy superpower.*"

Resurgent Russia? Rethinking Energy Inc.

Andreas Goldthau

Andreas Goldthau is the head of the Department of Public Policy and an associate professor at Central European University, an American graduate school based in Budapest, Hungary. In the viewpoint that follows, Goldthau refutes popular perceptions of Russia as an energy superpower. Goldthau acknowledges that Russia has large oil and natural gas resources, but he insists these assets are hampered by poor management and declining production. He maintains that Russia's growing economy, which is only partly influenced by energy profits, is more important to the country's strength and that restrictions on investments in oil

Andreas Goldthau, "Resurgent Russia? Rethinking Energy Inc.," *Policy Review*, no. 147, February/March 2008, pp. 53–63. Copyright © 2008 by Policy Review. All rights reserved. Reproduced by permission.

and gas have kept this sector from wielding more influence. In addition, Goldthau asserts that Russia's energy partnerships with former Soviet republics and Western nations are mutually beneficial and that stopping the flow of energy for political reasons may hurt Russia more than recipient nations.

As you read, consider the following questions:

1. Why does Goldthau claim that stopping the flow of Russian oil to a recipient nation would have no "major effect" on that nation?

2. How does Russia's dual pricing system for domestic and foreign markets hurt the country's profit potential and its political influence, according to Goldthau?

3. As Goldthau reports, how much money does the International Energy Agency think Russia will need by 2030 to develop new oil fields to ensure growth in that sector?

Russia is back on the international stage. After a decade of eroding political and economic power, the domestic economy flourishes and, as state budget revenues grow, so do egos in the Kremlin and Russia's global aspirations. The Russian resurrection is mainly attributed to high oil prices, which have enabled the country to overcome the 1998 meltdown, to maintain an average rate of economic growth of 6.7 percent for the past decade, and to build a $1 trillion economy, the basis of its new strength. At the same time, Russia's energy policy has become the subject of increasing controversy. Western observers regard energy as the Kremlin's major foreign policy tool, as countries like Ukraine or Georgia have come recently and painfully to learn. Fears have emerged that a looming Sino-Russian alliance, glued together by oil and gas deals, could challenge existing power structures—and U.S. dominance—on the international scene. In other words, as conventional wisdom reckons, the Western world is faced with a "corporate Russia" which is economically fueled by oil and gas, steered by a semi-authoritarian government with a clear geopolitical agenda, able to lubricate political alliances by oil and gas deals, and equipped with a foreign policy arm called Gazprom.

These common perceptions of Russia are understandable at first sight. Russia owns 26.6 percent of the world's proven gas reserves, and 6.2 percent of the world's proven oil reserves. In 2005, the country accounted for 21.6 percent of global gas production and for 12.1 percent of global crude oil production.[1] In that respect, Russia could in fact be perceived an "energy superpower." However, conventional wisdom is wrong on five counts. First, Russian energy is not primarily about geopolitics. Its rhetoric to the contrary, the Kremlin does not dispose of an effective "energy weapon." Second, the rationale behind Russia's recent "gas disputes" with its neighbors is to a large extent profit maximization, rather than punishing renegade governments in the neighboring Commonwealth of Independent States (CIS). Third, Moscow will not subordinate its economic interests in the name of a geostrategic Sino-Russian alliance. Fourth, Russia will have a hard time retaining the status of an "energy superpower" as it risks running out of gas instead. Finally, Russia is less reliant on oil and gas than assumed, at least as regards the drivers of its recent economic success story. In a nutshell: Western excitement about the Russian "Energy Inc." appears to be caused largely by a well-crafted piece of Russian PR.

By examining the five greatest "myths" of Russian energy, this article challenges some of the key assumptions underlying Western policy towards Russia. It reveals the limits of the prevalent argumentative lines on Russian energy, and offers an alternative explanation for some recent Russian policy choices. Finally, it draws some conclusions on foreign policy implications for the U.S. and the Western world.

Myth 1: Russia Has an Energy Weapon

The truth is: The Kremlin has only a limited ability to use Russian oil and gas as a "weapon." The Russian market is dominated by ten vertically integrated oil companies, which control 95 percent of Russia's crude production and more than 80 percent of its refining capacity. While the Russian state now controls a significantly higher share of the domestic oil industry than it did during the 1990s, state-controlled companies at present make up only around 25 percent of the country's oil production and around 16 percent of its refining capacity, thanks to a series of takeovers of private companies by state-owned Rosneft and Gazprom.[2] The domestic Russian oil market is fairly competitive, with prices determined by world markets and by the taxation policies of the Russian government.

From these few facts, three simple considerations can be deduced. First, given that the Russian state does not hold a majority in domestic oil production despite recent takeovers, the Kremlin is able to "steer" the oil industry for political purposes only indirectly, i.e., via tax incentives, export regimes, pipeline access, predetermined auctions on new fields, and the like. While these are by no means negligible instruments, they hardly render Russian oil an effective foreign policy tool. Second, Russian oil companies—state- or nonstate-controlled—trade their oil on a global market. Unless a majority of Russian crude is bound in bilateral contracts, a rather unlikely scenario in the foreseeable future, Russian oil companies do not have great leverage over individual consumers. Whenever Russia decides to cut oil supply to a consuming country, it will have no major effect, as the targeted country can purchase the shortfall on the spot market and circumvent the "blockade" (unless *all* producer countries, i.e., OPEC, decide collectively to block oil supply to their customers—which is unlikely to happen, especially if a non-OPEC member pushes for it). In the case of some Central European countries like

Slovakia, where the existing pipeline infrastructure does not allow replacing Russian crude oil in the short run, potential cutoffs can be largely absorbed by using alternative transport routes such as railroads.

Third, and related, the Russian state may well initiate further renationalizations of oil assets and expand state control over the oil industry in the future. But such moves will only diminish the performance of the Russian oil sector and reduce output growth rates, as similar experience in other countries has shown. Yet they will not affect oil markets as such, nor are they likely to render oil an effective foreign policy tool.

That leaves gas. True, Russia holds the world's largest gas reserves, and it has emerged as the most important supplier country to Western and Central Europe, where it covers up to 100 percent of imports for some countries. And, true, this dependence will become even more pronounced in the near future, when depleted European resources need to be compensated by higher imports—also from Russia. Despite this apparent dependence of European gas customers, however, there is no real case for an "energy weapon" for two reasons, both of which lie in the nature of the gas market. First, since exploration of gas fields and pipeline construction are extremely expensive and time-consuming, producers and consumers engage in long-term contracts that usually cover 20 years or more and entail destination clauses prohibiting secondary trading. Based on these take-or-pay contracts, the producer is able to invest in a multibillion-dollar project, as there is a constant and reliable return on investment. The consumer enjoys a guaranteed supply for several decades, thus reducing uncertainty and costs. Second, gas is a regional player, as it is almost exclusively transported via pipelines.[3] Hence, if either the producer or the consumer wants to opt for exit and start dealing with an alternative contractual partner, he has to make a high additional investment, i.e., build a new pipeline. Given extremely high up-front costs, it becomes very costly for either involved party to leave an established bilateral contractual gas relation. A quick look at the dense pipeline grid connecting Europe and Russia reveals that neither side can be interested in dumping all the money each has invested; nor do they have a real choice.

Russia does not have the option to sell its gas to, say, China, since the existing infrastructure is insufficient, at least in the short run. Nor can the Europeans simply turn away from their Russian provider. In other words, both sides are mutually dependent, from the very moment they have committed to a contract. What follows from the structural logic of the gas market is that there is only a limited possibility for Russia to use natural gas as a foreign policy instrument and unilaterally cut gas supplies to a consuming country without significantly and immediately affecting its own budget revenues. This does not look like an attractive move for a country whose largest share of federal budget income stems from hydrocarbon sales.

This is qualified somewhat with respect to small purchasers like Moldova or Georgia, where a cut in gas supplies hurts the affected country much more than the implied loss of revenues hurts Russia. This asymmetry provides Russia with a certain amount of leverage in the short run. As the past has shown, however, attempts to exploit this asymmetry have not caused major policy change in the affected countries. A strong limitation for Russia to make use of the asymmetry lies in the fact that many smaller purchasers are at the same time transit countries. This implies that a cut in gas supplies always affects the consumers in Western European markets—a market Gazprom aims at serving reliably, and which it has already severely threatened by the cutting of supplies to Ukraine.

Myth 2: Gazprom Is Instrumental in the Kremlin's Foreign Policy Agenda

The truth is: Gazprom and the Kremlin are intertwined, but the interests of both entities do not necessarily coincide. A case in point would be the recent gas disputes with Russia's "near abroad" (the 14 former Soviet republics that had declared their independence by the time the Soviet Union broke up at the end of 1991), which are to a large extent triggered by a regulated Russian home market, forcing Gazprom to adopt aggressive pricing strategies with foreign markets.

As gas makes up more than half of Russia's primary energy consumption, the domestic Russian gas market is highly politicized.[4] Gazprom, the gas monopolist, produces about 86 percent of Russian gas and also controls the entire domestic pipeline system. At the same time, it is obliged by federal law to ensure supplies for domestic consumption by households and industry. Russian gas consumption, which has been around 400 billion cubic meters (BCM) during recent years, is projected to continue to rise in all existing forecasts. To date, more than two-thirds of Russia's annually produced 600 BCM is already used in households, industry, transport, heating, and power plants. At the same time, Russia is a highly inefficient user of energy, using 3.2 times more energy per unit of GDP than the EU-25, most of this as gas.[5] The reason for this consumption pattern lies in Russia's dual pricing system, which is designed to subsidize Russian households and domestic manufacturers. Thus, domestic Russian gas prices are only a fraction of prices charged on foreign markets, amounting to only 17 percent of West European gas prices in 2006—29 percent when taking into account transit charges.[6]

In order to generate revenues, then, Gazprom has to tap foreign markets. Most of the easily accessible markets, such as those in Western Europe, are highly profitable. In fact, to date, Gazprom earns virtually all its profits from exports to Western Europe, although this market only accounts for 25 percent of total production.[7] In turn, if accessible foreign markets are not attractive for some reason, Gazprom tries to *render* them more profitable, and raises prices, if it can. This is what Russia's near abroad has had painfully to learn in recent times.

After heavily subsidizing its former Soviet allies throughout the past 15 years, Gazprom has increased gas prices in CIS countries and pushed to equalize prices net of transit fees with those it charges its West European clients. This policy has resulted in several gas disputes with neighbors such as Ukraine and Georgia. It has even hit Belarus, traditionally a strong Russian ally—a fact that presented the Kremlin with considerable problems when forced to explain suddenly raising gas prices on the last remaining pro-Russian government in Central Europe. In case an affected country is unable to pay the new price, Gazprom accepts in-kind payments, including shares of national or regional gas providers or pipeline grids—assets it would otherwise have to buy as an integral part of its expansion strategy.

Hence, the recent gas disputes appear to be about profits, not about politics. Indeed, they seem much less part of a geopolitical Kremlin game than the result of a rational strategic move by a company that has to compensate for a loss-generating home market. In that respect, and ironically, it may be that Vladimir Putin's foreign policy is increasingly driven by Gazprom's business interests rather than vice versa. At the bottom line, it is important to regard Gazprom and the Kremlin as two entities which, though deeply interwoven, do not necessarily share identical interests. If both players' interests coincide, as they have in the case of Gazprom's reclaims of Ukraine's $1.3 billion debt after the Ukrainian elections, the Kremlin might be able to use Gazprom for political reasons. But not necessarily at any occasion it would like to.

Myth 3: The Recent Russian Economic Recovery Is Due to High Energy Prices

The truth is: What has driven the Russian economic recovery has mainly been a boom in domestic consumption and investment, not energy. Russia has been growing impressively during recent years, at annual growth rates between 6 and 10 per-

The Problem of Making Energy the Basis of Superpower Status

Can oil really be used effectively as a 'weapon'? The global energy market is complex, fragmented and competitive. No single country or company is capable of exerting decisive influence over the market. Russia supplies less than 10 percent of global oil or gas; it is hard to imagine this market share could be leveraged into 'superpower' status. Only in collusion with other producers could there be some serious risk of the market being cornered.... The Organization of the Petroleum Exporting Countries (OPEC) showed that it was capable of radically increasing oil prices by restricting output. But nobody talked about a Saudi or Kuwaiti 'energy superpower'.... The Arab states were unable to use their oil wealth to achieve any of their political goals, such as the defeat of Israel. The conventional wisdom on the role of energy in state development is quite contrary to the 'energy superpower' idea: resource dependency usually means slower long-term economic growth and greater political instability. So it seems contradictory to argue both that Russia is dying from the 'resource curse' and that [it] is a dangerous energy superpower.

Peter Rutland,
"Russia as an Energy Superpower,"
New Political Economy, *June 2008.*

cent. The country's GDP hit $1 trillion in 2006, rendering Russia one of the world's ten largest economies again. True, due to the country's natural endowments, hydrocarbons are a major factor in the Russian economy and in state finance. The export of raw materials, mainly oil, gas, and refined oil products, has soared since the 1990s, accounting for about two-thirds of Russian exports overall in 2006.[8] Still, hydrocarbon sales account for a major part of state revenues, just as recent oil price increases have resulted in soaring tax revenues. The total share of government revenues stemming from hydrocarbon sales has more than doubled during the past four years, amounting to almost 40 percent in 2006.[9]

At the same time, however, oil and gas add less to overall Russian GDP and economic growth than the above figures would suggest. In fact, oil and gas presently contribute only about 20 percent of Russian GDP.[10] Moreover, the energy sector grew below the Russian average during recent years. The gas sector performed especially poorly.[11]

Moreover, the initial kick-start of Russian economic recovery did not lie in oil prices but in the 1998 financial crisis: As a consequence of the Russian government's default, the ruble was strongly devalued, which led to greater competitiveness of Russian products abroad, favored domestic over foreign goods, and thus spurred consumption of domestic Russian products.[12] In addition, the rise of oil and gas prices supported economic recovery, as did general improvements in management and technology of private companies, a cut in government spending, and the introduction of a new tax system in 2000. Double-digit annual increases in capital and labor productivity have further contributed to securing a stable Russian growth path.

Finally, while energy revenues are dominant on the income side of the governmental budget, they are far less important in financing governmental expenditures. In fact, as experts have noted, more than half of Russian oil and gas revenues are saved in a "Stabilization Fund." The latter, a lesson learned from the 1998 plunge in oil prices and its devastating effects on state finances, presently contains financial reserves equal to around 9 percent of GDP.[13] Hence, and counter to conventional wisdom, the six-year-long Russian economic growth has mainly domestic roots.

Myth 4: Russia Is an Energy Superpower

The truth is: Given heavy and unresolved investment challenges in the Russian oil and gas sector, it is questionable whether Russia will keep its current position on world markets, let alone increase its market share. True, Russian oil and gas reserves are impressive. The country owns nearly 50 trillion cubic meters of proven gas reserves, or 26.6 percent of the world's total, and proven oil reserves of 75 billion barrels, 6.2 percent of the world's total. In 2005, Russia accounted for more than one-fifth of global gas production and for 12.1 percent of global crude output. While Russian oil reserves will last "only" another 21 years at present production levels, its gas reserves will last another 80.[14] Russian oil production is expected to expand from current levels of 9.5 million barrels per day (MBD) to 10 MBD in 2010 and 11 MBD in 2030.[15] As for gas, projections differ somewhat according to source. While the Russian government's "energy strategy" defines a possible range of output of 680 to 730 billion cubic meters in 2020, other Russian sources see overall production between 770 and 901 BCM by that year.[16] Western sources project Russian gas production to run between 801 and 850 BCM in 2020, and to hit even 1 trillion BCM by 2030.[17]

However, a striking lack of investment makes these existing projections appear highly optimistic. The "giant fields" of Yamburg, Urengoy, and Medvezhye, which currently account for more than 60 percent of total Russian production, have started to decline. Production at Zapolyarnoye, a fourth giant field that came on stream in 2001, has recently reached its peak.[18] In order to compensate for declining output from these fields and to meet contractual commitments, Russia urgently needs to make new upstream projects start producing. But as most new fields are smaller than the depleting ones and, in addition, are located in the far north, costs for exploration and production (E & P) are about to rise significantly. The last known giant field of Shtokman, located off-shore in the arctic Barents Sea, is projected to cost $34 billion until it begins producing in 2013.[19] E & P costs for developing fields on the arctic Yamal Peninsula and on the Ob-Taz shelf will amount to $25 billion, and yet another $40 billion in pipeline infrastructure to connect these fields to the existing system.[20] On average, the Russian gas sector will have to spend $17 billion per year through 2030 in E & P projects and in the maintenance of current fields in order to meet domestic demand and to fulfill export commitments.[21]

As for the oil sector, the picture looks similar. As important fields have peaked, development of new fields will have to cover all of Russia's annual oil growth in the next five years. Projected accumulated investment needs range from Russian Ministry of Energy estimates of $240 billion until 2020 to IEA forecasts of $400 billion by 2030.[22] But while the largely private Russian oil sector can be expected to respond to market signals, the prevalent monopolistic structure of the domestic Russian gas market is susceptible to avoiding necessary investments. At present, Gazprom has only committed to a total of $13 billion of capital spending per year through the next years—considerably less than projected needs—and the rest has to come from private companies.[23] Yet, as Gazprom uses its control of the domestic pipeline grid to restrict third-party access and prevents independent producers from exporting gas, private gas companies have little incentive to invest in upstream projects. Moreover, as it is a declared part of Gazprom's business strategy to increase acquisitions abroad and to invest outside its core business, considerable parts of the company's capital spending will not flow into gas production or pipelines. Further, recent bids for foreign and domestic companies, such as the $13 billion takeover of Sibneft, have imposed a heavy debt burden on the company. Despite the fact that many of these bids have been carried out via asset swaps, they have considerably reduced Gazprom's financial scope. Finally, pullouts of Western companies from promising Russian upstream projects and recently approved laws restricting foreign ownership of oil and natural gas assets deprive Gazprom of foreign capital as well as managerial and technical expertise for developing new fields. Overall, due to heavy underinvestment, the Russian gas balance is at risk of turning negative.

In a nutshell, unless the Russian government adopts a fundamentally different domestic pricing strategy that prompts further investment, triggers significant gains in domestic energy efficiency, and frees supply potentials for exports, Russia will barely be able to maintain its perceived status as an energy superpower. Otherwise, and paradoxically, the country with the world's largest energy reserves may virtually run out of gas.

Myth 5: There Is a Looming Sino-Russian Alliance Based on Oil and Gas

The truth is: As Russia and China are primarily strong strategic rivals, especially with respect to central Asian oil and gas, there will be no long-term strategic alliance based on energy. After decades of strained bilateral relations, and having solved remaining border disputes over territories in Russia's Far East in 2005, Russia and China have improved their relations in recent years. This trend has become obvious in several joint military exercises in 2005 and 2007, in enhanced economic cooperation, and especially in collaboration in the Shanghai Cooperation Organization (SCO), which Moscow and Beijing have managed to render as a vehicle to limit Washington's influence in their common near abroad. This emerging Sino-Russian alliance has led to concerns. Several observers have suggested that oil is likely to be the glue between Russia, as a major energy producer, and China, as a rising consumer—enhancing the emerging cooperation and ultimately leading to a geopolitical partnership that challenges U.S. interests and power. Yet, while at first sight they may seem persuasive, these concerns lack substance at the second. In fact, the countries' strategic interests in oil and gas are antithetical, especially with respect to the upcoming "Great Game" over central Asian energy resources.

Russia's recent and successful efforts to enhance control over central Asian energy by committing Turkmenistan to ship its gas to Western markets via its pipeline grid was not only a blow to U.S. and European efforts to tap energy sources independent from Russian influence; it was also a step toward a fiercer Russian-Chinese competition on regional energy resources. China's recent oil and gas deals with central Asian countries, in turn, run counter to Russia's strategic goal of monopolizing central Asian gas. A 30-year natural gas deal with Turkmenistan on 30 BCM annually and an oil pipeline project with Kazakhstan on 1 MBD now provide China with access to the Caspian Sea's rich oil resources. And, most important, these Chinese deals deprive Gazprom of an indispensable fallback: Given looming investment gaps and Gazprom's hostility to independent domestic gas producers, additional purchases from central Asia are an indispensable factor in Gazprom's business strategy of keeping the overall Russian gas balance positive. In fact, if Gazprom is to cover projected Russian and European demand in 2010, it not only has to meet its entire production target and change access policy to its transport grids in order to allow for a considerable increment of output by other Russian producers; it also has to dispose of the entire central Asian export potential for re-export to Europe.[24]

Reflecting this emerging strategic competition, China has recently undermined Russian attempts to make the SCO the nucleus of a regional energy organization—in which Moscow would have been the dominant partner. Further, several high-profile energy contracts between Russia and China, including the much debated Altai gas pipeline, have been put on hold. Moreover, after having played China against Japan for years over the planned 1.6 MBD eastern oil pipeline that would connect the Siberian Angarsk oil fields with either the Chinese or the Japanese market, Russia has finally opted for Japan. Finally, given Moscow's efforts to strengthen the state's grip on strategic sectors, Beijing's desire to buy into Russian upstream assets by its state-owned oil companies—a dominant strategy in the country's push for energy supplies and its favored path to improved mutual economic relations—will not materialize.

At the bottom line, then, there is no looming geopolitical "axis" between Russia and China based on oil and gas. Neither Moscow nor Beijing will be willing to subordinate their geo-*economic* interests in the name of a geostrategic Sino-Russian alliance. At best, their bilateral relations will be characterized by classical, if strained, business contracts between an energy producer and an energy consumer—if not by a fierce competition over resources in their common near abroad.

It's About Rules, Not Geopolitics

In sum, Russia has not become the "Energy Inc." of Western predictions. While it has attributes of a petro-state, the country's economic future will depend much less on energy prices than on its ability to manage unfavorable demographics, contain still-rampant corruption, and improve poor public management. Given the strong growth of the non-resource sectors, Russia's economic future will probably be based on industry and services rather than on oil and gas. And while its government may have a strong geopolitical agenda, that may not be pursued with the help of a state-run gas industry. As a brief look at figures has shown, an effective energy weapon appears to be the Kremlin's wishful thinking rather than reality. Western policy toward Russia, therefore, should be based on thorough analysis of available data rather than on conventional wisdom. Instead of adopting a reflexive geopolitical perspective on Russian energy, Western policy makers should regard it as a commodity that, even if politicized, should be dealt with in terms of regulations on global or regional markets, through the means of dispute settlement mechanisms, and in the frame of investment regimes and trade agreements.

The answer to upcoming challenges stemming from Russian oil and gas will not lie in an "Energy NATO" or an "Energy OSCE," ideas that invoke the Cold War. Instead, Western policies should aim at establishing a framework providing reciprocal benefits for producers and consumers. Agreements like the Energy Charter Treaty (ECT), a legally binding document on rules in investment, transit, and trade of energy, would provide the needed planning security for (Russian) producers and (European) consumers alike. In particular, the ECT's dispute-settlement mechanism would prove helpful in preventing future disagreements from turning into conflicts. Major countries, including Russia and the U.S., have abstained from ratifying the document. Committing them to the ECT would go a long way to enhance energy security.

Notes

1. "Statistical Review of World Energy," British Petroleum (2006).
2. See, among others, Yulia Woodruff, "Russian Oil Industry Between State and Market," *Fundamentals of the Global Oil and Gas Industry*, Petroleum Economist Publications (2006).
3. Liquefied Natural Gas (LNG), commonly regarded as a panacea for European energy security, will not provide a real alternative at short sight, mainly due to prohibitively high up-front costs.
4. "World Energy Outlook," International Energy Agency (2004).
5. "Sustainable Energy in Russia," *Sector Factsheet*, European Bank for Reconstruction and Development. Available at http://www.ebrd.com/pubs/factsh/themes/eerus.pdf.
6. "Russian Gas," United Bank of Switzerland Investment Research (2006). Available at http://www.ubs.com/investment research.

7. *Gazprom Annual Financial Report 2006* (2007).
8. "Country Analysis Briefs: Russia," Energy Information Agency (2006). Available at: http://www.eia.doe.gov/cabs/russia.html.
9. "Russian Federation, 2006," Article iv Consultation. Staff Report, IMF Country Report 06/429, 35.
10. "Russian Economic Report, 13," World Bank (2006).
11. "Economic Survey: Russian Federation, 17," OECD (2006), 25.
12. "Economic Survey: Russian Federation, 17," (2006), 24.
13. "Russian Economy: Trends and Perspectives," Monthly Bulletin, Institute for the Economy in Transition (December 2006).
14. "Statistical Review of World Energy" (2006).
15. "World Energy Outlook" (2006).
16. A. Ananenko, A. Kontorovich, V. Kulezhov, O. Yermilov, A. Kozhubaev, V. Livshits, "Russia's Gas Strategy at a Glance," *Oil and Gas Vertical*. Available at http://www.ngv.ru/article_en.aspx?articleid=22326#16-2006-6_5.
17. "World Energy Outlook," (2004); "International Energy Outlook," Energy Information Agency (2006).
18. "Russia Energy Survey" (2002); "Russian Gas" (2006).
19. "Russian Gas" (2006).
20. Ananenko et al., "Russia's Gas Strategy."
21. The Russian Ministry of Energy forecasts investment needs of $120–200 billion between 2002 and 2020. V. Ivanov, "Energy Strategy of Russia for up to 2020: Balancing Europe with the Asia-Pacific region," ERINA Report, 53 (2003); the Asia Pacific Energy Research Centre estimates total investment needs between 2004 and 2030 at $295–401 billion. "APEC Energy Demand and Supply Outlook 2006," Institute of Energy Economics, Tokyo.
22. "Energy Strategy of Russia for up to 2020"; "World Energy Outlook" (2004).
23. "World Energy Outlook" (2006).
24. "Russian Gas" (2006).

> *"[Russia's leadership] habitually invokes a 'polycentric' or multipolar model of the world, with Russia working with her partners toward a future in which U.S. power is so diminished that it cannot act without Moscow's permission. Russia's vision of the Middle East is a case in point."*

Russia's Influence in the Middle East Threatens American Interests

Ariel Cohen

In the following viewpoint, Ariel Cohen argues that Russia is seeking to strengthen its influence in the Middle East by maintaining friendships with anti-American regimes and stalling democracy in the region. According to Cohen, the Russians are motivated in part by economic ties to their Arab allies but also by a desire to minimize American influence. In Cohen's opinion, Russia's double-talk in negotiating an end to the Arab-Israeli conflict, its support for tyrants, and its assistance in Iran's scientific and military programs prove the Kremlin's intentions to ex-

Ariel Cohen, "How the U.S. Should Respond to Russia's Unhelpful Role in the Middle East," *Heritage Backgrounder*, no. 2662, March 8, 2012. Copyright © 2012 by The Heritage Foundation. All rights reserved. Reproduced by permission.

*ert some control in the Middle East and to keep the United
States from doing the same. Ariel Cohen is a senior research fellow in Russian and Eurasian studies at the Heritage Foundation,
a conservative public policy institute.*

As you read, consider the following questions:

1. What does Cohen believe are the key Kremlin priorities
   that keep Russia from supporting the Arab Spring uprisings in the Middle East?

2. As Cohen states, who offered to sell Saudi Arabia
   "peaceful" nuclear reactors in 2007?

3. With what other leading natural gas producer has Russia
   sought to create a gas cartel, according to the author?

The U.S. and Russia have come to diplomatic blows in the
U.N. [United Nations] Security Council over Syria as political upheavals and transformations irrevocably alter the
strategic landscape in the Middle East and North Africa. In an
unprecedented rhetorical escalation, U.S. Ambassador Susan
Rice announced that the United States was "disgusted" with
Russia's veto of a Security Council resolution that condemned
the Syrian government: "The international community must
protect the Syrian people from this abhorrent brutality, but a
couple members of this council remain steadfast in their willingness to sell out the Syrian people and shield a craven ty-
rant."

According to State Department spokesman Victoria Nu-
land, prior to the crucial vote, Secretary of State Hillary Clinton tried repeatedly to reach her Russian counterpart, Sergey
Lavrov. He avoided her calls for 24 hours. He was in Australia
and said that the State Department gave him an inconvenient
time frame for the conversation. When asked why the Americans were complaining, he replied, "Probably this is due to her
manners." Hillary Clinton called the Russian and Chinese ve-
toes a "travesty."

Competing for Influence

As the diplomatic fights escalate, new actors and old rivals will compete for influence in the critical geopolitical landscape from the Atlantic to Iran. These include old neighbors, such as Iran and Turkey, and outside powers, China and Russia. Attempting to support its two allies Iran and Syria, keep lucrative arms contracts, and rattle American influence, Russia is playing a hardball, realpolitik game in the Middle East.

U.S. decision makers need to be fully aware of Moscow's motivation and modus operandi. With the U.S.-Russia "reset" failing, including in the Middle East, the White House needs to reassess its dialogue with the Kremlin and draw the appropriate conclusions about the realities of competition and cooperation, including in the Middle East. While some Russian concerns about the rising power of Islamists in Egypt, Libya, Tunisia, and Syria may be valid, Russia's anti-American zero-sum geopolitical game in the Middle East is not. Neither is the incessant anti-American propaganda.

Unless Russia fundamentally changes its zero-sum game approach, Washington should use diplomacy, economic sanctions, and "naming and shaming" from the bully pulpit to convince Moscow that its disruptive Middle East policy is self-defeating. Washington needs to conduct a bottom-up reassessment of U.S. policy toward Russia to ensure that in the future U.S. diplomats make clear to Russia what U.S. vital interests are and that undermining such interests will come at a price Russia cannot afford. . . .

Russian Support for Key Arab States

Syria has reached a critical point where not just the West, but also Arab leaders are condemning the [Bashar al-]Assad dictatorship. Yet Moscow is clinging desperately to its old client, even sponsoring a watered-down U.N. Security Council resolution to thwart passage of biting international sanctions against the Syrian regime. Russia, with its long-standing ties to the region, is an important player, which could be quite disruptive and destructive if it continues to view the region through the prism of competition with the United States. . . .

While Russian foreign policy in the Middle East is clearly anti-American, at times it also appears self-defeating. Russia is backing a losing Assad regime and siding with the isolated Shia Islamic Republic in Tehran [Iran]. The policy is almost incoherent, driven by a plethora of strategic relationships and commercial interests.

Russian leaders allege that the U.S. uses its "political technologies" with the intention of spreading them to Russia and the other former Soviet republics. In his 2011 annual address to the Duma, Prime Minister Vladimir Putin declared:

> In today's world, if you're weak, someone will surely come and give you advice on what direction you should take, what kind of policy you should pursue, and what path you should choose for your own development . . . and this, supposedly, well-meaning, unobtrusive advice may not seem that bad, but what's behind it is flagrant diktat and interference in the internal affairs of sovereign states.

Russia's veto of U.N. sanctions against Syria clearly demonstrated its distrust of and antipathy toward Western interventionism. Officially, Russia exercised its veto because the resolution was "based on a philosophy of confrontation," contained "an ultimatum of sanctions," and was "against a peaceful settlement of a crisis." Later on, Prime Minister Putin explained that Russia cast the veto to stop America's and the West's unilateral use of power, as in Serbia, Iraq, and Libya. Moscow-based commentators highlighted Russia's interest in the Syrian naval bases and arms contracts. Whatever the rhetoric, Russia's veto, along with China's veto, highlighted the countries' commitments to reinforce their influence in the region as well as their opposition to American and Western involvement.

Comparing Russian and Western Views of the "Arab Spring"

With a long history of political relationships and shared interests, especially with secular/socialist dictatorships, the Union of Soviet Socialist Republics (USSR) and later Russia supported the status quo in the Middle East. . . .

The dramatic revolts in Tunisia, Egypt, Libya, Syria, and Yemen have acted as a catalyst for a broader Arab awakening that has fundamentally altered the dynamics of the Middle East's political order, some aspects of which have been in place since World War I and World War II. Even so, U.S. engagement in the Middle East remains essential to global stability and economic interests. . . .

Russia does not view the Middle East uprisings through the same lens as the U.S. and the West. Its reactions to these developments demonstrate that foiling Western influence and protecting Russian arms sales and energy deals are key Kremlin priorities. The Putin administration has also apparently become concerned about the potential for uprisings erupting in Russia or in one or more of the former Soviet republics—the "near abroad" that the Kremlin considers its "sphere of privileged interests." Russian leaders also fear that an Arab Spring scenario in Russia might lead to a NATO [North Atlantic Treaty Organization] humanitarian intervention along the lines of what happened in Libya.

Russia supported the initial sanctions on Libya, but abstained on the Security Council resolution that authorized military intervention. Unsurprisingly, it subsequently criticized the NATO military intervention and vehemently denounced the killing of [Libyan leader Muammar] Qadhafi. Moscow continues to criticize in unambiguous terms any Western military interventions to stop human rights violations, which Russia perceives as a part of individual states' internal affairs. This reflects Putin's long-term foreign policy emphasis on sovereignty and nonintervention, even when it contradicts Russia's own commitments under Organization for Security and Co-operation in Europe [OSCE] agreements. Russia's political elites frequently criticize the West's support for democratization in the Middle East. During the 2007 visit to the Middle East, Putin himself wondered:

> I do not understand why some of our partners [Europe and the U.S.] . . . see themselves as cleverer and more civilized and think that they have the right to impose their standards on others. The thing to remember is that standards that are imposed from the outside, including in the Middle East, rather than being a product of a society's natural internal development, lead to tragic consequences, and the best example of this is Iraq.

Yevgeny Satanovsky, president of the Institute for Middle Eastern Studies in Moscow, argues that President [Barack] Obama's decision to participate in interventions in the region will only further escalate tensions and that assisting rebels may ultimately empower Islamic radicals, promote de-Christianization of the region (which is already in progress), and fuel the resurgence of populist Islamist movements. Satanovsky argues:

> Why American leadership would "shoot itself in the foot" is hard to explain. At worst, one would have to believe in earnest the conspiracy theory that the United States seeks to establish "controlled chaos" worldwide, for which it will support any protest movement and stage all sorts of "color revolutions" irrespective of who these may be for or against.

The Kremlin has long been skeptical about imposing democratic change from outside, especially regime change. In Russia, there has also been a tendency to overestimate the U.S. role in facilitating or encouraging the uprisings in Tunisia, Egypt, and Libya through nongovernmental organizations (NGOs) and social networks, including Facebook and Twitter. Russia's careful stance on Libya reflects the Kremlin's rejection of "the responsibility to protect"—a U.N.-construed, White House-supported duty to intervene (selectively) to protect endangered civilians from governmental abuses....

Soviet Support for Tyrants

Since the early 1950s, the USSR worked to develop close relations with Syria, Algeria, Iraq, and Egypt, influencing and assisting each regime in becoming increasingly nationalistic and socialist. Russia was the primary provider of modern heavy weapons to Egypt and Syria before the 1956, 1967, and 1973 wars with Israel and threatened to attack Israel directly during each of these wars. The Kremlin also extended massive political support to the Arab cause, including orchestrating a global propaganda campaign against Israel and training Palestinian terrorists in the USSR and the Eastern Bloc countries. The USSR was a major arms supplier to Iraq, Libya, South Yemen, and Sudan—all of which pursued anti-Western policies....

During the Cold War, the Middle East was a hotly contested arena of superpower competition. However, Soviet influence began to decline after the Egyptian president Anwar el-Sadat expelled Soviet advisers in 1972. The Israeli air force then devastated the Syrian air force and its antiaircraft missile batteries in the Lebanon War of 1982 without the USSR coming to Hafez al-Assad's aid. In 1991, the collapsing Soviet Union could not protect its long-term client Saddam Hussein during the Gulf War. After the war, Moscow's influence declined further in the Middle East amid domestic economic reforms and internal instability....

Putin Vies to Increase Russian Influence

After Putin became president in 2000, the Kremlin proceeded with a more vigorous strategy in the region. Soon after coming to power, Putin outlined a new Russian Middle East policy, which included supporting Iran's nuclear programs, forgiving Syria's $13 billion debt, and lifting export controls on chemical and biological technologies, which may have dual-use applications. Consequently, Moscow expanded bilateral relations with the anti-American regimes of Syria and Iran and pro-American states, such as Saudi Arabia, Israel, and Egypt. During his 2007 visit to Riyadh, Putin stunned the world with an offer to sell Saudi Arabia "peaceful" nuclear reactors. In addition, he offered 150 T-90 tanks and other weapons. The Russian president indicated Russia's willingness to sell helicopters, build rocket-propelled grenade factories, provide sophisticated antiaircraft systems, including the Carapace (*Pantsir*), TOR-M1, and *Strelets*. He also offered to sell the Saudis satellite launches and an opportunity to join GLONASS, the Russian satellite navigation system.

However, despite Putin's repeated assertions that Russia has returned to the world stage as a great power, its influence in the Middle East remains less dynamic than U.S. clout and is mostly limited to arms sales and cooperation in energy trade. Nevertheless, Moscow sees itself as a potential broker between the Muslim world and the West due to its Soviet legacy of good relations with the Middle East and Russia's own Muslim population (about 10 percent of Russia's total population). Russia is an observer member of the Organization of the Islamic Conference (OIC) and the Arab League. In addition, Russia would like to boost its involvement in mediating the Arab-Israeli conflict, although it is trusted less by the parties than the U.S. . . .

Seeking Its Own Agenda in the Arab-Israeli Conflict

In 2002, Russia, the U.S., the U.N., and the EU [European Union] formed the Quartet on the Middle East, which is attempting to mediate the Israeli-Palestinian conflict. After the 2006 Arab-Israeli conflict in Lebanon, Russia's leadership embarked on a stronger role in the quartet. . . .

However, President Dmitry Medvedev's talks with Hamas in 2010 and the Kremlin's enthusiastic support of the Palestinian push for unilateral statehood via the U.N. directly contradict U.S. interests, violate the quartet's road map for peace, and set back future prospects for an Israeli-Palestinian peace agreement. This suggests that Russia does not truly value its ties with Israel. This is not new. Russian-Israeli relations may have improved in recent years, but Moscow has not changed its broader foreign policy strategy, inherited from Soviet days, which has the United States as its target. The USSR always preferred the more lucrative opportunities in the Arab countries to good relations with Israel. Russia's perception of Israel's strong reliance on ties with the United States is another reason for it to abandon Israel, especially considering the consistent anti-American overtones of the Kremlin's foreign policy dialogue.

Russia as Iran's Protector

Russia has developed complex and close economic ties with Iran in energy, military, and technology. Since the Soviet era, a large number of Iranian scientists have been educated in Russian military academies and engineering colleges. Russian scientists and experts have continuously provided direct and indirect assistance to Iranian scientific and military development programs, while Russian state-owned and private companies have pursued their energy development and economic goals. At the same time, Moscow claims to support nonproliferation goals that are supposed to prevent Iran from developing nuclear weapons. At the height of the U.S.-Russian "reset" policy, Moscow vacillated between tactical concessions to the United States regarding Iran and a strategic commitment to Russian-Iranian ties. After Putin's expected return to the presidency in March [2012], the pendulum will likely swing more explicitly toward Tehran.

Thus far, Western and Russian efforts to prevent Iran from acquiring nuclear weapons have been woefully insufficient. President Mahmoud Ahmadinejad has publicly denied the Holocaust and threatened to wipe Israel off the map. However, Iran's nuclear ambitions threaten not only Israel, but also the entire Middle East because Iranian nuclear capability will likely trigger a regional nuclear arms race.

Furthermore, Iran can already threaten Israel and U.S. bases in the region with ballistic missile attacks, and Tehran is projected to have an intercontinental ballistic missile (ICBM) capability by 2015, which will pose an even greater threat to the U.S. and Europe. A nuclear-armed Iran would be a regional game changer and would significantly transform security dynamics in the Middle East. Already truculent, Iran will likely use its nuclear arsenal to bully its neighbors, deter other nuclear powers, and provide diplomatic cover for its terrorist proxies, such as Hamas and Hezbollah.

Iran currently returns spent uranium fuel from the Bushehr nuclear reactor to Russia. At the same time, it is feverishly developing its own uranium enrichment capability, ostensibly for civilian purposes, but most likely for making nuclear weapons. The September 2011 International Atomic Energy Agency (IAEA) report on Iran warns that "the agency is increasingly concerned about the possible existence in Iran of past or current undisclosed nuclear-related activities involving military-related organizations." The Russian foreign ministry slammed the report for alleged bias and intentional politicization of the issue, simultaneously accusing the United States of setting the stage for another war in the Middle East.

Russia's protective attitude toward Tehran is not surprising, considering it provided the technical expertise, nuclear fuel, equipment, parts, and other components to build the Bushehr nuclear power plant, which is an important component of Iran's nuclear infrastructure. Russia is also negotiating contracts for building additional reactors in Iran. Moscow's failure to denounce Iran's threats to block the Strait of Hormuz clearly demonstrates that Russia's interests in Iran directly conflict with those of the United States and the West.

While Moscow on some level may be uncomfortable with Iran as a nuclear power, its recent actions undermine the international effort to oversee Iran's nuclear program. In addition to its economic interest in continuing to develop Iran's nuclear capabilities, the Kremlin has used Russia's position on Iran as a tool to extract concessions on security issues from the U.S. and its allies, such as on the New START [Strategic Arms Reduction Treaty], European missile defense, and Russia's dominance of its neighbors. . . .

In addition, Russia has sought to strengthen its position by attempting to establish an [Organization of the Petroleum Exporting Countries] OPEC-style natural gas cartel with Iran and other leading gas producers. It is also engaged in oil and gas "swap" deals with Iran. Moscow and Tehran are also planning to create a massive energy and transportation north-south corridor to connect the Indian Ocean, the Caspian Sea, and Europe.

Moscow's ties with Tehran are a highly complex maze of military and economic partnerships and cooperation on nuclear and fossil energy issues, with the shared goal of reducing U.S. influence regionally and globally. If a nuclear-armed Iran is inevitable, Russia would rather be its friend than its enemy. In this sense, the Kremlin does not view Iran as a direct threat, but rather as an ad hoc ally and a rising regional power—one that could challenge U.S. influence.

The Future of Russia-Syria Cooperation

Russia maintains close relations with Syria, which is led by Bashar al-Assad and ruled by its socialist, nationalist Baath Party. Not long after the U.S. imposed sanctions on Syria in 2004 for supporting terrorism, Russia agreed in principle to sell Damascus war planes, air defense systems, and antitank weapons. In May 2010, President Medvedev signed the formal agreement during his first visit to Damascus, but only after Iran committed to pay for the weapons. In the past decade, Russia has sold well over $1 billion in arms to Syria, including antitank missiles, surface-to-air missiles, and MiG 29/31 fighter aircraft.

Russia also plans to construct a nuclear power plant in Syria, even though Israel destroyed a suspected nuclear reactor in the middle of the Syrian desert in September 2007. According to President Medvedev during his state visit, "Cooperation on atomic energy could get a second wind."

Despite Syria's growing isolation due to Assad's brutal crackdown on the increasingly violent protesters, Russia continues to supply weapons and nuclear technology to the crumbling Assad regime. Most recently, Russia decided to deliver SS-N-26 Yakhont antiship cruise missiles to honor an earlier arms deal.

Actions such as these are destabilizing and dangerous. In 2006, Hezbollah used Russian antitank rockets provided by Syria against Israeli forces. Since then, Russia has continued to deliver weapons to Syria despite U.S. and Israeli objections. Likewise, Iran continues to provide arms and training to Hamas and Hezbollah via Syria.

Syria is another example of the conflicting Russian and U.S. approaches to the Middle East. A longtime sponsor of terrorism and a close ally of Iran, Syria poses a number of challenges to U.S. interests in the region. Damascus has aided and abetted attacks of foreign fighters on American troops and U.S. allies in Iraq and the destabilization of Lebanon. . . .

Russia's Vision of the Middle East

The anti-American tilt of Russian foreign policy prevents diplomatic cooperation because the U.S. and Russia lack a shared threat assessment and mutual understanding in dealing with the changing dynamics of the Middle East. Despite clear statements to the contrary by Prime Minister Putin and Foreign Minister Lavrov, the Obama administration has repeatedly declared that the U.S. is not competing with Russia for regional influence. Regrettably, the Kremlin has not received this memo. Instead, Russian attempts to constrain U.S. policy have provoked little or no response from Washington. Lavrov habitually invokes a "polycentric" or multipolar model of the world, with Russia working with her partners toward a future in which U.S. power is so diminished that it cannot act without Moscow's permission. Russia's vision of the Middle East is a case in point.

> *"What Moscow is doing is positioning itself in such a way so as not to spoil relations with any other actor in the [Middle East], and to be able to exploit any possible emerging opportunities in case of further-reaching changes."*

Russia's Influence in the Middle East Remains Unclear

Marcin Kaczmarski

Marcin Kaczmarski is a member of the Centre for Eastern Studies, a research institution in Poland that addresses political, social, and economic change in neighboring countries. He is an expert in Russian foreign and security policy and has penned several papers on related issues. In the following viewpoint, Kaczmarski contends that although Russia's role in the Middle East has become more pronounced in recent years, its influence has not been used to broaden opportunities for political dominance in the region. Instead, Kaczmarski claims that Russia has chiefly sought outlets for arms sales and energy deals. According to the author, Moscow's reaction to the 2011 Arab revolutions in key states has exemplified its ambivalence. Initially fearful that the regime changes would lead to an expansion of radical Islam and

Marcin Kaczmarski, "Russia's Middle East Policy After the Arab Revolutions," *OSW Commentary*, July 26, 2011. © Ośrodek Studiów Wschodnich, Warsaw, Poland. www.osw.waw.pl/en.

thus threaten Russia's security, Moscow eventually supported these revolutions but used them as opportunities to criticize the West's "intrusive" involvement in Arab matters. Indeed, Kaczmarski believes that Russia will only engage in the Middle East when it has an advantage; otherwise, it will simply use its leverage to destabilize Western attempts to gain dominance.

As you read, consider the following questions:

1. Why does Kaczmarski maintain that Russian attempts to sell arms to Saudi Arabia and other Gulf countries did not meet with much success?

2. According to Kaczmarski, what is Russia's aim in involving itself in negotiations to settle the Iranian nuclear crisis and the Arab-Israeli conflict?

3. In the author's view, Moscow feared that the potential empowerment of radical Islam following the Arab revolutions might increase the threat of destabilizing central Asia and what Russian region?

R ussia's policy towards the Middle East is instrumental. Its activity in the region has been growing since the middle of the last decade, and its aim is to help Moscow achieve its objectives in other areas, particularly in its policies towards the US and Europe, as well as its energy policy. The establishment of these political influences constitutes a bargaining chip for Russia in its relations with the US. Russia's participation in resolving conflicts is aimed at building up its image as a supra-regional power. Russia's Middle East policy is a key element in its contacts with the Muslim world. At the same time, Russia's policy in the region remains cautious—despite its return to the region, Russia has not decided to 'play' for the Middle East, and its position and role in the region remain limited.

The balance of power in the Middle East has been shifting in the aftermath of the [2010–2011] Arab revolutions. However, it does not seem that they have opened up larger opportunities for Russian policy in the region. The Russian elite has been divided in its assessment of the consequences of these events. One part of it has displayed scepticism, treating the revolutions rather as a threat than a chance to strengthen their own position. The revolutions were not seen as democratisation processes, but rather as a destabilisation of the region and as posing an increased danger from radical Islam. For the other part of the elite, the revolutions were the natural consequence of the social changes occurring in the region. This internal dispute made it difficult for Russia to present a cohesive approach to the Arab revolutions, and its stance was reactive.

The defensive position which Moscow adopted showed that Russia did not have the potential to mould the political situation, either in the region as a whole or its individual countries; neither did it display any willingness to do so. What Moscow is doing is positioning itself in such a way so as not to spoil relations with any other actor in the region, and to be able to exploit any possible emerging opportunities in case of further-reaching changes.

Russia's Position in the Middle East Remains Limited

After having retreated from the Middle East following the collapse of the USSR [Union of Soviet Socialist Republics, or Soviet Union], Russia has begun 'returning' to the region since 2002, striving for a rapprochement with Muslim countries. The main cause of Moscow's involvement at that time was its efforts to cut off Chechen guerrillas from the Arab world's support. Since the middle of the previous decade (2005–2007), Russia's ambitions and political and economic presence in the Middle East have been growing substantially. The regional dimension of the commitment (the Arab-Israeli peace process and the Iranian nuclear crisis) was accompanied by intensified bilateral relations with practically all the actors, ranging from former Soviet-era allies (Syria), through actors with which

Moscow had previously had relations (Egypt, Jordan, the Palestinian autonomy, Algeria, Libya), to those countries with which contacts have been established almost from scratch (Saudi Arabia, the smaller Gulf countries). This policy has been complemented by close relations with non-Arab countries, namely Iran and Israel. In 2005 Russia gained observer status in the Organization of the Islamic Conference, and in 2006 established diplomatic relations with Hamas [Palestinian political party] after it had won the parliamentary elections.

Russia's activity in the Middle East has been 'auxiliary' compared to its main orientations in foreign policy, and has served above all to pursue its interests outside the region. Moscow sees the establishment of political leverage in the Middle East as a way of limiting American global domination, and was also intended as a bargaining chip in its relations with the US. Closer relations with both anti-American countries and US allies were meant to expand Russia's room for manoeuvre. At the same time, Moscow did not enter into military alliances with any of the countries in the region, and its geopolitical position there remained limited (in contrast to that of the USSR).

Bids for Arms Sales and Energy Markets

Arms sales have played an important role in building political influences; the main recipients were Iran, Syria, Algeria and Libya. These arms sales have constituted a bargaining chip in relations with the US, as was proven by the several years of bargaining between Russia and the US with regard to the former supplying S-300 anti-missile systems to Iran. On the other hand, technical and military co-operation with the countries of the region has been an element of Moscow's policy aimed at diversifying its arms exports. Moscow has also put great effort into promoting sales of its arms to the Gulf countries, particularly Saudi Arabia, but this did not bring results as these markets were already dominated by the US and other Western countries.

Energy is a significant area of Russia's activity in the Middle East due to its strategic and economic importance. By co-operating with the countries of the region, Moscow wanted to ensure a greater impact on the European Union, for which this area is the third largest supplier of natural gas and second largest of oil. Russia has made attempts at coordinating the policies of the largest producers, both from the Gulf (Iran, Qatar) and North Africa (Algeria, Libya), and has used the organisation of the Gas Exporting Countries Forum (GECF) for this purpose. However, due to Russia's inconsistent policy and the specificity of the gas market, these attempts brought about inconsequential results. In the context of producing and selling oil, relations with OPEC [Organization of the Petroleum Exporting Countries] have been important for Moscow, particularly with Saudi Arabia as the main (and most flexible) producer which is able to impact global oil supply. This co-operation was significantly hampered by Russia's lack of willingness to agree on the volume of its own production with OPEC. The region's economic importance for Russian energy companies as the place which provides access to resources and enables their extraction remains restricted (despite the fact that Russian companies are present in nearly every country in the region). Russia is also interested in entering the nuclear energy market emerging in the Middle East (Egypt, Jordan).

Contending with Islamic Radicalism and Russia's Image in the Islamic World

With regard to the large and dynamically growing Muslim population in Russia and the importance of the Middle East as the centre of the Muslim world, the policy aimed at the Muslim world has been another sphere of the Kremlin's involvement in the region. Moscow has been trying to ensure a legitimisation of its policy towards the North Caucasus and the Muslim population in general, as well as a restriction on the influx of Islamic radicalism to Russia. In this context,

Moscow has succeeded in preventing the situation of Muslims in the Russian Federation from becoming a pan-Islamic issue, and the improvement in relations with Saudi Arabia has brought about the legitimisation which it expected (among other events, Chechnya's President Ramzan Kadyrov was recognised as the legitimate leader of the republic by the Saudi monarchy). Equally, the position on the Palestinian issue—support for Palestinian statehood—constitutes an element of improving Russia's image in the eyes of the Muslim world. As for Islamic radicalism, attention should be paid to the close co-operation between Russian services with their counterparts in Arab countries (but also in Israel), which required political endorsement. Above all, Russia's policy in the region—acting as an intermediary in resolving crises—serves the purpose of building up its image as a global power (or at least a supra-regional power). Both the Kremlin's involvement in the Iranian crisis and in the Arab-Israeli conflict are intended to achieve this aim. At the same time, however, Moscow has not succeeded in persuading Tehran to accept its idea for settling the crisis, and Russia's initiatives regarding the Arab-Israeli conflict are not being implemented. Russia's *idée fixe* [obsession] is to organise a peace conference which would extend to all the actors, and serve as a manifestation of Russia's return to the region as an actor on an equal footing with the US.

The Middle East Is a Secondary Concern for Russia

So far, the balance sheet of Russia's 'return' to the Middle East has been equivocal. On the one hand, Russia has built up good relations with nearly all the actors, including those which had ignored it earlier. None of the countries sees Russia as an enemy power. Moscow has legitimised its policy towards Muslims in Russia and won a few new customers for its arms sales. On the other hand, Russia's successes remain limited: the rapprochement with Saudi Arabia has not translated into economic benefits; energy manoeuvres aimed at increasing its ascendancy over Europe have not brought any results; its actions as an intermediary in settling conflicts have been confined to declarations. In the face of American supremacy, Russia has not managed to develop its own sustainable influences, except on Syria, a country which is isolated in the West. This balance sheet proves that the Middle East orientation has played a secondary role, being used as an 'auxiliary instrument' for realising the objectives of its policy towards the US and Europe (as a sort of a bargaining chip) and for promoting restricted economic interests (support for foreign policy, limited importance for security policy). As a result of this approach and the 'auxiliary' character of the policy in the region—the consequent caution and the willingness to maintain good relations with all the crucial actors—and not committing important political and economic resources, the outcomes of Russia's 'return' have been limited, both in their political and economic dimensions.

Russia's Ambivalent View of the Arab Revolutions

The Russian government's cautious and sceptical reaction to the events in individual Arab countries, which soon came to be called the 'Arab revolution' by the Russian media, showed that Moscow was taken by surprise by the situation in these countries. The positions which the Kremlin formulated revealed important divergences among the Russian elite in their assessment of the nature and consequences of the events in the Middle East, and the dominant trend was scepticism.

On the one hand, the Russian government did not hide its distrust of the Arab revolutions. They were not regarded as processes of democratisation, but rather as a destabilisation of the region. Comparisons to the revolutions of 1989 were dismissed. The causes of the upheaval were attributed to external factors. Prime Minister Vladimir Putin hinted that it was the

North African branch of al-Qaida that stood behind the events in Libya. The Russian representative at NATO [North Atlantic Treaty Organization] Dmitry Rogozin pointed to the West's ill intentions and the lack of understanding of the situation in Libya itself, thus hinting that Western countries were deliberately painting a picture of a civil war. Deputy Prime Minister Igor Sechin accused Google of instigating the revolution in Egypt. As the situation in Libya deteriorated, the references to external factors intensified. The consequences of the revolution were seen as very negative. At the first stage of the revolution in Egypt in February 2011, representatives of the Russian government believed that if President Hosni Mubarak stepped down too soon, it would lead to radicalisation, divisions and destabilisation, and that similar scenarios could be reproduced in Tunisia, Jordan, Syria and Algeria. It was thought that the revolutions could pave the way for extremists, and result in the repetition of the collapse of the state, as happened in Somalia. In this context the revolutionary situation in the Arab countries was linked to a potential threat to the Russian state, above all from radical Islam. Soon after endorsing the changes in Egypt, President Dmitry Medvedev contended that the revolutions might cause fanatics to come to power, escalate extremism and provoke the disintegration of the Arab countries, which could also be dangerous for Russia. Foreign Minister Sergey Lavrov indicated that together with the destabilisation of the region, the risk was rising for central Asia and the Russian South Caucasus, as even during the period of stability this region was being infiltrated from the Middle East, and if the state structures collapsed, this infiltration would be even stronger.

At the same time, another trend has appeared in the Russian government's approach to the Arab revolutions which did not regard them as a threat. The revolutions' causes were seen in internal social and economic processes and in the situation of the individual countries. This stance was probably an attempt at adjusting to the new political situation. The statements made by President Medvedev and Minister Lavrov should be interpreted in this way as, contrary to their earlier critical comments, they both emphasised their support for the events in Egypt, for instance; they acknowledged that a strong democratic Egypt was important for the peace process, and that Russia would endorse related international efforts. Another example of a positive assessment of the shifts in the region was President Medvedev's statement in which he considered the transformations to be paving the way for reforms, and compared them to the implications of the fall of the Berlin Wall in Eastern Europe. At the same time, it is impossible to determine how sustainable this correction of the negative approach to the Arab revolutions is.

Warming to Revolution but Criticizing Western Intervention

The divergences in the Russian elite's evaluation of the Arab revolutions has given rise to inconsistency in the political measures taken by Russia.

At the initial stage (the upheavals in Tunisia and Egypt) Moscow distanced itself from the Arab revolutions, only issuing warnings against external intervention (although it did not take any action which could have prevented such a step). Russia also cautioned Western states against putting pressure on the Arab countries, or 'enticing' them to mount further revolutions and pro-democratic movements, deeming it counterproductive. Russia also evaded taking any unequivocal position, awaiting a relative 'clarification' of the situation (for example, Minister Lavrov went to Cairo only in March 2011, after President Mubarak had resigned from power).

The differences in the evaluation of the Arab revolutions had the strongest impact on Russia's position on Libya. Moscow vacillated between supporting the actions undertaken by the international community, headed by the Western countries, and criticism of the intervention in Libya's civil war. The first approach resulted in the condemnation of the actions taken by the regime of Muammar Gaddafi, voting for UNSC [United Nations Security Council] Resolution 1970 (which introduced the arms embargo, froze assets and submitted Libya's case to the International Criminal Court), and abstaining from voting for UNSC Resolution 1973, which introduced a no-fly zone. In the latter case, an important role was played by the Arab League which backed the idea of a no-fly zone. Furthermore, while supporting the approach of the Western countries, President Medvedev recognised that Gaddafi had lost all legitimacy to rule. At the same time, Russia severely criticised the actions undertaken by the West in Libya. Most critical was Prime Minister Vladimir Putin, who regarded Resolution 1973 as a call to a crusade, which led to a public polemic with President Medvedev. Nevertheless, both politicians quite unanimously denounced the way in which the no-fly zone was implemented, and consistently blamed the Western countries for abusing the UN resolution. . . .

Russia's Middle East Policy Remains Reactive

The Arab revolutions have been shifting the balance of power in the Middle East, both between the actors in the region and the position and importance of particular external actors. Due to internal disparities, Moscow has lacked a strategy in the face of the revolution, and its reaction has been defensive and adaptive. Most of its actions were taken in response to the evolution of the political situation in the region. This approach was reflected in Moscow's open position towards the opposition forces, even if it nominally supported a particular regime. Among its main achievements, then, Russia can therefore count the fact that it managed not to pit against itself any of the political forces in the region, especially in situations where further changes were possible. On the other hand, the policy Moscow has pursued to date shows that it does not have the potential to shape the political situation either in the region as a whole or in its individual states. Its policy remains reactive despite several bold diplomatic and political moves, such as the recognition of Hamas. Its reaction to the revolutions indicates a lack of willingness to shape the political situation. Moscow seems not to expect any geopolitical benefits as a result of the revolutions and the resulting weakening of the US position, but fears their detrimental implications above all. Russia's offer for the countries of the region has not been expanded (even in the categories of soft power, as Moscow does not have an attractive model of development, like Turkey does, for example). Moscow rather sees threats and risks than prospects for a new opening up and growth of its influences. In the long term, such an approach may lead to Russia's marginalisation in the region. At the same time, the long-term consequences of the revolutions for the Arab world remain undetermined. The main unknown is the share of influences between key political actors in the region and the role of political Islam, and thus the character of the governments which will be formed. As a result of further-reaching transformations, the context for Russia to realise its interests in the Middle East will change. Russia's capacities for further exploitation of the region in order to attain the supra-regional objectives of its foreign policy will to a great extent depend on the nature of the regimes which replace the current dictatorships.

| "Under New START [Strategic Arms Reduction Treaty], . . . the United States is compelled to substantially reduce its strategic forces—while Russia is allowed to build up its forces."

Russia Will Gain an Advantage in Nuclear Arms Under New Treaties

Robert G. Joseph

Robert G. Joseph is a senior scholar at the National Institute for Public Policy. He served from 2005 until 2007 as undersecretary of state for arms control and international security. In the viewpoint that follows, Joseph argues that the 2010 New Strategic Arms Reduction Treaty (New START) is a dangerous agreement that forces America to give up its advantage in nuclear weapons. The treaty calls for parity of strategic nuclear weapons but does not contain provisions for their tactical counterparts. Russia has more tactical nuclear weapons than the United States, according to to Joseph, and these weapons have a great significance in potential conflicts—especially to America's European allies, who would likely bear the brunt of any tactical nuclear exchange. In addition, Joseph maintains that the United States is currently com-

Robert G. Joseph, "Second to One," *National Review*, vol. 63, no. 19, October 17, 2011. Copyright © 2011 by The National Review. All rights reserved. Reproduced by permission.

mitted to reducing its warheads and not upgrading its delivery systems. Russia, Joseph claims, is taking the opposite path, building up its arsenal and improving its technologies.

As you read, consider the following questions:

1. How many warheads and delivery vehicles are the United States and Russia allowed under New START, according to Joseph?

2. As Joseph reports, how many new warheads can Russia and the United States make per year?

3. In the 2010 Nuclear Posture Review cited by Joseph, what does the Obama administration give as its reason for abandoning the notion of nuclear parity with Russia?

Since the start of the atomic age, from Harry Truman to George W. Bush, the United States has sought to maintain, in the words of John F. Kennedy, a nuclear-weapons capability "second to none." Each of these eleven successive administrations, Democratic and Republican alike, described its commitment to that principle differently, some insisting on superiority and others on parity or essential equivalence. But all—including those that took large and unilateral steps to reduce the U.S. nuclear arsenal following the Cold War—believed that it was vital for the United States not to concede nuclear preeminence to any country.

In pursuing the goal of a world without nuclear weapons, and notwithstanding his administration's stated commitment to maintaining an effective deterrent for as long as necessary, President [Barack] Obama has abandoned this bedrock of our national security. Under [2010's] New START [Strategic Arms Reduction Treaty], often heralded by the administration as its greatest foreign policy success, the United States is compelled to substantially reduce its strategic forces—while Russia is allowed to build up its forces, which Moscow has announced its intention to do. As a consequence of this treaty and of the significant advantages that Russia possesses in other measures of nuclear might, the United States will for the first time become a nation "second to one" in what remains a vital military capability in an increasingly dangerous world with ever greater proliferation.

Russia Will Seek Nuclear Advantage Under the New Treaty

Defenders of the Obama administration's policies are quick to assert that the nuclear posture of the United States today is superior to that of Russia and all other nuclear-weapons states combined. In support of this assertion, they cite the United States' current advantage in deployed operational strategic warheads and launchers. But this is the very advantage that is given up under New START. The United States currently deploys about 1,800 warheads on 822 strategic delivery vehicles. Russia, according to its initial declaration under the treaty, deploys 1,537 warheads on 521 delivery vehicles. Under New START, each side will be allowed 1,550 warheads and 700 deployed vehicles.

But by suggesting parity, these numbers mislead, because they do not accurately reflect the overall nuclear capabilities of the two countries—or perhaps even the capabilities of those forces covered under New START. One provision of the treaty is a change in counting rules: Each heavy bomber is counted as carrying one warhead, no matter what its actual load. While this rule applies to both sides, and will allow each to deploy a number of actual (as opposed to accountable) warheads well above 1,550, it is unlikely that both will take advantage of the rule. Russia has a record of fully exploiting such provisions in arms-control treaties and, if it does so again, it could deploy even more warheads than the 2,200 permitted under the [Treaty of] Moscow negotiated by the George W. Bush administration [in 2002]. The United States will likely want to set a different example by staying at or below 1,550.

Most important, thousands of Russian nuclear weapons carried by shorter-range systems—including everything from artillery to medium-range aircraft—are not counted under New START. With the notable exception of the 1987 INF [Intermediate-Range Nuclear Forces] Treaty, these weapons, referred to as "theater" or "tactical" nuclear forces, have largely been ignored by nuclear strategists and arms-control experts, who have focused almost entirely on weapons that can reach beyond 5,500 kilometers.

This division between "strategic" and "tactical" weapons is primarily a relic of Cold War arms control, based in large part on the inherent difficulties of verifying shorter-range, often dual-capable systems (that is, widely dispersed delivery systems that can carry both nuclear and non-nuclear warheads). To facilitate the negotiation of arms-control treaties, the United States and the Soviet Union agreed to categorize only specific long-range missiles and bombers as "strategic," while mostly ignoring nuclear-armed systems that were deemed "non-strategic"—an oxymoron, because the use of any nuclear weapon would have a strategic effect.

Adopting this convenient designation of "non-strategic" nuclear weapons seemed both necessary and acceptable. Necessary because including them in arms negotiations was considered simply too hard to do; and acceptable because the numbers of American and Soviet long-range weapons ran into the high thousands, making an agreement on shorter-range systems seem less urgent. But with today's much lower levels of strategic forces, the importance of theater weapons has increased substantially.

Russia Has More and Can Build More Nuclear Weapons

While both the United States and Russia deployed thousands of theater nuclear weapons during the Cold War, the current numbers show a dramatic disparity. As revealed by a key Obama adviser, the United States possesses a "few hundred" tactical weapons, while Russia deploys an estimated 3,500 to 4,000. When these thousands of weapons (which in some cases can strike the same targets as those delivered by longer-range systems) are included in the counting of nuclear arsenals, the emerging inferiority of the United States stands out.

And when total inventories of nuclear weapons are compared, the disparity is even starker. In May 2010, in the name of "transparency," the Pentagon took the unprecedented step of announcing that the active U.S. stockpile had been reduced to 5,113. While Moscow has not released a number for its total arsenal and is unlikely to do so in the future, the Congressional Commission on the Strategic Posture estimated the Russian operational warhead inventory in 2009 to be 7,900.

Beyond the numbers of weapons, any meaningful comparison must also take into account overall trends and weapons infrastructure. The United States not only trails but is falling further behind on both counts, even apart from the rapid vanishing of funding commitments the Obama administration made to secure ratification of New START. For example, Russia can produce about 2,000 new warheads each year, whereas the United States can produce just 50 to 80 under the best conditions. Russia retires and replaces its warheads, while the U.S. spends billions on stockpile stewardship, so these numbers exaggerate the difference—but nonetheless, they demonstrate Russia's dedication to maintaining its force at a time when America's weapons infrastructure is deteriorating. And while Moscow seeks greater military capability in its new warhead designs, the Obama administration has taken the unprecedented—and unilateral—position that the United States will forgo "any new capabilities" in future or redesigned warheads.

Russia's Commitment to Reaching START Limits

As for strategic delivery vehicles, while Russia's total will almost certainly continue to diminish in the near term because of the aging of its current forces, Moscow has begun to implement its stated commitment to reverse this trend, pledging to reach the New START limit of 700 by 2028. To meet this objective, Russia is constructing a new class of ballistic-missile submarines, two of which could be deployed by next year. It is increasing production of intercontinental ballistic missiles (ICBMs) this year [2011], with the goal of more than doubling production, to 30 per year, by 2013 and fielding a new missile by 2018. And it has announced that it will deploy a new strategic bomber by 2025 or 2030. While it is dubious that Russia will meet these ambitious timelines, for budgetary and other reasons, there is little doubt that, over time, it will build up at least to the New START limits—its self-image as a recovering superpower depends on it.

As for the United States, a new strategic submarine is planned for 2029. A new ICBM, for which there is no committed funding, will not come online until at least 2030, when the existing missile force will be 60 years old. And as for the new bomber announced by Defense Secretary Robert Gates before leaving office, not only is there no current program, but the Pentagon has not even established an official requirement for one—an essential step to moving forward. In fact, the recently retired vice chairman of the Joint Chiefs stated there is no need for such a bomber.

The U.S. Government Downplays the Importance of Nuclear Superiority

The Obama administration has responded to the emerging loss of parity in a variety of ways. First, it asserts that rough parity in overall nuclear forces still exists, despite the numbers and trends. Second, it suggests that parity is less important than it was in the past. Third, it has taken a number of steps that further erode parity, including unilateral reductions in nuclear forces. And perhaps most troubling are the sugges-

President Obama Mistakenly Views America as the Cause for Nuclear Proliferation

The [Barack] Obama administration is clearly committed to a policy that asserts that for every negative development in the area of nuclear proliferation the U.S. needs to take a substantive step in the direction of nuclear disarmament, and New START [Strategic Arms Reduction Treaty] is a product of this misguided approach. Ultimately, this approach effectively assumes that the possession of nuclear arms by the U.S. is the incentive driving other nations to pursue nuclear weapons programs. Not only is the assumption misplaced, but the policy will undermine deterrence and increase the likelihood of the use of nuclear weapons. At some point, the Obama administration will need to recognize that it is foolish for the U.S. to take substantive steps toward nuclear disarmament at the same time the nuclear proliferation problem is growing worse.

Baker Spring,
"Twelve Flaws of New START That Will Be Difficult to Fix,"
Heritage Backgrounder, *no. 2466, September 16, 2010.*

tions that even more reductions of this type are coming—all in pursuit of the president's vision of a world free of nuclear weapons.

To assert that parity is being maintained, one must ignore the facts. This is most commonly done in the context of minimizing the military and political value of "non-strategic" nuclear weapons. Today, even many who support the maintenance of an American nuclear force second to none have accepted the fiction outlined above that some nuclear weapons count in measuring overall capability ("strategic" weapons) while others do not ("non-strategic" weapons). When asked whether the United States is now inferior to Russia in nuclear weaponry, these members of the "nuclear priesthood" will often respond, "of course not," and cite the quantitative advantages in U.S. strategic forces, as well as what they present as qualitative advantages, such as reload capacity on ICBMs or better-built and -manned submarines. But when pressed about overall capabilities once tactical weapons are included, many concede that the calculus changes.

Others defend the strategic/non-strategic fiction. High-level Obama advisers have suggested that tactical weapons are mostly symbolic—having no real utility in the contemporary security setting. Shorter-range weapons don't matter as much, they argue, because they can't target the U.S. homeland. This is neither accurate, because many can hit targets in the United States, nor meaningful, because shorter-range weapons can strike forward-based U.S. forces as well as allies in Asia and Europe whose security we have long maintained to be inseparable from our own. In fact, as NATO [North Atlantic Treaty Organization] has incorporated new members in Central and Eastern Europe, the strategic significance of tactical nuclear forces has grown in the eyes of allies such as Poland.

Russia also sees the matter differently than we do—placing greater importance on tactical capabilities than ever before, as reflected in its published military doctrine and its intimidation of U.S. allies in Central Europe. Paraphrasing a warning from [Russian president] Vladimir Putin to these allies: If you deploy U.S. missile defenses, we will target you with short-range missiles.

Degrading or Abandoning America's Nuclear Weapons Programs

In providing its advice and consent to the ratification of New START, the Senate highlighted its concerns over the imbalance in tactical weapons. In its formal resolution, supported on both sides of the aisle, the Senate called on the president to pursue an agreement with Russia "that would address the disparity." Unfortunately, but understandably, Moscow has shown no interest in such an agreement, perhaps because the United States gave up all of its leverage by agreeing to a treaty eliminating its main nuclear advantage: a greater number of deployed strategic launchers and warheads.

In one of the less quoted but more revealing statements contained in its 2010 Nuclear Posture Review, the Obama administration intimated its willingness to accept a nuclear posture second to Russia: "Because of our improved relations, the need for strict numerical parity between the two countries is no longer as compelling as it was during the Cold War." In part, this judgment was based on the assumption that the United States would realize potential advantages in missile defenses and advanced conventional arms.

However, missile defenses, at least those capabilities intended to protect the U.S. homeland, were an early casualty of the Obama team's New START negotiations with Russia. Not only did the president cancel the third missile-defense site in Europe, sacrificing the security interests of key allies, but he also killed or greatly curtailed all the existing programs that were designed to meet long-range missile threats from states including North Korea and Iran. (Programs such as the multiple kill vehicle and the kinetic energy interceptor were ended; the airborne laser was relegated to the status of a science project; and the number of ground-based interceptors was reduced.) While the administration has supported the development and deployment of defenses against short- and medium-range threats, it has funded studies—but developed no real capabilities—when it comes to strategic defenses. As for advanced conventional programs, there has been no commitment to deploy long-range, prompt global-strike capabilities (which could attack targets at intercontinental range with nonnuclear payloads)—perhaps because, as with missile defense, Moscow has said that our deployment of such a capability would endanger its adherence to New START.

What guided the administration most in making deep, unilateral cuts was a desire to demonstrate the declining role of nuclear weapons and lead by example in placing nuclear reductions, in the words of the Nuclear Posture Review, "atop the U.S. nuclear agenda." But the nonproliferation dividends have been few, if any, and no country of concern has followed the example. Nevertheless, the administration argues that the United States still possesses too many nuclear weapons. The president's national security adviser, Tom Donilon, recently expressed this view in a forum sponsored by the Carnegie Endowment for International Peace, when he announced that the United States would conduct yet another study to identify even more reductions.

New START, although a bilateral agreement, is a clear step toward unilateral disarmament. While the Obama administration marketed New START as requiring 30 percent reductions in U.S. and Russian strategic forces, it simply does not. We now have definitive confirmation that only the United States must reduce its forces—a possibility raised by New START skeptics but strongly denied by the Obama administration during the ratification process.

In June, the State Department released the initial data exchange required by the treaty. As of February 5, the day the treaty entered into force, Russia was already below the ceilings for both delivery vehicles and warheads. Perhaps most telling, knowledgeable Russian observers have stated that American negotiators didn't even propose terms that would have required Moscow to reduce its stockpiles.

The same mind-set led to the administration's decision last year to give up all nuclear-armed Tomahawk missiles while asking for—and getting—nothing in return. It took this action despite its own consistent calls for negotiations with Russia on theater systems. Once again, leading by example left the U.S. empty-handed.

But that lesson continues to elude the administration. In a recent interview, the president's point man on arms control, Gary Samore, noted that, while we wait for the outcome of the study announced by Donilon, "there may be parallel steps that both sides could take or even unilateral steps that the U.S. could take." No doubt there are more steps that the United States could take. No doubt, as well, that for the Obama administration, it is more important to take these steps than to reverse the coming U.S. inferiority in nuclear capabilities.

> *"Washington and Moscow could easily reduce their nuclear forces to just 1,000 warheads apiece without any adverse consequences."*

Both Russian and American Nuclear Arms Should Be Reduced Further

Bruce Blair et al.

Bruce Blair is the president of the World Security Institute, a nonprofit organization that brings together research and journalism on global security issues. The following viewpoint, authored by Blair and four other US and Russian military experts, details the 2010 New Strategic Arms Reduction Treaty (New START) and its required reduction of strategic nuclear missiles. Blair and his colleagues argue in the viewpoint that the treaty does not go far enough and that further cuts in missile strength could be achieved without sacrificing assured nuclear deterrence. In addition, the authors maintain that most missiles could be "de-alerted," or taken off launch-ready status, and still provide a deterrent effect while reducing the likelihood of accidental catastrophe or theft by terrorists.

As you read, consider the following questions:

1. As Blair and his coauthors relate, how many urban targets would a country have to be able to retaliate against in order for deterrence to be stable?

2. How would de-alerting nuclear arsenals still ensure deterrence, according to the authors?

3. What is the authors' vision of a NATO-Russia cooperative venture on controlled missile defense?

On April 8, [2010,] sitting beside each other in Prague Castle, U.S. president Barack Obama and Russian president Dmitry Medvedev signed the New Strategic Arms Reduction Treaty (New START). Just two days earlier, the Obama administration had issued its Nuclear Posture Review, only the third such comprehensive assessment of the United States' nuclear strategy. And in May, as a gesture of openness at the Nuclear Non-proliferation Treaty Review Conference in New York, the U.S. government took the remarkable step of making public the size of its nuclear stockpile, which as of September 2009 totaled 5,113 warheads.

For proponents of eliminating nuclear weapons, these events elicited both a nod and a sigh. On the one hand, they represented renewed engagement by Washington and Moscow on arms control, a step toward, as the treaty put it, "the historic goal of freeing humanity from the nuclear threat." On the other hand, they stopped short of fundamentally changing the Cold War face of deterrence.

The Shortcomings of New START

The New START agreement did not reduce the amount of "overkill" in either country's arsenal. Nor did it alter another important characteristic of the U.S. and Russian nuclear arsenals: their launch-ready alert postures. The two countries' nuclear command, control, and communication systems, and sizable portions of their weapon systems, will still be poised for "launch on warning"—ready to execute a mass firing of missiles before the quickest of potential enemy attacks could be carried out. This rapid-fire posture carries with it the risk of a launch in response to a false alarm resulting from human or technical error or even a malicious, unauthorized launch. Thus, under the New START treaty, the United States and Russia remain ready to inflict apocalyptic devastation in a nuclear exchange that would cause millions of casualties and wreak unfathomable environmental ruin.

In the next round of arms control negotiations, Washington and Moscow need to pursue much deeper cuts in their nuclear stockpiles and agree to a lower level of launch readiness. These steps would help put the world on a path to the elimination of nuclear weapons—"global zero." And they can be taken while still maintaining a stable relationship of mutual deterrence between the United States and Russia, based on a credible threat of retaliation, and while allowing limited but adequate missile defenses against nuclear proliferators such as Iran and North Korea.

Assured Deterrence

A stable nuclear deterrent exists between the United States and Russia when neither country would choose to launch a nuclear attack against the other regardless of the level of tension that may arise between them. Deterrence would become unstable if either country acquired a credible first-strike capability—the ability to attack without fear of reprisal. The stability of deterrence, then, comes down to an assessment of the viability of both sides' retaliatory capacities.

Such a metric of stability was applied by nuclear planners in coming up with warhead limits for the New START treaty. After calculating the damage from a first strike against nuclear forces, they determined how many surviving nuclear weapons could be used in a retaliatory attack against targets of value—

economic and administrative centers. The planners assumed that in order for deterrence to be stable and predictable, a country had to be able to retaliate against 150 to 300 urban targets. These judgments played a key role in setting the warhead limit of 1,550 for each side in the New START treaty.

Many planners still contend that deterrence also requires the ability to retaliate against an opponent's leadership bunkers and nuclear installations, even empty missile silos. But this Cold War doctrine is out of date. Deterrence today would remain stable even if retaliation against only ten cities were assured. Furthermore, uncertainty and incomplete knowledge would make U.S. and Russian policy makers risk-averse in a crisis rather than risk-tolerant. So arsenals can safely be reduced much further than the New START level. But just how deeply can they be cut? And how can the reliance on a quick launch be eliminated while preserving strategic stability? To answer these questions, we created computer models that pitted U.S. and Russian strategic offensive forces against each other in simulated nuclear exchanges. We also modeled the thorny problem of missile defense systems to assess their impact on the stability of deterrence and to gauge at what warhead levels they become destabilizing.

A War Game Simulation Suggests Further Reductions

We used public estimates of U.S. and Russian nuclear forces—their number, accuracy, explosive yields, reliability, vulnerability—and manipulated their launch readiness to test the effects of de-alerting on their ability to survive a first strike and be available for retaliation against urban centers. Because some range of uncertainty is associated with each variable, we ran the model simulation at least 100 times for each possible set of characteristics.

Our modeling found that the United States and Russia could limit their strategic nuclear arsenals to a total level of

1,000 warheads each on no more than 500 deployed launchers without weakening their respective security. De-alerting these forces actually helped stabilize deterrence at these and lower levels. And the modeling showed that fairly extensive missile defense deployments would not upset this stability.

Dropping to 1,000 total warheads is the low-hanging fruit when it comes to arms control. To make further progress toward a nuclear-free world, it will be necessary to pursue even deeper cuts. These will depend on the state of relations between the United States and Russia, on the worldwide deployment of missile defense systems, on the precision of long-range weapons, and on the prospects of involving other nuclear states in the process of reducing and limiting nuclear weapons. It is hard to imagine, for example, that the United States and Russia would go below 1,000 total nuclear weapons if China was increasing its nuclear capacity.

The next stage in arms control negotiations should cover all the complex issues of nuclear weapons, including those surrounding both strategic and sub-strategic (tactical) nuclear weapons, as well as limits on strategic offensive weapons with conventional warheads. A realistic goal would be for the United States and Russia to agree to each have no more than a total of 1,000 strategic and tactical nuclear warheads combined. Taking into account the fact that for Russia tactical nuclear weaponry is a sensitive problem (primarily because of the superiority of China's conventional forces), this treaty should allow each side flexibility in determining its warhead mix. For example, Russia might retain 700 strategic warheads and 300 tactical warheads, whereas the United States might retain 900 strategic and 100 tactical weapons.

Because the delivery vehicles, or launchers, for tactical nuclear weapons can also carry conventional weapons, the treaty should place limits not on tactical launchers but on tactical warheads. It will be essential that all the tactical weapons in storage be inspected regularly to verify that the treaty's provisions have been implemented. Strategic nuclear warheads should ideally be kept separate from tactical ones. Since Russia currently stores these warheads together, the treaty should designate one or two monitored storage locations for tactical weapons on each side.

Further strides toward nuclear disarmament will be possible only if the other nuclear powers freeze their arsenals and join in the negotiation process to reduce their forces proportionately. For this stage, the United States and Russia could cut their arsenals to 500 nuclear warheads each in exchange for 50 percent reductions by the other nuclear weapons countries.

Moving Away from Launch-Ready Status

For almost half a century, about one-third of the United States' and Russia's strategic nuclear arsenals have been maintained on launch-ready alert. A massive salvo can commence just a few minutes after the combat order is received by the crews on duty. This posture has proved difficult to wind down, even though such high readiness comes with many dangerous risks.

Given the recent surge of terrorism and nuclear proliferation, the liabilities of maintaining such quick-launch postures are only increasing. In the future, the danger of mistaken or unauthorized use or of the exploitation of nuclear weapons by terrorists is likely to grow rather than diminish. War-ready nuclear postures keep hundreds of nuclear weapons in constant motion, changing combat positions or moving to and from maintenance facilities. This affords terrorists opportunities to steal them as they are transported and stored temporarily—the relatively exposed phase of their operation.

These postures also perpetuate a mutual reliance on nuclear weapons that lends legitimacy to the nuclear ambitions of other nations. When more states go nuclear, intentional use becomes more likely, and deficiencies in nuclear command and warning systems multiply the risk of accidental or unauthorized use or terrorist theft.

Given these dangers, going off launch-ready alert would yield major benefits—including opening up possibilities for still greater reductions in the size of arsenals. Although de-alerting was not on the table during the negotiations for the New START treaty, it should have been. The requirements of mutual deterrence between the United States and Russia are far less demanding today than they were two decades ago, even as the challenges of preventing proliferation and nuclear terrorism have grown.

To ensure stable deterrence with forces that are smaller and off alert, the nuclear forces of both countries should be divided into distinct components, each with a different degree of combat readiness. A stable deterrent whole would thus be constructed from more vulnerable, de-alerted parts. To demonstrate the stability of deterrence under such a setup, we again used simulations of nuclear exchanges. The latest U.S. Nuclear Posture Review concluded that de-alerting "could reduce crisis stability by giving an adversary the incentive to attack before 're-alerting' was complete." We found, in contrast, that de-alerting does not create incentives for re-alerting and launching a preemptive attack during a crisis. In fact, done properly, de-alerting stabilizes deterrence.

In our model, the primary group of de-alerted nuclear forces for each country is the "first echelon." It consists of equal numbers of U.S. and Russian high-yield, single-warhead, silo-based intercontinental ballistic missiles (ICBMs). These first-echelon ICBMs can be brought to launch-ready status in a matter of hours—for example, maintenance crews would re-enter missile silos to activate the launch circuits. Their primary role is that of peacetime nuclear deterrence for the United States and Russia, the day-to-day front line of deterrence.

The "second echelon" of de-alerted nuclear forces consists of a more diverse set of nuclear weapons, with equal numbers of warheads on each side but with asymmetry in the types of weapons. It includes both multiple-warhead and single-warhead weapons: submarine-launched ballistic missiles, silo-based ICBMs, and road-mobile ICBMs. In their day-to-day, off-alert status, second-echelon forces are quite vulnerable. But they are highly survivable when they are re-alerted and dispersed—submarines surge to sea, for example, and road-mobile missiles dash into Siberian forests. These second-echelon forces take much longer to re-alert—weeks to months—than first-echelon forces. Warheads, for instance, might have to be removed from storage and mounted on missile launchers. But our results show that no advantage could be gained by any re-alerting of either first- or second-echelon forces. Deterrence is robustly reinforced by the lack of incentives to re-alert.

Fear of Robust Retaliation

We looked at scenarios involving an attacking state and a victim state in which the attacking state secretly re-alerts its first-echelon forces and strikes the first echelon of the victim state—a so-called counterforce attack meant to disarm the adversary and gain a strategic advantage. In these scenarios, the attacker expends more warheads than it can destroy and must assume that the victim will respond by firing its surviving first-echelon forces at the cities of the aggressor. If the attacker used some of its first-echelon missiles to strike the victim's second-echelon forces, then the aggressor would expose additional cities to retaliation by the victim's first-echelon forces.

In our model, after the initial attack, both sides would re-alert their second-echelon forces (for example, deploying submarines to sea), and the second echelon of the attacking state would strike the second-echelon forces of the victim as they were being readied for use. Our model allowed for some ran-

The Importance of Multilateral Reduction of Nuclear Arms

As Russian and U.S. nuclear forces are reduced, other countries' nuclear arsenals will loom larger in security calculations. Regional conflicts also generate their own sets of impulses that affect nuclear decisions. The political dynamics of Asia and Europe are different today than during the Cold War. Eliminating the threat posed by nuclear weapons requires that many states actively participate in negotiations to reduce all nuclear weapons programs anywhere in the world.

The level of nuclear forces that Moscow and Washington may try to reach in the next phase could be achieved without the participation of other nuclear-armed states. Russia and the United States still will have by far the greatest numbers of nuclear weapons in their arsenals even after additional reductions. In practice, however, unless there is a widely and, preferably, universally shared commitment to progressively eliminate all nuclear weapons, the momentum necessary to sustain further Russian-U.S. negotiations will be lost.

James Goodby,
"A World Without Nuclear Weapons Is a Joint Enterprise,"
Arms Control Today, *May 2011.*

dom variability in the pace of re-alerting by both side's second echelons in a nuclear war. What was left of the victim's second-echelon forces could then conduct further strikes against cities of the attacker. This scenario is the way to test whether deterrence is stable when forces are off alert. If the victim has enough residual capability to deter an attacker contemplating a "bolt from the blue," then deterrence is stable.

If the United States' and Russia's nuclear arsenals were each limited to 1,000 (or even 500) warheads, and if their forces were de-alerted and partitioned into first and second echelons, an aggressor would still face the possibility of unthinkable devastation wrought by retaliation against more than 100 cities. That should easily be enough to deter any such attack, assuming the potential aggressor is rational enough to respond to the logic of deterrence in the first place.

Reducing Antiballistic Defenses

Missile defense, a divisive topic during the lengthy back-and-forth over the terms of the New START agreement, threatens to derail the next phase of negotiations. In September 2009, the Obama administration shelved plans for missile defense radars and other missile defense infrastructure in the Czech Republic and Poland. Russia welcomed this move. But the new U.S. posture keeps open the question of the U.S. missile defense system's capability against Russian strategic nuclear forces.

When antiballistic missile (ABM) systems are small enough, they do not distract from the arms reduction process. Russia, for example, is comfortable with having regional ABM systems near its borders that are designed to shoot down short- and medium-range missiles, and it sees merit in joining with other states in creating a cooperative regional system. It is especially keen on regional defenses because its nuclear-armed neighbors—China, India, and Pakistan—are not subject to the ban on nonstrategic missiles stipulated by the U.S.-Russian Intermediate-Range Nuclear Forces Treaty. These neighbors have been deploying nonstrategic missiles, and still other countries (such as Iran and North Korea) are likely seeking them.

Russia was therefore disappointed by Washington's plans to create piecemeal regional ABM systems—partnering with Israel in the Middle East, with Japan in the Asia-Pacific region, and with NATO [North Atlantic Treaty Organization] members in Europe—without consulting Moscow. Although the Obama team has suggested using Russian radar stations in the Azerbaijani city of Gabala and the Russian city of Armavir in a regional ABM system, the United States has shown little real interest in cooperating with Russia in such an endeavor. In Russia's eyes, the United States is intending to create not a true European system—including Russia as part of Europe—but a NATO system instead.

This noninclusive approach might lead to a new crisis in U.S.-Russian and NATO-Russian relations in a decade or so, when the United States' and NATO's new missile defense systems will likely be able to destroy significant numbers of Russia's strategic missiles. If this capacity is constrained in ways that reassure Russia that its nuclear deterrent will remain viable, then the process of nuclear weapons reductions will remain on track. But if Russia is not reassured, the New START agreement could become the end of nuclear weapons reductions rather than a step toward further ones.

That is why strategic missile defenses have to be kept from reaching a point where they can prevent retaliation by knocking out strategic offensive missiles. The results of our modeling for the 1,000-warhead level suggest that advanced missile defense systems, such as the SM-3 Block II that the U.S. Navy is testing, would not upset deterrence stability if their numbers do not exceed 100 interceptors deployed by each side. An attacking country could not expect to protect itself from retaliation against its cities if it possessed only 100 or fewer such interceptors. Under current plans, the United States will deploy fewer than 100 interceptors. Russia will strongly oppose expansion above this level.

Partnering in Global Nuclear Security

Even more important than such limits will be U.S.-Russian cooperation on the missile defense problem—namely, an agreement to share control of missile defense systems. This arrangement should go beyond bilateral control to a broader European arrangement that at minimum should entail NATO-Russia cooperation. A cooperative system like this would not be a dual-key system that would give Russia or any other country a veto over missile defense operations and thus over other countries' security. Cooperation could, and ideally would, involve only the joint detection, identification, and countering of emerging missile threats.

The same logic applies to national and regional ABM systems, given the widespread geographic impact of missile defenses. For example, ABM operations in the Asia-Pacific region might result in interception and explosions above other states' territories or in potentially radioactive debris falling onto another state's territory. Failing to coordinate national responses in such circumstances could lead to disaster.

In 2008, Russia proposed developing a joint database of missile attack threats, sought to create a common control body for the early warning and estimation of missile threats, and said it would be willing to engage in joint planning on a future regional missile defense system. There are small but significant steps toward that end that are worth taking: The United States and Russia could exchange military attachés, observe missile defense tests together, and establish a joint center for monitoring missile launches worldwide.

Toward a World Without Nuclear Weapons

Once the New START agreement is approved by the U.S. Senate [New Start was approved in December 2010], the arms control process between the United States and Russia needs to continue moving forward. Washington and Moscow could easily reduce their nuclear forces to just 1,000 warheads apiece without any adverse consequences. They could also de-alert their nuclear forces, diminishing the risk of an accidental or unauthorized launch. Eventually, in concert with other nuclear states and after progress has been made on missile defense cooperation, they should be able to reduce their arsenals to 500 weapons each. Even after these deep cuts, hundreds of cities would still remain at risk of catastrophic destruction in the event of a nuclear war.

Such changes to the nuclear relationship between the United States and Russia should be accompanied by a change in attitude as well as forces: Both countries must be more open in assessing nuclear threats and the requirements of deterrence. Secrecy about safeguards against unauthorized or mistaken launches and about estimates of first- and second-strike attacks hamper informed public debate and instill mutual suspicion. Open analysis can help inform the public and policy makers on the best way forward for nuclear policy, elevating the debate above the fray of politics, ideology, and secrecy to a higher plane of objective and transparent analysis. This openness could pave the way toward a safer and more stable world with fewer, and eventually zero, nuclear weapons.

Periodical Bibliography

The following articles have been selected to supplement the diverse views presented in this chapter.

Bruce Blair et al.	"Smaller and Safer: A New Plan for Nuclear Postures," *Foreign Affairs*, September/October 2010.
Ed Blanche	"Moscow Muscles In," *Middle East*, January 2010.
Misha Glenny	"Gas & Gangsters," *New Statesman*, February 28, 2008.
Rose Gottemoeller	"New START: Security Through 21st-Century Verification," *Arms Control Today*, September 2010.
Thane Gustafson	"Putin's Petroleum Problem: How Oil Is Holding Russia Back—and How It Could Save It," *Foreign Affairs*, November/December 2012.
Paul Johnson	"Vladimir Putin: The World's Most Unlovable Man," *Forbes*, October 3, 2012.
James Kirchick	"The Russian Reset: A Eulogy," *Commentary*, April 2011.
Alex Palmer	"Russia Rising," *Harvard International Review*, January 12, 2012.
Karen Smith Stegen	"Deconstructing the 'Energy Weapon': Russia's Threat to Europe as Case Study," *Energy Policy*, October 2011.
Fareed Zakaria	"How Oil Is Propping Up Putin," *Time*, February 20, 2012.

OPPOSING VIEWPOINTS® SERIES

CHAPTER 2

Is Russia Moving Toward Democracy?

Chapter Preface

In a 2000 interview with Mike Wallace on CBS's *60 Minutes*, former Russian president Boris Yeltsin said that he believed democracy was "firmly" established in Russia. During his presidency from 1991–1999, Yeltsin shepherded his country's post-Soviet restructuring. While he has had his tepid defenders, such as the BBC news service that praised Yeltsin in 1999 for having "carried his country through a turbulent transformation with far less bloodshed than many had feared," many critics in retrospect have questioned his commitment to democratic ideals. Only three days after Yeltsin's death on April 23, 2007, Katrina vanden Heuvel, for example, penned a decidedly negative appraisal of Yeltsin's tenure, claiming the president had illegally dissolved the Russian parliament in 1993 and used military force to crush resisters there, had instigated the bloody war against the breakaway republic of Chechnya in 1994, and in 1996 funded his reelection bid by selling off shares in Russia's government-run industries to wealthy financiers. According to vanden Heuvel, Yeltsin's policies were directly responsible for the economic collapse of Russia in the post-Soviet decades and gave birth to the political instability that the country faces today. Even more disastrous for the prospects of democracy taking hold, vanden Heuvel cites a "respected Russian survey" that "revealed that nearly 70 percent of Russians polled believe the country needs an authoritarian ruler," seemingly to rein in the turmoil.

To some Western eyes, Russia's president Vladimir Putin fits the bill of an autocrat. Most recently, in September 2012, Putin cut off United States Agency for International Development (USAID) funds to Russia—money that was earmarked for nongovernmental organizations working on building democracy and establishing civil society in Russia. According to a *Washington Post* report, the Russian foreign ministry stated that USAID had been suspended for meddling in elections. Putin has also cracked down on protestors in Moscow who are calling for reform. Many of these demonstrators represent the very organizations that formerly received US assistance. In May 2012, he accepted the presidency, a reprisal of the role since his last election win in 2000, while protestors took to the streets. As police collared anti-Putin activists outside the Kremlin, the president-elect told his assembled dignitaries, "We want to live in a democratic country, where every person has the freedom and space to apply their talent and labor." Putin's leadership still has the support of a majority of Russians, even as a Pew Research poll in May 2012 found that 56 percent of Russians supported the protests for fair elections.

In June 2012, demonstrators again congregated in Moscow streets, but according to the *Christian Science Monitor*, Putin's government pulled the plug on their Internet services and enacted a law imposing harsh fines on anyone taking part in a demonstration that harms people or property. Such acts did not stop the rallies. The publication asserts, "The protesters have no single leader on purpose. This prevents Putin from simply jailing the main organizers. It also reinforces the fact that the protests represent popular feeling." Assessments like the one provided by the *Christian Science Monitor* promote the belief that a desire for democracy is still alive in Russia today. The authors in the following chapter offer their opinions on whether that spirit survives and what chance it has to bring about reform under the current presidential administration.

> "Russia's educated and growing middle classes ... will continue to demand a real seat at the table in a system of democracy and pluralism, and they will not take no for an answer."

Russia Is Moving Toward Democracy

Mikhail Khodorkovsky

In the following viewpoint, Mikhail Khodorkovsky claims that the regime that has held power for so long in Russia must come to an end. In his opinion, the people of Russia want a greater voice in politics and more parties to choose from that represent their needs. Khodorkovsky expresses the view that the early 2012 presidential election would show that opposition to monopolistic rule is alive in Russia and that a more democratic government is not far behind. He writes that even if the centrist Vladimir Putin returns to power—and he did after Khodorkovsky wrote this piece—the budding opposition taking shape heralds change to come. Mikhail Khodorkovsky is a Russian businessman who was arrested under the Putin administration in 2003 for fraud and has remained a political prisoner since that time.

As you read, consider the following questions:

1. Why does Khodorkovsky think Russia's opposition will have to consolidate into two or three parties?

2. What Middle Eastern political upheaval suggests to Khodorkovsky that the common people worldwide are throwing off the yoke of oppressive regimes?

3. According to the author, why have Western nations been reluctant to advocate for democracy in Russia?

While this year [2012] promises hotly contested battles for the presidencies of France and the US, only in Russia does the outcome seem a foregone conclusion. But whereas we might be reasonably sure of the result, we should not assume that there is little at stake.

Russians Incensed at "Business as Usual" Politics

For Western eyes, the neat swap of titles from prime minister to president by Vladimir Putin—suitably circumventing Russia's rule that prevents a president from serving more than two terms consecutively—may appear to suggest business as usual in the closed world of Kremlin politics. But that was not the view taken by many Russians, insulted by the self-asserting proclamation of immovable presidential power stretching over the next decade and more. The poor, middle class and wealthy filled the streets, incensed by allegations of vote rigging and dirty tricks in the Duma [Russian parliament] elections in December [2011]. This movement, supported even by Russian elites, has exploded the long-held myth that the people want to stick with Putin just for the sake of stability.

Putin responded to the demonstrators with mockery and chauvinism, saying he mistook the white ribbon they wore for the condoms of safe sex campaigners. But the authorities also responded—quietly—with reform, permitting the registration of new political parties for future Duma elections, and election rather than appointment of regional governors. These steps are capable of changing much in Russia, a catalyst, perhaps unintended, for a more fundamental transformation.

A Gathering Opposition to Putin's Rule

They give hope that the seeds of modernity can be planted across the Russian Federation with the brightest and best coming forward as candidates for public office. Opposition figures capable of challenging existing power structures will grow—but the opposition will have to consolidate into two or three new parties, with the capacity and strength to challenge the status quo, avoiding the Kremlin trap of divide and rule among myriad rivals.

But if that is the vision for the future, what prospects for the presidential elections next week? I hope we will see a large turnout, with my fellow citizens taking a long hard look at the alternative four "candidates", even if many would have preferred different names, who were not allowed to be there. The last time Putin stood for president he won resoundingly in the first round. If he is forced into a runoff this time, it would be an altogether different situation.

A second round would confirm that the change we all seek is on its way: an evolutionary and not a revolutionary approach can be the way forward. We do not want the bloodshed on our streets seen elsewhere—but we do want things to be different. It must be the role of our generation to change the paradigm in Russia without a civil war.

Revolution in the Air

Abuse of power in Russian politics has been allowed to flourish too long. We need to modernise our economy, build a genuine civil society, end legal nihilism and stamp out corruption. We need to do this to build a better life for our children

Lilia Shevtsova, Senior Associate at Carnegie Endowment for International Peace: Russia Will Democratize on Its Own

I would say that the old model of democracy promotion that has been successful during the third tide of democratization [that saw the breakup of the Soviet Union] is now outdated and has lost its effectiveness. At that time, the Western foundations and governments were trying to help to promote democratic norms and rules of the game in transitional societies and in authoritarian societies as well. . . . In my view, Russian society does not need this kind of assistance. Western money coming to Russia to support different initiatives and to support democratic cells within the society could be counterproductive, because . . . the authorities can always present the recipients of such assistance as a kind of fifth column and thus discredit domestic routes to democracy. True, we have different groups and organizations that have no financial means and survive using foreign funds. . . . If the West cuts its financial help, those groups will cease to exist, so some external support is definitely needed. Western governments should not do anything more, though. It seems to me that Russian society already understands what democracy is, what party building is, what independent parliament is, what free media is. Thus, we really need to rely upon our own sources and create our own movement.

Jeffrey C. Goldfarb,
"Do Not Democratize Russia: We Will Do It Ourselves,"
Deliberately Considered, May 31, 2012.
www.deliberatelyconsidered.com.

and our children's children, and for the country we love to prosper and to be engaged usefully in a changed and changing world.

We have only to reflect on the Arab Spring [2010–2011 revolutions in several Arab states] to recognise the transformation taking place in the compact between the rulers and the ruled. While there are certainly many differences between those countries and Russia, there are some fundamental similarities.

From Cairo to Damascus, from Moscow to Magadan, people want to be treated with dignity and respect—and Russia is no exception!

The Arab Spring has shown us that nobody can hold back the power of modern technology to inform and to mobilise. Technology has empowered the people.

And Russia's educated and growing middle classes should comprise a majority in just 10 years. They will continue to demand a real seat at the table in a system of democracy and pluralism, and they will not take no for an answer.

A Monopoly on Power That Has to End

Nobody expects this to happen overnight—but next Sunday's [March 4, 2012] vote holds out the chance to end the would-be president's monopoly of power. We should not be afraid. By forcing a second round we will push our country down the path of positive change. Presidential power that previously answered to no one would have to start listening to the people it serves. The state that until now took the monopolistic presidential power for granted would be more wary of its hold and start moderating its behaviour. The politicians who gathered the opposition votes could become a force to be reckoned with, a voice for articulating the thoughts and views that have been ignored before. The establishment would have to start negotiating with the opposition and an evolutionary transition could meaningfully begin.

I would also welcome a change of position from Western countries. They should stop dancing to the whistle of the gas pipe. They need to speak loud and clear with one voice about real democratic reforms, recognising that the only way to secure our mutual interests in the long term is for governments to stop hiding behind the stability myth, legitimising a regime that is deceiving its own people—the people who are starting to wake up.

And so I ask you to watch with interest the results of this year's elections. In France and the US, the presidential vote is about choosing between differing political visions and outcomes. In my country the electoral calculus is a little simpler: choose Putin in the first round or in the second round. But do not be fooled! "President" Putin's return to the Kremlin, after either manipulating the first round or being forced into a second round, without doubt puts the world on notice that real political change in Russia is unavoidable. It will be welcomed.

| *"Many Russians despair about their country, its prospects and their own, but they say little and do less."*

Russia Is Moving Away from Democracy

Kathy Lally and Will Englund

In the following viewpoint, Kathy Lally and Will Englund report on the sense of disillusionment Russians have experienced since the days of the 1991 coup that brought about the end of the Soviet Union. In those days, the authors write, there was a fervent hope among the populace that Russia would become more democratic and open. However, after the end of reformer Boris Yeltsin's rule in 1999 and the rise of the conservative-minded Vladimir Putin, Russia has once again become an authoritarian regime, according to Lally and Englund. Furthermore, the authors claim that the people have lost hope in seeing the promised democratic change and have become passive in the face of reinstated autocracy. Kathy Lally is the Moscow bureau chief of the Washington Post. *Her husband, Will Englund, is a* Washington Post *correspondent.*

As you read, consider the following questions:

1. According to Lally and Englund, why is the opposition to Putin's rule publicly invisible in Russia?

2. What percentage of the Russian populace takes part in civil society, as Lally and Englund report?

3. According to Sergey Filatov, Russia is presently turning into a state that exists for what purpose?

Twenty years ago Friday [that is, on August 19, 1991], Communist hard-liners staged a coup here [in Moscow], sending tanks rumbling to the Russian White House in an effort to preserve the Soviet Union. Instead they touched off a powerful expression of democracy.

Boris Yeltsin, the first democratically elected president in Russia's thousand years, galvanized the resistance when he climbed atop one of the tanks and called on citizens to defend the freedoms he had promised to deliver. They mounted the barricades, unarmed, willing to risk their lives for democracy. The coup leaders lost their nerve. A few months later, the Soviet Union was dead.

All these years later, so is democracy.

Little Change, Much Disappointment

Today, Vladimir Putin presides over an authoritarian government in that same White House, a bulky 20-story skyscraper on the edge of the Moscow River. Occasional demonstrations in favor of democracy are small and largely ignored, except by the police.

Those who defended the White House thought they had changed the course of history, that in standing up so assertively the people had shaken off their Soviet subservience to the state and that the state would begin to serve the people. But today, elections are not fair, courts are not independent, political opposition is not tolerated and the reformers are widely blamed for what has gone wrong.

"The difference is this," says Georgy Satarov, president of the INDEM [Information Science for Democracy] Foundation and a former Yeltsin aide. "Then, people had hope. Now, they are disappointed and frustrated."

Yeltsin's voters wanted him to take them in a new direction, says Satarov, but the operative word was take. "We saw the old train was taking us in the wrong direction," he says, "but we thought all we had to do was change the conductor and we would have comfortable seats and good food. Democracy would take us where we wanted to go, not our own effort. Sometimes you have to get off and push."

Today, Russia works on bribes, and Putin's opponents call his United Russia party the party of crooks and thieves. People can say whatever they want to one another, unlike in Soviet times when they feared the secret police knocking in the middle of the night, but television is controlled and any opposition is publicly invisible.

"They cannot let people on television who will say Putin is a thief," says Igor Klyamkin, a scholar and vice president of the Liberal Mission Foundation.

Many Russians despair about their country, its prospects and their own, but they say little and do less.

A Silent and Passive Society

Not Satarov, who has made his life's work researching and writing about that corruption.

"During the last 300 years, there has never been such an inefficient government," he says. "The state is disappearing because those who have the job description of working for the state have much more important things to do. The problem is, the more they steal, the more they fear losing power."

In 1991, there were leaders who could inspire people to act, he says. "Now, there are none, and anything can happen."

Only a tiny percentage of the population takes part in civil society, about 1.5 or 2 percent, at the level of statistical error.

"Now, we can speak as much as we want," says Sergei V. Kanayev, head of the Moscow office of the Russian Federation of Car Owners, "but they don't listen. It's useless and very sad."

People feel powerless. "Nothing depends on us," they say in Russian.

"Ordinary people do not believe in anything, and they don't trust anyone," Kanayev says. "The entire society is silent and passive."

Reform Leadership Fails

For years, the independent polling and analytical organization called the Levada-Center has been studying Russian political and social behavior, watching disillusionment with democracy set in.

"At the end of the 1980s, anything to do with the Soviet system was reviled," says Boris Dubin, Levada's director of sociopolitical studies. "Then people lost everything in the economic upheaval of 1992 and 1993. They lost all of their savings. They were threatened with unemployment. There was a bigger gap between the more successful and the less successful, and this was very painful for anyone brought up in Soviet times."

Instead of blaming the legacy of the unsustainable Soviet economy for their suffering, Russians blamed the reformers. Democracy began to acquire a dubious reputation.

Long-entrenched interests proved more difficult to subdue than coup plotters. The old legislature, still sympathetic to the bloated industries sustained on a rich diet of state subsidies, opposed many reforms and refused to disband. Yeltsin turned his own tanks on them as they holed up in the White House in 1993, traumatizing the nation. Later he made what he would describe as his biggest mistake, sending tanks into separatist Chechnya at the end of 1994.

A Russian Research Organization Releases Poll Results Concerning the 2012 Elections

To what extent do regular elections make the government do what simple people want?

	April '07	March '08	April '11	Sept. '11
To a great extent	3%	7%	8%	8%
To some extent	28%	35%	32%	39%
To a minor extent	35%	26%	31%	33%
To no extent at all	28%	27%	25%	16%
Hard to say	6%	5%	5%	4%

After 2012, do you think that thievery and corruption in the country's leadership will increase, stay the same, or be less than it was earlier under Putin?

More	16%
The same	66%
Less	13%
Hard to say	6%

TAKEN FROM: Mark Adomanis, "Russian Opinion About the 2012 Elections, Democracy, and the Country's Future," *Forbes*, October 25, 2011. www.forbes.com.

"Yeltsin lost the support of most people," Dubin says. "There was a question of whether he could win the next election in 1996, and he dropped democratic tools step by step, drawing closer to the power structures."

The Return of Authoritarianism

By the end of the 1990s, many were feeling nostalgic for Soviet times. "They wanted a young strong leader who could create order," Dubin says. "So most were ready for Putin, and they did not think they should be frightened because he was a man of the power structure [the former KGB]."

Putin used state-controlled television to relentlessly send the message that life was better and Russia stronger under him than it was in the 1990s, a time of national humiliation. When he restored the old Soviet anthem, people hummed right along.

He dispensed object lessons, as in the case of former oil tycoon Mikhail Khodorkovsky, who financed political opposition to Putin and in 2003 was arrested on fraud charges. His jail term was recently extended to 2016. A few weeks ago [in July 2011], Khodorkovsky's business partner, Platon Lebedev, was denied parole because he had lost a pair of prison pants. In June, a liberal political party was refused the registration that would have allowed it to participate in the Duma [Russian parliament] elections in December.

"There are no leaders who can become symbols of change," Dubin says. "I don't see any change for 15 to 20 years."

Of course, today's Russia is not the Soviet Union, says Grigorii Golosov, a St. Petersburg political scientist. "But at the same time, it is an authoritarian regime that violates human and basic rights."

The next presidential election is in March [2012], and Putin has not declared who will run—the decision is considered his.

"Of course, it's our problem, and others can't solve it," Klyamkin says. "But if this regime is successful and Russia continues under the current system, it will be a threat to others. Even now it has visions of empire."

Remembering the 1991 Coup

Sergey Filatov, who recently turned 75, sadly ponders the question of how it has come to this, sitting in his office on the Avenue of the Cosmonauts, staring off into the distance, as if fixing his mind's eye on Aug. 19, 1991, when he rushed to the barricades in Moscow.

"Putin's election," he answers. "Russia is turning into a state that exists for the bureaucracy, and in many ways a closed state. And it started with Putin's election."

Yeltsin, inaugurated as president of the Russian Federation in July 1991, became president of an independent Russia when the Soviet Union dissolved at the end of the year. He resigned in weakness and ill health at the end of 1999, clearing the way for Putin's election. Putin has run Russia ever since, for eight years as president and since 2008 as prime minister, with Dmitry Medvedev as president.

The future had looked so different in 1991, and Filatov's voice grows strong and urgent as he describes the way Russians rose against the three-day coup.

Mikhail Gorbachev, president of the Soviet Union, was trying to save the Communist state with a policy of more openness and freedom when die-hard Soviet officials who thought it was all going too far imprisoned him in his vacation home and declared themselves in charge.

Everyone knew a coup was under way that Monday morning when normal broadcasting was suspended and Russians turned on their televisions and saw the ballet *Swan Lake*, the kind of calming fare Soviet authorities trotted out in times of crisis. "They danced and danced and danced," Filatov said.

Filatov, who runs the nonprofit Foundation for Socio-Economic and Intellectual Programs, would go on to become an important Yeltsin-era official and an architect of democracy. He still savors the moment that the three-day coup ended on Aug. 21, 1991.

"We raised the Russian flag over the White House, and there was huge euphoria," he says. Alexander Yakovlev, who had devised Gorbachev's policies of perestroika and glasnost, "had the briefest but strongest comment. He said, 'You are all very happy over your victory, but others will come and seize your victory.' And that's what happened."

Not Enough Gains

One day this summer in St. Petersburg, Oleg Basilashvili, a much-loved actor, sat brooding over the past, chain-smoking in his prewar apartment, a bay window at one end of the parlor and a baby grand at the other.

Basilashvili had spoken at Yeltsin's inauguration, summoning forth the magnificent Russian past, the land of Peter the Great, [Alexander] Pushkin, [Fyodor] Dostoevsky and [Leo] Tolstoy, and heralding the new, free life that lay ahead.

Today, there is no clear idea of where the authorities want to take the country, he says, no idea of what kind of Russia is being built on the ruins of the Soviet Union, only a sense that they are trying to destroy whatever happened in the 1990s.

"That's no basis for a state," he says in his actor's rich baritone voice.

Russians have forgotten much about that time when choices seemed so simple and hope lay ahead, untarnished.

"If, 25 years ago, someone had told me I could buy any book or even a computer without restrictions," says Dmitri Oreshkin, a political analyst, "that I could work or not work without going to jail for not working, that I would be able to write whatever I want, that I could travel wherever I want, I would have been very happy. And I probably wouldn't have believed it possible.

"Now, 25 years later, I don't think I have enough."

> "Putin's nationalism is not the cartoon-ish chauvinism of European or Russian nativists; it is Soviet at heart, focused on the state's role as the main vehicle of modernism and guarantor of stability."

Soviet-Style Nationalism Has Cemented Authoritarianism in Russia

Randall D. Law

In the following viewpoint, Randall D. Law argues that after democratic reform failed to take hold in post-Soviet Russia, a new authoritarianism has emerged under Vladimir Putin. According to Law, Putin has capitalized on the sense of moral waywardness and international humiliation that Russians felt after the fall of the Soviet Union to reinstate a strong nationalism that recalls the old order. Law claims that Putin has been able to maintain his rigid hold by using oil revenues to boost the national economy and also by controlling most Russian media outlets. Randall D. Law is an assistant professor at Birmingham-Southern College, where he chairs the Department of History.

As you read, consider the following questions:

1. According to Law, what debacle ended Boris Yeltsin's bid for a new Russian imperialism?

2. To what does Randall attribute Russia's new crop of billionaires?

3. What cracks does Randall see in the foundation of Putin's authoritarianism?

Don't let the recent public protests against Russian prime minister and presumptive president Vladimir Putin fool you: Authoritarianism remains firmly entrenched in Russia 20 years after the collapse of the Soviet Union, and there's more to it than meets the eye. It's not communism that lingers, but rather Soviet nationalism, which has formed the basis of a new social contract between the state and its citizens.

Soviet nationalism in its most influential form goes back to World War II, when the Soviet Union's victory was made possible by a new brand of nationalism: Russian in that it fit within a thousand-year-old history of expansionism, but Soviet in that it was achieved via modern technology, bureaucratic organization, and civic-mindedness. This new ideology kept the USSR [Union of Soviet Socialist Republics, or Soviet Union] afloat after 1945. Outsiders always emphasized the brutality and coercive power of the Soviet system, but the reality was more insidious and complex. For Soviet citizens during the Cold War, the carrot was a vast Eurasian empire, global power, domestic order, and a rising standard of living; the stick was fear of foreign domination and the consequences of internal disarray.

In the end, the sclerotic Soviet economy wasn't able to satisfy citizens' demands. [Former Soviet president] Mikhail Gorbachev had hoped to transform the Soviet Union into a modern socialist state "with a human face." Instead, he hastened its collapse, in large part by violating the post-war social contract amidst the chaos of glasnost and perestroika.

Class Divisions Spark Nationalism's Rise

Boris Yeltsin, Russia's first democratically elected post-Soviet leader, further eroded the underpinnings of the social contract tied to Soviet nationalism. Primarily concerned with his own quest to assert control, he swung wildly between pro-democracy demagoguery and authoritarian belligerence. His victory over parliament in 1993 established a presidency of far-reaching power but little popular support. Yeltsin tried to capitalize on the development of a new Russian imperialism, but the first disastrous war in Chechnya and humiliating peace treaty of 1996 showed it wouldn't work.

The corrupt and hastily executed privatization of Soviet infrastructure that Yeltsin oversaw ironically provided the state with one way to rebuild. Crony capitalism created a new class of billionaire "oligarchs" and young "new Russians," all deeply indebted to the Russian state. But on the other side of the economic and cultural gap, the older generation limped on, humiliated and impoverished. As the country experienced its freest years in history—varying political opinions became as easy to find as cheap imported goods, pornography and booze—many Russians were horrified by the sense of chaos, moral decline, and international humiliation. That horror paved the way for authoritarianism to return.

Enter Yeltsin's handpicked successor, Vladimir Putin. Much is made of the fact that he was a KGB officer, but he absorbed far more Soviet nationalism than communism. "I was a pure and utterly successful product of Soviet patriotic education," he told an interviewer in early 2000. Putin's nationalism is not the cartoonish chauvinism of European or Russian nativists; it is Soviet at heart, focused on the state's role as the main vehicle of modernism and guarantor of stability.

Putin Reasserts Russia's National Sovereignty During His First Presidency, 1999–2008

The same year as [Putin called for] the return of the Soviet anthem in 2000, Channel One reinstated a Soviet-era jingle for the main nine o'clock news programme, *Vremya*. Melodies, like smells, can be highly evocative. The tune signalled a return to Soviet-era news coverage. In fact, it was as if the state was sending signals to the country as a whole—signals of restoration and revanche.... As Russian troops moved into Georgia [in 2008], Russian television presenters talked with straight faces and straight voices about the hand of the West behind Georgia's attack on its separatist region of South Ossetia [the home of many ethnic Russians]....

In the absence of an indigenous liberal ideology, an old-fashioned nationalism ... has become the most powerful force in Russian society. It is this force that brought Russian tanks into Georgia and scares most of Russia's neighbours.

Arkady Ostrovsky, "Flirting with Stalin,"
Prospect, *September 28, 2008.*

Playing Ball with the New Boss

During his brief stint as prime minister in the fall of 1999, Putin renewed the war in Chechnya, calling it necessary to preserve Russia's sovereignty and protect its citizens against terrorists. After he became president less than a year later, his statist nationalism and emphasis on law and order undermined the legitimacy of anyone who spoke out against his increasingly authoritarian practices, especially journalists and democracy activists.

Putin found the way to a new social contract in the country's oil fields, which helped satisfy rising global energy demand. On the one hand, the country's oligarchs were put on notice: They could play ball with the new boss and continue to reap extraordinary profits, or they would be destroyed. Not surprisingly, the energy sector has produced the clearest winners and losers in Russia's pay-to-play business world. Sibneft owner and Putin pal Roman Abramovich has thrived, while Yukos owner Mikhail Khodorkovsky—once the richest Russian—was singled out over tax evasion charges. Energy revenue has also allowed Putin to revive some Soviet-style paternalism by encouraging greater domestic production of consumer goods and providing larger subsidies for those Russians left behind by the boom.

Putin's "Managed Democracy"

Putin's own term for the new phenomenon is "managed democracy." Nearly all Russian media outlets are controlled by the Kremlin's allies, who guide voters to Putin, his ally/ underling Dmitry Medvedev, and his party, United Russia. Government candidates and United Russia have never achieved embarrassingly one-sided majorities, but they have comfortably dominated. In the wake of United Russia's comparatively poor electoral showing this month [December 2011], Putin and his party might have to depend more on other progovernment groups, but the outcome will likely be the same.

Cracks have certainly emerged in the foundation of Putin's authoritarianism. His relationship with the energy and media barons is weakening, while the broader population is eager for national respect and material comfort, something that depends on growing oil revenue. And activists have become increasingly bold in denouncing the corruption, sham democracy, and police intimidation of the new Russia. But Putin's system has also shown its ability to deliver enough of the goods and deny the means by which an opposition can coalesce around a rival. It seems that Soviet nationalism still has some staying power.

> "It is in educating their fellow citizens, through self-organization and self-help, that [the grassroots organizations] see their most important contribution to the emergence of a new, dignified, and prosperous Russia."

Grassroots Organizations in Russia Are Leading a Civil Rights Movement

Leon Aron

Leon Aron is a resident scholar and the director of Russian Studies at the American Enterprise Institute for Public Policy Research, a scholarly collective focused on expanding personal and economic liberty. In the following viewpoint, Aron explains how interviews he and an associate conducted with Russian social activists illustrate that grassroots organizations in that country are fighting for political change. Aron argues that these small collectives—often based around civic and environmental causes—are battling bureaucracy and teaching people how to change the nation's laws for their benefit. Although Aron concedes that the

Leon Aron, "Following One's Conscience, Part 2: A Quest for Democratic Citizenship," *AEI Russian Outlook*, Fall/Winter 2011/2012. Reprinted with permission of the American Enterprise Institute, Washington, DC.

government often ignores these calls for reform, his interviewees attest that the experience is empowering citizens to band together and continue the struggle. Aron and those he interviewed hope this patient, peaceful activism may bring about real democratic change in Russia.

As you read, consider the following questions:

1. What does Marina Rikhvanova see as the key obstacle to environmental progress, as reported by Aron?

2. According to then president Dmitry Medvedev, what percentage of the state budget is stolen from the Russian treasury every year?

3. What are some of the similarities Aron sees between the US civil rights movement and the Russian struggle for civil rights?

Last July [2011], Daniel Vajdic and I traveled through Russia to interview leaders of six grassroots organizations and movements. Among the many fascinating themes that have emerged from the nearly forty hours of interviews, perhaps the most powerful is these individuals' conviction that the meaningful and lasting liberalization of the country may be ensured by only a mature, self-aware civil society, able and willing to control the executive. The main avenue for such a change would not be a political revolution in the conventional sense, nor would it be brought from above by a good tsar or a hero. Instead, the hope is predicated on a deeply moral transformation from within. Affecting such an evolution toward enlightened and morally anchored democratic citizenship appears to be the overarching meta-goal of the organizations, above and beyond their daily agendas. This objective is all the more remarkable because it diverges from the Russian historical tradition and political culture. . . .

"Overflowing into Politics"

At first blush, little that is overtly political can be found in the agendas of all six groups and movements whose leaders we interviewed.[1] "We are nonpolitical," Federation of Automobile Owners of Russia (FAR) president Sergei Kanaev told us,[2] and if asked directly, most of the others would have agreed. Indeed, national politics, not to mention regime change, seems to be completely outside their daily activities, which include slopping the pollution of Lake Baikal (Baikal Ecological Wave), improving road safety and helping automobile owners to fend off the rapacious traffic policy (FAR), fighting corruption (TIGR and Spravedlivost'), saving historic buildings from demolition (Bashne.net and Zhivoy Gorod), and protecting the Khimki Forest from development (ECMO). While TIGR and Spravedlivost' have occasionally strayed into politics by attempting to prevent fraud in elections, their efforts have been limited to local polls.

Moreover, all the movements have, with various degree of collegiality and effectiveness, cooperated with local authorities. Baikal Ecological Wave and FAR regularly produce data about pollution or road hazards and disrepair. Some leaders and activists (for instance, Marina Rikhvanova of Baikal Ecological Wave, Maxim Vedenev of TIGR, Sergei Kanaev of FAR, and Konstantin Doroshok of Spravedlivost') even have been invited to join "expert groups" or "consultation committees" advising mayors or governors.

Yet our interviews also made clear that, in the end, none of the organizations can avoid grappling with the nationwide issues rooted deeply in the nature of the regime. It is as if, having resolved to clean up your small apartment, you are almost immediately confounded by problems—faulty designs, leaking ceilings, lack of heat and hot water, crumbling walls— that are beyond your control and require a capital repair of the entire building. As the leader of ECMO, Yevgenia Chirikova, told an interviewer last year [in 2011], "I have no intentions of going into politics. It is the regime functionaries that make me into an opposition leader."[3]

Bashne.net and Zhivoy Gorod activist Dmitry Lynov called this phenomenon "overflowing over into politics" (*peretekanie v politiku*). Confronted with the regime's congenital defects, every leader we interviewed appears to have undergone a similar evolution. For instance, Chirikova denounced the absence of a normal judicial system and pointed out, "For the first time in Russian history we have in power people whose sole goal is personal enrichment at the country's expense." The leader of Baikal Wave, Marina Rikhvanova, condemned the "merger of power and property" as the key obstacle to environmental progress.[4]

In the same vein, a regional leader of the human rights and anticorruption watchdog group TIGR, Maxim Vedenev, saw one of the key goals of his movement as "working against the stranglehold (*zasil'e*) of corruption and the rampant lawlessness (*bespredel*) of state bureaucracy." . . .

Automobile Owners Seek Changes in the Law

Perhaps the most telling example of these organizations' encounters with national politics has been the evolution of FAR, which should have been the least "political" organization in the sample. Likely the largest grassroots organization in Russia, FAR's agenda includes redressing two major gripes of millions of Russian car owners: very high gasoline prices, almost identical to those in the United States though salaries are orders of magnitude lower, and the so-called "transportation tax" levied on every car in Russia. "Where does all this money go?," FAR began to ask, and instantly was confronted with two hallmarks of Putinism [i.e., Russia's system of government since Vladimir Putin first became president in 2000]: lack of transparency and rampant corruption.

Officially, the taxes and the duty collected at the pump are supposed to be spent mostly on improving highway safety and building more and better highways. Yet FAR quickly has established that these claims are largely bogus, the length of new roads constructed since 2000 has been miniscule, and Russia's traffic fatalities per one hundred thousand vehicles (seventy) remains the second highest in Europe (after Albania) and almost five times the US rate of fifteen. Instead, FAR concluded, the price of gasoline was inflated by the "corruption component": the between 20 and 30 percent (and sometimes as high as 50 percent) of the price of goods and services known as "administrative rent" and "kickbacks" (*otkaty*). This component is particularly large in heavily regulated industries such as oil.

Furthermore, as the organization's home page points out, the one trillion rubles (over $30 billion, or 12 percent, of the Russian state budget) that, according to President [Dmitry] Medvedev, is stolen from the Russian treasury every year is twice as much as the transportation tax and the gasoline tax combined. Hence, FAR demands "the end of corruption and [the introduction of] transparency, and public control over everything that is connected to the formation of monopolistic prices, state regulation, and duties."[5] They add, "It is not just the price of gasoline that will depend on how we act, but to what extent the authorities will take into consideration our interests in the future."

Similarly, highway safety has been compromised, often fatally, by another of the Putin regime's structural features: flagrant inequality before the law. In this instance, the law permits ill-defined categories of government officials to drive with blue flashing lights (*migalki*) and violate the rules, including driving on the wrong side of the road against the traffic. A source of many accidents, quite a few of them lethal, the law has been targeted for repeal by FAR's national campaign.

© 2012, Ollie Johansson and Cagle Cartoons, Inc.

The organization has sought, without success, to strictly limit the use of lights and allowable traffic violations to clearly defined and sharply reduced categories of top officials and medical and police emergency personnel.

While the movement thus far has failed to repeal or change the law, it has expanded its campaign into a broader affirmation of human dignity. One of FAR's most popular national campaigns has been the "blue buckets" protests: throughout the country, children's beach toys on car antennas and racks or protesters' heads have mocked the lights of the Russian officials' corteges. Popular bumper stickers that we saw in FAR's headquarters in Moscow tell a similar story: "For Equality and Security," "I Don't Give Bribes!," and "Flashing Lights Are Russia's Shame!" Shortly before our visit, FAR had released a letter to Putin demanding his resignation if he is unable to meet FAR's demands and improve the country's general economic conditions.

Finding the Political Will to Act

Although they almost daily confront structural problems that may be addressed only by radical reforms of the political system, for most respondents the regime was not the main culprit. Instead, they laid most of the blame at the door of the civil society that allowed the present regime to be established and to continue. In the words of a TIGR leaflet, "We have no civil society that would keep politicians to their promises . . . and would make government functionaries remember that they are servants of people who pay their salaries."[6]

The respondents saw this lack of a mature, self-aware and self-organized civil society able and willing to control the executive as the key obstacle to the country's meaningful and lasting progress. Those we interviewed articulated this theme with remarkable clarity, passion, and consistency. "Public control [over the executive] is the key," FAR's president, Kanaev, said:

> The system that we want to construct is a system of public control that would work no matter who is in power. Without this, nothing will change in the country. Everyone thinks that if only they [personally] come to power everything will change. But I tell them: by the time you get to power, you will already be just as the system wants you to be. . . . It seems to us that if we manage to work out a [new] system of control not by the state but by the society, everything will fall into place. We say, so long as there is no such control, no matter how many elections we hold, the power system will always remain the same [as it is now].

Chirikova's diagnosis was similar. She observed that the Soviet Union had collapsed because it was founded on violence, but was replaced by "a veritable kleptocracy," the "regime of swindlers and thieves." She added, "This is scary. I think the only way [out] is for our citizens to become real citizens. And in that case, we will be able to change the regime." At the moment, Chirikova continued, it would be "useless" to exchange Putin for someone else, "no matter who that person might be." Only when "people develop political will, if they are not indifferent to their fate, if they actively participate in the life of their country—only then we will have an entirely different regime in power."

Vedenev considered where the regime's impunity (*beznakazannost*) comes from: "It is a function of our indifference. Indifference breeds impunity, and impunity destroys everything. If people respected themselves more, we would have never had such impunity."

In the end, it is not change of regime, per se, that emerged from the interviews as the overarching "strategic" meta-goal, but an enlightened, active, and informed citizenry that would affect civic change and then remain vigilant. "Russia today does not have a mechanism for the effective defense of people's rights," TIGR states. "To create such a mechanism is precisely what constitutes our agenda. And this mechanism is called 'civil society.' . . . And then either the civil society will force the regime to pay heed to its demands—or it will change the irresponsible regime."[7]

The Meta-Goal:
"Changing People's Mentality"

The leaders and activists we spoke to had no illusion about the tall obstacles that must be overcome on the road to a mature democratic citizenship. For instance, calling on its members and supporters to participate in a March 2011 national protest against the gasoline prices, FAR's home page declared, "Nothing [provokes] the authorities [toward] lawlessness and impunity as the silence of society. . . . The parasite inside [us] thwarts all the attempts at civic activity. . . . Despair and laziness have shackled our society."[8]

The same reasons, according to Chirikova, accounted for the difficulty in mobilizing people for the defense of the Khimki Forest. "People are not ready to fight for their rights," she said. "Why do we have a situation where the 'party of thieves and swindlers' [United Russia] has a majority in the parliament? Because people cannot tear themselves from their sofas to vote in the right way or to [help] register a new party."

A consensus emerged among the respondents that lasting, effective change in the country can come only from *within* society. Nothing short of an evolution in people's attitudes—and, through it, of the country's political culture—will do. "The change of political regime is possible only through the change in people's mentality," said Chirikova. . . .

Motivating People to Help Themselves

No matter what their daily activities and short-term goals, the respondents see inculcating a new mentality as the essence of their effort and its ultimate moral justification. "We are no longer fighting just for the forest," said Chirikova. "Our struggle is a struggle for people's minds. . . . We are making [real] citizens out of citizens, which is why we publish newspapers, blanket the town with leaflets. . . . This is more important than any seizure of power, because this is the foundation for serious and long-term changes in the country."

The new civic mentality was defined, first and foremost, as self-respect and personal responsibility[10]—whether for one's neighborhood or for the entire country. Among several strategies to promote these attitudes, our interviewees judged self-organization and self-help to be the most effective. "Self" was the operational term. All were vehemently opposed to what Vedenev described as "dragging people along" toward any political or social order, no matter how progressive. Instead, they were determined to inculcate active, democratic citizenship through actual participation. Above and beyond any advance in their organizational agenda, this citizenship by action and by example was their ever-present objective.

"People come to our organization and ask for help," explained Vedenev. "I say, 'No, we can't help you.' They don't understand [and say], 'We know that you help people!' And I say, 'I help you to help yourself.' . . . I can explain what can be done and how we can help you do it. But it is you who must help yourself!" Similarly, according to the regional leader of FAR, Anastasia Zagoruyko, by increasing car owners' "legal literacy" (knowledge of laws), the group is able to "teach people how to defend their rights and to achieve justice."

The respondents believe that far more than informed civil society comes out of such efforts: These voluntary collective actions in pursuit of deeply moral objectives are key to building civic self-confidence and cohesion. . . .

Patient, Peaceful Change

Whatever other impact they seek to achieve in their work, by far the most satisfying effect for most respondents seems to be the change in their compatriots' attitudes. "I feel huge satisfaction when a man begins to talk seriously about the things that he considered foolish and impossible only a short time ago," Vedenev told us. "We have grown into a kind of family: we are family, we are friends, we . . . are a collection of individuals with [common] goals and ideas. . . . [In the end] I don't do what I do for the organization. The organization is only an instrument. The key is to forge a circle of people with a similar perspective on life, mentality, and understanding." In the expansion of such "circles," respondents saw hope for a peaceful and lasting change. "Many [like-minded people] gathered in one place can change a great deal," one of them said. "If people begin to self-organize, we won't need any revolutions. This will be the most peaceful revolution of all: people will simply stop submitting and begin to demand."

Chirikova saw "frightful historical parallels" in the current political regime, which is becoming "so deaf to the needs of the people, so incapable of meeting their demands, that the society could blow up." Such an outcome, she continued, "would not be good either for the people or the country," which in the past one hundred years have lived through "too many catastrophes."

"We've made this mistake once [in the Bolshevik Revolution of 1917], but we are more experienced now," she said. "Our condition is different. The world has changed, and so have our modes of communication, which is why I think that the key element of [political] change consists of citizens themselves changing. I think the chances are good to be able to change the structures of power regime by peacefully changing the conscience of our citizens."

Such change will not come overnight. It requires patience and steadiness of purpose. "It is paramount not to relax, to understand that this struggle may last our entire life," said Chirikova. A mother of two young children, she added, "It's like pregnancy. It will last nine months. No matter what you do, the baby will be born only in nine months. Laws of nature cannot be changed, and neither can the laws of societal development. We cannot skip over some processes: This is physically impossible. So all these quick, enthusiasm-fueled revolutionary transformations that many are dreaming of today—they will come to nothing. Only gradual change [will be effective]—and only work with individuals at every level we can."

Russia's Civil Rights Movement

In a break with the national tradition of political change born mostly out of violent political upheavals, the six organizations and movements we studied aspire to effect lasting progress by assisting in the emergence of informed, active, and self-confident citizenship. Again, in contrast to their political culture, which has prized quick—and usually illusory—results and what [Soviet dictator Joseph] Stalin called "great ruptures" (*velikie perelomy*) imposed from above, most respondents were convinced that needed change would come only through a sustained moral education. It is in educating their fellow citizens, through self-organization and self-help, that they see their most important contribution to the emergence of a new, dignified, and prosperous Russia.

It is clear that we are present at the birth of something new in Russian political tradition, at least since its evolution was interrupted by the 1917 Bolshevik Revolution. No historic parallel is perfect, but it is hard not to hear echoes of the civil rights movement in the United States. Of course, differences are many and formidable: from religious inspiration behind the movements (central to the US civil rights movement, but not present in Russia) to the institutional settings (a mature liberal democracy in the United States, as opposed to the authoritarian subversion of Russia).

Yet similarities are just as stark. Like its US counterpart more than half a century ago, the Russian movement's ultimate goal is dignity and equality for all people before the law. And just like the leaders of the civil rights movement, Russia's activists seek to effect vast political and social change by an example of personal and deeply moral effort. Both movements have rejected violence in principle.[12] Both have or had no time limits in which to achieve their goals, their supporters displaying quiet but unyielding determination and patience to persevere as long as necessary.

If Russia is lucky, another parallel may hold as well. In the beginning of the US civil rights movement, not even its leaders and most ardent supporters anticipated how quickly, by historical standards, their goals would be realized. At a time when deep and widening cracks are becoming visible in the icy carapace in which Putinism has enveloped Russian politics, the citizenship ethos spread by the movements we studied, and dozens like them throughout Russia, could provide the moral foundation for Russia's second breakthrough into democratic modernity in the past twenty years. It is far from a coincidence, then, that one of the most passionate advocates of democratic citizenship among our respondents, the thirty-four-year-old Yevgenia Chirikova, has emerged as a leader of the unfolding protest movement, which deserves to be called Russian Spring even if it was born in December.

Notes

1. See Leon Aron, "Following One's Conscience: Civic Organizations and Russia's Future, Part 1," AEI Russian Outlook, (Summer 2011), www.aei.org/outlook/foreign-and-defense-policy/regional/europe/following-ones-conscience-civic-organization-and-russias-future-part-1/.
2. All uncited quotations in this piece come from personal interviews with the author and his research assistant, conducted in July 2011.
3. See "Oolichniye aktsii: naskol'ko i komoo oni noozhni?" [Street actions: How much and for whom are they needed?], Ekho Moskvy, August 23, 2010, www.echo.msk.ru/programs/albac/706566-echo/ (accessed January 19, 2012). Chirikova has accused Vladimir Putin of having "blatantly violated and continuing to violate the laws of the Russian Federation," and in December 2010 she announced that "we are starting political struggle and will be insisting on the change of the current regime."
4. In the interview, I quoted to Rikhvanova her own statement: "The merger of state and business engenders conflicts of interest. And no matter how prettily the environmental policy is formulated, the state functionaries will not be interested in defending and expanding our common natural [and] cultural treasures." See "Marina Rikhvanova: 'Sliyanie gosudarstva i biznesa porozhdaet konflikt interesov.'" [Marina Rikhvanova: 'The merger of state and business engenders conflict of interests'], December 15, 2010, www.sibinfo.su/person/19.html (accessed June 3, 2011). Rikhvanova answered me, "When I've tried to delve deeply

into this, I understood that the merger (sliyanie) of [political] power and business is a real and serious conflict of interests."

5. Federation of Automobile Owners of Russia, Home page, n.d., www.autofed.ru (accessed January 19, 2012).

6. TIGR, "Prinuzhdenie k otvetsvennosti" [Forcing responsibility], Gazeta Tovarishchestva initsiativnykh grazhdan Rossii [The Newspaper of the Fellowship of Self-Motivated Citizens of Russia], February 14, 2009, www.phokprf.ru/info/9496 (May 12, 2011).

7. Ibid.

8. Federation of Automobile Owners of Russia, "20 marta-Vserossiyskaya aktsiya protesta protiv tsen na toplivo" [March 20—is the all-Russian protest event against the prices of gas], www.autofed.ru/?p=3863 (accessed May 15, 2011).

9. "If people had even a little bit of self-respect, then we would not have the impunity," said Vedenev.

10. Citizenship means "responsibility for what is happening in the country," said Chirikova. A citizen, she added, is someone who "to the best of his abilities does everything he can to ameliorate the situation in the country, in his yard, in his town, in his country—as far as he can reach."

11. "Prinuzhdenie k otvetsvennosti" (emphasis added).

12. Said Chirikova, "I think we look more like the Gandhi movement in India.... We lead many regular, rank-and-file people who understand that, to continue the parallel, we are not worse than the British, we are not worse than our authorities, that we are not slaves, and that, although the empire humiliates us, we continue to resist and do not respond with violence.... We quite consciously avoid violence, never resort to violent means in our struggle [because] when you don't respond to violence with violence you avoid multiplying evil.... If some of the people whom we support begin to resort to violence, of course we sym-

pathize with their [personal plight] after they are repressed. But ... I always tell them, 'Guys, I am very sorry that you are being punished like this, but our way is a way of peaceful resistance and it is the only way to change anything in the world.'"

> *"The last ten years have seen ... democratic institutions eroded in Russia."*

The Russian Government Undermines Civil Rights

Yury Dzhibladze

Yury Dzhibladze contends in the following viewpoint that the administration of President Vladimir Putin has chosen to abridge civil liberties in Russia and cut short the burgeoning power of nongovernmental democratic institutions. According to Dzhibladze, the government has embarked on this strategy to quell dissent and reinforce its own dominance. The author maintains that the government is using fear and the public's apathy to achieve its objectives. However, as Dzhibladze notes, more stringent laws could prompt those who now have had a taste of freedom to organize greater resistance. Yury Dzhibladze is a founder and president of the Center for the Development of Democracy and Human Rights in Moscow.

As you read, consider the following questions:

1. According to Dzhibladze, what do almost all of the new, punitive 2011–2012 Russian laws entail?

2. What does the author see as the intention of the "homophobic" laws passed in contemporary Russia?

3. Why does Dzhibladze think the Russian people have lost interest in politics?

In a very short space of time indeed [between June and July 2012] three fundamental freedoms—of assembly, association and speech—were subjected to ferocious legal restriction. Parliamentary procedures and the many protests were completely ignored; many experts consider, not without justification, that the new laws governing demonstrations, NGOs [nongovernmental organisations], defamation and the legal regulation of the Internet are proof that these three rights have not only been restricted, but effectively abolished. This 'bouquet' could also be said to include the medieval (in spirit) laws passed in several regions banning the so-called 'promotion of homosexuality', which openly introduce legal discrimination based on sexual identity. There is a considerable danger that a similar homophobic law, which has already been introduced in the State Duma [Russian parliament], will be passed at federal level.

Russia Is Not a Democratic State

These three fundamental rights—speech, assembly and association—are defined in international law as 'vital freedoms', serving as the basis for a democratic society. The principle informing them is fairly clear. If people are not able to express their opinions freely, to associate in groups in defence of their interests, to make their views known publicly at a demonstration without fear of being beaten up by the police, fined enormous sums or finding themselves behind bars for a long period of time, then the state cannot be considered democratic. Even the existence of such democratic institutions as regular elections, the separation of powers and an independent judiciary, etc., does not alter that fact....

The last ten years have seen these democratic institutions eroded in Russia. The supremacy of the law does not exist, laws are applied arbitrarily and most citizens are convinced there is no justice to be had in the courts. However, the existence in Russian law until recently of laws guaranteeing, albeit only on paper, these three fundamental rights and constitutional freedoms, allowed the political regime to be classified as 'hybrid', to be called an 'imitation of democracy'.

In June–July 2012 an important line was crossed. The new laws passed by the Russian government were an abnegation of what it had emphasized for many years. Russia is no longer a democratic state—not only in essence, but formally. Those who initiated these changes, introduced the draft laws in parliament, voted for them and publicly supported them have in effect signed up to the diagnosis formulated by the protesters in scores of towns and cities: The authoritarian nature of the current political system is acknowledged to be a denial of democracy as well.

Severe New Laws Aimed at Curtailing Freedoms

These new laws are anti-constitutional in spirit and fail to comply with Russia's international legal obligations (though the government cunningly asserts that these laws are based on the laws of democratic countries). There is another feature they have in common: Their vague drafting is typical of the 'ideological' legislation that we have seen throughout [Russian president] Vladimir Putin's rule. The 'political activities' in the NGO law on 'foreign agents', or the 'promotion of homosexuality', for example. It is not by chance that the laws are drawn up in this way: The catchall, woolly wording makes it possible to apply the law selectively, including for political or ideological reasons. It is the denial of the supremacy of the law and the equality of all before the law, and the selective application of the law that are at the heart of the authoritarian system.

Almost all the new laws entail the introduction of fines, the severity of which is unequalled in Russian law. This effectively serves as a brake on the exercise of rights and freedoms. Criminal liability has also been extended to cover defamation, and the 'gross violation' of the law on 'foreign agents' by NGO managers is likely to attract a maximum sentence of two years in prison. What is meant by gross violation is not, of course, clarified.

There is more than one example of legal discrimination as a principle in this repressive set of laws. The NGO law, for example, is aimed at certain kinds of NGO activity, landing them with an intolerable burden of financial reporting and inspections, and demanding of organisations involved in the defence of human rights and in education that they describe themselves as 'foreign agents', which in Russian means 'spies'.

In the case of the homophobic laws, the government's motives are clear: to mobilise the support of the most conservative section of Russian society. Putin's obsession with the supposedly important part played by human rights NGOs in organising the protests (using foreign money), their mythical 'unacceptable meddling in politics', remains on the whole a mystery. . . . Whatever the case, NGOs were actually not involved at all in organising the protests of winter 2011 and spring 2012. . . . Times have changed and the civil society leaders—or at least that part of civil society which protests loudly against the existing order—are no longer the traditional NGOs, but the informal public movements and the 'disgruntled citizens' united by social networks.

The new laws are often described as unconstitutional in nature because they limit vital freedoms. It is unclear, however, if the Russian Constitutional Court has enough power to protect basic constitutional rights.

The vague drafting of the laws gives rise to another important problem: It is very difficult to elicit from the text of the law which activities it is that will mean you are breaking it so it is impossible to predict the legal consequences of one's behaviour. In jurisprudence this is known as the 'violation of the principle of legal clarity'. This, together with the amorphous definitions not grounded in law, gives good reason for these laws to be described as unlawful.

Characteristically, the government soothed the anxieties of the civil society by assuring them that the law on 'foreign agents' would not be applied to all NGOs. Just to this organisation, and to that one too, because they are harmful to the state. The government does not want, after all, to put the whole of the opposition behind bars or to close down all independent organisations. Their aim is somewhat different—to scare the discontented with severe penalties by organising some widely publicised reprisals.

Using Fear as a Weapon

It is interesting that the ruling class is trying to scare society, because it itself has taken fright. The new laws were clearly passed in haste to quell the waves of protest, which were on the increase from December to June. Provoked by the mass rigging of the elections, no fewer than 250,000 took part in unprecedented protests all over the country and the government obviously took this very seriously.

The change in the relations between the state and society dates from Putin's very first day as president. One has only to remember the police aggression on 6 May during the demonstration on Bolotnaya Square [in Moscow], the arrests of the demonstrators, the investigation of the opposition leaders, the pressure on human rights organisations, such as 'Golos' ['Voice'] and the Committee Against Torture and, finally, the inquisition and trial of the girls from the punk rock group Pussy Riot. The three young women have just been sentenced to two years in prison for their flamboyant, nonviolent political protest [of Putin's reelection] in the Cathedral of Christ

Licensing and Monitoring Civil Organizations in Russia

The Kremlin has worked to create a system that gives them considerable discretion over which groups and which individuals are able to operate in Russia. Groups that accept a role within the licensed system have seen their opportunities for funding and their institutionalized access to policy making improve significantly, whereas groups that the regime deems oppositionist in orientation are either eliminated or live a tenuous existence at the mercy of the authorities.

Central to the new system is Federal Law No. 18-FZ ... signed into law on 10 January 2006. . . .

In part the law is intended to clean up the NGO [nongovernmental organization] sector, which had previously been awash with organizations that were either simply badly run or that were operated more as fronts for commercial or even criminal activity than as NGOs. . . .

However, the other part of the administration's strategy is to make sure that the government is able to keep NGOs, and in particular foreign and foreign-funded NGOs, on a very tight rein. All NGOs have been required to reregister with the authorities, and the law provides for several grounds on which registration might be refused. The reporting requirements of NGOs have been significantly increased, and, in particular, NGOs are required to report all funds received from foreign sources and to provide details on how these are used.

Graeme B. Robertson, "Managing Society:
Protest, Civil Society, and Regime in Putin's Russia,"
Slavic Review, *Fall 2009.*

the Saviour. A more obvious signal that the government cannot stomach criticism and will come down heavily on it is difficult to imagine.

The tone of utterances by the political leadership has changed too: both the form and the content have become much harsher and more scornful. They have effectively declared 'cold war' on the civil society. Many have noticed that the atmosphere in Russia changed within the space of a few weeks: Calls for the restitution of the death penalty, a new surge of Stalinist apologetics, and medieval bigotry disguised as religious principles have suddenly all become possible.

But the Russian government no longer has at its disposal the functioning social contract of Putin's first two terms: People have lost interest in politics and are more concerned with improving their standard of living, backed up by foreign loans and high hydrocarbon prices. They are fed up with the same old faces in the government and President Putin's popularity ratings are the lowest they have been since 2001.

As levels of dissatisfaction with rampant corruption and the lack of social justice increase, the government has to turn to its last weapon—fear. The ruling class is not prepared to embark on the path of real democratic change, because it realises that the chances of being able to hang on to its positions of power, not inconsiderable property and, for some, liberty itself, are extremely dubious. It is, however, also not prepared to take a decisive step towards dictatorship because it forms part of, and is dependent on, the global economy.

Government Clampdown May Spark More Resistance

What might be the consequences of these extraordinary measures to 'tighten the screws'?

Well, a section of society has indeed taken fright. The emigration option has become more popular. According to Levada-Center data, by the middle of August 2012 people were significantly less willing to take part in demonstrations. Some NGOs have announced that they feel compelled to refuse funds from abroad.

There is, however, also the opposite reaction. Active participants in protest rallies on the one hand, and human rights organisations on the other, have for the last month been engaged in discussing reaction strategies. They make no secret of the fact that they consider the new laws anti-constitutional and unlawful and, in the case of the 'foreign agents' law, also absurd. Various activities are planned: from the legal, material and moral defence of certain activists and organisations (a strategy for preservation and survival) to campaigning for an open boycott of the unlawful laws (a strategy for defending the supremacy of the law).

For these actions to be successful, a greater degree of self-organisation and social solidarity than currently obtains will, of course, be essential. 100 or 500, rather than 5, NGOs must announce that they will not comply with an anti-constitutional law, and several thousands more must support them publicly. Hundreds, rather than scores, of courageous people will be needed to turn out without preliminary permission in defence of their constitutional right to peaceful assembly. Many passionate supporters of LGBT [lesbian, gay, bisexual and transgender] activists will be needed to contribute their own money to a fund for the defence of activists and organisations being prosecuted, and barristers prepared to defend them on a pro bono basis. In the event of such a leap forward in civil self-organisation, the government will find it very hard to apply the new laws as they had planned—selectively and for the purpose of instilling fear.

The 'constitutional coup' of the summer of 2012 could, unexpectedly for its initiators, awake powerful forces of resistance. The scenario is by no means as hopeless as it might seem today.

Periodical Bibliography

The following articles have been selected to supplement the diverse views presented in this chapter.

Daniel Beer	"Russia's Managed Democracy," *History Today*, May 2009.
Ben Coleridge	"Russians Voting Against Democracy," *Eureka Street*, December 12, 2007.
Dmitri Furman	"Imitation Democracies: The Post-Soviet Penumbra," *New Left Review*, November/December 2008.
Laura A. Henry	"Redefining Citizenship in Russia: Political and Social Rights," *Problems of Post-Communism*, November/December 2009.
Ivan Krastev	"Putinism Under Siege: An Autopsy of Managed Democracy," *Journal of Democracy*, July 2012.
Alex Nice	"Politics Returns to Russia," *World Today*, December 2011.
David Remnick	"The Civil Archipelago," *New Yorker*, December 19, 2011.
Mikhail V. Savva and Valerii A. Tishkov	"Civil Society Institutions and Peacemaking," *Anthropology & Archeology of Eurasia*, Spring 2011.
Victor Sonkin	"Gloves Are Off," *New Internationalist*, September 2012.
Metta Spencer	"Peace and Democracy in Russia," *Peace Magazine*, July–September 2011.

OPPOSING
VIEWPOINTS®
SERIES

CHAPTER 3

What Relationship Should the West Foster with Russia?

Chapter Preface

In an April 3, 2012, article for *U.S. News & World Report*, John T. Bennett argues that Russia is "proving to be a major obstacle for America's foreign interests." According to Bennett, Russia has hampered the President Barack Obama administration's efforts to pressure Iran into giving up its nuclear ambitions, and it has rejected a United Nations measure calling for the resignation of Syrian president Bashar al-Assad, a ruler who has used his military to brutally crush populist protests in his nation. Bennett claims this posturing is part of Russian president Vladimir Putin's desire to show that his country is still a superpower two decades after the collapse of the Soviet Union in 1991. The stubbornness, he writes, emphasizes that "Moscow fundamentally opposes Western efforts to boss around the world's strongmen, with which Russian leaders have much in common."

Under President Obama, the United States has avoided adopting a confrontational attitude with Russia. The administration worked to broker a new treaty to reduce nuclear arsenals in both countries, revealing its preference for negotiation and foregrounding Obama's 2009 promise "to reset U.S.-Russian relations, so that we can cooperate more effectively in areas of common interest." The White House has also sought Russian cooperation in stabilizing the new government in war-torn Afghanistan, where America and its allies have been fighting the autocratic Taliban regime since 2001. Such diplomacy, Obama has stated, is "paving the way for more progress in the future."

Not all politicians, however, are content with the administration's approach. In a March 2012 CNN interview, Mitt Romney, Massachusetts governor and Republican candidate in 2012's presidential election, claimed that Obama was being too soft on Russia. Describing Russia as America's "number one geopolitical foe," in part because it "always stands up for the world's worst actors," Romney expressed concern for the current administration's foreign policy. He criticized the new nuclear treaty because its only result was to decrease American missile strength since Russian warhead numbers were already below treaty limits. He also fretted over the president's decision to push for a European missile defense system that was weaker than the one proposed during the presidency of George W. Bush. A September 1, 2012, article in the *Economist* observes that "Mr Romney's advisers see things differently: they have no wish to accept limitations on US development of missile-defence capabilities, and show little interest in new arms-control agreements." What plans Romney had for US-Russian relations were unclear because his campaign made no definitive statements, but his comments on the election trail suggested a different strategy in dealing with Putin's assumed intransigence.

In the following chapter, several commentators and analysts offer their perspectives on how the United States and its Western allies should deal with Putin's Russia. Some advocate building a strong relationship to keep Russia from backsliding into Soviet-era autocracy. Others believe the Putin government has already shown a willingness to revert to older Cold War models of leadership and therefore should be confronted with human rights abuses and other poor choices in domestic and international affairs in an attempt to further Russia's move toward democracy. Whichever path the West takes will be determined by President Obama and European leaders who face growing economic and energy ties with the former superpower.

> "We believe the Magnitsky legislation
> should be the starting point for a sec-
> ond phase of [improved U.S.-Russian
> relations], one that focuses on Russian
> respect for universal human rights stan-
> dards and its integration in the open
> international economy."

The United States Should Pass Legislation to Discourage Human Rights Abuses in Russia

Robert Kagan and David J. Kramer

*In the following viewpoint, Robert Kagan and David J. Kramer
assert that Congress should pass the Russia and Moldova Jackson-
Vanik Repeal and Sergei Magnitsky Rule of Law Accountability
Act of 2012, also known as the Magnitsky Act. This piece of legislation attempts to restrict Russian officials from living or doing
business in the West if they have engaged in human rights abuses,
the authors state. Kagan and Kramer believe that, despite
Moscow's opposition to the act, the time is right to bring human
rights issues to the forefront of US-Russian relations in order to*

help end corruption and improve the lot of the Russian people. Robert Kagan is a senior fellow at the Brookings Institution, a public policy research organization. David J. Kramer is president of Freedom House, a US-based nonprofit that researches and promotes global democracy.

As you read, consider the following questions:

1. Who was Sergei Magnitsky, as Kagan and Kramer report?

2. Why do the authors contend that the Magnitsky Act is not an intrusion into Russian affairs?

3. What piece of legislation do Kagan and Kramer believe should be lifted because its restrictions are out of date?

The House Foreign Affairs Committee is scheduled today [June 6, 2012] to take up the most consequential piece of legislation in years related to Russia: the [Russia and Moldova Jackson-Vanik Repeal and] Sergei Magnitsky Rule of Law Accountability Act of 2012. With strong bipartisan support, led by Rep. Jim McGovern (D-Mass.) and Sen. Benjamin L. Cardin (D-Md.), the Magnitsky bill is the most serious U.S. effort to address human rights and the rule of law in Russia since the collapse of the Soviet Union.

The legislation is named after the 37-year-old lawyer who was jailed unjustly in 2008 after exposing a massive tax fraud by officials of Russia's interior ministry. While in jail for almost a year, Magnitsky became ill but was denied medical treatment. In the end he was brutally beaten and left to die.

A Bill to Hold Human Rights Abusers Accountable

The proposed legislation is not about one man, however. It is about a Russian system choking on corruption, illegality and abuse. The new law would impose a visa ban and asset freeze against the officials responsible not only for Magnitsky's murder but also for other human rights abuses, including [abuses] against individuals who "expose illegal activity" carried out by Russian officials or who seek to "defend or promote internationally recognized human rights and freedoms." This includes journalists who have been murdered when they have dug too close to powerful officials or oligarchs. It includes human rights activists who have been beaten and crippled or killed for exposing the mistreatment of their fellow Russians.

Senior Russian officials have protested vigorously against the legislation, claiming it is an unwarranted intrusion into their country's internal affairs. But the legislation denies only Russian officials who engage in human rights abuses the privilege of traveling to, living in or studying in the West, and of doing their banking in Western financial institutions. Russian officials who respect the rule of law in their country, who do not engage in the torture and beating of journalists, lawyers, human rights advocates and opposition figures, have nothing to worry about. Moreover, the legislation will not impede a visa facilitation agreement between the United States and Russia that is nearing completion, one that will strengthen people-to-people ties.

An Attempt to Stem Russian Corruption

Foreign Minister Sergey Lavrov and other senior Russian officials have described the legislation as "anti-Russian." Actually, it's just the opposite.

The Russian people today live in a system where corrupt officials spirit their ill-gotten gains to safe havens outside the country, where they can neither be taxed nor accounted for. Capital flight out of Russia totaled $84 billion last year, and it is on pace this year to far surpass that. This corruption, and the forces who defend it by imprisoning or killing those who expose it, are gnawing away at Russian society from the inside. What the people of Russia need is a free and open public dis-

Maryland Senator Benjamin L. Cardin Introduces the Magnitsky Act

Mr. President [of the Senate], private and even public expressions of concern are not a substitute for a real policy nor are they enough; it's time for consequences. The bill I introduce today sends a strong message to those who are currently acting with impunity in Russia that there will be consequences for corruption should you wish to travel to and invest in the United States. Such actions will provide needed moral support for those in Russia doing the really heavy lifting in fighting corruption and promoting the rule of law, but they will also protect our own interests—values or business related.

We see before us a tale of two Russias, the double-headed eagle if you will. To whom does the future of Russia belong? Does it belong to the Yevgenia Chirikovas, Alexei Navalnys, Oleg Orlovs and countless other courageous, hardworking, and patriotic Russians who expose corruption and fight for human rights or those who inhabit the shadows abusing and stealing from their fellow citizens?

Let's not put aside our humanity out of exaggerated and excessively cautious diplomatic concerns for the broader relationship. Let's take the long view and stand on the right side—and I believe the wise side—with the Russian people who've suffered so much for the cause of liberty and human dignity.

Benjamin L. Cardin,
"Sergei Magnitsky Rule of Law Accountability Act of 2011,"
Proceedings and Debates of the 112th Congress, 1st session,
May 19, 2011.

course where government officials can be held accountable. That kind of climate will attract the foreign investment Russia needs to grow and to diversify its economy.

Those Russians who oppose this legislation are no friends of a prosperous Russia. They are part of the problem.

Russian authorities have warned Washington that their government's participation in President [Barack] Obama's "reset" of relations will end if Congress passes the Magnitsky legislation. Right now, it is not clear how committed Moscow is to the reset, with or without Magnitsky. President Vladimir Putin's decision to skip last month's Group of 8 summit [of the most economically developed countries] at Camp David; the recent threat by Gen. Nikolai Makarov, Putin's armed forces chief of staff, to launch a preemptive strike against NATO [North Atlantic Treaty Organization] over an ongoing missile defense dispute; and the continuing harassment of U.S. ambassador Mike McFaul, the author of the reset, all raise some doubts.

Modern Legislation for Today's Russia

But in any case, we believe the Magnitsky legislation should be the starting point for a second phase of the reset, one that focuses on Russian respect for universal human rights standards and its integration in the open international economy, from which average citizens stand to benefit.

One element of that is Russia's expected entry into the World Trade Organization. That is why we favor lifting the Jackson-Vanik amendment, legislation dating to 1974 that denied most-favored-nation status to countries, including the Soviet Union, that restricted the ability of its citizens to emigrate and travel. That legislation has long outlived its utility, since Russian authorities for years have eliminated such restrictions. The Obama administration and U.S. businesses that operate in Russia have been pushing Congress to lift Jackson-

Vanik; doing so, and thereby granting Russia most-favored-nation status, would level the playing field for U.S. companies.

But these measures can't succeed if Russia continues on its current path. The human rights situation in Russia in the last dozen years has deteriorated significantly, as documented both by Freedom House and by the State Department's human rights report. These abuses are a symptom of the larger problem in Russia, which is the endemic corruption of people in high places. That is why Congress should replace Jackson-Vanik with modern legislation that addresses today's Russia.

> "The [Magnitsky] bill has no real chance
> of reducing corruption or human rights
> abuses in Russia's criminal justice sys-
> tem."

US Legislation
Will Not Be Effective in
Combating Human Rights
Abuses in Russia

Raymond Sontag

*In the following viewpoint, Raymond Sontag, a former officer for
the National Democratic Institute's political party program in
Moscow, claims that the Russia and Moldova Jackson-Vanik Repeal and Sergei Magnitsky Rule of Law Accountability Act of
2012 is a poorly conceived piece of legislation. While not denying
the importance of promoting human rights in Russia, Sontag believes the bill—which freezes assets and denies travel privileges to
Russian officials who engage in human rights abuse—will have
no effect on ending corruption or improving human rights. Sontag claims that corruption is too entrenched in the Russian government and that officials will go to any lengths to maintain the
status quo. A law passed in the United States, therefore, is not*

likely to convince corrupt Russian officials to end the abuses of power that keep them in luxury and security, Sontag asserts. In addition, the author insists that the United States is not engaged or concerned enough with Russia to enforce any stringent human rights laws.

As you read, consider the following questions:

1. In Sontag's view, why has the United States not sought to hold China accountable for its human rights abuses?

2. How does the Magnitsky Act itself reflect that human rights are not a primary concern for policy makers, according to Sontag?

3. What force does Sontag assume may eventually prove sufficient to compel the Russian leadership to do something about containing corruption?

Russia's accession to the World Trade Organization [WTO] has created a quandary for Congress. On the one hand, members want to respect WTO rules and allow free trade with Russia, thereby further integrating that country into the world economy. On the other hand, many in the policy-making community have concerns over the Russian government's human rights record and do not want, in effect, to reward an undeserving Moscow with unfettered access to American markets. For this reason, Congress has yet to repeal the 1975 Jackson-Vanik amendment, which stipulates that the United States cannot grant permanent normal trade relations to non-market economies that restrict emigration, a practice the Soviet Union once engaged in. The Soviet Union disappeared in 1991, and Russia long ago removed all impediments to citizens who wish to leave the country, but Congress has kept Jackson-Vanik in place, hoping to use it as leverage with the Russian government. As a result, the United States cannot engage in unrestricted trade with Russia, and Russia, of course, is responding in kind by limiting American access to its markets.

Substituting One Bill for Another

Congress, though, seems to have found a way out of this impasse by swapping one piece of human rights legislation for another: Several leading members of Congress have said they would vote to repeal Jackson-Vanik if the so-called Magnitsky bill [officially known as the Russia and Moldova Jackson-Vanik Repeal and Sergei Magnitsky Rule of Law Accountability Act] is passed. This bill seeks to bar from the United States, and freeze the assets of, Russian officials responsible for the November 2010 death of lawyer Sergei Magnitsky and for "other gross violations of human rights." Magnitsky was investigating tax fraud by Russian officials, who in turn apparently sought to silence him by charging him with fraud, locking him up in pretrial detention and denying him medical attention that likely would have saved his life. Magnitsky's death sparked international outrage, and the Magnistky bill is Congress's attempt to hold the guilty parties responsible. By substituting the Magnitsky Act for Jackson-Vanik, the United States would seem to accomplish both its goals: getting free trade with Russia and keeping up the pressure on the Kremlin to respect human rights.

The Magnitsky bill, however, is very unlikely to improve human rights in Russia, and it is also reflective of a broader problem affecting U.S. foreign policy: an impulse to engage in self-righteous posturing rather than in crafting serious strategy. The problems the bill aims to address, corruption and abuse in Russia's criminal justice system, are far too entrenched and lucrative to those involved to be seriously impacted by denying officials entry to Western countries or access to their Western bank accounts. U.S. ambassador to Russia Michael McFaul, himself a vocal proponent of American democracy promotion in the former Soviet Union, opposes the Magnitsky bill, claiming that it is redundant to steps the State Department has already taken to bar officials responsible for Magnitsky's death from the United States. The administration's resistance to the legislation is understandable. The law would tie its hands in its dealings with Russia and make what is already a contentious bilateral relationship that much worse—all while doing nothing to actually improve human rights in Russia.

Focusing on China, Not Russia

In truth, though, further deterioration of relations with Russia would mean little to most in Washington. This is the bigger problem that initiatives such as the Magnitsky bill reflect. Since the end of the Cold War, Russia has not asserted itself as a power to be reckoned with, as China has done, nor has it democratized and integrated itself into Euro-Atlantic political and economic structures, as the countries of Central Europe have done. Russia's lack of hard power and its failure to cooperate more closely with the West leave American policy makers without a clear agenda for dealing with it. Many in the United States are disappointed with Russia's failure to democratize, but few take Russia seriously as an economic or military force. This disappointment produces impulses to correct the course of Russian politics, and Russia's seeming insignificance means there is little to check these impulses.

This approach to Russia stands in sharp contrast to the one Congress has taken to the other formerly Communist nuclear power that Jackson-Vanik covered: China. Congress lifted all Jackson-Vanik restrictions on trade with China before it joined the WTO in 2001 and did not find it necessary to replace them with other measures to ensure that Beijing observed human rights. Obviously, this was not because there were no concerns over how China treats its citizens, but because economic relations with China were simply too important to make them hostage to human rights concerns. The volume of U.S. trade with China is about 16 times larger than U.S. trade with Russia and China's U.S. Treasury securities holdings are nearly ten times larger than Russia's. When one weighs China's and Russia's human rights records against their relative importance to the U.S. economy, it is hard not to conclude that Congress is ready to push for human rights abroad only when no real interests are at stake.

Human Rights Are a Secondary Concern

That human rights promotion is at best a secondary consideration for the United States is reflected by the Magnitsky bill itself, which includes so-called "waivers for national interest." These waivers stipulate that the administration can allow Russian officials guilty of human rights abuses into the country or have their assets unfrozen if it deems that doing so is in the national interest. In a similar vein, while the [Barack] Obama administration is lobbying to make the bill's rules apply to all countries and not just Russia (and thereby lessen tensions with Moscow) unnamed congressional aides told *Foreign Policy* that such an expansion might be problematic, as it could create conflicts with some foreign governments. In other words, while there are countries where the U.S. Congress sees promoting human rights as a secondary consideration to maintaining good relations with their governments, Russia is not one of them.

Of course America's inconsistency in its promotion of human rights abroad is not, by itself, a reason to never promote them; perhaps if the Magnitsky bill had a real chance of accomplishing its stated aims, one could support it despite its being redundant and self-contradictory. But the truth of the matter is that the bill has no real chance of reducing corruption or human rights abuses in Russia's criminal justice system. In fact, those who believe it does have such a chance are actually underestimating the scope of the problem. Corruption in Russia is not just a matter of a handful of unscrupulous bureaucrats misusing their posts; it is a mainstay of the economy. According to Moscow's [Information Science for Democracy (INDEM) Foundation] think tank, Russian businesses paid about $462 billion in bribes in 2010, which is around 31 percent of the country's gross domestic product. With this much money available to officials through graft, it is not surprising that, according to a 2010 poll conducted by the Public Opinion Foundation, more than half of Russians aged 18–30 want to pursue careers in civil service. President Dmitry Medvedev himself said that these numbers showed young people were looking to become bureaucrats because, despite low official salaries, this career was "a way to get rich quickly," and that this was "very disturbing."

Russia's Hesitancy to Tackle Corruption

As these comments suggest, Russia's leaders are aware of the corruption engulfing government agencies. Medvedev devoted much of his time as president to passing anticorruption measures and reforming the police force. Magnitsky's death, in fact, was a catalyst for some of these reforms. About a month after the lawyer died, Medvedev proposed changes to the law that would prevent the police from keeping people accused of financial crimes in pretrial detention, thereby removing officials' primary tool for pressuring and extorting business figures. This measure was passed into law, but, like all of Medvedev's efforts to reduce government abuse and corruption, it proved to be more cosmetic than real and failed to change fundamentally how law enforcement functions in Russia. Those responsible for Magnitsky's death remain unpunished and Russian law enforcement continues to churn out grim stories of abuse on a near daily basis. The country's leaders may realize how serious the corruption problem is and they may want to change it, but they have not shown any willingness to go after the problem aggressively.

Part of the reason for their hesitancy to tackle corruption earnestly is that they or people close to them benefit from it. There is evidence, for example, that top officials have been shielding the perpetrators in the Magnitsky case and allowing them to engage in theft of budget funds on a massive scale. The larger impediment to a real anticorruption campaign, though, is that corruption is so central to how law enforcement agencies work in Russia, and these agencies are so essential to how the [president-elect Vladimir] Putin regime exercises power, that if the leadership did truly tackle the problem, it would find itself in a serious fight with a key constituency.

At some point the Russian people's outrage with this corruption may prove sufficient to force the leadership to do something about it. In large part, anger over corruption motivated the recent anti-Putin street protests, but the long-term prospects for this sort of bottom-up change are unclear. What is clear is that publicly barring officials from the United States or freezing their assets will not be sufficient incentive for Russia to crack down on abuses by law enforcement.

A Bill That Misses Key Points

The Magnitsky bill's backers point to the fact that corrupt Russian officials like to travel and keep their money abroad as evidence that denying them these privileges will make them less corrupt. But these arguments miss the rather obvious point that if these officials did not engage in this corruption, they would also be effectively barred from Western banks and trips abroad not by American laws but by the fact that they could never afford such luxuries on their meager official salaries in the first place. These arguments also miss the point that, however irritated Russia's leaders may be with the Magnitsky bill, its sanctions are nowhere near sufficient to get them to take on their own security services.

Those who wish to see human rights as the cornerstone of U.S. foreign policy may respond that we should have even tougher measures than the Magnitsky bill that are applied more broadly. But aside from the question of whether or not this would be desirable, the U.S. relationship with China shows that it is impossible. Even the United States is not immune to the need to pursue its material interests. This only appears to not be the case when, as with the relationship with Russia, there appear to be no real interests at stake. Russia's lack of integration into American-led international institutions, its apparently knee-jerk opposition to many Western initiatives and its relative lack of economic or military power may make it hard to see how or why the United States should engage with it. Should the perception in Washington of Russia's importance to the United States change, one can be fairly sure measures such as the Magnitsky bill will fall by the wayside.

> "The conviction of Pussy Riot will do much to boost Mr Putin's reputation as a thug."

Western Support for the Punk Band Pussy Riot Draws Attention to Russia's Authoritarianism

Gideon Rachman

In the following viewpoint, Gideon Rachman, the chief foreign affairs correspondent for the Financial Times, *claims that Russian president Vladimir Putin has made a public relations blunder by jailing the punk band Pussy Riot for speaking out in protest of his reelection in 2012. Rachman insists that it is unwise to turn artists and musicians into political martyrs because they have a celebrity appeal that can rally both national and international support. Indeed, Rachman maintains that while Pussy Riot has so far only released a single, the controversy surrounding the band's sentencing has tarnished Putin's reputation at home and has drawn criticism from Westerners who are now looking more closely at the regime's other "unattractive features."*

As you read, consider the following questions:

1. What trademark "look" does Pussy Riot have that Rachman claims can be easily emulated by fans and supporters?

2. As Rachman reports, what American pop singer showed support for Pussy Riot during her August 2012 concert in Moscow?

3. According to Rachman, the Pussy Riot incident has convinced some Putin loyalists to conclude what about the new president?

Congratulations Vladimir Putin. Just four months back in the Kremlin and you have inflicted the worst blow to Russia's international image in more than a decade.

Few can doubt that the Kremlin had a hand in the decision to sentence Pussy Riot to two years in prison [in August 2012]. The punishment is grossly disproportionate to the band's "crime"—singing a raucous anti-Putin ditty in a Moscow cathedral.

Still, professional Russia watchers know that there have been far worse human rights violations in the Putin years. The difference is that Sergei Magnitsky, a murdered lawyer, Anna Politkovskaya, a murdered journalist, and even Mikhail Khodorkovsky, a jailed oligarch, have never really become household names in the outside world. Pussy Riot members, by contrast, are all set to become global celebrities.

Celebrities Make Dangerous Political Opponents

Writers and musicians can be far more dangerous opponents for authoritarians than mere politicians or controversial businessmen such as Mr Khodorkovsky. They often have a wit, panache and integrity that makes rulers look ridiculous. Václav Havel, a playwright, became the rallying figure for the opposi-

© 2012 Petar Pismestrovic, Kleine Zeitung, and Politicalcartoons.com.

tion in Czechoslovakia. Around the world, Ai Weiwei, an artist, has become the flamboyant face of opposition to the identical apparatchiks of the Chinese Communist Party.

Pussy Riot has only just released its first single. But it has courage and a gift for performance art. Its name deftly combines two of the major preoccupations of teenage boys. And, as outspoken women, its members embody the idea of "girl power"—as lauded by the Spice Girls. The band's trademark balaclavas [knit caps] also provide an easily imitated "look" that has already been emulated in demonstrations from Berlin to New York.

Yet those tempted to dismiss the three imprisoned members of Pussy Riot as simply clever marketeers should read their statements from the dock, which are intelligent, articulate and moving.

Condemnation from Human Rights Watch and pursed lips at the Swedish foreign ministry are one thing. But when Madonna and Yoko Ono are on the case, the Kremlin is entering a different league of international odium. Madonna, in particular, has played an admirable role. In a recent concert in Moscow, she donned a balaclava, wrote the band's name on her back and spoke out in their support. The crowd at the concert cheered wildly—while Dmitry Rogozin, a Russian deputy prime minister, betrayed the Kremlin's anger by labelling the singer a moralising "slut".

It cannot be long before concerts in support of Pussy Riot are held outside Russia. The obvious model would be the "Free Nelson Mandela" concerts of the 1980s, which so acutely embarrassed South Africa's apartheid government.

Tarnishing the Regime's Image

The Putin government may try to pretend that it does not care about the outrage of musicians and intellectuals in the West. But it has spent many millions hiring Western public relations firms to burnish Russia's image. Any one of these hired guns could have warned Mr Putin that the Pussy Riot sentence is an unqualified PR disaster.

The danger for Mr Putin is that bashing the Russian government may now become cool. Until recently, critics of Russia were often cast as outdated Cold War warriors. When [Massachusetts governor and Republican presidential candidate] Mitt Romney recently declared that Russia was America's "number one geopolitical foe", his statement was widely taken as evidence he was living in the past.

The conviction of Pussy Riot will do much to boost Mr Putin's reputation as a thug. In the process, it may draw much wider attention to many other unattractive features of Putin's Russia—from widespread corruption to its protection of brutal regimes such as Syria and the frequent unpunished murders of government critics such as Mr Magnitsky or Alexander Litvinenko, the former Russian agent, who was poisoned in London.

Keeping Protest Alive

The Russian government will insist that Mr Putin is far more representative of the Russian people than some avant-garde musicians from Moscow. There may be some truth in that. Russia is a socially conservative place and there are certainly many religious people in Russia who were genuinely offended by Pussy Riot's performance.

Nonetheless, independent opinion polls suggest that the government's heavy-handed treatment of the band has not convinced a majority of Russians. Less than half (44 per cent) said that they regarded the case against Pussy Riot as just.

One of the important questions, when Mr Putin returned to the Kremlin in May, was whether he would be able to put behind him the popular protests that had greeted the rigging of legislative and presidential elections a few months earlier. The initial signs were encouraging for the Kremlin. The demonstrations in Moscow—and the popular movement that had formed around them—appeared to have largely fizzled out.

Now, however, the conviction of Pussy Riot has re-energised the Russian opposition and inflicted a grave blow to Mr Putin's international image. Even some former Putin loyalists are concluding that the president is now an international embarrassment and a hindrance to Russia's modernisation. There are signs that the Kremlin realises it has made a mistake with Pussy Riot—and may seek to get the band released early. However, the damage to the president's standing is done. Pussy Riot is going to prison. But the band still has the power to rock the Kremlin.

> *"American celebrities are right to be out-raged about Pussy Riot's treatment, but it's a shame that so few seem to have investigated what happens to the activ-ists who aren't Western media darlings for their all-women punk bands with sexually suggestive names."*

Western Support for the Punk Band Pussy Riot Has Obscured the Plight of Other Russian Dissidents

Joshua Foust

A correspondent for the Atlantic *and a columnist for PBS, Joshua Foust is a fellow at the American Security Project, a nonprofit organization focused on issues of national and global security. In the following viewpoint, Foust asserts that the sentencing of the Russian punk band Pussy Riot for demonstrating against the re-gime of President Vladimir Putin is a travesty. Although Foust maintains that it is unjust for the band to suffer such a harsh penalty, he regrets that the women activists have become Western media darlings not because of their dissent but because of their unique status as female punk musicians. Foust worries that the celebrity attached to the band's name says little about the real issues that need to be addressed in Russia—the kinds of issues that have led to the deaths and imprisonment of resisters who don't happen to have the cult allure of a trio of young women rock stars.*

As you read, consider the following questions:

1. According to Foust, Western fans of Pussy Riot are mistakenly turning a serious issue (abridging civil liberties) into a celebration of what?

2. Whose plight does Foust say has been unfortunately ignored in the aftermath of the May 2012 anti-Putin protests?

3. In Foust's view, if Pussy Riot is seen as representing regular Russians, how might that benefit the Russian people?

Pussy Riot have been found guilty of "religious hatred" for their February 21 [2012] protest at the Christ the Saviour Cathedral [in Moscow]. . . . The case itself is troubling for many reasons. For one, Pussy Riot are clearly not expressing hatred of Orthodox Christianity, but they are protesting the church's close relationship to Vladimir Putin and his regime. Hating Putin is not hating religion, unless Putin is now religion in Russia.

The world wants to help, and that's great, but that effort may actually misunderstand both Russia and its challenges in ways that are not always constructive. Pussy Riot have been turned into a *cause célèbre* by Western pop culture mavens. Madonna, Paul McCartney, Björk, even Sting—who apparently learned his lessons after screwing up in Kazakhstan, where he once sold his services to a dictator—have publicly issued statements supporting the fem-punkers.

Feminist punk is great, but it's not the solution to this problem. Pretending it is takes away from more worthwhile efforts.

Commercializing Political Activism

Pussy Riot are being unjustly persecuted (in a free society, they'd have been given a slap on the wrist and a fine, then let go), and that's appropriate and good to protest. But the support movement also carries some uncomfortable echoes of the Kony 2012 campaign and its many less infamous predecessors, repeating an unfortunate practice of activism for the sake of activism, of enthusiastic support for someone who seems to be doing the right thing without really investigating whether their methods are the best, and privileging the easy and fun over the constructive.

The Kony 2012 campaign, by an American NGO [nongovernmental organization] called Invisible Children, was the most successful social media effort ever. Centered around a short movie of the same name, it was meant to raise the international profile of Joseph Kony, a notorious warlord in central Africa famous for conscripting child soldiers and other horrific atrocities. While the Western celebrity efforts around Pussy Riot don't have the same ring of neocolonialism as the Kony 2012 videos and events—Russia was a perpetrator of colonialism and not a victim, after all—they do suffer from similar fundamental problems of commercializing political activism.

In a real way, Kony 2012 took a serious problem—warlords escaping justice in central Africa—and turned it into an exercise in commercialism, militarism, and Western meddling. Local researchers complained about it, and a number of scholars used it as an opportunity to discuss the dos and don'ts of constructive activism.

In Russia, Pussy Riot's newfound Western fans are taking a serious issue (Russia's degrading political freedoms and civil liberties) and turning it into a celebration of feminist punk music and art. Feminist punk music and art are great, but they are not the solutions to this particular problem, and pretending that they are takes attention away from more worthwhile efforts. Pussy Riot might have made punk music, but they got themselves imprisoned for an act of political dissent. Their unjust imprisonment doesn't necessarily make anything done in their name—or, particularly, in the name of their punk music—a step forward for Russian political rights.

Overshadowing Constructive Dissent

Ask yourself, how much have you heard about Pussy Riot's two-year sentence compared to the much harsher sentences facing their not-famous, not-female co-protesters? Radio Free Europe reports:

> With the eyes of Russia watchers trained on Pussy Riot, the feminist punk performance-art group whose now-famous trio is bracing for a verdict over their iconoclastic performance at a Moscow cathedral, the plight of Artyom Savyolov has drawn little attention. . . . Sixteen of the demonstrators remain in custody and at least 12 of them, including Savyolov, have been charged with calling for mass disorder and assaulting police officers. They could each face up to 10 years in prison if convicted.

When Sergei Magnitsky, a lawyer in Russia who was arrested after he drew attention to what he says was widespread political corruption, died from the abuse he suffered in prison—having never even gotten the courtesy of a trial, as did Pussy Riot—there were some peeps of protest by some politicians but nothing on the scale of the Pussy Riot movement. Russian authorities acted suspiciously after his death, leading many to suspect they may have had something to do with it.

Magnitsky's death did prompt some movement in the U.S. Congress, where a bill named after him, which would sanction foreign officials found to have been involved in human rights abuses, now awaits enactment. It's great that Pussy Riot can stand in for the regular Russians who face far worse brutality and mistreatment by Putin's government every day, perhaps drawing some attention to that much larger problem. But the obsessive focus on these three women, not for their activism or political dissent, but for their status as female punk rockers, risks drawing attention away from other Russian activists or political prisoners and focusing it instead on the plight of all-women punk bands, which is decidedly less dire.

Spectacle Obscuring Real Issues

That's not to downplay these three women or their plight. Focusing on the *spectacle* of Pussy Riot actually obscures the real issues that prompted their trial in the first place. Pussy Riot are not peasants grabbed off the road and put on trial for being women—they are rather famous (at least in Russia) political activists who got arrested for political activism. That is a horrible, ludicrous thing for Russia to do, but making them into innocent everymen misunderstands both their actual efforts and why they matter.

Pussy Riot are part of a larger movement within Russia to demand political freedom, one that Putin's regime thugs are literally, physically beating back. American celebrities are right to be outraged about Pussy Riot's treatment, but it's a shame that so few seem to have investigated what happens to the activists who *aren't* Western media darlings for their all-women punk bands with sexually suggestive names. Rather than the Pussy Riot trial catalyzing a broader Western awareness of Russian authoritarian backsliding or even a popular movement to pressure Moscow to loosen its restrictions, it seems to have inspired little more in the West than outrage about how sad it is for some punk rockers to go to jail for a silly little church concert.

| *"The myth that Russia and the U.S. have a mutually useful strategic partnership has been promoted by the Americans for years, but the fiction is becoming harder to maintain."*

The United States Should Not View Russia as a Strategic Partner

Garry Kasparov

Garry Kasparov is the leader of the Russian pro-democracy group the United Civil Front and chairman of the New York-based Human Rights Foundation. In the following viewpoint, Kasparov questions the US government's stance toward Vladimir Putin's rule in Russia. According to Kasparov, the United States has recently praised Moscow's continuing commitment to democracy despite Putin's obvious crackdown on political protest and his strategic relationships with dictators. Kasparov insists that it is not in America's best interest to seek a partnership with Putin's regime and instead should use its diplomatic pressure to hold Putin accountable for his misdeeds.

As you read, consider the following questions:

1. As Kasparov states, what US government official claimed that "Russia will be able to continue democratizing" under Putin's new term as Russia's president?

2. Why does Putin's government supply Iran with arms but not antiaircraft missiles, according to Kasparov?

3. What power would the Magnitsky Act give to the US government if the law was passed, as the author contends?

After four years of Dmitry Medvedev keeping the czar's throne warm, Vladimir Putin is once again Russia's president. There were no public celebrations to accompany Mr. Putin's inauguration on May 7 [2012]. Quite the opposite. Moscow's streets had been cleared by a huge security presence; the city turned into a ghost town. This scene came the day after massive protests showed that the Russian middle class rejects Mr. Putin's bid to become their president for life. With no independent legislature or judiciary at our disposal, Mr. Putin's impeachment will have to take place in the streets.

Clearing the Opposition

Meanwhile, this modern czar is using the full power of the state to stamp out Russia's growing democracy movement. Two young movement leaders, Alexei Navalny and Sergei Udaltsov, were arrested on May 6 and are still in jail [as of May 21] on 15-day sentences. They've been charged with "violently resisting arrest," even though several videos of the arrest show Mr. Navalny with his hands in the air shouting, "Don't resist! Don't resist!"

Naturally, the court has forbidden the admission of any video evidence in the case. It is possible that a criminal case will be added against them for "inciting mass violence"— Kremlin code for a political trial.

A similar case in St. Petersburg has even grimmer overtones of KGB repression. Activists of the Other Russia coalition were recently charged with "extremist activity" based on the testimony of agents and informants all in the employ of the interior ministry. Their crime is officially described as organizing "public events focused on inciting hatred toward high leaders of state authority"—just the sort of phrase that sends chills down the spine of anyone born behind the Iron Curtain [an ideological barrier that cut off the Soviet Union from non-Communist countries].

The American reaction to the protests and the Putin regime's vicious response to them was not long in coming. On May 8, with security forces still clearing the streets and raiding cafes, Secretary of State Hillary Clinton gave an interview with CNN that made the [Barack] Obama administration's position frightfully clear. In a phrase that quickly became infamous here, Mrs. Clinton said she hoped "Russia will be able to continue democratizing" during Mr. Putin's new term.

Allying with Tyrants

The 12 years of Putin rule have marked a steady slide away from democracy in every way, so what message was this outrageous statement intended to convey? Are Russians still supposed to act grateful that we no longer live under [Soviet leaders Leonid] Brezhnev or [Joseph] Stalin? Or is this the Obama administration's way of telling Mr. Putin to carry on, that matters of human rights and democracy are safely off the table as long as NATO [North Atlantic Treaty Organization] can use Russian territory for Afghanistan supply lines?

The myth that Russia and the U.S. have a mutually useful strategic partnership has been promoted by the Americans for years, but the fiction is becoming harder to maintain. Mr. Putin abruptly canceled his trip to the G8 summit [of the most economically developed countries] at Camp David and will

Conflicting Foreign Policies in the Early Twenty-First Century

The post-9/11 [referring to the September 11, 2001, terrorist attacks on the United States] activist U.S. foreign policy, which perceives the promotion of liberty and democracy as the key strategic means of ensuring America's security, cannot but be increasingly at odds with the Kremlin's post-imperial "restoration," the essence of which is political and economic recentralization at home and an omnivorous realpolitik abroad. Even on the territory of the former Soviet Union, where under different circumstances the United States may have been more inclined to be indulgent of the Russian interests, Moscow's opposition to democratization and liberalization in the post-Soviet space, which tends to create pro-Western regimes (Georgia and Ukraine)—now viewed by the Kremlin as inherently anti-Russian—and its support for some of the region's most repressive governments (Belarus and Uzbekistan), cannot but cause serious friction with the United States.

Leon Aron, "The United States and Russia: Ideologies, Policies, and Relations," American Enterprise Institute, Russian Outlook, Summer 2006.

instead make the first foreign excursion of his new term to the unalloyed dictatorship of Alexander Lukashenko's Belarus.

Perhaps Mr. Putin should continue and make a tour of all of his dictator brethren, to whom he provides both direct and indirect support. The Kremlin is desperate to keep Syria's Bashar al-Assad in place and continues to sell him "defensive weapons"—since any conflict in the region sustains the high oil prices Mr. Putin and his cronies need to maintain power.

Aiding Iranian strongman Mahmoud Ahmadinejad's nuclear quest serves the same purpose. Mr. Putin is more than happy to provide Iran's mullahs with arms, and when he agrees not to sell them advanced antiaircraft missiles it is only because he does not want to entirely dissuade Israel from a military strike against Iran, his dream scenario being open conflict in the region and ever-higher oil prices.

Other Putin-friendly dictators hold the line along the soft central Asian underbelly of Russia where radical Islam is an ever-growing threat and where Russian generals manage the drug trade. Further afield, the U.S. government has accused members of Hugo Chávez's government in Venezuela of aiding and abetting Mexico's drug cartels, and there is no doubt Mr. Chávez's close relationship with Kremlin fixer Igor Sechin comes in handy there.

Holding Putin Accountable

If all this sounds to the Obama administration like a Russian partnership with America, perhaps my understanding of strategy is not what it once was. Franklin Roosevelt, Winston Churchill and Joseph Stalin joined forces [during World War II] because they faced a shared existential threat. Mr. Putin's clandestine agenda serves only his own purposes.

Opposing Mr. Putin's activities is also a matter of upholding international law. The epic proportions of public-private corruption in Vladimir Putin's Russia spilled over our borders long ago.

So what can be done to aid the cause of Russian democracy in the face of obstruction by the Obama administration? The U.S. Congress should, at the earliest possible date, pass the 2011 [Russia and Moldova Jackson-Vanik Repeal and] Sergei Magnitsky Rule of Law Accountability Act to hold Mr. Putin's thugs and bureaucrats accountable. Named for a Russian attorney who died in police custody in 2009 while investigating official corruption, the Magnitsky Act would bring

visa and asset sanctions against Russian government functionaries culpable of criminal and human rights abuses.

Unlike the charade of cooperation between the Kremlin
and the White House, passing this law will be something truly
in the best interests of both the American and the Russian
people.

Periodical Bibliography

The following articles have been selected to supplement the diverse views presented in this chapter.

Barry Blechman and Jonas Vaicikonis — "Unblocking the Road to Zero: US-Russian Cooperation on Missile Defenses," *Bulletin of the Atomic Scientists*, November 2010.

Emily Cadei — "U.S.-Russia Diplomacy: From 'Reset'; to Pause," *CQ Weekly*, September 8, 2012.

Ben Cardin — "U.S.-Russian Ties Need a Human-Rights Focus," *Washington Jewish Week*, August 9, 2012.

Stephen F. Cohen — "Obama's Russia 'Reset': Another Lost Opportunity?," *Nation*, June 20, 2011.

Nikolas K. Gvosdev — "Parting with Illusions: Developing a Realistic Approach to Relations with Russia," *USA Today*, November 2008.

Timothy Hopper — "Pressing for Change," *Harvard International Review*, January 12, 2012.

Garry Kasparov and Boris Nemtsov — "The Right Way to Sanction Russia," *Wall Street Journal*, March 15, 2012.

Mikhail Khodorkovsky — "Stop Coddling My Country's Rulers," *Newsweek*, September 25, 2011.

Robert Legvold — "The Russia File: How to Move Toward a Strategic Partnership," *Foreign Affairs*, July/August 2009.

Katrina vanden Heuvel — "Pussy Riot and the Two Russias," *Nation*, August 27, 2012.

Dean A. Wilkening — "Cooperating with Russia on Missile Defense: A New Proposal," *Arms Control Today*, March 2012.

OPPOSING
VIEWPOINTS®
SERIES

How Is Russian
Culture Changing?

Chapter Preface

Patriotism has always had a place in Russian civic mindedness. As V.V. Gavriliuk and V.V. Malenkov argue in a February 2008 issue of *Russian Education and Society*, "Traditionally, an individual considered his highest duty to be a citizen of his country and a patriot whose activity would bring benefit and glory to it." These Russian sociologists contend that "the [ethnic] Russian [russkii], the citizen of Russia [rossiianin], has always had more trust in the state than in society (and very often simply did not distinguish them), and the idea of service was something that he associated with his relation with the Motherland." Gavriliuk and Malenkov advocate that this sense of patriotism is still alive in Russia, but it needs the backing of traditional values—from personal manners to political awareness to an interest in the nation—in order to flourish in the twenty-first century. They assert that "the revival, production, and development of these traditions must serve as the foundation of the national culture, the future of Russia's creation."

In recent years, Russia has experienced a wave of ultranationalism espoused by a loose collective of extreme right-wing groups that have pushed for certain agendas under the banner of patriotism. Though not the patriotism that Gavriliuk and Malenkov affirm, the ultranationalists are stressing a return to traditionalism and to a strong motherland that, above all, can find jobs for the millions who are unemployed and adrift in the economic chaos that has persisted since the fall of the Soviet Union in 1991. When President Vladimir Putin first took the reins of statehood in 2000, he openly dubbed himself a patriot. Speaking to the Indian newspaper *India Today* in September of that year, Putin clearly defined what he stood for: "[Russian] basic values are none other than patriotism, love of one's motherland, love of one's home, one's people, one's cultural values. . . . Everything that makes us a nation, that is the source of our uniqueness, everything that we can be proud of—all this will be the foundation of [the national] idea." Many ultranationalists rallied around Putin's words, taking them to mean "Russia for the Russians" and therefore sanctioning their belief that immigrants should be expelled for taking scarce jobs. Though Putin has repudiated his link to the rise of such xenophobia and the violence that has erupted between "pure" Russians and other ethnic groups, some observers believe Putin's rhetorical emphasis on a national mission and the reemergence of Russia as a great power has incited ultranationalist fervor. According to a May 3, 2009, article in the *Independent*, "Some surveys show that up to 60 per cent of Russians agree with the slogan 'Russia for the Russians.'"

After an August 2012 incident in which supporters of a soccer team from the Islamic province of Dagestan were attacked by nationalists, Putin condemned the perpetrators of such violence at a meeting of his Council on Interethnic Relations. He insisted, "It is important to confront their dangerous influence. . . . We should understand that conflicts may not only weaken the state and society but destroy its foundations." Some critics were rankled by his focus on preserving the state, and others were dismayed that, while disparaging the attacks, Putin subsequently called for tougher immigration laws in Russia. After Putin's dismissal of ultranationalist tactics, these groups largely abandoned the president, hoping instead to carry on winning support from those who still keenly feel the economic hardships and believe the solution resides in a strong, ethnically unified patriotism.

The impact of ultranationalism on Russian society is one topic debated in the following chapter. The chapter also addresses other aspects of the nation's culture that are undergoing change in the twenty-first century.

"The massive persecution of the church under communism has been followed by what seems to many Orthodox a miracle of rebirth."

Orthodox Religion Is a Socially Unifying Force in Post-Soviet Russia

John P. Burgess

Under Communist rule, Orthodox religion in Russia along with all other faiths became targets for elimination. While the Communist Party succeeded in marginalizing religion while the Soviet Union existed, John P. Burgess argues in the following viewpoint that in the years since the fall of the Soviet Union and communism, Orthodox religion has been slowly regaining its cultural importance in Russia. Burgess maintains that the Orthodox Church has solidified its significance in part by establishing its role in addressing social issues in addition to fostering close ties with the government, as evidenced by the presidential cooperation with and participation in the church. Even though the church has made strides in reintegrating itself into Russian life, Burgess concedes that the majority of Russians do not identify

John P. Burgess, "Orthodox Resurgence: Civil Religion in Russia," *Christian Century*, vol. 126, no. 12, June 16, 2009, pp. 25–28. Copyright © 2009 by The Christian Century Foundation. All rights reserved. Reproduced by permission.

religion as an important factor guiding their daily lives. Still, in a seeming contradiction, most Russians identify themselves as Orthodox, according to the author, showing the unique position of religion in Russia. While Burgess concludes that Orthodoxy in Russia will likely remain one of many identities with which Russians can identify, he maintains that the church has reestablished itself as an important voice within Russian culture. John P. Burgess is a professor of systematic theology at the Pittsburgh Theological Seminary.

As you read, consider the following questions:

1. According to the author, what institutions do Russians believe should be responsible for shaping citizens' moral values?

2. What percentage of "self-identified atheists in Russia" also identified themselves as Orthodox, as stated by the author?

3. What does Burgess believe Orthodoxy offers Russia in the face of globalization, social inequality, and national demoralization?

Immediately after inauguration as president of the Russian Federation in May 2008, Dmitry Medvedev proceeded to a Kremlin church, where Patriarch Alexy II blessed him and gave him an icon of the Vladimir Mother of God, to which Russians over the centuries have turned for national protection. Medvedev, along with former president Vladimir Putin, was again present when Metropolitan Kirill was enthroned as the new patriarch of the Russian Orthodox Church on February 1 [2009].

In light of such events, some Russian Orthodox anticipate a return to the ancient conception of a "symphony" between church and state in Russia: The church infuses the state and society with spiritual values, while the state protects the church. Critics of the church, however, charge that the church is simply returning to its historic role of being aligned with the state in return for social and political privilege.

The situation is complex. Although there is a renewal of Orthodox life in some ways, at the same time Russia is becoming religiously pluralistic—and it remains highly secular.

When Alexy died in December 2008, his supporters could point to the impressive changes of the past 20 years since the fall of the Soviet regime. The number of monasteries had jumped from 22 to 804, the number of parishes from 7,000 to 30,000 (as many as half of these, however, lie outside of the Russian Federation, many of them in Ukraine). The number of Orthodox churches in Moscow alone rose from 40 to 872. Moreover, the percentage of Russians identifying themselves as Orthodox increased from 20 percent to perhaps as much as 80 percent. The massive persecution of the church under communism has been followed by what seems to many Orthodox a miracle of rebirth.

The Rebirth of Russian Orthodoxy After the Soviet Union

Dramatic evidence of this rebirth can he found at the monastery in Solovki, located 100 miles south of the Arctic Circle on an island in the White Sea. In the early 1920s, the Soviets transformed the monastery into their first concentration camp, where they refined the methods that they would apply to the entire gulag system. Thousands of people died from cold and disease before the camp was closed in 1939. Two outlying churches served as hospitals—in reality, holding pens—for prisoners who had contracted typhoid. Until the recent restoration of these buildings, one could still see the prisoners' blood that had soaked into the floorboards.

In the early 1990s, the government began returning parts of the monastery complex to the church. Today monastic life has been reestablished both in the main monastery, where 30 monks celebrate a full cycle of services every day, and in two smaller, semi-hermetical communities. Two churches in the main complex have been restored and re-consecrated, and memorials have been dedicated to the many believers who died a martyr's death here. As many as 30,000 Russian pilgrims and tourists now visit Solovki annually.

The renewal of parishes and monasteries has been complemented by the church's commitment to addressing social needs and issues, as reflected in a major document adopted at a bishops' council in 2000 and titled "The Basis of the Social Concept of the Russian Orthodox Church." Patriarch Kirill, who at that time was chair of the church's Department for External Church Relations, was its principal author. The document includes chapters on law, work, property, politics, war, family, health, bioethics, ecology, education, media and globalization.

The Russian Orthodox Church has reestablished hospitals, orphanages and nursing homes. It is negotiating with the state about providing religious education in the public schools and supplying military chaplains. It has privileged access to the mass media. On Saturday mornings Kirill is featured in a half-hour television program about Orthodox belief and practice.

In their book *Russian Orthodoxy Resurgent*, John and Carol Garrard argue that the Russian Orthodox Church "has achieved a cultural dominance akin to Western Christianity's in the United States." They depict Alexy as adroitly protecting the church from state manipulation and positioning it to offer society key symbols for a post-Soviet Russian identity. In "an almost perfect parallel to Constantine's slow and careful substitution of the symbols of Christianity for those of pagan Rome," Orthodox narratives, holidays and moral values, they argue, have quietly but inexorably replaced the discredited social ideology of Russian communism.

Typical Russians Do Not View Religion as Important

But this view is at best half of the story. Orthodox identity in Russia today has to be reconstructed from a tradition that was decisively shattered. A typical Russian is Tanya, who lives with her husband in a large apartment in a northwest suburb of Moscow and works as an adjuster for an insurance company. I met her at Solovki, where she had come to immerse herself for a week in the rhythms of monastic life and prayer.

Tanya does not attend church in Moscow. Most of Moscow's churches are in the historic city center, and attending one of them would involve a commute of an hour or more for Tanya. She did not grow up in the church and knows little about Christian belief and practice. She is so busy with work that she would not get involved in the life of a congregation if she wanted to.

Yet her time at Solovki touched her deeply. She experienced a spiritual power that she wanted to hold on to but knew that she would lose as soon as she returned home. Life in the monastery represented a reordered world in which the problems and conflicts of her everyday world vanished. The ancient rhythms of the liturgy swept her up into Russia's great spiritual past.

Sociological studies illuminate the paradoxes of Tanya's religiosity. Russians, more than almost any other people in the world, see religion as insignificant for their everyday lives. When asked which institutions should shape their moral values, only 4 percent mention the church—about the same percentage as those who look to the mass media. (The vast majority, 67 percent, cite the family.)

Russian Identity Is Closely Tied to Orthodox Religion

Priests commonly told me that at most 5 percent of the population are regularly in church. Last year, 83 percent of Russians said that they would not fast at all during Lent, and only 3 percent that they would fast in full accordance with the church's rules. This year's survey indicated that more Russians intended to keep the fast at least partially. But it also revealed that only 30 percent of Russians see it as a spiritual exercise, whereas 24 percent regard it as a cultural tradition, 19 percent as a way of cleansing the body, and 22 percent as no longer having any special meaning.

Just what kind of social identity, then, do Russians find in Orthodoxy?

For many Russians, to be Russian is to be Orthodox. Nineteenth-century Slavophile ideas are still influential, casting Catholicism and Protestantism as Western imports that have belonged historically to invaders from abroad (such as Catholic Poles or Protestant Swedes and Germans). Many Russians are suspicious of Western pluralism and the notion that the individual can construct an identity, including a religious identity. Russians assume that individuals inherit a historical identity from the ethnos to which they belong. Russians are more readily able to acknowledge the unique religious identity of other ethnic groups within the Russian Federation (such as Muslim Tartars) than to accept the fact of a plurality of religious identities among ethnic Russians.

Kirill reinforces such ideas when he, like his predecessor, speaks of the unique place of Orthodoxy in Russian history, or refers to the Orthodox Church's "canonical territory," presumably off-limits to other Christian churches. Alexy took particular umbrage at Pope John Paul II's creation of new Catholic dioceses within this canonical territory and supported state legislation to limit Catholic and Protestant missionary work. When the Russian Orthodox Church speaks of religious education in the public schools, it proposes alternatives for members of other religious groups, such as Islam, but not for members of other Christian churches.

If to be Russian is to be Orthodox, it is not surprising that Alexander Lukashenko, the dictatorial leader of Belarus, can call himself, with no tongue in cheek, "an Orthodox atheist." Indeed, according to the Garrards, a whopping 42 percent of self-identified atheists in Russia claim that they are also Orthodox.

Equating Russia and Orthodoxy is troubling, however. First, it is simply not true historically. Catholicism and Protestantism, while never as large or influential as Orthodoxy, have nevertheless had a historical presence in Russia, in some places for centuries. They not only guarded immigrants' ethnic identity but also helped shape Russian culture (whoever learns a little Russian soon discovers the number of words appropriated from languages like German). Surely, too, there is a Christian solidarity in suffering, for the Soviet persecution affected these little churches as much as the Orthodox Church.

Christianity itself has never been monolithic in Russia. The history of the country's Baptist churches is instructive. While Baptist missionaries came from Germany into Russia in the late 19th century, small indigenous religious groups with free-church characteristics (Molokans, Stundists) shaped the Baptist movement there into a distinctively Russian phenomenon.

Second, equating Russia and Orthodoxy easily underwrites xenophobia. Russian Catholics and Protestants continue to suffer under a general social (and Orthodox) suspicion that they are being financed and used by Western political interests. They often have difficulty in getting building permits, holding public rallies or conducting evangelistic campaigns. Kirill, like Alexy, has been careful in public statements to call for religious toleration and to honor the leaders of other Christian groups. But he has not embraced a vigorous social pluralism that would recognize the necessary and legitimate place of these groups in Russian society.

Third, equating Russia and Orthodoxy reduces Christianity to a cultural identity. Orthodox, Catholics and Protestants agree that the heart of their religion lies in people's faithful response to God's call to a new way of life in communion with the risen Lord.

Echoing statements of Alexy and Kirill, priests with whom I spoke emphasized that the most pressing challenge before the Russian Orthodox Church today is education. Too few people know the basics of the faith or what it means to commit themselves to the life and work of the church.

Unity in Russia Derives from Orthodox Identity

Orthodox identity provides for social harmony and unity in post-Soviet Russia. The fall of communism and the integration of Russia into the global marketplace have brought about tremendous social dislocation and demoralization. Once able to think of itself as a superpower, Russia today is perceived both domestically and internationally as a second-tier nation. The United Nations ranks its standard of living at approximately 73rd in the world, below that of Mexico (51st) or Romania (62nd). International watchdog groups classify Russia as among the world's most corrupt places for doing business.

Huge social inequities stir up public resentment: Russia ranks third among countries with billionaires (after the U.S. and Germany), yet elderly people barely survive on minuscule state pensions. The general economic infrastructure lags decades behind the West's (there is not yet a fully built controlled-access four-lane expressway between Moscow and St. Petersburg). With breakdowns in the health care system and widespread abuse of alcohol, the average age at which men die has declined since the fall of communism to 59.

In a society that can be hard and cruel, Orthodoxy offers a socially unifying ideology. It promotes personal values that make community possible: committed work, honesty in rela-

Young Russians Value Private Religiousness

One of the common features of religiousness among today's young people is its passive nature, with no relation to church. On the scale of values, for example, going to church is certainly not more important than finding entertainment. This kind of religiousness that is not related to church is a phenomenon that the German sociologist [Thomas] Luckmann has given the name "invisible" or "private" religiousness. Under our own conditions, this is manifested in the fact that young people, who have grown up with no real association with the Orthodox tradition, believe in the possibility of personal belief in God and communion with God without the mediation of church and priests. And so, the tendency to prefer private life has also taken the upper hand in the sphere of religion.

S.M. Klimova and G.V. Martynova,
"College Students' Attitudes Toward Religion,"
Russian Social Science Review, *September/October 2009.*

tionships, and concern for one's neighbor. Russians increasingly want the church to guide them through life's major transitions. They know little or nothing of Christian theology, but the church's rituals give them a sense of healing and peace. Slavophile ideas are again at work here: The Russian identity as shaped by Orthodoxy represents a powerful alternative to Western individualism and social competition.

Sociologist Robert Bellah has argued for the virtues of American civil religion, and perhaps Russians, by way of Orthodoxy, are trying to construct a viable civil religion for themselves. One nevertheless has reason to doubt that Orthodoxy in Russia can fulfill its Christian responsibility to society except as it engages in the hard work of rebuilding vital congregational life. Russian Orthodoxy's prominence as a social ideology seems curiously out of proportion with the realities on the ground, where the work of familiarizing people with the scriptures, the liturgy and basic church practices is still at the beginning and is seriously hampered by the secularizing forces that communism let loose and that continue in a different way under conditions of the global market economy.

Russian Ideas of Exceptionalism Are Rooted in Orthodox Religion

Orthodoxy gives Russians a sense of national mission. Contemporary Orthodoxy's cultural relevance goes even further: It gives Russians a sense of their place in world history. Russian Orthodoxy has traditionally viewed Russia as a great nation with a divine appointment to defend civilization itself. Like Americans, Russians have believed in their exceptionalism—that they are not subject to the vices of other nations but are uniquely able to realize a more perfect political order, which God calls them to offer to the world. In both countries, religious language has easily gravitated into political rhetoric.

Historians have often noted that Marxism itself has roots in biblical eschatology, and Soviet ideology was filled with religious-like language of sacrifice, personal transformation ("the new human") and a perfected social order. With the fall of communism, this eschatology has been reconstructed within an Orthodox worldview that looks back to words that Abbot Filofei of Pskov wrote to Czar Vasili III several decades after the fall of Constantinople in 1453: "[You alone are now] lord and protector of the altars of God and of the holy ecumenical Catholic and Apostolic Church. . . . Two Romes have fallen, the third stands, and a fourth there will not be."

Russia Appears to Be a Concretely Christian Nation

Moscow as the Third Rome has a new lease on life in post-Soviet Russia. On September 1, 2004, Chechen rebels took hundreds of children and their parents and teachers hostage at a school in Beslan in the Russian republic of North Ossetia. When Russian troops stormed the building two days later, more than 300 people, including 186 children, died. As all Russia mourned these events, Russian television broadcast footage of President Putin, alone in a Kremlin chapel with an Orthodox priest, saying prayers for Beslan's dead. The camera panned in close as Putin, wearing a tired, grim look, crossed himself and bowed. Consciously or unconsciously, he seemed to be invoking the historical mythology that places Christian (Orthodox) Russia against godless barbarian hordes.

Putin and Medvedev have been careful to avoid the language of religious war and have emphasized that the Russian Federation is a multiethnic, multireligious nation in which different groups must respect each other and work together. But Orthodox notions of Russia's unique historical mission are never far from the surface as the church bestows awards on military leaders and blesses their troops and weapons. The potential for religious conflict remains real in a country in which the ethnic Russian population is rapidly declining while the Muslim population is increasing.

Patriarch Kirill also gives expression to Russia's unique historical mission when he calls for the church (and the nation) to defend Christian moral values. His statements resonate with pronouncements from John Paul II and Benedict XVI, and have spawned widespread speculation that he will make common cause with Rome in defending "Christian Europe."

But the Russian Orthodox Church has traditionally been less willing to speak a critical word to its own state. No American should render judgment on the path of political accommodation that all the Russian churches took under the heavy hand of communism. The Orthodox Church did everything that it could to protect the liturgy, and one can argue that as long as it preserved the liturgy, it also preserved the seeds of the alternative politics that Christ sets forth over and against the ideologies and powers of this world. But one might wish that Kirill and other church leaders would provide for more vigorous debate and analysis of the church's past and present relationship to the state than currently seems to be the case.

The Place for Orthodox Religion in Russian Culture Remains Uncertain

An Orthodox culture is reappearing in contemporary Russia. It is evident not only in renewed religious life and the church's social initiatives but also in such phenomena as music (every monastery sells CDs of its chanting, and the traditional chant of the famous Valaam Monastery has won popular recognition), film (a recent movie, *Ostrov* [The Island], won popular acclaim for its portrayal of Orthodox monastic life), church newspapers, museums, youth clubs and summer camps.

Nevertheless, it seems unlikely that Russia as a whole is on its way to embodying an Orthodox culture in the way that it did up to 1905 or 1917. A reconstructed Orthodox culture will likely be nothing more than one subculture among many. In such a world, the church's social and political influence will wax and wane, as has that of mainline and evangelical Protestant churches in North America, which, despite their deep roots in U.S. history, are now but one voice among many in the spiritual marketplace.

Many Russians—including many Russian politicians—will formally bow to Orthodoxy and even regard it as a special part of Russian identity. But they will increasingly try on other, sometimes competing cultural identities. The new Russia is a place in which not only Orthodoxy thrives, but also

Western-like consumerism, Western sexual mores and a multitude of religious, ideological and lifestyle subcultures, all of which the Russian state gladly tolerates so long as they do not threaten its hold on power.

Most Russians are probably not on the way to claiming Orthodoxy as their primary identity. Whatever being Orthodox will mean to them, it will not lead them into the deeper experience of faith that every Christian community seeks to nurture. At best, the reconstruction of Russian identity as Orthodox identity will open up social space in which the church can do its proper work. At worst, it will tempt the church with worldly power (as managed by the state) and divert it from shaping congregations in which people hear the gospel, participate in the sacraments, shape a more faithful life together and work for a more just society.

In the end, the opportunities and perils that face Russian Orthodoxy and its new patriarch are no different from those that face Christian churches in the pluralistic West. We are always tempted to overestimate our cultural significance and relevance, and to underestimate the demands of the gospel and the difficulty of thinking about our lives theologically. The Russian Orthodox Church faces these enduring challenges even as it tells Russians that they are part of a great tradition with far deeper historical roots than communism, that they both belong and do not belong to the West, and that they still have a unique mission to the world.

> "On the verge of a systemic—that is,
> all-encompassing—crisis, instead of
> trying to overcome it, we risk succumb-
> ing once more to the delirium of totali-
> tarianism, starting with the schools."

Teaching Orthodox Religion in Russian Schools Is a Return to Totalitarianism

Mikhail Sitnikov

Following the extended period of government-promoted atheism that existed under the government of the Soviet Union, government and church relations under Russian presidents Vladimir Putin and Dmitry Medvedev have warmed considerably. The ties have become so close that in 2012 Putin approved a law requiring compulsory religion classes in schools. In the following viewpoint, Mikhail Sitnikov argues that these classes threaten to instate a new form of religious totalitarianism not dissimilar from the government-instituted atheism that dominated the Soviet era. Sitnikov contends that the methods used by the church to promote religious teachings in schools mirror those used by the Communist Party, and they set up all other views as so undeni-

Mikhail Sitnikov, "Orthodox Bolshevism," *Russian Politics and Law*, vol. 49, no. 1, January/February 2011, pp. 83–90. English translation copyright © 2011 by M.E. Sharpe Inc. Reprinted with permission. All rights reserved. Not for reproduction.

ably negative that when compared with the alternative, only the Orthodox seems acceptable. The author further opposes the favored methods of teaching because the church does not provide objective religious education but rather offers only a dogmatic view that seeks to cultivate believers. Mikhail Sitnikov served as a council member of the Russian Department of the International Association for Religious Freedom.

As you read, consider the following questions:

1. What are the two points the author believes to be asserted by the church "behind its veil of flowery language" about Orthodox teaching in schools?

2. Why, as stated by the author, is it futile to try to figure out what the church means when it states that it seeks to give children lessons in "religious security"?

3. According to the author, what are the problems with the way in which religious supporters of clericalization want to teach religion in schools?

As the attempts to clericalize secular institutions in Russia become increasingly clear, the supporters of this process ever more openly flout legal and moral norms. The introduction of the teaching of religion into the secular school system seems in this sense a sufficiently indicative theme, especially in view of the ongoing argument over the proposed school course "Foundations of Orthodox Culture" (FOC). People artificially redirect this argument from the clericalization of education to the question of whether Orthodoxy, or religion in general, is "good or bad." This turns the discussion of an urgent problem into nonsense, for attitudes toward religion are purely individual, and coercion in this regard always violates the law. The result buries a genuinely urgent problem in endless chatter. In lieu of open discussion of the meaning of the proposed introduction of religion into the secular school system, we see the issue removed from public view and left to the arbitrary discretion of secular and church officials. This merely exacerbates the problem.

The Church Is Calling for a Clerical Revolution

Only rarely does material suddenly appear in a semiofficial church source—an Orthodox publication—that openly confirms the fears of those who oppose the clericalization of Russian society. "FOC as a Challenge to the Pokémons" [OPK kak vyzov pokemonam], an article published on 23 July on the Orthodoxy and the World [Pravoslavie i mir] site, sets out—probably for the first time, in a frank if somewhat vulgar manner—the ideological premises of the campaign to teach religion in the secular school system. The article could not be more worthy of attention: It contains practically everything that is required for a sober view of the range of problems associated with the clericalization—or, if you will, the ideologization—of faith-based education. . . .

I quote from the article: "Russia is not a label or a map; it is a culture. Replace its people—their language, views, and customs—with others, and it will no longer be Russia. Culture sustains itself over time through the family and the school. A formal education transmits, passes on, the cultural tradition that defines Russia. Orthodoxy forms Russia's backbone, its watershed (which is not to insult other faiths with less influence on history)."

But we can use different words to say the same thing: "Russia is not just a name and a territory but the level of development that characterizes its public self-awareness. Russia's circumstances correspond to those of its society, which are determined by the level of culture. A formal education aims to transmit the essence of Russia from generation to generation, and Orthodoxy constitutes its foundation."

Already this formulation raises a host of questions. Behind its veil of flowery language the article asserts that (1) our chief task is to "adhere constantly to the past," where we will find the true Russia; and (2) the quintessence of Russia is Orthodoxy, and nothing else merits attention. Any sober-minded person will immediately understand these points and object to them, because they posit a clerical revolution in ideology.

Totalitarian Methods Are Being Used by the Orthodox Church

Let us set aside the political and economic causes underlying the rise of a clericalist tendency in contemporary Russia, because in view of the systemic crisis we may regard this tendency as inevitable. Let me draw attention to the special characteristics of the methodology to which the clericalists resort. This methodology is traditional for all totalitarian tendencies—whether party-based, corporate, or religious—and distinct only in terms of its scale and target. The scale, as is well known, is national, not intragroup (as in the Communist Party or any Western corporation), while the target is not the church's own adepts or even potential adepts among the descendants of its followers but those outside its influence—that is, Russian society as a whole and all areas of national public and state life. In other words, supporters of clericalization openly seek to expand into "outer space," in the broadest sense. In this respect, incidentally, the clericalists are not violating the law—unless they stop preaching and start speculating with this "freedom of speech," using it not to express their own convictions, opinions, and assessments but to conduct ideological propaganda forbidden by the Constitution.

What kind of speculation do I have in mind? Merely the "small inaccuracies" that supporters permit themselves in commenting on certain details associated with changing the public understanding of certain established facts. The article provides a good demonstration of a model that works on a broader scale.

The Religious Indoctrination of Russia Violates the Law

For example (I quote the subtitle of the article): "The president has given Russia a chance to survive the twenty-first century: in the schools it will be possible to study the foundations of Orthodox culture, and in the armed forces not to fall away from church life." The subtitle immediately raises several questions:

(1) Is "church life" as understood by the Moscow Patriarchate the sole or chief condition for Russian citizens—believers and nonbelievers, Orthodox, Muslims, Protestants, agnostics, and so on—to survive the twenty-first century?

(2) What is the relationship between "Orthodox culture," which implies the inculcation in all schoolchildren of the foundations of "ethno-ideological Orthodoxy," and the multidenominational culture of Russia as a whole, which synthesizes within itself a host of diverse subcultures?

(3) From what kind of "church life" can conscripts who profess various faiths or none "fall away" and how, when freedom of religion is guaranteed to all Russian citizens, religious institutions are separated from the state (in this case, from the armed forces), but servicemen are free to attend places of worship while on leave?

(4) And, finally, how consistent with the Constitution, which separates church and school, is the probably compulsory teaching of religion in the secular school system, declared "by approval of the president"?

From this example we can see a high official's throwaway remark, one that contradicts the law and other objective factors, being presented to society as something wholly positive and used to justify an attempt to organize—in violation of the law and moral standards—the systematic cultic-ideological indoctrination of the country's population from childhood onward.

Methodologically, this is in no way different from the teaching of God's law in prerevolutionary Russia, which—let us recall—undermined a proper attitude toward the Orthodox religious tradition and, as is well known, led to the subsequent tragic fate of Orthodoxy in our country. Nor does it differ from the teaching of *The History of the Communist Party [of the Soviet Union (Bolsheviks): Short Course]* in the Soviet Union or of the Juche Idea in North Korean schools, where a formula set by local totalitarian regulations expresses a uniquely correct worldview for everyone.

Religious Education Resembles the Moral Education of the Soviet Union

The authors of the article also refer to the tragedy of the Russian Orthodox Church and to the period of Bolshevik repression against the population, declaring that the "Bolsheviks turned Russia into a zone" [of forced labor camps—Trans.]. Like scholars, artists, and representatives of almost all Russian institutions, the authors complain about the mangling of our native language. They remind the reader that "thieves' jargon is heard from the highest rostrums: kickbacks, raids, showdowns." "No revolution," they proclaim, "can return to us this ... bright 'Rus in Rus' ... except one, the inner revolution that is accomplished in God."

Perhaps this refers to a spiritual awakening like the one that, according to the gospels, happened to Saul, after which he became known as the apostle Paul? That is, something like the awakening that occurred, for instance, in Germany after 1945, when that country realized the horrors of the World War that it had unleashed—an awakening that has yet to dawn in post-Soviet Russia? In other words, something that would bring such a serious revelation to the individual and to society that they will find in it a value and an ideal, in whose light our traditional deception and self-deception will fade?

But what do you think? What are we really talking about here?

Here's what (I quote): "To reach this point, one must learn at least something about God—not from fortune tellers and Satanists, not from sex educators and pseudo-liberals, but from those who cherish God."

If one accepted such a statement at face value, one might think that in Russia, as in a nightmare, all these "fortune tellers, Satanists, and sex educators" do nothing but "talk about God." But those familiar with brainwashing techniques will immediately understand that by setting up an absurd series of negative images the authors are creating a phobia in the reader against any source other than the one that they themselves are about to offer. Do you remember how this was done with "enemies" in Soviet times? "Fascists," "Uncle Sam," "Israeli militarists," "religious obscurantists" (this was meant to include believers in our own country), "traitors to the homeland" (that is, human rights defenders), and so on—these were all lined up in a single column and thrown into battle against the "normal Soviet person and patriot." To ensure that people would assimilate this frame, it was echoed on every street corner and drummed into children's heads from their first day at school. This was called the "moral education [*vospitanie*] of a Soviet citizen at school."

A New Totalitarianism Could Begin in the Schools

And now? Now, with the light touch of the new ideologists (again I quote): "This, too, requires school lessons in religious security." The declaration is then rammed home. These lessons, supposedly, will help clarify: "What is what and how to name it correctly. That's the first thing. And second, how may all this knowledge concern me? Where is my entrance to the 'only building whose blue cupola the sky cannot rival'? The school can only point to this entrance; you have to pass

Government Suppression of Religious Dissent Poses a Danger to Society

The [Russian] state authorities must base their actions [regarding religion] on the Constitution. They must not only stay within but also try to bring the whole country inside constitutional bounds (which for our country are not natural law). Church leaders must rely on their own authority and not involve the state—contrary to its assigned purpose—in resolving ideological and religious problems. It is necessary and in certain—even political—respects permissible to unite the efforts of the state authorities with those of all social forces, including the diversity of religious associations, for the democratic development of society. But joint efforts by state and church authority to suppress religious dissent pose a danger to state and society and lead to the strengthening of this dissent.

A.E. Sebentsov, "Religion in the System of State Power,"
Russian Social Science Review, *January/February 2012.*

through yourself. Or not pass through. But then you will no longer have the excuse that you were not told, did not know, did not hear, and therefore you turned into a drunk or an addict or got so depressed you hung yourself."

Not a word has yet been said about what kind of "knowledge" will be conveyed, which if rejected will make you get "drunk, addicted to drugs or depressed to the point of suicide" but which you are already starting to accept (in other words, on which you are starting to depend psychologically). It is not worth even trying to determine from this passage what "religious security" means—the security of religion from something else or vice versa? Because here we have a typical if primitive example of the neurolinguistic programming that was and is used by almost all the world's political parties, advertising agencies, and, of course, religions. It is a method of propaganda—that is, of inculcating into the masses convictions that someone considers they need to hold by instilling a certain worldview into individual and public consciousness. If it is a single worldview, then, of course, that means a totalitarian worldview.

As history has shown, anything may become the basis of such a totalitarian worldview. We know how German Nazism emerged and developed, what made it famous, and how it ended. We know where the Cultural Revolution in China led and what kind of "progress" resulted from the all-embracing Juche Idea in North Korea. We ourselves lived through Bolshevik totalitarianism with all its "delights"—repression, the "devouring" of natural resources, and hatred for the part of the world that we failed to subordinate to ourselves. As a result, we ended up with a genetically, intellectually, and spiritually exhausted nation, a corrupt society, and an economy, science, and educational system in ruins. And on the verge of a systemic—that is, all-encompassing—crisis, instead of trying to overcome it, we risk succumbing once more to the delirium of totalitarianism, starting with the schools.

Schools Will Engage in Ideological Expansionism

It turns out that our children (Russia's future citizens) need "lessons in religious security" more than they need to learn their native language, literature, history, art, and other humanities and scientific disciplines and acquire knowledge of the world and themselves! In other words, they need to view all disciplines without exception from the church's current religious-ideological perspective.

Experts—students of religion, educational specialists, psychologists, and psychiatrists—know well what this training in "security" amounts to. The vast majority of the population, whose educational levels remain confined by ideological stereotypes of the Soviet type, does not. In a similar fashion, the Bolsheviks introduced their "security" under the guise of a universal doctrine to "secure" future citizens, starting in childhood, from the risk of genuine independent thinking. As is well known, this doctrine was "Marxism-Leninism," which bore little relation to Marx and Marxism. Today we observe a mirror image of the same phenomenon under the guise of religious education—"under the guise," because catechization (teaching of the foundations of religious belief) cannot be introduced on a mass scale in a society that is formally multidenominational but in essence unenlightened about religion—a society of "superstitious nonbelievers." Unless, of course, some religion is profaned by being used as the basis for an ideology, as one more "uniquely correct worldview" that someone has chosen to replace a "Marxism-Leninism" that has lost its influence.

It is interesting that the religious supporters of clericalization firmly oppose acquainting students with religion as a grandiose historical phenomenon of our entire civilization—a phenomenon much more mature than science and comparable only with art. They want to limit how much students learn about religion. The clericalists are the ones categorically against children studying the history of religion and of religious organizations and against teaching of the natural sciences if they contradict the denominational ideology that corresponds to the needs of the "current political moment."

According to banal factology—that is, the comparison of obvious facts by applying common sense—this is called ideological expansionism or, in this case, the introduction, under the guise of "spiritual revival," of a totalitarian ideology into public consciousness, using the instrument of a formally religious but actually state-ideological organization.

Religious Teachings Must Be Balanced

The authors barely conceal the methods with which they plan to inculcate this totalitarian ideology. What cause could there be for confusion when they declare that

> Russia's educational community and the church face the task of writing textbooks that will not direct but acquaint, not speak of "prayer to our Lord Jesus Christ" but say that "Christians pray to their Lord Jesus Christ." In this case, a child need not call the God of the Christians his god. A textbook must be aimed at the broadest possible audience. That is why it must be not an imperative from the church ("Come on, believe, get baptized, and attend church!") but a cultural studies introduction to a space of meanings that does not oblige children to agree with them. Nonetheless, after becoming acquainted with the world of [Andrei] Rublev and [Fyodor] Dostoevsky, they will no longer be able to confuse the Orthodox tradition with imitations of it and will at last have the capacity to become themselves in the space of European high culture, to obtain from their schooling that which atheist ideology, which permeated the entire humanities curriculum, deprived the Soviet schoolchild.

All this is absolutely reasonable and indisputable, including the reference to the possibility of thereby catching up with European children in their knowledge of the winged sayings of the Bible. There should be no need to explain the source of the inscription in the Harry Potter novel: "For where your treasure is, there your heart will be also" [Matthew 6:21]. Because, as the article tells us, the "envisioned course in the foundations of Orthodox culture will serve our children as a key to all the riches of European culture, of which the culture of Russia is also a part." Especially as then, thanks to FOC, "educated Russians will be able to share the values and meanings of Christianity with Chinese, Arabs, Europeans, and anyone else who is not overjoyed at the prospect of the total pokémonization of the world." That is all very well, except that no honest teacher would ever reduce Russia's multifaceted culture and "space of meanings" to the ethnic aspect of church culture, which has left many highly ambiguous vestiges in our national history.

Only Comparative Religion Is Appropriate for Secular Schools

We must note that the ideas in this article can be found in many other clerical articles and speeches. But everyone knows that in our country there are always great differences and contradictions among what people say, think, and do. For example, the desired goal of raising the level of knowledge about Christianity and other religions can be achieved—as everyone understands—only via systematic teaching within the framework of a factologically justified and therefore exclusively scientific approach—that is, through the study of comparative religion. To instill cultic and denominational habits in a person who professes any religion—and everyone understands this point, too—it takes only religious training. There is a third kind of instruction in the field of religion—namely, the improvement of religious knowledge in the context of a specific faith, that is, religious education. The appropriate form for transmitting knowledge about religion in a secular school system is the teaching of comparative religion. The appropriate places for religious training are family, church, and Sunday school. For religious education there are religious (denominational) educational establishments under the aegis of religious organizations. But if all these things are mixed together in a heap, then no amount of good intentions will compensate for the damage inflicted by such experiments— the formation of a new Bolshevism on a "quasi-Orthodox" instead of a "Marxist-Leninist" basis.

> "We are now reaping the fruits of the TV anti-culture that is instilling destructive sociocultural experience in the young."

Television Is a Threat to Russian Youth and Culture

Mikhail N. Berulava

Mikhail N. Berulava argues in the following viewpoint that television influences Russian youth negatively and can be blamed for many of the destructive and harmful tendencies seen in the younger generation. Berulava, a Russian scientist, politician, and member of the Russian Academy of Education, contends that Russian youths emulate the models they see on television, and he identifies these as being antisocial, unconcerned with morals or family, and detrimental to society in general. Further, he maintains that the Russian education system and other traditional institutions of morals have failed to recognize and combat the threat of television and to mitigate it by proposing more appealing, socially acceptable alternatives. Berulava concludes that, left unchecked, television will continue to degrade Russian society and culture.

Mikhail N. Berulava, "The Nation Is in Danger," *Russian Education and Society*, vol. 52, no. 3, March 2010, pp. 30–36. English translation copyright © 2010 by M.E. Sharpe Inc.

As you read, consider the following questions:

1. How have the traditional instillers of morals failed in educating the youth of Russia, according to Berulava?

2. The author lists preoccupations of a typical individual portrayed on television. What are some of the examples given of interests not portrayed on Russian television?

3. What does Berulava envision as the role of state-run public television?

Our society faces many tasks: the intensification of economic reforms, the development and adoption of new technologies, military reform, the fight against corruption, and health care; the list could be made longer. Work is being done in all of these areas. However, the problems need to be examined from the scientific point of view, comprehensively and systematically. It is cadres that represent the deciding factor in solving them.

It will not be possible to deal with a single one of these problems without young specialists trained to work in the new economic conditions, specialists who have acquired a body of knowledge and the ability to put that knowledge to effective use, and who also possess the necessary moral qualities. If a person is not a patriot of his native land, if he is not honest and decent, not interested in helping those who are weaker—women, children, and the elderly; if the values of the family do not mean anything to him, if he is full of aggression, malice, and envy, then none of his knowledge will help find solutions to the tasks facing the country.

The Moral Qualities of Russian Youth Are Failing

The persistence of the problems indicates that the moral qualities of many people, in particular our young people, constitute the stumbling block. What are the life values of today's youth—the desire to do something useful for our country, or to leave and go where the pay is higher? To have a family and raise children or to spend every hour seeking amusement in pursuit of a glamorous life? To become a professional in some craft and be proud of it, or to look for ways to make easy money, very often through unlawful means?

Why have we such an overabundance of people who do not want to become mechanics but, instead, lawyers and bureaucrats, although the official pay of a worker is a great deal higher? It is no secret that today we are being treated by young doctors who have purchased their diplomas. They prescribe fake medicine and operations that we do not need because they want to make a lot of money. We hire college graduates who have diplomas from prestigious higher educational institutions in the capital cities, only to find out that they got their education in some far-off little town where no one ever saw a candidate of science. For some reason, the Ministry of Education and Science has decided that diplomas held by the graduates of prestigious institutions of higher learning and their branches in little towns that no one has ever heard of should be rated the same. What we are getting as a result is the kind of "specialist" who does not even know how to fill out a job application properly.

No Institution Instills Morals in Young People

To solve all of these problems it is necessary to answer who or what is supposed to instill in young people the moral qualities necessary for life in society. And where and how is this to take place?

In the family? Very rarely. Many parents must hold down two jobs in order to take care of their children. They have to spend a lot of time on the road. When the parents finally do make it home late in the evening (and must attend to a lot of household chores), they do not have any energy left to interact with their children, who are usually already asleep in any case.

How about kindergarten? As we know, there are not enough municipal preschool child-care institutions; applicants have to wait many years. Not all parents are able to pay for the private kindergartens. It also must be acknowledged that preschool teachers' level of training is below average: All too often, totally unqualified people are working in these positions. If you walk into a kindergarten you see children left to their own devices and teachers standing around discussing their personal problems.

Nor are the schools taking care of upbringing. They have long since stopped doing that. As is well known, some time ago schools were told to forget that the term "upbringing" even existed. And earlier, upbringing was just a kind of dogmatism indoctrination: It consisted of nothing more than events held for appearances' sake. Even though the situation is different today, not much has changed in the schools.

The colleges and universities never were oriented toward the process of upbringing; they figured that they had other tasks to do. Today their main problem is to get accreditation, and the level of students' moral qualities was never included among accreditation indicators. For this reason, the institutions of higher learning are not oriented toward the opinions of students and employers but, instead, the opinion of the ministry, the sole entity that decides which institutions are to be kept open and which are to be closed.

Television Plays a Decisive Role in Youths' Upbringing

Just who or what is actually involved in the upbringing of the individual? The answer is simple and self-evident: It is the mass media, in particular television and the Internet. And just what are electronic media teaching? This is a very important question, because, after all, we are living in an information society, where the individual is dealing not with real images of events and things but with their virtual substitutes.

Sadly, the system of education is far out of touch with the realities of present-day society. In particular, it fails to take account of all the sociocultural experience that children, adolescents, and young adults receive. On the television screen, in politics, and on the streets, the priorities are very different from the values that teachers propound.

It is well known that an essential role in the development of the personality is played by the models to be emulated. The most significant ones on the psychological plane are the models of behavior and interaction that are shown on television, because they are always emotionally charged. The behavioral stereotypes that become internalized are primarily those that are mediated via image and feeling. This is why the decisive role that television plays in the upbringing of young people has to be recognized. The model that is to be emulated today is the kind of individual who is constantly eating and drinking and preoccupied with sex, whose goal in life is to win a million. The range of his interests does not include patriotism, a desire to start a family and raise children, to help other people, to have respect for the elderly, the ability to get pleasure not only from drinking and eating but from cultural pursuits, from the things that make a person human.

Unfortunately, today, whether deliberately or not, TV is working assiduously to destroy everything that is human in the younger generation. We are now reaping the fruits of the TV anti-culture that is instilling destructive sociocultural experience in the young.

There Are No Positive Models for Behavior on Television

The ability to have a sense of humor is an important sign of wit, a quality that is highly valued among the young. It represents a litmus test of the intellectual potential of young people.

We cannot help noticing that increasingly, humor is being replaced by a depressing vulgarity, insolence, and stupidity. Young people are being taught to laugh at anything that an intelligent person could not and should not laugh at in principle.

A very important quality that is a decisive factor in success in life is an orientation toward work. Success in one's profession provides social status and respect, factors that are among the most important psychological needs. However, interaction with television fails to instill in the young person that vital competence. TV encourages idleness, and since there cannot be anything more boring and useless, it encourages increasing degrees of pathology. Television is forced to keep coming up with new anti-examples, because very quickly they are accepted by young people as the norm, they are no longer attractive, and they lose their audience.

It is worrisome that the voice of scientists, educators and psychologists is not being heard loud and clear in regard to this topic. It is society, the public at large, that has been much more insistent on sounding the alarm—clergy members, leading figures in culture, the [Youth] Public Chamber and the State Duma [government body]. But it is scientists who should point out that if a young person's range of interaction does not include positive models, there will essentially be nothing for him to internalize except pathological forms. Demagogic statements such as "if you don't want to watch, then don't watch" lack scientific foundation. People's needs are formed on the basis of stereotypes of behavioral activity that have come to be established in the unconscious. If no other models are offered, it is only natural that the ones that become firmly fixed are those shown on TV.

State-Run Public Television Is Necessary

It may seem that we are just going along in the same direction as European countries. But that is not true: Not a single one has the kind of television that we have. They are concerned about the psychological health of their people.

Great hopes used to be pinned on the Kultura [Culture] channel. But it failed to justify those hopes. Culture does not consist only of classical music. It involves a way of thinking, but we hardly ever see on the Kultura channel the kind of people whose thinking can serve as a model of spirituality, morality, and creativity, any more than we see examples of enriching interaction.

It is essential to create a genuinely state-run public television, in the best meaning of that term, a system that employs people who are genuinely interesting and creative, rather than the same old characters of weird appearance who show up simultaneously on all the TV channels, talking nonsense. Meanwhile, we still have plenty of intelligent and profound people. Why are they not working in television?

Education Cannot Compete with the Appeal of Modern Media

We must understand that the present stage in the development of our society is conditioned by the constant effect of the mass media and the Internet on the development of the personality of children, adolescents, and young people. We are surrounded by huge volumes of information disseminated with great speed. It is a situation that is fundamentally new, but the system of education is not responding flexibly enough to these changes. It continues to think of itself as the only source of influence on the student, whereas in actuality it is becoming less and less significant and attractive to youth. An increasing role in that development is played by an alternative value scale that often is in conflict with the precepts and attitudes offered by schools. The advantage of information "out of school" is that its perception is always individualized: A person can take it in under the conditions and at the pace that are convenient to him. There is significant motivation, since only those things that are interesting are chosen. The instruction purveyed in the schools and institutions of higher learning is not able to offer these things. The information provided by the media is given priority by young people; its influence on their development is colossal.

It has to be realized that the mass media represent the main agent of upbringing and instill an aggressive and warped image of the world. Young people are beginning to think that in normal society human life is not worth anything, there is no love or human interests but only physiological instincts. From our mass media, today's youngster never learns that the chief happiness comes from the opportunity to realize his creative impulses, a feeling that those around him care about him. Instead, television is making our young people preoccupied with sex; it is turning them into cruel and depressive individuals.

Young Russians Live in a Virtual World

This is not only sad, it is actually frightening. Young people are basically living in a virtual world, one in which they are starting to hate people of other nationalities, people of other cultures and levels of education, who are more successful and wealthy, who may have something a bit better. Their inner energy is not oriented toward self-development but toward self-destruction. And if this aggression continues to increase, the consequences will be irreversible.

In fact, representatives of the public at large occasionally raise their voices to protect children against the negative influences of television, but TV directors and producers take offense and declare that they are being deprived of their creative freedom (in truth, no one has seen any creativity for a long time, and many do not even know what it looks like) and are being deprived of the advertising without which, supposedly, television would die.

Russia Is Destroying Itself

Today the issue must be looked at in a different way. The situation can only be characterized in these words: The nation is in danger. It is impossible not to see this. Unless this task is fundamentally solved, there never will be any reforms. This is the key problem in our country. It cannot be solved through penalties and bans alone. We are steadily and systematically corrupting our young people, and then we are shocked to find that corruption and crime are rising in all professional groups; we wonder why our young women are not having children and why our young men do not feel a need to have a family and be responsible for it.

We have to say, in all honesty, that our television is not capable of teaching the things that are good and eternal. We do not need to fear outside enemies; we are ourselves destroying our society better than anyone else could.

> "Nationalism and xenophobia have a deep and broad appeal, particularly to the three-fourths of the country that hasn't yet entered the emerging middle class."

Skinhead Violence Rising in Russia

Mark Ames and Alexander Zaitchik

In the following viewpoint, Mark Ames and Alexander Zaitchik argue that a strong undercurrent of racism and xenophobia exists in Russia today, driven by both extreme ultranationalist citizen groups as well as factions within the government. While the authors concede that the government has passed legislation in an apparent attempt to rein in the violence, they point out that government manipulation of such groups and ideas to control the populace would not be a new phenomenon, with these types of tactics being used by both late Soviet and early Russian Federation leaders. Still, the authors do not place the blame solely on the government. Ames and Zaitchik identify a variety of sociocultural factors, including the discrediting of Western liberalism, the collapse of the economy, and the continued marginalization of religion, as merging to create an atmosphere where

ultranationalism can flourish. Mark Ames is an American jour-
nalist who spent a large portion of his career based in Moscow;
Alexander Zaitchik is an American journalist who contributed to
Ames's satirical biweekly the eXile *when it was in print.*

As you read, consider the following questions:

1. According to the authors, what are some possible motivations for the Russian government to incite or support ultranationalist violence?

2. What would the Kremlin hate speech and crime law prohibit, as stated by the authors?

3. How has Putin's presidency, in the authors' view, contributed to the current state of ultranationalism in Russia?

Beheadings posted on the Internet used to be a trademark of Chechen separatists in this part of the world. But on August 12 a video surfaced on several neo-Nazi Russian websites showing the brutal execution of two men from ethnic groups frequently targeted by Russia's ultranationalists—one of whom had his head sawn off with what appeared to be a Russian army knife.

Both victims came from southern Muslim regions: one from Tajikistan, the other from the Russian republic of Dagestan, which borders Chechnya.

The video marks the first time that neo-Nazis—in this case, a previously unknown group calling itself the National-Socialist Party of Russia—have turned to copying the sorts of radical-Islamist beheading videos that have come out of Chechnya, Pakistan and Iraq in recent years.

The three-minute clip, accompanied by a heavy metal soundtrack, was a grisly late-summer addition to what has been a banner year for skinhead violence in Russia. According to SOVA, a Moscow-based organization that tracks hate crimes in Russia, the recent executions push the number of race murders to more than forty. This is twice the number of race murders at this point last year.

To give another example of how racial violence has grown, as late as November 2001, the Moscow branch of the Anti-Defamation League estimated[1] that there had been a total of twenty killings by skinheads in recent years.

Along with targeting dark-skinned people from central Asia and the Caucasus, Russia's neo-Nazis have increased their assaults on Russian antifascists and other associated progressive activists. Last month, gangs of pipe-wielding skinheads attacked a peaceful antinuclear camp protesting in Angarsk, Siberia, resulting in the death of a 21-year-old environmental activist and a number of injuries requiring hospitalization. Some suspected that local authorities may have helped organize the attack, although others claim it was just another round in local skinhead versus AntiFa (antifascist) gang fights that ended up deadlier than usual.

The big question here is whether the rise in skinhead violence is a strictly organic phenomenon or whether it is being manipulated or even encouraged from above. Russia is holding parliamentary elections in December and presidential elections next March, and with President Vladimir Putin preparing to step down, the battle among various clan elites is turning increasingly nasty. The website kavkazcenter.com[2] isn't alone in suggesting that the FSB (formerly the KGB) may have had a hand in the beheading video with the aim of destabilizing the political situation, which presumably would empower the *siloviki*, or security services, who form one of the two most powerful clan elites. Alternatively, the Kremlin could be trying to discredit extremist nationalists beyond its power, in order to draw voters closer to the Kremlin's brand of somewhat more staid nationalism.

Such plots aren't that far-fetched. Going back to Yeltsin's and even Gorbachev's time, neo-Nazi organizations like Pamyat and Russian National Unity have been manipulated by (and in some cases invented by) Russian security organs to serve as convenient bogeymen who scare both the West and the local population into supporting the government in power.

Others see a more insidious link between the spike in racist violence and the Kremlin. By fostering a xenophobic mood and passing increasingly harsh antiforeigner legislation, the Kremlin may allow skinheads to feel more comfortable, even justified, in their violence.

"The skinhead violence has clearly gotten worse with the rise to power of Putin and his team," says Alexander Vinnikov, of the St. Petersburg–based group For Russia Without Racism. "Since 2000 there has been an increase in xenophobia and nationalist propaganda in the media at every level. It's created a favorable atmosphere for the development in young people of a chauvinistic worldview. For Putin the question is not how to fight racism but how to use it as a political tool without letting it slip from the Kremlin's control."

Indeed, it can be confusing. Officially, the Kremlin is taking an increasingly hard line against racially motivated hate speech and crimes. Some members of the ruling party in the Duma have drafted a law that would make it illegal to mention "in mass media and on the Internet any details concerning the ethnicity, race or religion of the victims, perpetrators, suspects and accused of crimes." In theory, the law is meant to ban race-based criminal stereotypes from the media, but many fear that it will serve as just another way to manage coverage of rising hate crime or that it will be loosely interpreted to target a broad range of articles and reports unfriendly to the Kremlin. Even without the law, say observers, coverage has dropped way off. State-run Russian media have reported far less on hate crimes over the past year, even as their numbers have risen, forcing observers like SOVA to rely increasingly on witness and victim accounts.

Nationalist Beliefs and Democracy Are Incompatible

The [Vladimir] Putin decade has witnessed a large growth of nationalist ideas of the type that turn easily into Nazism. And the regime is responsible for much of this, since it has no ideology other than statism tinged with nationalism. The structural immaturity of society, the lack of freedom in social life and the lack of developed political culture also favor the propagation of such crude ideological substitutes. This has resulted in the expansion of xenophobia, inseparable from nationalism, ethnic pogroms against migrants from the Caucasus, Nazi terror in the streets, thuggish violence of nationalist football hooligans around Manege Square in the center of Moscow (2010), etc. The mass protests against electoral fraud called forth feverish activity among the nationalists, who tried to attach themselves to the democratic movement so as to ride on the rising wave. Their main goal is to be recognized as a political force by public opinion. But behind the "democratic nationalists" hide genuine Nazis. Indeed, the very phrase "democratic nationalism" is an empty notion: The claim of superiority of "true Russian nationality" over other ethnic groups (made by the nationalists and now by Putin) is profoundly incompatible with the principles of democracy.

Alexei Gusev, "The Return of the Russian Revolution:
Nature of and Perspectives on the Wave of
Social Protest in Russia," New Politics, Summer 2012.

Meanwhile, the Russian government continues to play the populist race card. In recent months, nonethnic Russian migrants have been banned from selling produce and other goods in Russia's outdoor markets—which have traditionally been dominated by immigrants from Russia's southern border regions. A pamphlet published in June by a Moscow city government-affiliated youth group, Mestnie (or "Locals"), urged ethnic Russian women not to accept taxi rides from dark-skinned drivers (many immigrants moonlight as gypsy cab drivers).

And then there is Nashi, the thousands-strong Kremlin youth movement that professes to fight against fascism yet attacks liberal dissidents and puts on mass parades of youths marching in uniform Putin T-shirts and doing calisthenics, in scenes reminiscent of the 1930s. A few years ago, the muckraking newspaper *Novaya Gazeta* published an investigative report detailing links between skinheads, Moscow police and Nashi's previous incarnation, a pro-Kremlin youth organization called Walking Together.

And yet the skinhead problem is not a manufactured phenomenon. Nationalism and xenophobia have a deep and broad appeal, particularly to the three-fourths of the country that hasn't yet entered the emerging middle class. Over the past few decades, communism and Western-style liberalism have been thoroughly discredited, first by the collapse of the Soviet Union and then with the collapse of the Russian economy by the end of the 1990s. Christianity has never recovered from the Bolshevik Revolution. All of this, put into the context of social, economic, cultural and geopolitical decline, has helped foster growing ultranationalism, including neo-Nazism— which seems strange in a country that lost 27 million people to the Nazis.

Since Putin came to power in 2000, Russia has experienced an unexpectedly rapid yet uneven revival, and his government's overt patriotism, as well as its ambivalent attitude toward Western liberalism, reflects and enables the growing appeal of ultranationalism.

The Kremlin has thus been working not simply to manipulate ultranationalism but also to control it, though its motivations are not always clear. In recent years, several major pieces of legislation have been passed to address the problem. Article 282, for example, criminalizes the incitement of "ethnic, racial, or religious hatred" and has led to the successful prosecution of more than a dozen distributors of neo-Nazi literature. But these laws, ostensibly passed to control hate crime, are often used for anything but. Just this week, a member of the right-wing Rodina party threatened to bring Article 282 against Issa Kodzoyev, a novelist from the southern region of Ingushetia. The writer's crime? A character in his novel *The Landslide*, which is set in the 1940s, calls on the Ingush people to resist Joseph Stalin's persecution of them.

And early in 2005, several members of the Duma petitioned to have Judaism banned in Russia after accusing the religion of preaching ethnic hate.

"The truth is that many Russian politicians believe in a 'cultural racism,'" said Alexander Vinnikov, of For Russia Without Racism. "And even if extremist activists are from time to time arrested, on the whole, racist ideas do not meet the rejection of the Russian population. This problem is not going away."

Links

1. http://www.exile.ru/2001-November-15/feature_story.html
2. http://kavkazcenter.com/

> "Through the democratic process, Euro-
> pean ultranationalists are relegated to
> a small corner of the political field. In
> Russia, they become martyrs."

A More Open Political System Would Thwart the Ambitions of Russia's Ultranationalists

Daniil Davydoff

In the following viewpoint, Daniil Davydoff blames the Vladimir Putin government for the growth of ultranationalism in Russia, not because the president supported these views, but because he arrested those who expressed them and suppressed those who opposed them. Davydoff believes that unlike other European countries such as Sweden and France, where nationalism is marginalized by the democratic process, nationalism and its followers in Russia are sometimes seen as martyrs for their cause, persecuted by an overly harsh government. Thus, while the author emphasizes the need for the government to take action to limit hate speech, crimes, and beliefs, he also stresses the need for balance so as not to increase the nationalists' power. Daniil Davydoff is an independent consultant for Eurasia Group's Comparative Analytics practice, which analyzes potential business opportunities in various countries.

As you read, consider the following questions:

1. What does Vladimir Putin's record on Russian-Jewish issues illustrate, according to the author?

2. As stated by the author, why is it dangerous to persecute the National Bolsheviks and similar organizations?

3. What "potent mix," according to the author, would make it possible for nationalist groups to take over in Russia?

If freedom-loving France expels ethnic minorities and open-minded Sweden elects a quasi-fascist party to its parliament, is it really so surprising that the far-right movement is alive and well in Russia, a country that has reclaimed its nationalism so effectively in recent years? For many, the December [2010] riots by ultranationalists in Moscow are simply an affirmation that Russia is, like the rest of Europe, flirting with xenophobia. This view has merit but ignores the fact that Russia's closed political landscape makes the far right a bigger threat there than anywhere else on the continent.

Nationalists Become Martyrs in Russia

The ultranationalist Sweden Democrats and the knife-wielding soccer hooligans of Moscow are fringe elements in their countries' politics. Whatever one thinks of Russia's soft authoritarianism, far-right sentiments have never been part of the "modern Russia" narrative that has been spun by the authorities over the last decade.

Vladimir Putin's record on Russian-Jewish issues alone illustrates this. During his presidency, Mikhail Fradkov, a Jew, was nominated to the post of prime minister and extremism laws were passed to target and disband hate groups. Putin himself attended the opening of a Jewish community center as well as the 60th anniversary of the liberation of Auschwitz. In 2005, Putin visited Israel, making him the first leader of either Russia or the Soviet Union to have done so.

What makes the Russian ultranationalists different is not their aspirations or their methods, but the political environment that they operate in. All over Europe, far-right groups rail against foreigners, with splintering extremists even committing heinous acts of violence. But for such groups the avenue of political action is wide open; in Russia it is not. Through the democratic process, European ultranationalists are relegated to a small corner of the political field.

In Russia, they become martyrs, attracting unwarranted interest for their persecution at the hands of the ruling regime. How else does one explain how the notorious National Bolsheviks—a far-right organization whose ideology is at the nexus of the 20th century's dangerous "-isms"—have been able to align themselves with respectable opposition groups?

The Possibility for a Nationalist Takeover Exists in Russia

Being a victim does not grant an individual or group special powers by default. Just ask the Russian parties with platforms most resembling those of mainstream parties in the U.S. or Europe. Ask also the freshly reconvicted oligarch Mikhail Khodorkovsky, whose internationally reported trial was reportedly followed by a little more than a third of all Russians. Yet it is important to remember that liberals and oligarchs have never been well liked in Russia.

That is why the persecution of the National Bolsheviks and similar organizations could actually pose a threat: The ultranationalists are ideologically closer to the broadly popular Communist Party and Liberal Democratic Party, the highest represented parties in the country's parliament after Putin and [Dmitry] Medvedev's hegemonic United Russia.

To be sure, few Russia watchers would say that the peripheral ultranationalist groups, victims or not, could achieve political power anytime soon. But consider that a century ago [Vladimir] Lenin's Bolsheviks—who would come to rule over

Nationalism Influences Russian Politics

Nationalist ideology in Russia has a constantly shifting purpose, determined by the political ends toward which it is applied. There is no single, large-scale nationalist movement uniting the Kremlin elites and the far-right neo-Nazi parties; ideologically they are too disparate ever to be completely reconciled. Even a populist demagogue like [politician Vladimir] Zhirinovsky, known for his xenophobic attitude toward minorities, was an eager supporter of Russia's policy of handing out passports to Abkhazians, because he saw this as an opportunity to expand Russia's influence. Russian fascists are unlikely to accept such a policy: For them a true Russia means one purified of all foreign elements. Despite this divergence, both groups have actively perpetuated an aura of hostility and mistrust, which has only been intensified by the government's rhetoric. Nationalism is a dangerous political tool, and the Kremlin's resentment over its loss of empire and the encroachments of the West into its traditional sphere of influence makes for dangerously virulent politics.

Rafael Khachaturian,
"The Specter of Russian Nationalism,"
Dissent, Winter 2009.

a Communist empire for over 80 years—were but a small faction of the Russian Social Democratic Labour Party, itself barely represented in the legislative assemblies of the late tsarist Russia.

Nevertheless, the potent mix of able leadership and the skillful use of violence quickly elevated them to ultimate power in a time of national crisis. Should circumstances change, something comparable could happen in Russia today.

Russian Authorities Must Open the System to Combat the Nationalists

It is easy to understand the predicament facing Russian authorities, because repression of political groups with unsavory views is always a gamble: Subdue too little and their beliefs get an audience, stifle too much and their cause gets consideration. Thus far, the authorities have tried to address the dilemma by sanctioning token opposition parties which have nationalist elements, but such a strategy is likely to fail in the face of genuine discontent.

While the focus on preventing and prosecuting actual hate crimes should be strengthened, the Russian leadership needs to realize that opening the political system to competition from the ultranationalists may actually be the best way to prevent their grievances from getting unjustified attention and traction.

Periodical Bibliography

The following articles have been selected to supplement the diverse views presented in this chapter.

Liubov' Borusiak	"Soccer as a Catalyst of Patriotism," *Russian Social Science Review*, January/February 2010.
Jonathan E.M. Clarke	"Orthodoxy and the Search for Identity in Contemporary Russia," *Journal of Religion & Society*, vol. 13, 2011.
Charlie Gillis	"Putin the Terrible," *Maclean's*, September 3, 2007.
Rafael Khachaturian	"The Specter of Russian Nationalism," *Dissent*, Winter 2009.
Alexey D. Krindatch	"Religion, Public Life and the State in Putin's Russia," *Religion in Eastern Europe*, May 2006.
Alexei V. Malashenko	"Islam in Russia," *Social Research*, Spring 2009.
Owen Matthews	"Dumbing Russia Down," *Newsweek*, March 22, 2008.
Timothy C. Morgan	"From Russia, with Love," *Christianity Today*, May 2011.
Nicu Popescu	"The Strange Alliance of Democrats and Nationalists," *Journal of Democracy*, July 2012.
Jeffrey Tayler	"Russian Hangover," *Atlantic*, November 2011.
Nathan Thornburgh	"Russia's Long (and Brutal) War on Terror," *Time*, August 22, 2010.

For Further Discussion

Chapter 1

1. Randall Newnham maintains that Moscow uses its country's oil and natural gas resources to reward or punish neighboring states based on their allegiance to Russia. Andreas Goldthau, however, contends that Russia's energy sector is poorly managed and suffers other problems that keep it from wielding much power. What kinds of evidence does each author use to support his claim? Whose evidence do you find more convincing? Explain why.

2. After reading the viewpoints by Ariel Cohen and Marcin Kaczmarski, explain what you think Russia's motives in the Middle East might be. In answering the question, first identify all the major reasons both authors give for Russia's engagement with the region. Then, clarify which you think are probably the most important to Russia's aims as well as the results the nation hopes to achieve through its Middle East policies.

3. The New START treaty signed by the United States and Russia was designed to reduce both states' nuclear arsenals. Robert G. Joseph believes the treaty is dangerous to US interests because it limits American strength and does not account for tactical nuclear weapons, of which Russia has an advantage in Europe. Do you think Joseph's warning is worth considering, or are you, like Bruce Blair and his colleagues, in favor of more cuts to stockpiles of nuclear weapons? What do you think should be the guiding principle for advocating or resisting cuts to America's nuclear capabilities? Explain.

Chapter 2

1. The 2012 presidential election in Russia has been the subject of great controversy. United Russia candidate Vladimir Putin won the election in spite of protests that the voting was unfair and that Putin's strong, centralized rule would lead Russia further away from democracy. Writing on the eve of the elections, Mikhail Khodorkovsky believes that Russians, indeed, favor democracy and are willing to stand up against Putin. Kathy Lally and Will Englund, however, claim that most Russians support strong leaders and will let democracy slip away because they have lost hope that meaningful change can occur. Do you think the results of the 2012 election signal the end of democracy in Russia, or do the continued protests suggest Russians are committed to change? Use the viewpoints in this chapter and other opinions you find to support your answer.

2. A May 2012 Pew Research Center poll reported that Russians believe a strong economy is better for Russia than a good democracy. Randall D. Law supports this conclusion by claiming that Russians fear the economic chaos that followed the collapse of the Soviet Union and are willing to sacrifice some facets of democracy to ensure that the shocks of the immediate post-Soviet era do not return. What evidence does Law provide to buttress his argument? Do you think the evidence is convincing? Why or why not? Use arguments from other viewpoints in the chapter to support or counter Law's conclusion.

3. The Vladimir Putin government has passed laws to hinder protests and to stifle opposition parties from forming. Yury Dzhibladze argues that while these restrictions may curb some demonstrations in the short term, they might foster greater resistance to Putin's rule over time. Using the viewpoints in this chapter, describe whether you think Putin's apparent infringement of civil rights will lead to a

backlash or a quiet acceptance of such laws. Draw on quotes from the viewpoints to support your claims.

Chapter 3

1. Do you think the United States should view Russia as a strategic partner? Russian dissident Garry Kasparov believes the United States should condemn Vladimir Putin's government for thwarting democracy in Russia and should not seek a partnership at this time. After examining Kasparov's argument, explain what course you believe America should take.

2. After reading the viewpoint by Robert Kagan and David J. Kramer and the counterargument by Raymond Sontag, explain what place human rights issues should take in US-Russian relations. In addition, explain how effective you think US legislation could be in addressing human rights abuse in Russia.

3. The punk band Pussy Riot has garnered a lot of attention for its protest of an Orthodox religious leader's endorsement of the election of Vladimir Putin. After the band members were arrested for a demonstration at Moscow's Cathedral of Christ the Saviour, the fledgling performers were flooded with support from human rights activists and Western celebrities. Joshua Foust argues that this support, though well intentioned, masks the plight of noncelebrity dissidents in Russia who have worked for years to bring about reform. After reading his viewpoint and the one by Gideon Rachman, do you think Western praise for Pussy Riot will help focus attention on dissidents in Russia or perhaps obscure the efforts of those who don't have the ear of entertainers and the media? Explain your answer.

Chapter 4

1. In the first two viewpoints of this chapter, the authors examine the impact of the increasing influence of the Russian Orthodox Church on life in Russia. John P. Burgess, a professor of systematic theology, has a seemingly positive view of the transformation and ties Russian Orthodoxy closely to individuals' sense of identity in that country. Mikhail Sitnikov views it as damaging in its ability to create a new kind of totalitarianism if religious classes are established in secular schools. After reading both viewpoints, which do you agree with more? Do you think the increase of religious influence will benefit or harm Russian society? Use examples from the viewpoints to support your reasoning.

2. Mikhail N. Berulava presents an analysis of the ways in which Russian youth obtain information and use entertainment media. Reread this viewpoint and consider the ways in which you consume information. Do you think differences exist between American youths' media use and the use of media by Russian youth? Use quotes from the viewpoint and details of your own examples in your answer.

3. This chapter's final two viewpoints assess nationalist violence and sentiment in Russia today. Mark Ames and Alexander Zaitchik provide an analysis of the current problem and some possible sources for the ultranationalist sentiment, while Daniil Davydoff offers a possible course of action to stem the rising tide of ultranationalism. After reading these two viewpoints, do you believe that a more open political system is the best way to combat ultranationalism? If so, explain why. If not, conduct some outside research to find other possible solutions. Support your answer by using quotes from your sources.

Organizations to Contact

The editors have compiled the following list of organizations concerned with the issues debated in this book. The descriptions are derived from materials provided by the organizations. All have publications or information available for interested readers. The list was compiled on the date of publication of the present volume; the information provided here may change. Be aware that many organizations take several weeks or longer to respond to inquiries, so allow as much time as possible.

American Enterprise Institute for Public Policy Research (AEI)
1150 Seventeenth Street NW, Washington, DC   20036
(202) 862-5800 • fax: (202) 862-7177
website: www.aei.org

The American Enterprise Institute for Public Policy Research (AEI) is a nonpartisan public policy institute that researches and provides education pertaining to topics such as US government, politics, economy, and social welfare. The institute views Russia as a continuing challenge for the United States due to its authoritarian government and its defiant policy choice that stands in opposition to the West. Further, AEI is critical of the Russian government's unwillingness to enact meaningful democratic reform. Articles covering a range of topics including US policy toward Russia, democracy and protest in Russia, and missile defense policy can be found online and in the monthly magazine of the organization, the *American*.

Amnesty International (AI)
5 Penn Plaza, New York, NY   10001
(212) 807-8400 • fax: (212) 627-1451
e-mail: aimember@aiusa.org
website: www.amnestyusa.org

Amnesty International is a coalition of members, activists, and supporters who work worldwide to end human rights abuses and ensure that all humans are guaranteed the rights granted in the Universal Declaration of Human Rights and by other human rights standards. The organization provides analysis of human rights by country. The 2012 Amnesty International report on the state of human rights in the Russian Federation can be read online along with articles such as "The Russian Federation Continues to Strangle Freedom of Peaceful Assembly," "Deadly and Dangerous Arms Trade," and "Russian Federation: A Human Rights Agenda for Russia." Detailed articles outlining specific cases of human rights abuses in Russia can also be found on the Amnesty International website.

Arms Control Association (ACA)
1313 L Street NW, Suite 130, Washington, DC   20005
(202) 463-8270 • fax: (202) 463-8273
e-mail: aca@armscontrol.org
website: www.armscontrol.org

The Arms Control Association (ACA) has been working since 1971 to educate the public about and promote effective arms control policies. It encourages nuclear nonproliferation and disarmament. Information on the site can be searched by country, with overviews of the country's nuclear programs and treaties accessible on the country page. Russian articles include "Arms Control and Proliferation Profile: Russia," "Cooperating with Russia on Missile Defense: A New Proposal," and "Russian Strategic Nuclear Forces Under New START." *Arms Control Today* is the official magazine of ACA.

Council on Foreign Relations (CFR)
The Harold Pratt House, 58 East Sixty-Eighth Street
New York, NY   10065
(212) 434-9400 • fax: (212) 434-9800
website: www.cfr.org

Since 1921, the Council on Foreign Relations (CFR) has served as a nonpartisan, independent public policy think tank seeking to provide reliable analysis of current international issues for policy makers, business leaders, journalists, students, and citizens. CFR's coverage of Russia spans a range of issues including economics, national security and defense, and human rights. Articles such as "Foreign Policy: Yes, Russia Is Our Top Geopolitical Foe," "Russia: Politics, Protests and the Presidential Election," and "Impact of Russia's WTO Entry on U.S." can all be read online. Additional articles can be found in *Foreign Affairs*, the bimonthly publication of CFR.

Embassy of the Russian Federation to the United States of America

2650 Wisconsin Avenue NW, Washington, DC   20007
(202) 298-5700 • fax: (202) 298-5735
website: www.russianembassy.org

The Russian Embassy is the diplomatic representation from that country within the United States. The physical embassy houses the Russian ambassador and provides a voice for Russia in the United States. The Russian Embassy's website provides information about Russian-American relations—political, economic, and cultural—in addition to details about the structure of the embassy and general information about Russia. Travel guidelines and needed documents are also provided on this site.

Federation of American Scientists (FAS)

1725 DeSales Street NW, Suite 600, Washington, DC   20036
(202) 546-3300 • fax: (202) 675-1010
e-mail: fas@fas.org
website: www.fas.org

The Federation of American Scientists (FAS) is an independent public policy research organization that provides evidence-based policy analysis regarding national and international security as it relates to applied science and technology. Founded in 1945 by scientists who participated in the creation of the first atomic bomb, FAS is particularly concerned with nuclear arms. With regard to Russia, it has published comprehensive guides to Russian and Soviet nuclear forces, analyses of current arms holdings, and assessments of US-Russian relations on nuclear weapons. These articles, along with additional information about Russian weapons programs, can be read on the FAS website.

Human Rights Watch (HRW)
350 Fifth Avenue, 34th Floor, New York, NY   10118-3299
(212) 290-4700 • fax: (212) 736-1300
website: www.hrw.org

Human Rights Watch (HRW) is an international organization concerned with ensuring the observance and protection of human rights for all people worldwide. With regard to Russia, HRW is particularly concerned with the government's unwillingness to hold individuals responsible for human rights abuse, its continued suppression of dissent, and human rights abuses in Chechnya. Reports such as "An Uncivil Approach to Civil Society" and "Choking on Bureaucracy," as well as the photo documentary "Acting Up: Russia's Civil Society," provide insight into the human rights problems that exist in Russia today and the actions citizens are taking to prevent further abuses.

Institute for Democracy and Cooperation
655 Third Avenue, Suite 2010, New York, NY   10017
(212) 922-0030 • fax: (212) 922-1555
e-mail: info@indemco.org
website: www.indemco.org

The Institute for Democracy and Cooperation is a nongovernmental think tank working to increase understanding and cooperation between Russia and the United States in government, finance, economics, and culture. Information about the institute's projects relating to democracy, immigration, local governance, and xenophobia can be found online. Additionally, articles relating to the institute's work, such as "The Anti-Putin Campaign" and "Russia Elections Won't Pave the Way for a Putin Dictatorship," can be accessed under the Works by Institute tab.

National Endowment for Democracy (NED)
1025 F Street NW, Suite 800, Washington, DC   20004
(202) 378-9700 • fax: (202) 378-9407
e-mail: info@ned.org
website: www.ned.org

National Endowment for Democracy (NED) is a private, non-profit organization that works to foster the growth and improvement of democratic institutions worldwide. Within Russia, NED provides large amounts of money in the form of grants to help strengthen the fight for democracy. Details about the grants and amounts given can be found on the organization's website. NED has also discussed freedom of speech and censorship laws extensively with reports and articles accessible from its website.

Russia Profile
4 Zubovsky Boulevard, Moscow   119021
   Russia
+7 (495) 645-6486
e-mail: info@russiaprofile.org
website: www.russiaprofile.org

Russia Profile is a Russian-based, English-language website dedicated to providing current, accurate information about topical issues in Russia relating to business, economics, politics, and culture. In addition to daily updates to its website, the service publishes the quarterly *Russia Profile Special Report*, which provides detailed assessments of specific issues in Russia. The Russia Profile website offers access to current and archived articles, as well as background information on many of the topics covered.

US Energy Information Administration (EIA)
1000 Independence Avenue SW, Washington, DC   20585
(202) 586-8800
e-mail: infoCtr@eia.gov
website: www.eia.gov

The Energy Information Administration (EIA) is an agency within the US Department of Energy focused on conducting research and collecting data, analyzing that information, and producing independent, unbiased information to provide a basis for policy making, sound markets, and public knowledge about energy. Country overviews provide detailed analysis of world players in the energy market, among them Russia. The Russia analysis assesses oil production and exports, natural gas production, electricity, and coal. Additional articles about Russian energy can be found on the EIA website.

World Policy Institute (WPI)
108 West Thirty-Ninth Street, Suite 1000
New York, NY   10018
(212) 481-5005 • fax: (212) 481-5009
e-mail: wpi@worldpolicy.org
website: www.worldpolicy.org

The World Policy Institute (WPI) has been working for half a century to provide trusted nonpartisan, international policy leadership. The institute's goal is threefold: ensure a stable global market economy open to all, foster informed global civic participation to create effective governments, and encourage international cooperation on national and global security issues. Articles outlining topics such as US policy toward Russia ("Reset with Russia: Not as Easy as It Sounds") and Russian censorship ("Digital Freedom & Control: Russia & Asia") can be read on the organization's website along with details about the WPI Russian Project, which spanned five years and examined changes occurring both within the country and with regard to its international relations.

Bibliography of Books

Anders Åslund — *Russia's Capitalist Revolution: Why Market Reform Succeeded and Democracy Failed.* Washington, DC: Peter G. Peterson Institute for International Economics, 2007.

Ronald D. Asmus — *A Little War That Shook the World: Georgia, Russia, and the Future of the West.* New York: Palgrave Macmillan, 2010.

Peter Baker and Susan Glasser — *Kremlin Rising: Vladimir Putin's Russia and the End of Revolution.* Washington, DC: Potomac Books, 2007.

Robert H. Donaldson and Joseph L. Nogee — *The Foreign Policy of Russia: Changing Systems, Enduring Interests.* Armonk, NY: M.E. Sharpe, 2009.

Orlando Figes — *Natasha's Dance: A Cultural History of Russia.* New York: Metropolitan Books, 2002.

Masha Gessen — *The Man Without a Face: The Unlikely Rise of Vladimir Putin.* New York: Riverhead, 2012.

James M. Goldgeier and Michael McFaul — *Power and Purpose: U.S. Policy Toward Russia After the Cold War.* Washington, DC: Brookings Institution Press, 2003.

Marshall I. Goldman — *Petrostate: Putin, Power, and the New Russia.* New York: Oxford University Press, 2008.

David E. Hoffman — *The Oligarchs: Wealth and Power in the New Russia.* New York: PublicAffairs, 2001.

James Hughes — *Chechnya: From Nationalism to Jihad.* Philadelphia: University of Pennsylvania Press, 2007.

Adeeb Khalid — *Islam After Communism: Religion and Politics in Central Asia.* Berkeley: University of California Press, 2007.

Jeffrey Mankoff — *Russian Foreign Policy: The Return of Great Power Politics.* Lanham, MD: Rowman & Littlefield, 2011.

Michael McFaul, Nikolai Petrov, and Andrei Ryabov — *Between Dictatorship and Democracy: Russian Post-Communist Political Reform.* Washington, DC: Carnegie Endowment for International Peace, 2004.

Anna Politkovskaya — *Putin's Russia: Life in a Failing Democracy.* New York: Henry Holt and Co., 2007.

Thomas F. Remington — *Politics in Russia.* Boston, MA: Pearson, 2012.

Susan Richards — *Lost and Found in Russia: Lives in the Post-Soviet Landscape.* New York: Other Press, 2010.

Angus Roxburgh — *The Strongman: Vladimir Putin and the Struggle for Russia.* New York: I.B. Tauris, 2012.

Lilia Shevtsova   *Russia Lost in Transition: The Yeltsin
                         and Putin Legacies.* Washington, DC:
                         Carnegie Endowment for
                         International Peace, 2007.

Martin Sixsmith   *Putin's Oil: The Yukos Affair and the
                         Struggle for Russia.* New York:
                         Continuum, 2010.

Daniel Treisman   *The Return: Russia's Journey from
                         Gorbachev to Medvedev.* New York:
                         Free Press, 2011.

Andrei P.   *Russia's Foreign Policy: Change and
Tsygankov   Continuity in National Identity.*
                         Lanham, MD: Rowman & Littlefield,
                         2013.

Christoph   *The Post-Soviet Wars: Rebellion,
Zürcher   Ethnic Conflict, and Nationhood in
                         the Caucasus.* New York: New York
                         University Press, 2007.

Index

CPSIA information can be obtained
at www.ICGtesting.com
Printed in the USA
FFOW02n0618031013
1958FF

Resources from MOPS

Books

Beyond Macaroni and Cheese
Children Change a Marriage
A Cure for the Growly Bugs and Other Tips for Moms
Getting Out of Your Kids' Faces and Into Their Hearts
In the Wee Hours
Loving and Letting Go
Make Room for Daddy
Meditations for Mothers
Mom to Mom
A Mother's Footprints of Faith
Ready for Kindergarten
Real Moms
What Every Child Needs
What Every Mom Needs

Little Books for Busy Moms Series

Boredom Busters
Great Books to Read and Fun Things to Do with Them
If You Ever Needed Friends, It's Now
Juggling Tasks, Tots, and Time
Kids' Stuff and What to Do with It
Planes, Trains, and Automobiles ... with Kids!
Time Out for Mom . . . Ahhh Moments

Books with Drs. Henry Cloud and John Townsend

Raising Great Kids
Raising Great Kids for Parents of Preschoolers Workbook
Raising Great Kids for Parents of Teenagers Workbook
Raising Great Kids for Parents of School-Age Children Workbook

Gift Books

God's Words of Life from the Mom's Devotional Bible
Mommy, I Love You Just Because

Kids Books

Little Jesus, Little Me
My Busy, Busy Day
See the Country, See the City
Mommy, May I Hug the Fishes?
Mad Maddie Maxwell
Zachary's Zoo
Morning, Mr. Ted
Boxes, Boxes Everywhere
Snug as a Bug?

Bible

Mom's Devotional Bible

Audio

Raising Great Kids

Curriculum

Raising Great Kids for Parents of Preschoolers Zondervan*Groupware*™ (with Drs. Henry Cloud and John Townsend)

MOTHERS OF
MOPS®
PRESCHOOLERS
...because mothering matters

Shelly Radic

CREATIVE WAYS TO CELEBRATE
YOUR CHILD'S SPECIAL DAY

ZONDERVAN™

GRAND RAPIDS, MICHIGAN 49530 USA

ZONDERVAN™

The Birthday Book
Copyright © 2002 by Shelly Radic

Requests for information should be addressed to:
Zondervan, *Grand Rapids, Michigan 49530*

Library of Congress Cataloging-in-Publication Data

Radic, Shelly.
    The birthday book : creative ways to celebrate your child's special day / Shelly Radic.
       p. cm.
    Includes bibliographical references and index.
    ISBN 0-310-24704-7
    1. Children's parties. 2. Birthdays. I. Title.
GV1205 .R36 2002
793.2'1—dc21

                                       2002007547

All Scripture quotations, unless otherwise indicated, are taken from the *Holy Bible: New International Version*®. NIV®. Copyright © 1973, 1978, 1984 by International Bible Society. Used by permission of Zondervan. All rights reserved.

Published in association with the literary agency of Alive Communications, Inc., 7680 Goddard Street, Suite 200, Colorado Springs, CO 80920.

Interior design by Susan Ambs

Illustrations by Nick Carrubba appear on the chapter title pages and on pages 21, 30, and 34.

All other illustrations are by Tom Ungrey.

Printed in the United States of America

02 03 04 05 06 07 08/❖ DC/ 10 9 8 7 6 5 4 3 2 1

To my five special gifts from God—
Brittany, Natalie, Danielle, Dillon,
and their daddy, Bruce

Table of Contents

A Quick Guide to Theme Parties

Acknowledgments

With special thanks to the following who shared their birthday experiences with me:

To the mothers of twins: Tina, Jill, Andrea, Alicia, Mary, and Sheila

To twins: Kristy, Alyssa, Kelly, Jessica, and Jennifer

To mothers of special needs children: Claudia and Joelle

To mothers who have or have had teens: Debbie, Jeny, Laurie, Jan, Lil, and Beth

To mothers around the country: Thanks to my sister MOPS Area Coordinators, Sharon, Sylvia, Laurie, Joy, Lisa, Andrea, Robyn, Eve, and Debbie

To the mothers and friends who were my first readers: Linda C., Stephanie, Rosemary, Jamie, and Linda L.

To Beth Lagerborg for your encouragement, advice, and enthusiasm. I would have never accomplished this project if you had not planted the seed, watered it, and nurtured its growth from start to finish.

Why Celebrate?

HAPPY BIRTHDAY TO YOU

Parties are fun,
Cake is great.
But YOU are why we celebrate!

Her big brown eyes twinkled with joy as she filled her cheeks so full of air they looked like pink birthday balloons. Her ears drank in the sweet sound of those who loved her best of all singing the familiar words, "Happy birthday to you, happy birthday to you." Wishing for a hundred more wishes, she blew the three candles out with a mighty puff of air to the delight and applause of her adoring audience. "Happy birthday, dear Janie, happy birthday to you!"

ONE OF MY FAVORITE THINGS about being a mother is celebrating my children's birthdays. Each birthday is an opportunity to reflect on what a unique, special creation each child is. As I look back over the previous year, I can see how God has been working in their young lives, bringing growth and maturity while he patiently molds them into his own image. My children's birthdays have provided a day for me to say "I love you" in some special way. A day to say, "You are special to me." Birthdays seem to naturally provide opportunities for us to have fun together.

What makes a birthday a special day? Is it a cake with some candles? A pile of gifts wrapped in brightly colored paper? A houseful of guests singing the birthday song? While cake, gifts, and special guests can make the day special, they are not what a birthday is all about. What makes a birthday special is the child himself. Birthdays are about focusing our attention on that special little person God has blessed us with, to zoom in for one day each year on that child's growth, interests, and accomplishments. To let that child know, without a doubt, that he or she is a unique creation, truly special and dearly loved.

I entered motherhood in the mid-1980s, a decade of excess everything! My daughter attended her first birthday party when she was nine months old, and was it ever something. Two dozen kids, even more adults, loads of decorations and food, a pile of gifts, and lots of fun stuff to do. Mothering magazines in the 1980s emphasized the importance of building self-esteem in your child. I love a great party, and took great pride in the special first birthday I planned for my little girl. Being the overzealous first time mother I was, I thought giving my child a blowout birthday party was an ideal way to build her self-esteem.

Forty birthdays later (it really adds up fast when you have four children!) I've come to some different conclusions about celebrating children's birthdays. Excess and success are not synonymous, and while blowout birthday parties can be an incredible gift for a child, they are not the only way to celebrate a birthday. It took me awhile, but I finally figured out that the most important birthday gift a mother can give her child is not self-esteem, or a blowout party, but an appreciation for the unique and special person God created him to be. Now my goal for each birthday is to celebrate the unique life God has created in my child, to give her a glimpse of who God is shaping her to be, to let her know I am thankful for the special gift God entrusted me with, and to have fun celebrating her special day.

Why celebrate birthdays? Celebrating birthdays provides an opportunity to meet the needs of our child in some unique, memorable ways. In their book *What Every Child Needs*, Elisa Morgan and Carol Kuykendall share with us the nine basic needs of our children: security, affirmation, belonging, discipline, guidance, respect, play, independence, and hope. Celebrating a child's birthday gives us an opportunity to meet many of these needs in memorable ways.

Security

Your child's need for security can be met when on his special day, you give him just a little bit more of yourself—a little more time, a few more hugs. While a one-year-old will not remember anything about his first birthday, the sound of his mother's voice singing the birthday song and whispering a prayer of thanksgiving for her little child will be etched forever in his brain. As a child grows older and watches his mother consistently plan and carry out special birthday celebrations, he will be reminded of her continuous love and care. Celebrating birthdays is an opportunity to hold your child close in the security of your love.

Affirmation

Cello virtuoso and conductor Pablo Casals asks a thought-provoking question of parents when he writes, "When will we also teach them [our children] what they are? We should say to each of them: Do you know what you are? You are a marvel. You are unique. In all the years that have passed, there has never been another child like you. Your legs, your arms, your clever fingers, and the way you move." Children learn who they are by watching how those around them react to them, and by listening to the things we say about them. In the hustle and bustle of daily life, moms sometimes forget how important it is to affirm their child as a unique, God-created human being. View your child's birthday as a chance to tell her what you really like about her. Show her how she is uniquely and wonderfully made. Whether it's learning to walk, sort socks, or write her name, praise your child for the accomplishments she's achieved in the past year. On your child's birthday, join her in activities she is interested in, or use her unique interest as the theme for her birthday party. Celebrate the birthday of your child by finding ways to affirm her. Fran Scott, dean of the Erickson Institute for Advanced Study in Child

Development says, "Children need more than food, shelter, and clothing. The bottom line is: Every child needs at least one person who's crazy about him."

Belonging

Cheers, a popular television series in the 1990s, was a big hit because it gave us a glimpse of a place where "Everybody knows your name!" It was about a place people liked to go because they felt a sense of belonging. You can build your child's sense of belonging in your family when you celebrate his birthday. Often birthdays are a time to talk about when your child entered the family—a day worthy of celebration! Extended family members, grandparents, aunts, uncles, and cousins often send a birthday greeting letting the child know how thankful they are the birthday child is a part of the family. Special family birthday traditions (we'll talk more about these in the next chapter) help your child know he is an important part of your family unit. Your child has a place where he belongs!

Discipline

Birthday celebrations offer an opportunity to meet your child's needs for discipline. Other than their first birthdays, each of my children had the opportunity to practice delayed gratification during their birthdays. Gifts and cards came in the mail, but were not opened until the special day. Special treats prepared in the morning for a birthday party could not be eaten until the appropriate time. Sometimes a special privilege such as playing in the front yard without mom would be granted on a milestone birthday. There is a sense of excitement that builds with this type of waiting. Birthdays give the opportunity to teach a child limits in social settings as well. Taking turns, serving your guest before you serve yourself, and treating others with respect all build good manners, an important component in the life of a well-disciplined child.

Guidance

The way you handle celebrating your child's birthday offers an opportunity for you to meet your child's need for guidance in some unique ways. As your child sees you valuing her life, she learns her life has value. As she sees you thoughtfully preparing a special cake, she observes the value of doing kind things for others. As she listens to you share about the importance of saying thank-you for a gift, she learns to be grateful. As she helps you prepare for any special guests, she develops the art of hospitality. As your child plays games, hears stories, or listens to special music, she discovers the joy of having fun with someone she loves. Celebrating a birthday can provide many unique teachable moments for guiding your child.

Respect

In *Eight Traits of a Healthy Family*, Bill Hybels writes, "One day your children should be able to look back and say, 'My family was the one place where I felt I could be myself—and be loved for it.'" A child's birthday is a perfect opportunity to take a close look at your child and let him know you like what you see. Celebrating a birthday by doing some of your child's favorite activities, welcoming his specially chosen friends, or decorating your house with dinosaurs (or whatever your child's current passion is) sends a message of respect for your child. In a sense you are saying, "The things you do are so fun, I want to do them too. The friends you chose are such great people, I want to get to know them better. The stuff you are enthusiastic about is so interesting, I want to discover more about it!" Valerie Bell writes about "loyal delight." She says, "A parent's job is to celebrate the child, as he or she is."

Play

Possibly the easiest need to meet on your child's birthday is the need for play. Children whine when they're hungry, yawn when they're sleepy, and cry when they're hurt. Sometimes I think we moms need a flashing light on our child's face that says, "I need to play!" It's so easy to forget about this important need in the midst of meeting all the others, and yet meeting this need is often the most fun for both mom and child. When I meet my child's need to have fun, I find myself meeting so many of his other needs as well. Birthdays are often a time when a child receives a few gifts. Take the time to choose at least one gift that will encourage play between you and your child. No need to spend a fortune—beach balls, Play-Doh, bubble wands, and refrigerator boxes can provide hours of playtime for under five dollars. Choosing to engage in a few of your child's favorite activities, whether it be blowing bubbles or climbing a jungle gym, will not only meet your child's need to play, but will be fun for you as well.

Independence

Every birthday is a milestone towards your child's independence. While moms don't always want to admit it, our children do have a need for independence. As your children get older, they can be progressively more responsible for the planning of their birthday celebration. When my children were toddlers, they loved to "help" me bake their birthday cake. By age four they were capable of doing many of the baking tasks on their own. At age seven, they begged to be allowed to decorate the cake themselves. By allowing them to take charge of this task, I helped their stretch towards independence. Moms, each birthday should be a reminder to us our child is growing up and needs us to leave more of life's daily tasks and decisions in his increasingly capable hands.

Hope

Finally, celebrating your child's birthday offers an opportunity to give hope. A birthday is a day of looking forward, a chance to ask your child what she thinks it will be like to be three or five or eighteen, to imagine with her the exciting new adventures awaiting her as she grows up. It is a chance to look back as well, to remind your child of the wonderful things God has blessed her with during the past year. It is a chance to tell your child again that God loves her and has a unique plan for her life. It is a chance to offer a prayer of thanksgiving for God's continued guidance, love, and protection. Birthdays offer an opportunity to slip your child's name into Jeremiah 29:11–12 and offer a prayer such as this: "Dear God, thank you for the special plans you have made for my sweet [Natalie]. Help her to always understand your plans are for her well-being, designed to keep her from harm. Your plans offer [Natalie] a hope and a future. Thank you, Lord, because [Natalie] can always call upon you at any time in her life, and you will listen to her and answer her prayers."

Learn to view your children's birthdays as an opportunity to meet their basic needs in creative, memorable ways. Celebrate by saying, "I love you, you are special to me," in several different ways. At the close of his or her special day, every child should know without a doubt that he or she is a unique creation, truly special, and dearly loved.

Chapter Two

Ways to Celebrate

i'm glad there are
So many ways
To celebrate your special day.

As he awakened, the first thought flitting through his brain was, *I'm five today! A whole handful!* He bounced up in bed, eyes wide open, looking for the brightly decorated gift bag he knew would be at the foot of his bed. Grabbing the bag, he raced into his mommy's room and tugged at her pillow. With an excited whisper he asked, "Are you awake? Can I open it now?" His mommy was expecting him. With a smile she said, "Happy birthday, buddy. Go ahead, open your gift." Throwing the sparkly tissue aside, he pulled out a pair of khaki pants with huge cargo pockets and zippers that transformed the pants into shorts. His arms wrapped around his mommy's neck as he whispered into her ear, "Thank you, Mommy, I really wanted pants like these!" Delighted to feel his little face so close to her own, his mommy whispered, "I know."

LEAVING A GIFT BAG with new clothes on the birthday person's bed is a favorite tradition at my house. It is one of the ways I say, "I'm happy it's your birthday," to my children. I try to pick something extra special, something they've really wanted that I might not normally buy, to welcome in their special day. My children eagerly anticipate their new clothes, knowing I have put special thought into our early morning birthday ritual. During the weeks preceding their birthdays, I enjoy turning into a fashion sleuth as I solve the mystery of what they would like to wear most of all. I have to confess I've often uncovered evidence that my child is growing up during my sleuthing. No longer does my little boy want a shirt with a fire engine or a big yellow bird. Now he wants pants like the cool big guys wear! My little lady is no longer interested in a dress with lace. She now prefers jeans with frayed edges and patches! As my girls hit the preteen years, I began letting them accompany me on my fashion mission. They now value our shopping time as well as their early morning "surprise."

As I mentioned in the previous chapter, when I was a new mom I thought a child needed to have a big party to feel truly special on his birthday. Over the years, I've learned there are many ways to say, "I'm glad that it's your special day. You are God's special gift to me." Sometimes it involves a tradition, like the giving of new birthday clothes each year, but just as often it might be something unique you do just one time. While I still love to give birthday parties, I've discovered that there are other ways birthdays can be celebrated that will also leave a positive, permanent imprint on a child's life.

Before deciding how to say I love you, it's important to think about your child. What would he enjoy the most? Which of his needs most need to be met on this special day? It's also important to think about yourself. Some moms (I include myself in this category) struggle with the fear that if we don't do everything possible for our child, we will ruin his life forever. For instance, I have a beautiful memory album for each of my children, and I take pictures and save mementos of their special events—but the albums and the picture and mementos have yet to meet! I can't tell you how many times I've raked myself over the coals for my failure to provide my children with these special books. Fortunately, I have friends who remind me of the other things I do for and with my children. (I also remind myself that my own mother made me a memory book when I was in my thirties, which gives me hope that someday my children's books will get done!)

Please don't think that just because an idea is mentioned in this chapter, you need to use it for your child. Pick the idea or ideas that work best in your situation and leave the others for another birthday (or another mother!). Avoid the trap of turning your child's birthday into one giant mommy to-do list.

Create a Memory Book or Photo Album

Although I am indeed "memory-book challenged," I would be the first to say a memory book or photo album offers several wonderful opportunities to celebrate a birthday. Two of my children are adopted, and to celebrate the adoption of my daughter, I created a little memory book for her. It's a simple little album, but I included pictures of her birth mother and sister, a picture of the three of them together, and pictures of some of the other special people in her life. The last picture is the family picture, taken outside the court building immediately following her adoption. I included some captions for the pictures, and wrote down some of her favorite things. My daughter, who was almost five on her adoption day, helped me add special stickers to decorate the pages. This little album is among her favorite possessions. It

Warning

Fulfilling all of the following birthday suggestions will lead to a stressed-out mommy and tearful birthday child! Please, choose carefully and prayerfully.

gives her a sense of who she is, where she belongs, and the reminder she is loved by not one, but two mommies. Her little memory book is worth every minute of effort I put into it. Many mothers create special birthday pages in their child's album; some even create entire albums dedicated to birthday celebrations. These pages offer a creative way to document the growth, interests, friendships, and activities of the child. Through the pages of these books a child gets a sense of who he is and what has happened during his life. A child's album might be displayed in a prominent place in the home during the birthday week, allowing plenty of opportunities to explore the pages together. Time might be devoted to working on new memory pages together, recording the people, places, and things important to your child at this stage in his life.

Take Birthday Pictures

Whether you work on a memory book or not, it is fun to use a birthday as a reminder to take pictures of your child. This might be a professionally photographed image or just pictures you snap yourself. Many families have a hallway gallery where these pictures are displayed, or a special frame that holds the most current picture of the child. Children love to see how much they've grown up in the past year. Digital photography and computer scanners now offer new and exciting ways to display pictures. Consider creating a birthday collage your child could hang in his room or send electronically to Grandma. Some children even have their own webpages. Please give careful consideration to the content of a webpage. Safeguard your child by not giving out any contact information, or use a password for admittance to the webpage so only those you invite can view your child's pictures and information.

Create a "How You've Grown" Poster

At my children's school some of the teachers celebrate a child's birthday by making them "Star of the Week." When her child is so honored, mothers are asked to create a poster about the child. It's been fun to sit down with my children and go through their pictures together, choosing which ones to include on the poster. Together we look through magazines or newspaper ads for pictures of their favorite things. We choose stickers, colored paper, or special artwork to decorate the poster. After the child shares the poster at school, you could put it up in the child's room, preserve it with other special items, or take a photo before dismantling it.

Measure Your Child's Growth

Purchase or make a growth chart for your child, or utilize a doorway molding to keep a permanent record of your child's growth. In our previous house I used the doorway to my sewing room for this purpose. Kids love to be measured, and it is fun to see just how much they've grown since their last birthday and how they compare to their siblings and parents. (If you have a record of your own growth or your husband's, consider marking these on the wall as well.) Be sure to put the date and child's name next to the mark. If you move or decide to paint, take a long strip of paper, tape it to the wall next to the growth marks, and copy the information. Reverse the procedure in your new home or after the molding is repainted.

Make Handprints and Footprints

Another way to document your child's size at a particular age is to make an imprint of his hand or foot. Clay is a popular medium, with several kits available at craft and toy stores. When my children were small, I coated their hands with acrylic paints and pressed them onto a matte board. I framed these to hang on the wall with their baby pictures. An inexpensive white tablecloth can also be used to preserve your child's handprint or footprint. Coat your child's hand with fabric paint, then press it onto the tablecloth. Write the date next to the print. If your child is old enough to write, let him use a fabric pen or Sharpie marker to "sign" the print. If you hang a framed handprint or footprint, be prepared to take it down occasionally, as your child will want to see how much he's grown.

Making a handprint or footprint of a child under the age of three can be challenging! Here are some hints to make your project a success.

1. Have all supplies out and within reach before starting.
2. Prepare a sink of warm water and have paper towels ready for cleanup.
3. Enlist an assistant to hold your child while you paint his hand.
4. Dress mommy, child, and assistant in old clothes.
5. Use your index finger to paint the hand rather than using a brush.
6. Spread the fingers of the child's hand apart right before pressing onto fabric or matte board. Gently roll each finger back and forth for a more complete imprint.
7. Press gently on each individual toe and roll the foot slightly to get a complete footprint.

Some children are sensitive to the feel of paint on their hands and feet, especially if the paint is cold. Try rubbing the paint bottle between the palms of your hands to warm it. If your child seems frightened or distressed, save this project until he is a little older.

Record Your Child's Voice

Not only do your child's hands and feet change, her voice changes as well. Purchase a high quality blank cassette tape. Record your child singing or talking. Be sure to clearly label the tape and keep it with your child's baby book so you don't accidentally tape over the precious sounds.

Select a Special Birthday Meal

Make your child's birthday special by allowing her to select the menu for one or all of the meals on her birthday. It's important to respect your child's choices, but you may have to meet her need for guidance by helping her choose some foods from the different food groups. If the birthday girl picks pizza, corn nuts, and chocolate cake for dinner, consider agreeing to those items while giving her the option of choosing between carrot sticks or green beans to build up her muscles. If you can, bring your child along to the grocery store when you purchase the supplies for the meal. Also, encourage your child to help you prepare the food. The birthday child could spread the pizza sauce, sprinkle the cheese, or place pepperoni slices on the pizza. As your children mature, celebrate their growing independence by letting them prepare more and more of their birthday meals.

A variation on having your child choose the food for her birthday meal is to let her choose a favorite restaurant. My middle daughter's birthday falls in the middle of December, a difficult month to schedule birthday activities. Last year, her birthday fell on a Wednesday night, an evening when my three younger children needed to be at church for a Christmas play rehearsal. To make her birthday special I asked her to pick a place to eat her birthday dinner. On her birthday night, I packed up a store bought cake, candles, decorated napkins and plates, her birthday cards and gifts, and, of course, my camera. The waiters made a big fuss over her (one even came up with a lighter to light the birthday candles, as I had forgotten matches!), sang an enthusiastic rendition of the birthday song, and oohed and aahed over her birthday gifts. The evening was such a success that my youngest daughter, whose birthday falls one month later, asked for a repeat performance!

One final variation on birthday meals is for the birthday child to have a special meal with Grandma and Grandpa during his birthday month. Several years ago, my parents began taking the birthday grandchild out for a meal alone with them. They ask the birthday grandchild where she would like to go, often offering several suggestions. Together my parents and the birthday grandchild have enjoyed pancake houses, hilltop restaurants with valet service, and just about everything in between. My children look forward to this special date with their grandparents, and I am thankful for the strong bonds and memories being created during each cross-generational meal.

Consider a Birthday Clothes Tradition

If you'd like to share my family's tradition of new birthday clothes, put on your detective hat and figure out what your child would really like. Younger children often like clothes that reflect a current interest. When my daughter was one, I painted her a teddy bear T-shirt. When my son was two, I purchased a shirt with a Tonka truck on the front. All three of my girls wore the lace and pearl trimmed lavender T-shirt and leggings I purchased for my oldest daughter's third birthday. Part of what makes the new clothes tradition fun at my house is the way the clothes are presented. They lay waiting in the morning on the birthday child's bed. The ritual of waking up to the clothes is as important as the gift itself!

For older children, a particular style or brand of clothing may be important. As your child grows older, you may want to make shopping together for the surprise part of the tradition. Taking increasing control over clothing choices is an important step toward independence. For a teen or preteen, sometimes just knowing your mother picked an item out is enough to make it unwearable!

Decorate for Your Child's Birthday

A fun way to celebrate your child's special day is to decorate her room or spot at the table. On the eve of her birthday, after your child goes to sleep, quietly sneak into her room and put up streamers, balloons, and a birthday banner in her favorite colors. Or wrap streamers around her chair at the table, tying balloons at the corners. Hang a banner on a wall by the table that says "Happy Birthday, Susie!" Your child will be delighted with this special attention. This is an idea best saved until your child is at least two years old. A baby might be frightened by the sudden change. Also, be sure balloons and streamers are firmly attached so they don't become choking hazards to a younger child.

Write a Birthday Letter

Writing a birthday letter to your child, sharing your special insights about his life, is a birthday gift your child will surely treasure. A letter provides a permanent record for your child of what you love about him, how he's grown, or where you see him going in the next year. My husband had written birthday letters a few times, but I'd never tried it until this past year. I wrote the following letter on my youngest daughter's tenth birthday, and presented it to her right before the close of her special day. As you may know or remember, ten is an awkward age for a girl. Her body and mind are just beginning to change into their womanly forms, yet the girl is still in most ways a child. My daughter was going through a particularly awkward phase and my letter meant a great deal to her. Upon finding out about Dani's birthday letter, both of her sisters cried, "No fair!" and extracted my solemn promise to write them letters on their next birthdays. I guess birthday letters are now an official birthday tradition at my house! With her permission, I am sharing Dani's letter with you, hoping it inspires you to consider writing a birthday letter to your own child.

> *Dearest Danielle,*
>
> *Happy birthday, honey. Ten years old today. I can hardly believe it's true. What a blessed gift you have been to me this past decade. From the very first moment I looked into your shining eyes, I knew God had created someone very special.*
>
> *Last June, when I learned you had been selected by your teacher to receive the Christian citizenship award, I was so proud. Not only because you were receiving an award but because of the reasons your teacher gave for selecting you. She said you always seem to be thinking of others, trying to make their lives a little better. Your generous spirit made you willing to share what you had with someone else who needed it. (You also now know that should not include test answers!)*
>
> *Dani, you're not just generous but also funny, creative, and hardworking. I think of how hard you worked last summer to learn how to dive in the pool and the way you'll practice a piece of music (the ones you like) over and over until it sounds just right.*
>
> *Honey, this year my prayer for you comes from Luke 6:46–48. I pray this year you will not only hear and read God's Word, but put it into practice in your life. When you do this, you are digging a deep foundation for your life, carving it into all God's promises. I pray you will dig such a deep foundation that nothing can ever destroy your faith in God. No matter what life has in store for you, your "house" will be unshakable!*
>
> *Precious Danielle, wherever you go, whatever you do, I will always love you.*
>
> *Love, hugs, and kisses,*
> *Mom*

Select a Scripture Verse for the Year

Each year, your child grows not only physically and mentally, but also spiritually. The Bible contains many beautiful words of affirmation, security, wisdom, guidance, and hope. One way to hide these words in your child's heart is to select a special verse each year for your child. You and your child can memorize, study, and put into practice the birthday verse throughout the entire year. The verse can be printed or handwritten on a decorative piece of paper, then framed and placed in the child's room so it is constantly in sight. The verse could be included in a birthday letter to your child or written in the child's memory book.

Deuteronomy 6:6–9 instructs parents, "These commandments that I give you today are to be upon your hearts. Impress them on your children. Talk about them when you sit at home and when you walk along the road, when you lie down and when you get up. Tie them as symbols on your hands and bind them on your foreheads. Write them on the doorframes of your houses and on your gates." Proverbs 6:22–23 offers this promise to children who know God's Word, "When you walk, they will guide you; when you sleep, they will watch over you; when you awake, they will speak to you. For these commands are a lamp, this teaching is a light, and the corrections of discipline are the way to life." It is important to share God's Word with our children every day, but a birthday offers an opportunity to make a specific verse apply in an intimate, personal way.

Write or Record Your Child's Birthday Story

Children love to hear stories about themselves. An interesting birthday activity is to have your child dictate

Suggested Prayer Verses

Consider the following Scriptures when choosing a Bible verse to pray for your child. A Bible concordance can help you find other verses on specific topics you would like to pray for your child.

A Strong Relationship with God
Proverbs 3:5–6
Mark 12:30
Ephesians 3:16–19
Philippians 2:16–18
Colossians 2:6–7

Godly Attributes
Psalm 19:14
Proverbs 3:1–4
Romans 12:2
Galatians 5:22–23
Philippians 4:8
1 Peter 1:5–7

Wisdom
Proverbs 2:10–12

The Future
Jeremiah 29:11–12

Protection
Psalm 23
Psalm 91:11–16

Relationships
Ephesians 4:32
Philippians 2:4

Blessings
Numbers 6:24–26
Philippians 4:7

her birthday story to you. (When she gets older, she can write the story herself.) Your child's story could include all the things she liked and disliked about being a certain age, what she thinks her life will be like in the coming year, a description of her favorite person, or a record of what she did on her birthday. If your child is a storyteller, you might want to have her tell you an imaginative story. Consider having your child illustrate her story as well. Put a construction paper "cover" around the story to make it look like a real book. Another option is to record your child's story on a blank cassette tape. As mentioned earlier, be sure to clearly label the tape and put it in a safe place so you don't inadvertently tape over your child's voice.

Crown the Birthday Child King or Queen for a Day

At one time or another, I think we all wish to be queen or king for at least one day. A fun way to celebrate a child's birthday is to make her queen (or king if a boy) for the day. The queen might start her day off with a birthday crown and special robe. She is asked what she desires to eat and drink. Other family members do her regular chores for her. The queen may choose the activities she would like the family to participate in (within reasonable limits, of course). If the queen wants to spend the morning playing Candyland, the entire family plays Candyland. If she wants to ride bikes at the park, the family rides bikes in the park. Should the queen desire pancakes for dinner, pancakes will indeed be served. If this sounds like something you'd enjoy, make sure your child knows Mommy also wants a chance to be queen on her birthday too!

Provide a Child-Centered Activity or Outing

As a busy mom of four, I've discovered the lyrics to that old Jim Croce tune ring all too true: "There never seems to be enough time to do the things you want to do once you find them." I love spending time one-on-one with my children, but music lessons, doctor appointments, piles of laundry, and needy siblings make one-on-one time an infrequent luxury. Before my older two girls hit adolescence, I used their birthdays as a time to get away, just mother and daughter, for a "growing up" weekend. Both girls selected San Diego as our destination. I booked rooms at a nice, but not too expensive, hotel near the water. Over a period of three days we listened to Dr. Dobson's "Preparing for Adolescence" tapes and explored the concept of becoming a teenager.

I asked the birthday girl what she would like to do and where she would like to eat during our weekend trip. Between tapes, we shopped, had our nails done, went to the movies, had makeovers, rode the ferry, and went bike riding. One of the best parts about these weekends away was the opportunity for uninterrupted conversation and play.

While going away and staying in a hotel was a wonderful experience, spending two or three uninterrupted hours with your birthday child doing something he loves can also provide wonderful birthday memories. If airplanes fascinate your child, park near an airport and watch the planes take off and land. If you ask at one of the boarding desks, you might even be able to get a little pair of wings. A child who loves to engage in pretend play might enjoy seeing a children's play performed. I've included an idea list of things to do with your child, but remember, it is best to choose the activity or outing that matches your child's current interests. Whether one-on-one or with the entire family, a thoughtfully chosen activity or outing can be an exciting way to celebrate your child's special day.

Fun Things to Do on a Birthday

- *Visit a petting zoo*
- *Ride a train or bus*
- *Play at the beach*
- *Paint ceramics*
- *Go skating*
- *Take a hike*
- *Go camping*
- *Attend a children's production*
- *Visit a children's museum*
- *Fly kites at a park*
- *Go to an amusement park*
- *Play miniature golf*
- *Work on a puzzle*
- *Build a fort in the living room*
- *Run in the sprinklers*
- *Attend a sporting event*
- *Make homemade ice cream*
- *Go for a boat ride*
- *Work on an art project*
- *Plant a tree or some flowers*
- *Go fishing*
- *Visit Grandma and Grandpa*
- *Have a tea party*
- *Film a "this is your life" video*
- *Visit a dude ranch*
- *Go on a bug hunt*
- *Pitch a tent in the backyard*
- *Arrange a fire station tour*

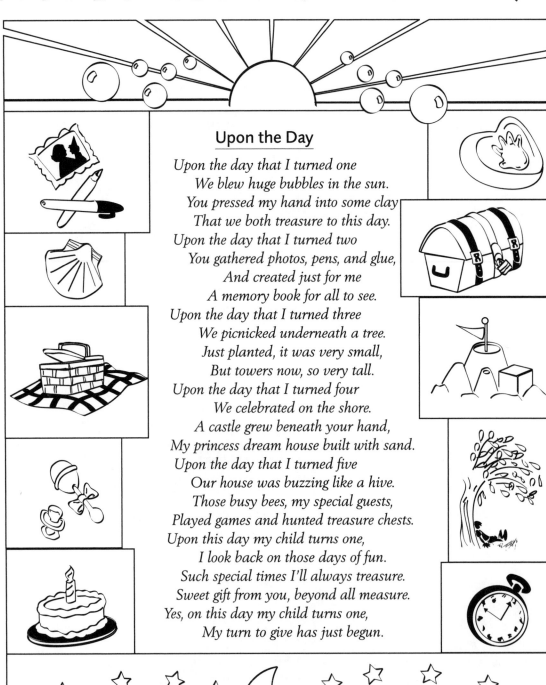

Upon the Day

Upon the day that I turned one
  We blew huge bubbles in the sun.
  You pressed my hand into some clay
  That we both treasure to this day.
Upon the day that I turned two
  You gathered photos, pens, and glue,
    And created just for me
  A memory book for all to see.
Upon the day that I turned three
  We picnicked underneath a tree.
  Just planted, it was very small,
    But towers now, so very tall.
Upon the day that I turned four
  We celebrated on the shore.
  A castle grew beneath your hand,
My princess dream house built with sand.
Upon the day that I turned five
  Our house was buzzing like a hive.
  Those busy bees, my special guests,
Played games and hunted treasure chests.
Upon this day my child turns one,
  I look back on those days of fun.
  Such special times I'll always treasure.
  Sweet gift from you, beyond all measure.
Yes, on this day my child turns one,
  My turn to give has just begun.

Chapter Three

Let's Plan a Family Party

The table's set,
The gang's all here,
Time for some family birthday cheer!

"All right, Gardiner gang, it's Candle Compliments time. Allison's celebrating five glorious years, so we each get a candle this time. We'll go around the table, starting with Daniel. Share a nice thing about Allison and then put your candle on the cake."

"I like that Allison can read me stories now," lisped little Danny.

"I'm proud of how Allison has made so many new friends in preschool this year," Mommy said with a warm smile.

"It's cool how well Allison can ride her bike—no training wheels!" chimed in big brother, Chris.

Grandma added, "Allison, I appreciate how you've patiently learned so many new Bible verses with me this year."

"And Allison, I'm proud of the way you've taken care of Pup, feeding and walking him every day," Dad said, completing the circle of compliments. He added, "Okay, everybody, all together now as I light these candles."

As the candles blazed, the family cheered, "Allison, you really light up our life!"

TAKE A FEW MINUTES to grab a cake and a package of candles and you'll have the basic ingredients for a family birthday celebration. Take a bit more time to plan a favorite meal, add some birthday table talk and a special activity, and you'll have a cherished family memory. Family birthday celebrations are a tradition for many families. They provide a string of memories that tie family members together. Family birthday celebrations are usually intimate times of conversation, laughter, gift giving, and looking back over a child's life. Sometimes the family party guest list includes only the immediate family, and sometimes extended family members, grandparents, aunts, and uncles are present. (If hosting your extended family is more like hosting New Year's Eve in Time Square than an intimate gathering, you might want to consider incorporating some of the planning ideas in chapter 4.) Intimate family birthday parties strengthen family ties, provide family memories, cultivate a child's sense of identity and belonging, and offer an opportunity for family-oriented fun.

Come Up with a Plan

Even when planning a simple family birthday party, there are a myriad of small decisions to be made and usually a number of things needed from the store. A family party planning sheet and a shopping list are provided in the appendix to help busy mothers keep track of everything with minimal stress. Planning a family birthday celebration a week or two in advance leaves plenty of time to organize and complete the details without too much frustration. Use the timeline in the appendix as a guideline for planning your family celebration.

Focus on Favorites

Birthdays are a wonderful opportunity to focus on some of a child's favorites. Make a quick list of the things your child likes best; include favorite foods, songs, games, hobbies, and activities. Consider choosing one of your child's favorites as the theme of his party. If your child is old enough to participate, be sure and include him in this planning session. Choosing a theme will give the party a focus, making it easier to plan and create with pizzazz. Sometimes simply Rosie's Second Birthday (slip in your child's name and age) is the best party theme. Once a theme is chosen, consider how to fit in some of the child's other favorites. For instance, if your child loves cowboys, pizza, and Legos, a cowboy party theme might be a good choice. Serve Wagon Wheel Pizza, and have the family join together to build a ranch house and corral out of Legos. Family members could dress for the party in jeans, bandannas, and cowboy hats. And if the child has cowboy playthings, use them to create a great centerpiece.

Carry On Traditions

A child's first few birthdays provide an opportunity to establish a family birthday tradition or two. Talk to your mother, mother-in-law, or older family member to ascertain any traditions already established in the extended family. Take a walk back through time (why not include Daddy in this activity) and reminisce on those birthday traditions that were most meaningful to each of you as a child. Pick out one or two activities to become a traditional part of your family's birthday festivities. (The activities in chapter 2 may provide some useful ideas.) A tradition might be as simple as the Candle Compliments that started out this chapter, or as elaborate as taking a trip together. Keep in mind that if you have more than one child, you'll be repeating these traditions several times in the same year, maybe even several times in the same month.

> *"Times have changed and we can probably count on their continuing to change. So it's up to us to seek out the little pieces of life that will become our children's memories."*
> —Sylvia Harney, Every Time I Go Home, I Break Out in Relatives

Create a Festive Environment

Decorations

Creating a festive birthday environment in your home helps to distinguish a child's birthday from every other day of the year. Party decorations provide the visual aspect of the birthday environment. Decorations can include either items found around the house, items created by you or your child, or items purchased from a party, discount, or toy store.

Once you've established a theme, take some time to meander through your house, looking for items that could be used as party decorations. Chances are, if you've picked a theme from your child's current interests, there will be several useful items available. Also consider what you might be able to borrow from a friend or relative. For instance, if you've selected an ocean theme, an aquarium, a pop-up book about ocean creatures, a stuffed shark, and a pair of goggles or fins would add to the party atmosphere. Note all the items discovered on the party planning sheet.

Next, think about decorations you and your child could create. For an ocean theme, for instance, a length of butcher paper or a light blue paper tablecloth could be the backdrop for an under-the-sea mural. Construction paper fish could be painted with glitter glue to create sparkling sea creatures. Note what you'd like to create and make a list of any needed craft supplies on your planning sheet.

Finally, you might choose to purchase decorations. Party stores, craft stores, discount stores, and toy stores usually carry a large assortment of streamers, balloons, and theme decorations. Affordable decorations and party supplies are also available on-line. (See the appendix for resources.) Decide on a budget before you shop. Purchased party decorations can add up fast! However, simple streamers and balloons, used creatively, can be inexpensive. For an ocean theme, green and blue streamers could be transformed into seaweed and ocean waves, while clear round balloons might be bubbles floating to the surface. Make a note of any decorations to purchase on your shopping list.

The Food Table

Another important part of the party environment is the table where the food is served. Use a plain white tablecloth or a purchased theme tablecloth for your background. A package of party napkins on top of everyday dishes transform any table setting inexpensively, or, if party napkins for your theme aren't available, purchase plain napkins and stickers and let your child decorate them. A few of the theme items found around the house or the decorated birthday cake will provide an inviting centerpiece. Some families purchase or make a special plate for the birthday person to use; others choose to decorate the birthday child's chair with streamers and balloons.

Auditory Additions

A visually festive environment can be enhanced by auditory stimulation. Giggles, chuckles, guffaws, and big belly laughs are perhaps the best forms of auditory enhancement! Theme related music or music from the birthday child's favorite tape or CD will also add to the festivities. Perhaps the greatest impact in the auditory department, however, will come from the words spoken throughout the birthday celebration. Conversation centered on the growth and accomplishments of the birthday child is a welcome addition to any family birthday celebration. Here are a few ideas to consider:

- *Peak and Pit*. Ask the birthday child to describe the best (peak) and the worst (pit) thing that happened to them in the past year.
- *Special Object*. Ask each family member to bring one item to the table that describes the birthday child and explain why the item was chosen.
- *"You Are Special" Notes*. Ask each family member to write a note (younger family members can dictate this to mom or dad) telling something special about the birthday child. Read each note aloud.
- *Birthday Blessings*. Ask each family member to think of a way they would like the birthday child to be blessed in the coming year. Pray these blessings for the birthday child.
- *Focus on the Future*. Ask each family member to predict what they think the birthday child will be doing in twenty years and why. Write predictions down for the baby book or put into the child's scrapbook.
- *How You've Grown*. Place a picture of the birthday child on a blank piece of paper (scrapbook or poster size). Brainstorm all the ways the birthday child has matured since her last birthday and write them all around the picture.
- *A Verse to Grow On*. Select an annual birthday Bible verse. Share why this verse was selected and pray this verse for your child.

Choose the Menu

Food plays an important role in a family birthday celebration. At my house, the birthday child chooses the menu for her birthday party meal. As discussed in chapter 2, sometimes Mommy has to give nutritional guidance to help the child select a well-balanced (or at least semibalanced) menu. Most children choose foods that are familiar. Renaming a familiar dish to go along with the birthday theme can add to the fun. For example, spaghetti and meatballs might be renamed "buried treasure" to enhance an ocean theme. Add a side dish of goldfish crackers for a touch of whimsy. Jell-O is a versatile and often requested side dish from younger children. A single serving of purple Jell-O could become a jellyfish, and blue Jell-O, combined with fresh fruit in a tall cup, becomes an ocean scene. Jell-O jigglers, those firm, wiggly pieces of Jell-O, can be cut into just about any imaginable shape, including the letters in a child's name or their initials. For recipes, go to www.kraftfoods.com/jello. Involving your child in food preparation can be as much fun as eating the food. Children are always proud to say, "And I made the . . ."

For many children, the birthday cake is the highlight of the meal. Cakes can be made at home or purchased from the grocery store, a bakery, or an ice cream shop. After you decide whether to bake or purchase the birthday cake, consult the birthday child to discern what flavor of cake she desires and write this information on the planning sheet. For most of us, a child's birthday is not the time to try an innovative new cake recipe. Stick with a tried and true recipe (or a cake mix) for best results. If baking and decorating the cake at home, list the needed ingredients and decorating supplies on your shopping list. (More ideas for decorating cakes are given in chapter 5.) When purchasing a cake, write down the phone number, order number, and date ordered, pick-up time, cost, and required form of payment on your shopping list. Call two or three hours before pick-up time to ensure the cake will be ready as promised. Remember, cakes cannot be kept in the car for long, and some cakes must be stored in the refrigerator, or in the case of an ice cream cake, in the freezer, until serving time.

Have Fun as a Family

A family birthday celebration is clearly an opportunity for fun. The specially planned food, festive decorations, warm conversation, and rousing rendition of the birthday song are all parts of the fun. And what child doesn't have fun opening a few gifts! Some families like to extend party fun by playing a few games or enjoying an activity together. The birthday child can again exercise her decision-making skills by choosing the activity. For the very young, peekaboo or finger games are fun. Older children enjoy games like Hide and Seek or Simon Says. (Many of the games in chapter 7 can be adapted for family playtime.) A favorite game or sport could also be incorporated. The creative birthday child might want to organize and perform a dance or play. Another idea for family fun is to pull out family pictures, videos, or movies of the birthday child. Children enjoy seeing what they looked like as an infant or toddler. Whether you choose to play a game, make a home movie, or do an art project together, be sure to write down all the supplies you will need on your planning sheet.

Make Time for December Birthdays

Finding time to celebrate a December birthday in a meaningful way is challenging for most families. The calendar is full, the wallet is thin, and the days between Thanksgiving and New Year's move past at the speed of light. Some families successfully meet this challenge by celebrating the child's birthday early or late in the month. Others move the celebration to another month altogether, possibly six months later on the half birthday. For me, this was not a satisfactory solution. I feared moving the birthday celebration would send my daughter the message that holiday activities were more important than celebrating her special day. With some creative time management, advance planning, saying no to certain holiday happenings, and at times, burning the midnight oil, each December my family has been able to give my daughter Natalie the gift of a family celebration on her actual birthday. Many years she has also celebrated her birthday with a party for her friends. Natalie and I usually start planning the party early in November, setting aside a date and time early in December for the party.

Cross-Generational Activities

Here are some activities to enjoy with the extended family:

- Puzzles
- Bingo
- Charades. *Try animals for very young children and allow them to make the sounds of the animals.*
- Clap, Snap, Concentration. *In case you've forgotten, the rhyme for this classic game is, "Concentration now begins. Keep the rhythm, keep the beat."*
- Dominos *(use several sets for larger groups)*
- Family Photo Concentration. *Make copies of fifteen to twenty family snapshots. Shuffle the photos, and then lay them face down. Players take turns finding the matches. Players get to keep any matches found.*
- Hangman
- Hunts. *Hide pennies, plastic eggs, birthday candles, or a unique (unbreakable) family artifact. Children enjoy hiding things almost as much as they enjoy hunting for them!*
- Name That Tune
- Pictionary
- Simple Board Games
- Telephone. *The first player whispers something about the birthday person to the player on the right. Players continue to whisper the message, one by one, around the table. The last person to receive the message says it aloud.*
- To Tell the Truth. *A family member makes two statements, one true and the other false. The rest of the family must guess which one is true.*

Involve Siblings

While the birthday child basks in all the individual attention and new gifts, siblings sometimes sense they are being left out, or become jealous of the attention the birthday child is receiving. Children have been known to "act out" to regain the attention of the family. Parents can do a variety of things to involve siblings without taking the spotlight off the birthday child. One of the best ways to help a sibling who is feeling left out is to involve him in party preparations. Ask the sibling to create a special birthday decoration, prepare a special birthday song, or organize a game or activity. Take siblings on a shopping trip to select a gift for the birthday child. Remind siblings of their own birthday celebrations. Show pictures or videos of their birthday parties. Take out a favorite toy the sibling received on his birthday and talk about how fun it was when he received the special surprise. My children all experienced some of these feelings when they were young, but by the time they were six or seven years old, each had enough positive memories of past birthdays and enough experience in sharing siblings' birthdays that there were no longer any problems. As a matter of fact, they often eagerly anticipate each other's birthday festivities.

Make Memories with Multiples

In some families, two or more wonderfully unique individuals share a common birthday. Celebrating the life of each child in a multiple set adds to the excitement of the day, but also presents a few challenges. Several twins and mothers of twins shared with me how they make these birthdays special for each child. I was amazed at both the similarity and wisdom of their responses. One idea woven throughout each response was the importance of celebrating the life of each individual child. It may take some extra effort, but endeavor to consider the needs of each individual child when planning a birthday celebration for multiples.

Most parents of multiples celebrate their birthdays with one party. There are several advantages to doing this. Obviously, it is easier to plan one celebration than two or more. As one mother said, "One party, one theme, one mess!" The first two or three years, it is fairly easy to plan a celebration that pleases each child. Usually at this age, multiples have similar interests and friends. However, as children reach their preteen years, they begin to enjoy different people, interests, and ideas.

At this age, multiples may desire to celebrate independently. Don't be surprised if the decision on how to celebrate varies from year to year. Listen to your children and endeavor to accommodate their wishes.

The following is a compilation of advice from twins and their mothers.

- During the early years, multiples enjoy celebrating birthdays with a common party or celebration, incorporating the favorites of each child.
- Give each child an individual "cake and candle" moment. Present the cake or cupcake, light the candles, and sing the birthday song to each child individually.
- Bakeries can provide cakes that are two different flavors. Some families purchase one large cake along with a small cake or cupcake for each birthday child.
- Explore birthday celebration wishes with each multiple. Spend time discovering what is important to each child, then discuss the celebration ideas together and come up with a party plan. Consider using two themes, the favorite colors of each child, and a combination of favorite foods.
- Multiples' birthday celebrations are often bigger and more elaborate than others. Be careful to limit the number of guests and keep plans manageable. One mother shared that her twin's first birthday celebration included fifty family members in a two-bedroom apartment. This is not an experience she recommends to other mothers of multiples!
- Begin planning well ahead of the birthday. It takes time to get input from each child, reach an agreement on how to celebrate, and plan either a joint celebration or two separate celebrations.
- Multiples of different genders are more likely to need or desire separate celebrations.
- If it seems important to the multiples to have separate celebrations, consider celebrating one birthday the day before the actual date and one the day after (back-to-back weekends are another option). Plan a few special surprises for the children on the actual day as well.
- When inviting guests, allow each multiple to invite the same number of friends, choose the same number of games, and select the same number of snacks. Keeping things fair is very important to children!

- When planning separate celebrations, remind children that guests outside of the immediate family may not be able to come to both parties. This is because of scheduling conflicts, not because the guest loves one child more than the other.
- As gifts from the same source are often duplicates, arrange for the multiples to open them at the same time. If possible, without sounding rude, request that the multiples receive separate gifts. Other families choose to have their multiples open gifts at different times during the celebration.
- Try to choose at least one unique gift for each child. A few identical gifts can be fun, but multiples don't want to share everything!
- Take photos of the children individually as well as together.
- When celebrating the birthday of multiples, remember to consider each child as a unique individual creation. Spend one-on-one time with each child, reviewing the events of the past year and dreaming together of the future.

Chapter Four

Let's Plan a Birthday Party

Munchies, and favors, and games, oh my, Best keep my party plans close by!

Riley's four-year-old eyes peered over the edge of the counter as he watched his pirate party supplies move across the store's scanner. "Blip, blip, blip," the scanner recorded each item for Riley's party.

"Mommy, how do you know we got everything we need for my party?"

Riley's mommy shifted his baby sister to her other hip and brought her shopping list down to Riley's eye level. "See Riley, as we planned your party, I wrote everything we would need down on this list. Cake supplies are here, decorations are over here, and right here I wrote down all the supplies we'd need for the games and prizes. That way, when your friends come over, we'll have everything we need for a great pirate party."

"That's a great idea! You're the smartest mommy in the whole wide world and this is going to be the bestest party ever!" exclaimed Riley.

PLANNING A BIRTHDAY PARTY, complete with youthful guests, yummy food, amusing games, imaginative activities, and fabulous favors is a delightful way to celebrate a child's birthday. But planning a birthday party can be intimidating. All those little details to see to, and, more often than not, only fragments of time found throughout a busy day available for party planning. In order to prevent the myriad of details involved in hosting a birthday party from overwhelming the entire family, it is important to develop a party plan that keeps all the details in order and provides a map for accomplishing them. A few busy moms will be able to do this in their heads, but most of us need to write our ideas, plans, and supplies on paper to keep all the details straight. To assist you in maintaining order as you plan, prepare, and host your child's birthday party, a party planning sheet, shopping list, and safety checklist are included in the appendix. These may be copied for your personal use. By utilizing the planning sheets and the information in the following chapters, even the busiest mom can confidently host a successful, fun-filled birthday party for her child.

How Often Should I Host a Major Party for My Child?

There is no hard-and-fast rule as to how often to host a major birthday party for a child; each family must determine what works best for them. Some families host a major party every year, others prefer to celebrate as a family or with one or two close friends. Here are some other common alternatives:

- *Host a major party every other year.*
- *Host a major party for the first, fifth, tenth, thirteenth, and eighteenth years.*
- *Host a major party those years it best meets the family and child's needs.*
- *Host a major party every other year and plan a birthday activity with one or two close friends the alternate years.*

Decide on a Realistic Budget

An entertaining party can be accomplished with almost any budget. Keep in mind that the purpose of a birthday party is to create an opportunity for your child and her friends to have fun together, not to impress other moms with your decorating talents or culinary abilities. Forget about what everyone else has done at birthday parties (unless it's a great idea you want to borrow) and focus on planning a party your child will enjoy.

Even the simplest parties cost money, and a huge party with all the trimmings can cost a bundle, but both simple and extravagant parties can be memorable and fun. Decide how much you can afford to spend, and plan accordingly. Use the three sample budgets to assist you in setting your own birthday party budget.

Sample Budgets

Party 1 (8 guests)

Invitations/thank-you cards/stamps	$9.00
Food	
Kool-aid	$2.00
Homemade cake/ice cream	$6.00
Decorations	
6 helium balloons/streamers/handmade poster	$7.00
Paper goods	
White plates/cups/birthday napkins	$6.00
Games and prizes	
Small prizes for 2 games	$4.00
Treasure for hunt	$4.00
Party favors	$8.00
Film/batteries/developing	<u>$10.00</u>
Total cost	**$56.00**

Party 2 (12 guests)

Invitations/thank-you cards/stamps	$16.00
Food	
Juice boxes	$ 6.00
Homemade cake/ice cream	$ 6.00
Sandwiches	$ 4.00
Vegetables/dip	$ 5.00
Decorations	
12 helium balloons/streamers/banner	$13.00
Paper goods	
Party lunch plates/cake plates/napkins/tablecloth	$20.00
Games and prizes	
Small prizes for 2 games	$ 5.00
Treasure for hunt	$ 8.00
Party favors	$12.00
Film/batteries/developing	<u>$10.00</u>
Total cost	**$105.00**

Party 3 (12 guests)

Invitations/thank-you notes/stamps/stickers	$18.00
Food	
Juice boxes	$ 6.00
Purchased ice cream cake	$25.00

Pizza	$24.00
Fruit kabobs	$ 5.00
Chips/dip	$ 6.00
Decorations	
Helium tank and 24 balloons	$25.00
Streamers/banner/centerpiece	$15.00
Paper goods	
Lunch plates/cake plates/tablecloth/plastic ware	$20.00
Games and prizes	
Small prizes for 3 games	$12.00
Treasure box/treasure	$20.00
Jump house	$80.00
Party favors	$24.00
Film/batteries/developing	$20.00
Total cost	**$300.00**

Name That Theme

Once you've settled on a budget, snuggle up with the birthday child and brainstorm possible birthday themes. A theme brings focus to all the elements of the party and generally makes planning easier. When celebrating baby's first birthday, parents get to choose the theme. Children turning two or three may need some suggestions to help make an appropriate decision. From the fourth birthday on, a child usually has decided opinions about the party theme. Whenever possible, use the theme your child likes best, even if it wasn't the one you had in mind. Should your child choose a theme the family considers inappropriate (for instance your son has his heart set on an army party and you are a confirmed pacifist), explain why you consider the theme inappropriate and ask the child for other ideas. If your child has trouble deciding on a theme, try the following:

Cost-Cutting Tips

- *Invite fewer guests.*
- *Make food from scratch.*
- *Create your own decorations.*
- *Use everyday dishes/silverware.*
- *Use plain paper plates/cups.*
- *Use game prizes or crafts as party favors.*
- *Use a computer to create prize certificates/invitations/thank-you notes/decorations.*
- *Hand make and deliver invitations/thank-yous.*

- Think about the child's current interests and favorites (toy, doll, book, music, sport, game, location, food, hobby, person, movie, television show, holiday, song, cartoon character, etc.).
- Look through the party plans offered throughout this book and the list of theme ideas in the appendix.

- Visit a local party supply store or go on-line (see the appendix for suggested sites) and look at the available themed party supplies.
- Check your local library for books on hosting children's parties and look through them for possible themes.

As you and your child discuss the party theme, take the opportunity to highlight his unique, God-given interests and abilities. Tell your child you are thankful God created such a special person and placed him in your care. Encourage the child to plan a birthday celebration that reflects God's incredible creative ability!

Plan the Day, Date, and Time

Plan the party for a day suitable to your family's calendar, your child's activity and nap schedule, and for a time help is readily available. For school-age children, take school schedules into account as well. While it's fun to host the birthday party on the child's actual birthday, weekend parties are often easier. If serving only cake and ice cream, plan the party for early or midafternoon. Set a fixed starting and ending time for the party, keeping the party between one and three hours in length. If planning a sleepover party for a school-age child, include the date and time the party starts and ends. These parties will obviously be longer than three hours! Generally, the younger the child, the shorter the party should be. Don't hesitate to check with parents about the availability of a favorite friend or relative.

Choose a Location

Birthday parties are held at a variety of locations. Many parties are held in the child's home or yard. Outdoor parties offer plenty of space to play, easy cleanup, and less wear and tear on furniture and carpet, but weather can be uncooperative at times, so have an alternate plan in mind. Indoor parties provide a safe, secure environment. Rearrange furniture to allow for large play areas and be firm about setting and maintaining physical boundaries. Confine the guests to one or two rooms (plus the bathroom) for best results. When the child's home isn't a viable alternative, ask if a grandparent, aunt, uncle, or family friend would possibly be willing to share their home for the occasion. If a friend or family member offers his or her home for the party, be sure to set clear expectations as to where the guests will be entertained, when you will arrive to set up for the party, and when you plan on being finished and don't forget to leave the party area in

Locations to Consider

Local park
Children's museum
Zoo
Child-oriented restaurant
Fast-food restaurant
Pizza parlor
Gymnastics center
Beach or lake
Community pool
Community recreation center
Bowling alley
Miniature golf course
Skating rink
Sports center
Ceramics studio
Athletic event
Movie or children's theater
Theme park
Local farm for pony or hayrides

tip-top condition after the party! Giving flowers or some other small token to the homeowner is a great way to say thank-you for their generosity.

Birthday parties are also held away from home. Hosting a party at a location away from home has some obvious advantages. For example, these locations may offer more space for play, on-site entertainment, and there is no wear and tear on your own home. Parties away from home are usually more successful for children four and older. Younger children (including the birthday child) can be overwhelmed by the noise and activity of an unfamiliar location.

Consider the following tips and questions to think about when hosting the party at a location other than your home:

- Call ahead. Some sites book six to eight weeks in advance.
- When calling, have an estimate of the guest count (adults and children) and the hoped-for date and time for your party. Have an alternate date in mind in case your first choice is taken.
- For parks or community centers, contact your city's parks and recreation department for information on obtaining a permit, party rules, and regulations. Find out how, where, and when any fees need to be paid. Be prepared to leave a deposit. Bring all paperwork to the party in case there is someone else using the reserved site.
- For restaurants, find out exactly what choices are available for food. Choose the same menu for everyone.
- Ask what food, decorations, favors, and activities are available on-site. What is the cost per child?
- Inquire whether there is a minimum or maximum number of guests required. Can the original number of guests be changed after the reservations are made?
- Is there a suggested age range for the facility?
- Does the birthday child receive special recognition?
- What assistance does the facility staff provide?

- How long will the facility be reserved for the party?
- Can outside food (such as a birthday cake) or drinks be brought in?
- What accommodations have been made to keep the children safe and secure?

Invite the Guests

Once the party theme, time, and location are finalized, it's time to invite the guests. As a general rule of thumb, invite one guest for each year of a child's life, plus one more. For example, if a child is five, invite six guests. Of course, this is just a guideline. You may be able to accommodate more children if you have plenty of help, adequate space, and an ample budget. Invite fewer guests if your child is more comfortable in a small group. Parents of children under the age of four are likely to accompany their child to the party, adding to the number of people involved. Make your child aware of guests who must be invited, but allow her the freedom of choosing her own guests whenever possible. Write each guest's name in your planner along with pertinent contact information.

Deciding on a guest list may bring opportunities to teach your child sensitivity to the feelings of others. Help your child understand how hurtful it is to feel left out of the fun. Teach your child to refrain from talking about the party in front of those she couldn't invite.

Once a guest list is established, you are ready to invite guests to the party. An invitation can be extended by mail, phone, e-mail, or hand-delivered two to three weeks before the party. Unless you are inviting the entire group of children, avoid handing out invitations at playgroup, school, or Sunday school. As invitations seem to mysteriously disappear out of cubbyholes, backpacks, and little hands, give the invitations directly to a parent or send them by mail. When inviting guests by phone, write out all party information before calling. If the birthday child makes the call, speak to the guest's parent as well to ensure information was accurately communicated.

Invitations help set the party mood. Select or make invitations compatible with the party theme. Ready-made invitations are available in a wide variety of themes. Check a local party store or an on-line party supply site for invitations. Creative, handmade invitations are fun to make, give, and receive. Making invitations might even be a fun family project. Each of the party plans in this book offer ideas for handmade invitations. Use these ideas to spur your own creativity. Here are some ideas for invitations:

- Computer-generated invitations.
- Invitations printed on themed paper.
- Heavy paper cut, stamped, stenciled, embossed, or decorated in the party theme. Stickers are fun and easy to use!
- A precut, blank puzzle or a small puzzle in the party theme. (Write party information on back.)
- A recent photo of the birthday child used like a postcard.
- A balloon with the invitation slipped inside. (Blow up the balloon, slide the information inside, and deflate.)
- A balloon with the party information printed on the outside. (Blow up the balloon, write the information with a Sharpie marker, deflate.)
- A blank cassette tape. Record the party information on the cassette and send it in a padded envelope to each guest.
- A plastic bib. (Write party information on the back.)
- A homemade candy wrapper with the party information printed on the outside. (Slip over a candy bar and mail in a padded envelope.)
- A bag of microwave popcorn with the party information taped on the outside. (Include instructions to remove the party information before popping!)

On vacation one year, I carefully cut, stamped, and embossed adorable pink teapot invitations for my daughter's upcoming birthday tea. When we returned home, I hurriedly stuffed the invitations in their envelopes and had my daughter give one to each of the girls in her class. A week before the party, I had heard from only half of the guests, so I decided to call and see who would be coming. Imagine my embarrassment upon discovering I had forgotten to print the party information inside half of the invitations! My lovingly created invitations were adorable, but useless!

Whatever type of invitation you choose, be sure to include the following party information:

- Child's name
- Purpose of celebration (Sam's fifth birthday)
- Day, date, time (start and end)
- Location with address
- RSVP or regrets date/phone number/ parents' names
- Special instructions (cake and ice cream will be served, pizza provided, dress like a cowboy, bring a favorite doll, be ready to get wet, bring a sleeping bag, etc.)
- Directions to the party if needed

Include Children with Special Needs

Our children are blessed to live in a world in which people with special needs are increasingly mainstreamed into society. If your child is fortunate enough to be friends with a special-needs child, be sure and include him or her in party plans. Children with special needs and their mothers are often frustrated by the word *can't*. "I can't do this because…" "You can't come because…" When planning for a child with special needs, learn to lean heavily on the word *can*. "Carter can, so we will…" As much as you are reasonably able, plan a party that is accessible to all children invited. This can be challenging when also trying to honor the birthday child's wishes. Remember to keep "I can" in mind. "I can plan a party that is fun for all the children involved." Consider the mother of the special-needs child as a resource when planning.

As I researched this book, each mother I asked had different opinions on the protocol to follow when inviting a special-needs child. This is most likely because each of their children had different special needs! One mother preferred being consulted before the invitation was sent, stating that an invitation can be a two-edged sword. On the one hand, being invited to a "regular" friend's party is a tremendous blessing, but at times it can be challenging for a special-needs child to succeed in a party environment. One mother suggested inviting the child to the party site before the party in order to gain a better understanding of the child's capabilities. Another mother said she would be thrilled to have her child receive even a single invitation. If in doubt about invitation protocol, consult the mother first. Each mother I interviewed expressed a willingness to answer questions about her child's special needs and emphasized the importance of being honest about any concerns or questions.

> "Give the gift of acceptance. Step out of your comfort zone and realize how much joy you will bring to the mother whose child may never have been invited to a single birthday party."
>
> —Mother of a special-needs child

For the safety of the special-needs child and your own peace of mind, ask the following questions. (Not all questions may apply to every situation.)

- Does the child have any special dietary needs?
- Are there any sensory or emotional issues to take into consideration?
- How can I create a safe physical environment for the child?
- What activities does the child enjoy participating in?
- How can I involve the child in (name specific activity)?
- Does the child need one-on-one supervision?
- If anything could go wrong medically, what would it be? What should I watch for? What should I do if this situation arises?

Celebrating a birthday together can be a positive experience for the birthday child, the special-needs guest, and all other party guests. Together, the children can have a wonderful time.

Enlist Extra Help

Even Super Mom needs extra help at birthday parties. Snapping pictures, taking videos, overseeing crafts, refereeing games, serving cake, and nursing boo-boos all at once is too much for any one person to handle. Enlist dad, older siblings, parents of party guests, a close friend, grandparents, or other relatives to help. Pay the teen or preteen down the street to help with selected activities. I recommend at least one helper for every four guests, with a two-adult minimum. Also consider having someone available to tend to the needs of young siblings during the party. Before the party begins, inform each helper exactly what he is expected to do.

Prepare a list of desired shots for the person helping with video or photography. You may want to include a picture of the birthday child with each guest, a photo of the birthday child blowing out the candles and opening gifts, a snap of the decorated table, and group shots of guests playing games and making crafts. Make sure your photographer knows how to adjust the camera, use the flash, and rewind and replace film. Have a fresh supply of film and batteries on hand.

Plan for Safety

A trip to the emergency room or even just a skinned knee can put a damper on a birthday celebration. Consider the suggestions in the party safety checklist in the appendix as you create a safe environment for your child's party.

HOSTING A SUCCESSFUL birthday party involves planning a festive environment, fun activities, and delicious food. The following three chapters are filled to the brim with ideas to help you create a memorable birthday experience with your child. As ideas for your child's party come to mind while reading these chapters, jot them down on the party planning sheet in the appendix.

When Your Child Is the Guest

- *Respond as soon as possible to the invitation. If necessary, ask the host parent for directions to the party.*
- *Make the host family aware of any special needs your child might have. (If your child is on a restricted diet, offer to provide alternative food for your child.)*
- *See to it that your child arrives and departs on time.*
- *Remind your child that he or she must obey the host parent and be courteous and kind to the birthday child and other guests.*
- *Ask well in advance if you would like to bring a sibling to the party.*
- *Provide a gift for the birthday child.*

   Families typically spend between five and twenty-five dollars on birthday gifts for friends.

   Ask the birthday child's parents for gift suggestions, or ask your child for ideas.

   Make sure the gift is age-appropriate.

   Avoid toys that might be controversial unless you're sure the host family approves. (Live animals, toy weapons, Barbies, violent action figures, and media-based items are some commonly controversial toys.)

   If you take your child gift shopping, clearly define your gift budget before you step into the store.

   School-age children and teens enjoy receiving cash and gift certificates.

- *Leave an emergency contact phone number with the host parent in case of emergency.*

Chapter Five

Fun Fixin's for Festivities

Ice cream and a super cake,
Pizza shaped just like a snake.
I can't wait to fill my tummy
With party food that tastes so yummy!

Maria and Guillermo stood on two chairs on either side of their mother, wrapped in oversized aprons to protect their clothes from sticky frosting fingers. Patiently the twins helped their mother add candy details to a choo-choo train cake for their birthday party. Maria's car was frosted bright purple, her favorite color, and provided transportation for her plastic kitten collection. Guillermo's car, festooned with his favorite dark green frosting and licorice ropes, provided camouflage for a group of brave plastic soldiers. The newly minted four-year-olds chattered back and forth about the unique details their mommy had created: a Hershey's kiss smokestack, Oreo cookie wheels, and the special caboose car with their names inscribed on opposite sides. Maria and Guillermo could hardly wait to show their friends the distinctive cake they'd helped create.

BUSY MOTHERS WILL BE HAPPY to know the list of required foods for a successful birthday party is actually rather short: a great cake, frosty-cold ice cream, and a plentiful supply of drinks. Anything else served is, well, icing on the cake! Unless the party falls during a traditional mealtime (before 10 A.M., noon, or between 5 and 6 P.M.) children will not be expecting a meal, although snacks and food seldom go uneaten. If the party falls on or near a traditional mealtime it's a good idea to state on the invitation what will be served (e.g., "cake and ice cream will be served" or "a pizza lunch will be provided"). Whether you plan to serve cake and punch or a complete meal, the following pages will provide ideas, recipes, and handy hints for festive party fare.

Serve with Guests in Mind

Whether you're serving cake and ice cream or an entire meal, provide a place for young guests to sit while they eat and a place to set their dishes other than a lap. Very young guests will need a low table and chair, high chair, or booster seat (telephone books stacked on a chair work too). If you will be sitting at backless picnic benches, closely monitor children under three years old. Preschool and school-age children can sit around the dining room table, at card tables, or on a blanket, picnic style. Seat the children and bring the food to them. Save buffet-style serving for teenagers and adults.

Using paper plates and plastic utensils saves wear and tear on dishes and makes cleanup easier. Themed paper goods are attractive, but inexpensive white supplies work just as well. When providing a meal, be sure to purchase large plates for the meal and small plates for cake. Guests will also need two forks apiece. If you use silverware, watch the trash can carefully. When helpful guests dispose of paper plates and napkins, often forks and spoons fall in as well. One solution is to place a large container with a sign reading, "Dirty silverware here!" alongside the trash can. When serving drinks in recyclable containers, provide a labeled container or trash bag for these next to the trash can as well.

Celebrate with Cake!

Children love birthday cakes! They delight in selecting the cake, eagerly join in to help decorate it, take pleasure in admiring it, and relish tasty bites of the sweet concoction. Additionally, the birthday child savors the moment, once a year, when his name appears, surrounded by lights, on the birthday cake! Although many a mother has found great satisfaction in baking and decorating a birthday cake to her child's specifications, modern day mamas don't have to be experts in the kitchen to provide a great cake. Cakes can be purchased ready-made, ordered from a bakery, grocery store, or on-line, made from a cake mix, prepared using a favorite family recipe, or baked from a new recipe culled from a chat room friend.

Like every other component of the birthday party, the birthday cake should be just what the birthday child orders. Usually children want a cake to go along with their party theme, but not always. Last year, my son wanted to go bowling for his birthday, but desired a skateboard ramp birthday cake! Do your best to accommodate the child's wishes. Ask your child to share his favorite cake flavor, frosting flavor, colors, and decorating ideas. Write down this information on your party planning sheet.

There's no need to do without a birthday cake if your child is on a restricted diet, allrecipes.com lists several recipes for cakes and frosting that are gluten-free, dairy-free, or sugar-free. I recommend testing any new recipe before using it as a birthday cake.

Skateboard Ramp Cake

Bake a 9"x 13" cake and a loaf cake. When cool, frost the 9"x 13" cake in chocolate icing. Cut a half circle out of the loaf cake as shown. Cut the half circle in half as shown. Assemble according to diagram on top of the 9" x 13" cake. Frost in white and add miniature skateboards and flags.

Ordering a Cake

Delicious cakes can be ordered from individual bakeries or the bakery department of large grocery stores. Ask friends, neighbors, or relatives for recommendations as taste and quality vary. Many bakeries, including those in grocery stores, will provide a sample slice of cake or a cupcake upon request. Bakeries usually have a sample book of cake pictures showing a wide variety of cakes. In addition, most bakeries can create a custom cake decorated to your specifications.

Many bakeries today have the technology to copy a photograph or picture onto a cake top. Prices of bakery-made cakes range from fifteen dollars for a simple, quarter sheet cake serving ten to twelve people, to fifty dollars or more for larger, more elaborate cakes. See the sidebar for information to have on hand when ordering a cake.

Cake Specifications

- *Flavor of cake*
- *Type of icing*
- *Type of filling*
- *Number of servings needed*
- *Shape desired (round, oblong, square, rolled)*
- *Theme or design*
- *Colors*
- *Inscription*
- *Pick-up date and time*

Two other options when ordering a bakery cake are to either purchase an undecorated cake or to purchase an already decorated cake. An undecorated cake usually has white frosting and a white border around the perimeter. You can add your own decorations at home. If you purchase a decorated cake, be sure to ask the baker to inscribe a personalized birthday message to your child. This takes only a few minutes and can be accomplished while you wait.

Delicious ice cream cakes can be ordered from most ice cream shops. These cakes usually contain two layers with ice cream between the layers, or are a block of decorated ice cream. Ice cream cakes are often more expensive than traditional cakes, but you don't have to purchase or scoop ice cream! Ice cream cakes must be kept in the freezer until approximately fifteen to twenty minutes before serving. Be sure your freezer can accommodate the cake before ordering it.

One other source of ready-made cakes is the internet. Cakes are pricier, and there are not many options for decorating, but for ultra-convenience, this method can't be beat (unless you're blessed with a grandma who will bake, decorate, and deliver the cake!) In most cases, website orders are filled by local bakeries which bake, decorate, and deliver the cake. Most sites recommend cakes be ordered at least five days before the party, but for an additional fee, cakes can be made and delivered within twenty-four hours. Expect to pay sixty dollars or more for a decorated quarter sheet cake. Cakes must be paid for by credit card.

Baking and Decorating a Homemade Cake

Despite the many times I've taken advantage of the convenience of ordering cakes for my children from a local bakery or ice cream shop (they especially like ice cream cake), there is something unmistakably sweet about creating a homemade cake. Perhaps it's being able to watch the almost magical way goopy cake batter and frosting can be transformed into puppies, doll dresses, an ocean, or a turtle, or maybe it's the camaraderie of two "pastry chefs" working together in the kitchen. Most likely it is simply the act of creating something special for the child you love.

Birthday cake ideas exist for bakers of all experience levels. The cakes suggested in this book were selected with the novice baker in mind. Most are designed so the birthday child, even if he's only two or three, can help with decorating. If the cake your child desires isn't mentioned in this book, several websites and cake cookbooks that feature easy-to-make cakes are listed in the appendix. The cake ideas in this book use variations of three techniques: decorating with children's toys or cake decorating items, shaping cakes with simple cutting techniques, and cakes with edible decorations. Any of the cakes used can be made from a favorite scratch recipe, a cake mix, or purchased cakes. For instance, the volcano cake in chapter 10 was made using purchased angel food cakes and a jumbo muffin.

Tips for Successful Birthday Cakes

- Use fresh ingredients at room temperature.
- Generously spray the bottom and sides of the cake pan with cooking spray. Cut a piece of parchment or waxed paper to fit the bottom of cake pan. Fit in place and dust with flour (cocoa for a chocolate cake). Wilton sells a nonstick spray that works without flour.
- Fill cake pans no more than two-thirds full.
- Bake cake until toothpick inserted in center of cake comes out clean.
- Cool cakes for ten to fifteen minutes on a wire rack or pot holder.
- To release cake from pan, run a knife or narrow spatula along sides of pan. Put a plate, cake board, wire rack, or small cutting board on top of cake and gently turn pan upside down. Slowly remove pan and carefully remove wax paper. Place a second plate, cutting board, or wire rack over the cake and gently turn right side up.
- Allow cake to cool completely before cutting or decorating.
- Use a sharp, serrated knife or dental floss to cut off rounded cake tops for ease of layering and decorating. Doing this allows layers to lie flush against each other. This prevents the cake from cracking and the top layers from sliding off to one side.

- Use a sharp, serrated knife or dental floss for cutting shaped cakes.
- To make cake assembly and frosting easier, freeze each layer or cake piece individually for three to five hours before assembling. Place the layer or piece on a cake board or cookie sheet and wrap loosely with plastic wrap.
- To move cake layers or pieces into place, first run a spatula under the piece. Then gently slide the fingers of both hands under the cake, fingers spread out to keep the piece level. Center the piece in the desired location and slide fingers away. Smaller pieces can be moved with a spatula.
- Before frosting a cake, especially one cut into a shape or a chocolate cake frosted white, frost with a thin layer of white frosting. Let frosting dry before final decorating. This keeps crumbs away from top layer of frosting.

Basic Yellow Cake

2 1/2 cups all-purpose flour
2 1/2 teaspoons baking powder
1 teaspoon salt
1/2 cup butter
1 3/4 cups granulated sugar
1 1/2 teaspoons pure vanilla extract
2 eggs
1 1/4 cups milk

1. Preheat oven to 375°.
2. Spray bottom and sides of two 9-inch round pans or one 9" x 13" pan with nonstick cooking spray.
3. Cut parchment or wax paper to fit bottom of pan. Spray again, then dust with 1 teaspoon flour.
4. In a medium bowl combine flour, baking powder, and salt. Set aside. In a large bowl, beat butter about 30 seconds, add sugar and vanilla; beat till well blended. Add eggs, one at a time, beating 1 minute after each addition. Then add flour mixture and milk alternately. Pour into pans.
5. Bake 9-inch rounds 30–35 minutes, 9" x 13" pan 35–40 minutes, cupcakes 18–20 minutes. Cool 10 minutes on wire rack; remove from pans. Cool completely before decorating. Serves 12–16.

- Spread a thin layer of frosting between layers or pieces of cake to "glue" them together.
- Trace a design or lettering in frosting with a toothpick first.
- Add decorating items (sprinkles, candies, cake toppers, figurines) before frosting dries or they won't stay put.
- To transport a cake, set the cake into a cake box (available at many party and craft stores), cake carrier, the lid from a copy paper box, or a cookie sheet with edges. When using the lid or cookie sheet, put the candles in place on top of the cake, then loosely cover the cake and lid or cookie sheet with plastic wrap. If there are only a few candles, use toothpicks as well (remove them before serving) to keep the plastic wrap off the cake. Be sure to take along a cutting knife and spatula for serving.

Chocolate Fudge Cake

1 tsp cocoa (to dust bottom of cake pan)
2 cups all-purpose flour
1 1/4 teaspoon baking soda
1/2 teaspoon salt
2/3 cup butter
1 3/4 cups sugar
1 teaspoon vanilla
2 eggs
3 ounces unsweetened chocolate, melted and cooled
1 1/4 cups cold water

1. Preheat oven to 350°.
2. Spray bottom and sides of two 9-inch round pans or one 9" x 13" pan with nonstick cooking spray.
3. Cut parchment or wax paper to fit bottom of pan. Spray again, then dust with 1 teaspoon cocoa.
4. In a medium bowl, combine flour, soda, and salt. Set aside. In a large mixing bowl beat butter on medium speed about 30 seconds. Beat in sugar and vanilla. Add eggs, one at a time, beating 1 minute after each addition. Blend in cooled chocolate.
5. Add flour mixture and cold water alternately to beaten mixture, beating after each addition. Pour into pans.
6. Bake 9-inch rounds 30–35 minutes, 9" x 13" pan 35–40 minutes, cupcakes 18–20 minutes. Cool 10 minutes on wire rack. Remove from pans. Cool completely before decorating. Serves 12–16.

Butter Cream Frosting

6 tablespoons butter, softened
4 1/2 cups sifted* powdered sugar (measured after sifting)
1/4 cup milk
1 1/2 teaspoons vanilla

Beat butter until light and fluffy. Gradually add half the powdered sugar, beating well. Beat in the milk and vanilla. Gradually beat in remaining sugar, adding milk if needed. This will frost a 9" x 13" cake, a two-layer 9" cake, or 24 cupcakes.

*Frosting made without sifting sugar tastes and spreads just fine, but it will be slightly lumpy.

Variation: For chocolate butter cream frosting, add 2 ounces of melted, cooled unsweetened chocolate along with the vanilla.

A myriad of cake and frosting recipes are available, including ones that read: open a box, add eggs, oil, water, and bake. On pages 58-60 are two basic cake recipes and a frosting recipe.

Serving Cupcakes Instead of Cake

Young guests tend to have small appetites. Keep servings small and don't be surprised if guests don't eat everything. Chances are the cake is delicious but the guests are eager to return to the fun party activities you've planned. As an alternative to a cake, serve cupcakes. Here are three popular cupcake suggestions.

- *Cupcake caterpillar.* On a cake or cutting board, arrange cupcakes like a caterpillar. Frost the lead cupcake with gumdrop eyes and lollipop antennae. Use M&M candies to decorate remaining cupcakes.

- *Cupcake balloons.* Find a clown picture or flat plastic clown decoration (available on-line, at cake decorating stores, or party supply stores). Place picture or decoration on the bottom right of cake or cutting board. Arrange cupcakes frosted in different colors to look like balloons at top left. Connect to clown decoration with licorice whips.

- *Ice cream cone cupcakes.* Set flat-bottomed ice cream cones into a cupcake tin. Place crumpled foil around each cone to prevent tipping. Fill cones halfway with cake batter. Bake as instructed for cupcakes. When cool, remove from pan and frost. Add sprinkles and a maraschino cherry on top.

Guest-Decorated Cake

One year, when I ran out of time to decorate the cake before the party (oh, those December birthdays) I accidentally discovered how much school-age children like to decorate cakes. Set the cake in a spot where several children can work at one time (pull out a cutting board or use a card table). Sometimes it helps to assign each child or team of children a specific task. Provide several bowls or cans of frosting, plastic knives, sprinkles, decorator tubes of gel icing, edible letters, and themed plastic cake decorations for guests to use. Other options include providing each guest a cupcake or cookie to decorate, or dividing the guests into teams and giving each team a cake to decorate. Be prepared for sticky hands, countertops, and floor!

Scoop Up Some Ice Cream

Ice cream is the second essential menu item for birthday celebrations. Choose the birthday child's favorite flavor. (If the birthday child has an affinity for an unusual flavor, consider providing vanilla ice cream as an alternative for guests!) For ease of serving, take the ice cream out of the freezer about ten minutes before serving, or place in microwave on medium power for eight to ten seconds. Dipping the ice cream scoop in warm water between scoops also makes serving easier. Some hostesses scoop the ice cream

Ice Cream Clowns

1/2 gallon ice cream
16 chocolate chips
8 maraschino cherries
2 red licorice whips
8 ice cream cones (the pointed, sugar variety)
1/4 cup coconut
Red food dye
8 mini marshmallows or small gumdrops
1 can of whipped cream

1. *Line a cookie sheet with waxed paper. Place 8 round scoops of ice cream on sheet. Freeze again if soft.*
2. *When hardened, decorate each scoop with 2 chocolate chips for eyes, a maraschino cherry for the nose, and a piece of red licorice for mouth. Place an ice cream cone on top of head for hat. Press red coconut* on top for hair. Stick a marshmallow or gumdrop on top of hat for pompom.*
3. *To serve, place "clowns" on individual plates. Squirt canned whipped cream around bottom of clown for neckpiece.*

*To make red coconut, place 1/4 cup shredded coconut in a Ziploc bag. Add 3 or 4 drops of red food coloring and shake until the coconut is evenly colored.

ahead of time, place individual servings on a cookie sheet, cover with plastic wrap, and stick it back into the freezer until a few minutes before serving. Another alternative is to purchase ice cream in a square container and cut slices. Individual ice cream cups are easy to serve and clean up! When guests are very young, consider serving the ice cream and cake in a bowl instead of on a plate.

The ice cream clowns (pictured on p. 61) are a favorite party treat for preschool children.

Bring on the Beverages

Party guests seem to work up a thirst as they play games and participate in birthday activities. I've found the easiest way to quench thirst is with individual containers of juice, soda, or water. Before the party begins, layer the drinks with ice in an ice chest or other large container. Provide several permanent markers to label unfinished drinks. Less expensive alternatives include those old summer standbys, Kool-aid and lemonade, as well as frozen concentrate juices or large containers of soda, punch, or juice.

Sometimes it's fun to serve a special punch that fits the party theme, such as Lava Nectar or Safari Cooler. (These are simply fancy names for red punch and green punch!) When serving punch, have a second batch ready to go in the refrigerator and an extra adult prepared to serve the punch to little guests. Fill cups half full and label cups so they can be reused. Provide young children with lidded cups. Older kids love fancy straws. Licorice whips with hollow centers make great straws too!

Serve Simple Snacks

Children are always happy to see snack foods provided at parties, especially when offered treats that aren't normally served at home. When choosing snacks, provide some nutritious selections along with items like chips and candy. Vegetables or sliced fruit with an accompanying dip are usually kid-pleasers. Pretzel sticks or trail mix is a nutritious alternative to chips or candy. Many children enjoy preparing their own snacks. Shaped sugar cookies, soft pretzels, trail mix ingredients, and celery sticks can provide activities that are both fun to do and delicious to eat.

Removing Drink Stains from Carpet

Avoid serving brightly colored punch or juices if children will be eating in a carpeted area. Colored drink stains are very difficult to remove from carpeting. If a stain does occur, blot immediately with a clean white rag or several layers of white paper towels or napkins. Cover the area with additional white toweling until it can be properly cleaned after the party. Use a carpet stain remover immediately following the party to completely remove stain. Many homemakers use hydrogen peroxide on these stains with great success. Test on a hidden corner of carpet first to make sure the peroxide won't damage your carpet.

Bugs in the Sand

Ziploc bag for each guest
3 tablespoons graham cracker crumbs for each guest (sand)
Mini chocolate chips (ants)
Raisins (sow bugs or rolly-pollies)
Red hots (lady bugs)
Gummy worms (worms)

Pour crushed graham cracker crumbs in Ziploc bags. Give each guest a bag of crumbs and allow them to fill the "sand" with desired bugs.

Low-Fat Vegetable Dip

$2/3$ cup low-fat cottage cheese
8 ounces reduced fat cream cheese, cubed
1 teaspoon cider vinegar
$1/2$ teaspoon Worcestershire sauce
1 teaspoon minced garlic
$1/8$ teaspoon each dried basil, savory, and thyme
1 tablespoon minced parsley
Raw vegetables of choice, cut into strips

Process cottage cheese in blender until smooth. Add remaining ingredients and process until smooth. Chill at least one hour before serving. Makes about 1 1/2 cups.

Fruit Dip

8 ounces reduced fat cream cheese, softened
1 jar marshmallow crème
1 teaspoon ground cinnamon
Variety of fresh fruit, sliced or whole

Process all ingredients in blender until smooth. Serve with sliced fruit or whole berries. Makes about 2 cups.

Variation: Omit cinnamon. After transferring cream cheese mixture to serving bowl, pour about 1 cup caramel ice cream topping over top. Serve with apple slices.

Celery Wagons

4 celery stalks
4 carrots
Peanut butter or cheese spread
Raisins
Toothpicks

1. Cut each celery stalk into 3 pieces. Cut each carrot into 12 "coins."
2. Run 2 toothpicks through the bottom of each celery piece to serve as axles. Push a carrot coin onto each toothpick end to serve as wheels.
3. Spread peanut butter or cheese onto celery. Place 3 or 4 raisin "passengers" aboard. Enjoy. Makes 12 celery wagons.

Variation: Celery boats. Omit carrot wheels. Instead cut a slice of American cheese twice diagonally to form 4 triangles. Attach the cheese to a toothpick to form a sail. Poke the sail into the celery.

Trail Mix

8 ounces M&M candies
8 ounces peanuts
4–6 ounces pretzel sticks
8 ounces raisins or other dried fruit
8–12 ounces cereal (Crispix, Cheerios, or child's choice)
8 ounces small fish crackers

1. Give each guest a Ziploc bag with his or her name written in permanent marker.
2. Place the above ingredients in separate bowls and allow guests to create a unique trail mix blend. (You may need to limit the M&Ms!) For a fun twist, rename the ingredients to match the party theme.
3. Decorate bags with stickers. Makes about 8 bags.

Giant Soft Pretzels

1 tablespoon yeast
$^1/_2$ cup warm water
1 teaspoon honey
1 teaspoon salt
1 $^1/_3$ cups flour
Coarse salt
1 cup very cold water

1. Preheat oven to 425°.
2. Dissolve yeast in warm water. Add honey and salt. Stir in 1 $^1/_3$ cups flour. Knead until smooth.
3. Divide into 8 portions. Give each guest a portion on a piece of waxed paper. Have them roll dough into a "snake" and then form letters or shapes. Brush with cold water, sprinkle with coarse salt, and place on a baking sheet.
4. Bake for 10 minutes. Cool for 5 minutes. Remove from baking sheet and serve. Makes 8 pretzels.

Sugar Cookies

3/4 cup butter, softened
1 cup sugar
2 eggs at room temperature
1 teaspoon pure vanilla extract
2 3/4 cups all-purpose flour
1 teaspoon baking powder
1/2 teaspoon salt
Frosting or colored sugars for decorating

1. Preheat oven to 375°.
2. In a large mixing bowl, cream butter and sugar until light and fluffy; add eggs and vanilla.
3. Combine flour, baking powder, and salt in a medium bowl; gradually add to creamed mixture. Mix well.
4. Divide the dough into 12 portions. Wrap in waxed paper and chill at least 1 hour.
5. Give each guest 1 portion of dough and a small amount of flour for hands. Press dough with floured hands until 1/4" thick. Cut with assorted cookie cutters, coated with flour.
6. Bake on ungreased cookie sheets for 8–10 minutes. Cool 1 minute before removing from pan. Allow guests to decorate.

Variation: Cut and bake the cookies before the party and allow guests to decorate. Makes about 6 dozen.

Dirt and Worms

1 box instant chocolate pudding
1 box chocolate wafer cookies, crushed
Gummy worms
6 (4-inch) flowerpots

1. Wash flower pots the day before using and dry thoroughly. Line flowerpots with foil to prevent leakage.
2. On the day of the party, mix pudding according to package directions. Layer pudding and crushed cookies, adding gummy worms as desired.
3. Top with a plastic flower and 1 or 2 gummy worms coming out of "dirt."
4. Refrigerate at least 1 hour before serving. Makes 6 pots.

Finger Jell-O

2 envelopes unflavored gelatin
1 (6 ounce) package flavored gelatin

1. *Dissolve unflavored gelatin in 1 cup cold water.*
2. *Dissolve flavored gelatin in 1 cup boiling water.*
3. *Combine and add 1/2 cup cold water. Chill in a pan sprayed with cooking spray until solid. Use cookie cutters to cut shapes.*

Monkeys on a Stick

1 craft stick per guest
1 banana per guest
1 jar peanut butter
Chocolate sprinkles or chopped nuts

Push a Popsicle stick into banana. Coat banana with peanut butter. Roll in chocolate sprinkles or nuts. Freeze for at least 1 hour before serving.

Make Meals Kids Love

If you've decided to offer a meal to birthday guests, stick to familiar foods that can be prepared ahead of time and are easy to serve and eat. Add to the party fun by renaming foods to fit the theme. Sandwiches cut into the shape of stars can be called "Stellar Sandwiches," and mini–corn dogs can be renamed "Dinosaur Eggs." Top English muffin pizzas to look like a clown face and call them "Circus Pizzas." After rising, pizza dough can be shaped into a snake, a teddy bear, or a monster head. Remember to keep food portions small for young guests. They can always ask for more if they're still hungry. The following are some suggested main dishes kids love.

- Pizza (homemade or delivered)
- English muffin pizzas
- Hamburgers
- Hotdogs (children three years and older)
- Pigs-in-a-blanket (hot dogs covered with biscuit dough and baked)
- Grilled cheese sandwiches
- Sandwiches cut into shapes with cookie cutters
- Chicken nuggets

- Macaroni and cheese (shaped pasta adds to the fun)
- Spaghetti and meatballs (this can be messy)
- Quesadillas

Cleaning Up

If you've used disposable party goods, it will be easy to clean up the mess. First remove any decorations you plan on keeping. Then remove any partially filled beverage containers (I like to dump the contents into a plastic pitcher, then pour down the sink), fold the ends of the tablecloth together, and place the entire mess into a plastic garbage bag. Carry the plastic garbage bag around the party area, adding any trash to the collection. If soda cans were served, carry an additional bag for those. Even a small child can help with this.

If you've used reusable goods, collect the dishes in a plastic tub and dump trash into a plastic trash bag. Immediately place dishwasher safe things in dishwasher; everything else should go into a sink of hot, soapy water. After the party, wash, dry, and put away hand washables and run dishwasher. Put a stain remover on any tablecloth stains, and then launder.

Chapter Six

Creating a Festive Environment

**Canopy of streamers,
Balloons plump with air,
Help set the stage
For a festive affair.**

Brittany sat in the middle of the living room, costumed for her birthday tea in mommy's pink, shiny party dress. Her daddy stood at her side, uniformed in a white dress shirt and dark pants, a white dish-towel over one arm. In his best British butler's accent he asked each bright-eyed girl seated with Brittany, "How may I serve you?" The girls, dressed up in costumes like Brittany's, giggled as they ordered finger sandwiches, Earl Grey tea or apple juice, and teapot or teddy bear cookies. While Brittany's daddy filled their orders, the girls admired the pretty china cups and saucers, the vase filled with garden roses, and the costumed bear print of the cloth on their table. All around the room sat the other party guests, the girls' teddy bears, decked out in hats lovingly created by each girl earlier in the party. As her daddy poured from a hand-painted teapot, Brittany overheard her friend, Charmese, sigh and say, "This feels like a real grown-up tea party."

CREATING A FESTIVE ENVIRONMENT is an important component in planning a successful birthday party. Playful decorations, distinctive music, ingenious costumes, creative party favors, and good manners transform an ordinary time and place into a fun-filled party. Making decorations and party favors, choosing the perfect music, selecting costumes, and practicing party manners provide opportunities to be involved in fun activities and learning experiences with your child. Working side by side, you have the opportunity to teach your child hospitality, the art of creating an environment where guests sense they are welcomed and loved.

Playful Decorations

Probably the most obvious element in creating a festive environment involves decorations. Working with a theme keeps decorations focused, making a strong visual impact. If your party theme is "Taylor's Fourth Birthday," set the stage with streamers in Taylor's favorite colors, balloons tied in bunches of four, an enlarged picture of (or by) Taylor, and a home-made sign that says, "Happy 4th Birthday, Taylor." If you choose a car or truck theme, for example, you could decorate with black and white "road" streamers, balloons in stoplight colors (red, yellow, green), the birthday child's own cars and trucks, a table covered with inexpensive road maps, and a large construction paper stoplight that says, "Happy Birthday, Chris," in the three light circles.

When choosing decorations, there is no need to overdo; a few well-chosen decorations provide enough visual focus and fun to set a festive tone for the party. But if you and your child enjoy decorating and have the resources to plan, prepare, and/or purchase more deco-rations, by all means enjoy this aspect of birthday party fun by creating a more elaborate "set" together. Each of the party plans in this book gives specific suggestions for decorating.

Party stores, discount stores, and children's toy stores, either in your community or on-line, provide a wide variety of items to enhance the party environment. (See the appendix for a list of on-line and mail-order sources.) Latex and helium balloons, streamers in a variety of shapes and colors, banners, signs, centerpieces, tablecloths, decorative paper goods, props, hats, music, and just about every imaginable party supply can be purchased. Carefully watch your budget— it's amazing how fast these small items can add up to a big purchase!

Some party items can be reused. As a young mother, I worked in a Vacation Bible School with a seasoned mom. The theme for VBS was "Let's Celebrate!" When we discussed decorations, this experienced mom told me she'd just pull out her boxes of party decorations. By keeping her reusable or unused supplies in a specific place, this experienced mom was able to create a festive environment with little expense and effort. Following her lead, I've kept a variety of party supplies in two labeled boxes. Although I have to carefully pack these away after each party, I've been able to use them many times.

When planning decorations, take the birthday child on a treasure hunt through the house to find theme-appropriate items. Either note these items on the party planning sheet or immediately place them in a "party idea" box. Think about decorating items your family or friends own that could be borrowed for the party. Brainstorm ways to use each item. Thumb through the party ideas in this book or other party books for easy decorating ideas. Write down ideas on the planning sheet. Look through the list of birthday supplies on the shopping list, considering any items you might want to purchase for the party. Choose the decorating items that fit the following criteria:

Balloon Basics

- *Use caution with balloons around pets and children under three.*
- *Helium balloons can be purchased filled or you can rent or purchase a tank and fill balloons at home. When using more than two dozen, it is usually cheaper to purchase or rent a helium tank.*
- *Bringing helium balloons home from the store can be a challenge. Have the shop tie the balloons together and use a heavy object to hold the strings down so the balloons don't hinder visibility while driving.*
- *Latex helium balloons only float for three to six hours, depending on balloon quality. Filling them the night before results in limp, low-lying balloons. Mylar helium balloons last several days without drooping.*
- *When filling a large quantity of regular balloons, consider purchasing an inexpensive handheld pump. This alleviates one source of party headaches!*
- *Balloon clips are available at many party supply stores. These make tedious tying unnecessary and speed up the decorating process.*

- The birthday child likes this idea.
- You have the resources to carry out this idea.
- This idea will enhance the party.

Once you have decided on a decorating plan, collect and purchase needed supplies and ready-made items. Arrange to obtain any items you will borrow. Keep all decorating items together in a box or closet. Check your calendar and set aside time to work on the decorations with your child (if age-appropriate). Be generous in estimating how much time it will take to finish projects so you and your child can enjoy the time spent creating decorations without feeling hurried and harried.

Thinking out of the Box

With a bit of creativity, imaginative decorations can be devised out of ordinary materials. A refrigerator box turned on its side, cut to resemble a fire truck, and painted bright red is not only an eye-catching decoration, it will also provide a fun place to play during the party. Stand

Ten Ways to Transform a Box

1. *Create a fire truck*
2. *Build a barn*
3. *Make a car or airplane for each child*
4. *Paint a school bus*
5. *Design a dog house*
6. *Put together a maze or tunnel*
7. *Construct a gingerbread house*
8. *Set up a puppet theater or carnival booths*
9. *Flatten and design a backdrop for photo opportunities*
10. *Assemble a train*

the same box straight up, cut a large square out in the top half of the front, and you have a puppet stage or a carnival booth. Take an old sheet, dye it dark blue, use glow-in-the-dark paint to create stars and planets and voila, a night sky. The same sheet draped over furniture or sawhorses can create a tent or a dark cave. Inexpensive crepe paper streamers can be hung to make a traditional party canopy or twisted across boxes to create animal cages. Take those same streamers hung from the ceiling and attach paper fish to them randomly, and you have an instant ocean for mermaids or sharks to swim through. Construction paper can be cut, folded, glittered, and glued into stars, footprints of all varieties, sea creatures, trees, flowers, and speech balloons. The possibilities are endless!

Curbside Appeal

Arriving guests can experience a festive environment right away when decorations are placed at the curb or front door. Helium balloons tied to the mailbox or attached to a rock or fencepost let guests (and their chauffeur) know right where the party is taking place. Construction paper footprints, funny little signs, or a balloon path leads guests straight to the fun. A purchased or computer-generated banner hanging over the doorway or between two trees at the park alerts guests to the fun-filled activities in store for them.

The Food Table

Whether you serve cake and punch, pizza and watermelon, or a more elaborate meal, the food table is often a focal point for party decorations. At some parties, food is served buffet style, and at others, guests are served at the table. If you choose to serve buffet style, I recommend providing another table where children can eat. That way the housekeeping staff (you) will have fewer spills to clean up.

Setting a Buffet Table

Whenever possible, arrange the buffet table so that guests can serve themselves from two sides (see diagram on p. 74). Place plates at the start of the line, then the main dish, side dish(es), salad(s), and salad dressing, then bread and butter. Place napkins and utensils next. If space is limited, wrap individual sets of needed utensils in a napkin, tying closed with a piece of ribbon. Arrange these in a basket or other container. If possible, use a second small table or counter for beverage serving. If this is not possible, locate cups, ice, and beverages at the end of the table, as shown. Place the beverages far enough from the edge of the table that a guest has room to set her plate down while pouring her beverage.

Plates	Main Dish	Side Dish	Salad & Dressing	Bread & Butter	Napkins & Utensils	Cups Ice
					Beverages	
		Centerpiece			Beverages	
					Beverages	
Plates	Main Dish	Side Dish	Salad & Dressing	Bread & Butter	Napkins & Utensils	Ice Cups

Table Coverings, Place Settings, and Centerpieces

A tablecloth provides the foundation for a well-decorated table. Party stores offer a wide variety of themed paper cloths; however, I've been disappointed in the past with these because only the sides are printed and the middle section that covers the top of the table is plain white. I also find these tear easily when wet. A cup of punch or a cold juice box will quickly make a hole in the cloth. My favorite party cloths are the inexpensive, plastic colored ones. These do a better job of protecting the table and make a colorful background for themed plates or napkins. A washable white tablecloth, white butcher paper, or old twin sheets provide other cover options. Further protect the finish of a dining room table by using an extra tablecloth, an old blanket, or table pads. My dining room table now has an "unfinished" portion, the result of nail polish remover spilled at a daughter's sleepover.

Colorful plates, cups, and napkins provide quick, easy decorations for the food table. Stack them attractively on a buffet table or set up individual place settings for a sit-down meal. Place cards can be purchased, decorated with stickers, or designed on the computer. This is a wonderful area to let the birthday child apply her creativity. Place cards tell each guest you've prepared especially for her and alleviate arguments over who will sit by the birthday child.

The focal point of the table is the centerpiece. A centerpiece might be the birthday cake, an arrangement of toys or books that fit with the theme, a bunch of balloons or flowers, a basket filled with party favors or a purchased decoration. Surround the centerpiece with confetti, pieces of curled ribbon, or brightly wrapped pieces of candy to complete the arrangement. Be sure guests can see each other around the centerpiece.

Create a Keepsake Birthday Tablecloth

Purchase a white, washable tablecloth and fabric marker or paint. Invite the party guests to trace their handprints, draw a picture, or write a message to the birthday child. Have guests sign and date their work. This could be done for one special year or brought out each year so guests can add to the design.

Place a plastic cover or strips of waxed paper under the cloth to be painted to save the table underneath from paint damage.

Music to Play By

Have you ever attended a birthday party that did not include some rendition of "Happy Birthday to You"? Music is part of virtually every birthday party. Two years ago a CD full of 1950s music favorites was a key element in the environment for my daughter's Sock Hop. During an Under the Sea party, young party guests could enjoy the soundtrack from *The Little Mermaid*. Depending on how it is used, music can help make a party lively, calm young guests after a lively activity, or be an important element in a game or activity. Here are some ideas.

- Play appropriately themed music as children arrive and throughout the party to help set the tone for the party.
- Play soothing background music to calm excited guests while eating or enjoying quiet activities like crafts.
- Invite children to sing along with a tape, video, or live musician (I'm thinking along the lines of a favorite friend playing his guitar, not a hired musician!) while waiting for birthday treats or for their parents to come pick them up.
- Make or order a personalized cassette tape of "Happy Birthday to You" to play during part of the festivities.
- Check your local library, children's bookstore, or the internet for a tape of favorite children's party songs to enjoy during the party.
- Provide a set of children's instruments and have the children create their own music. Allow them to perform as they parade around the party area. Videotape the parade and let the children watch themselves perform.
- Each year, record the party guests singing "Happy Birthday" on a cassette tape reserved for this special purpose.

Costumes

Children, especially three to seven year olds, take great pleasure in dressing up. One of the highlights of my son's dinosaur party was the plastic safari helmet each guest decorated with dinosaur stickers and wore as they searched for dinosaurs in the yard. And my daughter's ballerina birthday would not have been the same without the tutus, garland wreaths, and Styrofoam star wands. Costumes don't need to be elaborate. Often a simple hat can transport children into the world of make-believe. Inexpensive hats are available from many party supply stores or can be created from poster board and covered with fabric, foil, paint, and other embellishments. Here are instructions for five easy hats.

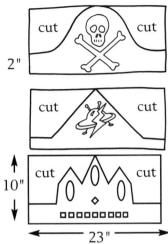

Crown, Pirate Hat, and Alien Hat

Cut a 23" x 10" rectangle out of poster board. Use gold poster board for crown, black for pirate, and silver for alien. For pirate hat, from the center of hat, cut down into a curve leaving the ends about 2" wide. Using white paper or felt, cut out a skull and crossbones and glue to front. For the alien hat, cut from center to create a triangular peak, leaving the ends about 2" wide. Cut a green, shiny lightning bolt and glue to center. For a crown, cut a series of evenly spaced triangles, leaving the ends about 2" wide. Glue shiny rhinestones or shiny paper jewels to crown. Glue or staple the 2-inch ends to fit child's head.

Princess Crown and Clown Hat

Out of poster board, cut a half circle with a 17" radius. Cover with metallic fabric for a princess hat or brightly colored fabric for a clown hat. After checking your child's head for size, glue the two straight ends together to form a hat. Sew or staple 1/4" elastic to fit under the chin. For a princess hat, sew or staple a 20" x 10" piece of fabric to the top of the hat. For a clown hat, glue felt circles and stars around the hat. Glue a large pompom on the top of the hat.

Face Paints

Face paints offer an easy dress-up option. Party stores, toy stores, and costume shops sell face paints. I like to use face paints in "crayon" form. Green paint creates a camouflage face for a young soldier or skin color for a dinosaur or space alien. Black is used to make mustaches, beards, dark eyebrows, animal noses and whiskers, to outline a clown face, or create a special design. Most face paints are easily removed with soap and water, baby oil, or petroleum jelly, but check the instructions before using to avoid problems. Provide a large mirror so guests can see their new "look." Do not use tempera paint as it flakes off and is itchy.

Of course, the easiest way to have costumed guests is to invite guests to come to the party dressed for the theme. As guests RSVP, ask if they have clothes to fit the theme. Provide a few dress-up options for guests who don't have anything to wear or forget to dress up. If there aren't enough dress-up options in your child's dress-up box, borrow from friends or search through the racks at the local thrift store. If a child balks at donning a costume, don't press him. Assure him his regular clothes are fine and let him know the dress-up things are available if he changes his mind. Be sure to have the camera ready for pictures of costumed guests.

Young guests love it when the adults dress up too. Don a poodle skirt, put on a party hat, or paint a happy clown smile on your face. Your young guests will admire the outfit, and you'll have more fun too.

Party Favors

When planning birthday parties for my children, I've always regarded party favors as an important element in creating a festive environment. Favors are a great way for the birthday child to thank guests for coming and a way to send a "piece of the party" home with each child. Not long ago, however, I was confronted with a different view of party favors when I opened the *L.A. Times* to an article entitled "Mom's New Status Symbol: Goody Bag." The article presented a story of mothers desperate to make a positive impact on their child's friends (not to mention their own friends) by spending hundreds of dollars on birthday party favors! The following week I was relieved to read the letters to the editor about this article, in which readers pointed out how detrimental this was to children.

I was shocked at how out-of-hand the "goody bag" competition had come to be, and certainly do not believe it is healthy for our children, but I can relate to those mothers' desire to please young guests. Unfortunately, in a desire to please today's children, it's easy to fuel the attitude of entitlement so evident in our society. Here are some hints on providing favors that will enhance the festive party atmosphere without engaging in the goody bag wars!

- Set a price limit per child.
- Choose favors well in advance to avoid last-minute "desperation" purchases.

Fifty Nifty Favors

1–3 years	3+ years
Plastic animal	*Autograph book*
Stuffed animal	*Baseball cards*
Animal crackers	*Hair accessories*
Bubble solution	*Hat*
Board book	*Bug box*
Beach ball	*Art supplies*
Sand toy	*Candy*
Water toy	*Cookie-pop*
Sunglasses	*Fruit roll*
Animal ears	*Finger bike/board*
Duplos	*Gift certificate*
Framed photo	*Frisbee*
Decorated T-shirt	*Jacks*
Modeling clay	*Jump rope*
Sipper cup	*Key chain*
Sing-along tape	*Kazoo*
Hat	*Kaleidoscope*
Puppet	*Magnet*
Pinwheel	*Magnifying glass*
Toothbrush	*Fancy shoestrings*
Crayons	*Whistle*
Colored chalk	*Water toy*
Raisins	*Sports bottle*
Teething toy	*Puzzle*
Stickers	*Yo-yo*

- Buy favor(s) in bulk from party stores, mail-order companies, or websites.
- Choose an item(s) that is fun to give and receive.
- Give all guests the same favor.
- Use crafts or game prizes as favors.
- Choose an item that goes with the theme.
- Think of something you can make yourself. Bake cookie-pops (cookies with a lollipop stick inserted before baking), make homemade modeling clay, or stir up a batch of bubble mix.
- Package the gift in an eye-catching way: use colored lunch sacks, Chinese takeout cartons, plastic party hats, beach pails, comic paper wrap, or purchased party bags.
- Label each favor with the guest's name.
- Personalize a classic favor with themed stickers, a picture, or a computer-generated tag or label.

There are various theories on the appropriate time to pass out favors to guests. I have experienced the most success with presenting favors at the end of the party, either while waiting for parents to pick up guests or as a parting thank-you when saying good-bye. Whatever you decide, instruct the birthday child to give the favor to each guest, taking the opportunity to thank him or her for coming to the party.

Manners

Good manners enhance a party environment, and a party environment provides a natural venue for children to practice the many little rules of etiquette mothers endeavor to teach. With some guidance from mom and dad, a child can learn to welcome and introduce guests, allow others to go first, show appreciation for gifts, and thank guests for attending the party.

Several days before the party, begin giving your child guidance in appropriate party behavior. Share with him what is expected and provide him with opportunities to practice through role-playing. Use stuffed animals to practice greeting guests. Introduce each "stuffed" guest to the other "stuffed" friends in the room. Practice what to do when opening gifts. Younger children can be taught to simply say thank-you to the giver after opening a gift, possibly bestowing a grateful hug. Older children should be taught several responses to give when receiving gifts, especially gifts he already has or does not really care for. Teach your child to use phrases such as, "Thank you for giving this to me," "This looks like a lot of fun," or "I'm not surprised I received two of these. It's one of my favorites."

During the party be gentle with reminders about manners. A festive environment is extremely stimulating to some children and they may have a difficult time with self-control. Some families arrange in advance a special signal to give to a child who needs to remember manners. A mother might tug on her ear or say "Chris, MYM" (mind your manners) as a quiet reminder to her child. Remember, children are not born with good manners; good manners are acquired through time and practice. Rather than embarrassing a child in front of guests by mentioning poor manners, make a mental note of what needs to be reinforced and work on it another day.

Thank-you Notes

Writing thank-you notes is a good way for a child to show gratitude towards those who do something special for her. Thank-you note writing is a skill a child will be able to use throughout adulthood. Unfortunately, thank-you notes are often neglected in the hurried life of today's family. I must admit I have not been as diligent in this area as I should have been. Thinking back through past birthday experiences, I've come up with the following list of suggestions for getting those thank-you notes written, addressed, and mailed.

- When planning the party, set aside a specific period of time afterward for writing thank-you notes.
- Before a child plays with a gift, require him to write a thank-you note to the giver.
- Purchase thank-you cards, stamps, and some cute stickers for envelopes at the same time as you purchase invitations.
- Make a list of gift and giver as gifts are opened.

- When addressing envelopes for invitations, address envelopes for thank-you notes. (Finding an address again has at times been my downfall.)
- Take Polaroid pictures of the birthday child with each gift. Send the picture with a note on the back.
- Children who cannot yet write their own name can scribble a picture and/or use a rubber stamp to imprint their own name.
- A gift of personalized notepaper can encourage an older child to write thank-you notes.
- Allow older children to design a thank-you note on the computer, but make sure they sign the notes by hand.

Party in a Box

Do you long to create a festive, fun-filled party environment for your child's next birthday, but the thought of planning, shopping, and crafting gives you a massive headache? On-line and mail-order entrepreneurs have the answer for you. With just a few clicks of the mouse you can order what is commonly referred to as a "birthday in a box." Priced at around twenty-five to seventy-five dollars for eight guests, several on-line vendors offer a box that includes everything from invitations, paper goods, and decorations to party favors and tips for games and activities. As the contents of party boxes can vary widely, I recommend ordering well in advance. (Rush delivery will also add to the cost.) I used a 1950s party box from American Girl with great success. The decorations, especially the cake decorations, were easy to use and the paper goods were eye-catching and of good quality. Our only disappointment was with the enclosed cassette tape. There were just not enough songs to last an entire party. The party favors were a big hit, although it was expensive to add for extra guests. Overall, I appreciated the time I saved by not having to think up and search out all the elements to fit the theme, the guests oohed and aahed over the decorations and party favors, and my daughter considered her ninth birthday party a great success. Check the resources in the appendix if you're interested in hosting a "birthday in a box."

Chapter Seven

Great Games and Activities

**Play Pin the Tail, then Simon Says,
A game of Blind Man's Bluff!
Fill every party moment
With oodles of fun stuff.**

Ten children stood poised in two straight lines, ears attuned for the word "Go!" Laughing, the first player in each line raced toward a red bucket filled to the brim with cooked spaghetti, scooped up a handful, and ran back to the team. Gleefully the players passed the wet noodles hand over hand to the end of the line, where they were deposited in a plastic bowl. Upon depositing the pasta in the bowl, the last player raced to the bucket, grabbed more slimy spaghetti and headed back to the team. Cries of "Don't drop it," "Hurry up, they're ahead," and "Oh, this feels so disgusting!" were heard as each team attempted to transfer the most spaghetti from bucket to bowl. "Run, Antonio, you can do it!" "Wow, that's a big handful of noodles!" the players encouraged their teammates as they enjoyed a rousing birthday relay.

LAUGHTER, SINGING, AND GIGGLES—those beautiful sounds of children having fun. It's what every mother hopes to hear during her child's birthday party. But how to draw out those happy sounds? How to fill the hours of a successful birthday party? The secret to success lies in planning plenty of age-appropriate crafts, games, and activities to occupy birthday guests from the minute they arrive at the party until it's time to say good-bye. Careful advance preparation allows guests to transition quickly and smoothly to each activity, maximizing the amount of fun they can experience during the party and minimizing the opportunities for boredom to set in. A variety of activities including crafts, quiet and active games, and even thinking games for older children creates a sense of anticipation as guests try to guess what will happen next. Incorporating activities the birthday child enjoys will provide an opportunity to share favorites with friends.

Develop a Game Plan

Consider the amount of time guests will spend at the party, then estimate how much time to allot for each component. Use the schedule on page 83 as a guide, adjusting for the number of guests and their ages. When serving a meal, add ten to fifteen minutes for serving and eating. Post the party schedule on the refrigerator or another prominent place for easy reference. Wear a watch during the party to keep track of the time.

Vary the Pace

Vary the types of activities throughout the party. Start with a quiet activity such as a craft so guests have time to chat and become comfortable in the party environment. Plan one or two active games such as Musical Chairs or a relay race, and then slow the pace down with a quiet game or craft. Plan a few more active games, and then have children participate in a quiet table activity like coloring place mats or playing "Wink" while you prepare to serve the snacks. Close the party with an open-ended activity. If you've videotaped the party, guests will enjoy watching themselves on television!

Party Schedule

Age: 5 years   Length of party: 2 ¹/₂ hours   # Guests: 7
Theme: "Who Let the Dogs Out?"

1:00–1:20	Arrival activity—Make dog collars, tails, and dog-ear hats
1:20–1:30	"Go Fetch" relay
1:30–1:40	Dog bone hunt
1:40–1:50	Obedience school (Simon Says)
1:50–2:00	Tail tag
2:00–2:15	Table activities—Make pretzel dog bones, tape-record barking contest
2:15–2:25	Play "Doggie, doggie, where's your bone?"
2:25–2:45	Enjoy cake, ice cream, and dog bones
2:45–3:00	Open gifts
3:00–3:15	Listen to recorded barks, give out prizes and favor bags
3:15–3:30	Watch party video and free play
3:30	Pick-up/extra game: Hidden puppy (hide-and-seek)

Let the Games Begin!

Plan an activity to engage guests immediately upon arrival. As most guests arrive during the first fifteen minutes of the party, arrival activities should be open-ended. Ask another adult or helper to supervise this activity so you and the birthday child can focus on greeting guests. A themed craft is one excellent choice. When early birds finish the project before other guests, allow them to use extra supplies to create something else or help another guest finish his project. Other on-site resources like a sandbox filled with buckets, shovels, and cars, or the family collection of Play-Doh and cookie cutters will entice guests to join in the fun. Some guests, especially those less than five years, may prefer to sit with a parent or other adult and watch awhile before joining in.

Plan More Than Enough

Plan at least two or three more activities than you think will be needed to fill the time. Keep in mind that many party activities take less than ten minutes to carry out! If you're uncertain how long an activity will take, time your child doing the activity. Ask a sibling or friend to participate if the activity requires more than one child. With extra activities planned, when an activity doesn't appeal to guests, there is the option of ending it quickly and moving on to another activity.

When children are enthusiastically involved in an activity, allow them to continue enjoying it a bit longer. And if guests clamor to go back to an activity they especially enjoyed, allow them to do so. The most important thing during the party is the ability to be flexible!

Although you will be tempted to schedule every minute of your child's party, don't forget that children of all ages enjoy time for free play. Provide the children with clear instructions about what is available for use during free play. As children approach the preteen years, they will desire more free time to hang out together.

Organize All Supplies

Carefully organize the necessary supplies for each activity at least one day before the party. Place the supplies in separate boxes or bags labeled with the activity's name or description. I like to use the large handled paper bags distributed by some stores. If a helper will be in charge of the activity, write out instructions on the outside of the box or bag. Organizing supplies will alleviate stressful last-minute searches for stray supplies and keep the party running smoothly.

Plan around the Theme

Planning activities around the party's theme adds to the pizzazz. If your computer-loving twelve-year-old chooses "Surfin' through Cyberspace" as the party theme, brainstorm together for activity ideas to carry out the theme. Often traditional games like scavenger hunts or art projects can be easily modified to fit a theme. For this party, the scavenger hunt could be renamed Search Engine Scavenger Hunt and the classic party game Hot Potato becomes Mouse Byte. Some activity suggestions for a "Surfin' through Cyberspace" party might include:

Opening Activities

- Decorate a party hat
- Create a party costume
- Make a puppet
- Decorate cookies or cupcakes
- Make edible jewelry
- Design a card for the birthday child
- Decorate a party tablecloth
- Chalk a sidewalk mural
- Put up the decorations (older children)
- Sculpt with modeling clay
- Build a frame from tongue depressors and decorate with stickers
- Decorate a light switch cover
- Trace each child's body on butcher paper and have them decorate
- Hunt for pennies, buttons, or age-appropriate puzzle pieces (ages three and up)
- Build a town with various types of blocks
- Play on playground equipment
- Dig in a sandbox
- Play bingo
- Make music with a collection of children's instruments
- Play Follow the Leader or Simon Says
- Create a page for a party memory book
- Blow bubbles

- Provide art supplies and host a surfboard design contest with prizes for best use of computer pictures in design, best graphics, best rendition of a virus, best use of a logo, most likely to be forwarded, or most creative illustration of an e-mail address.
- Create a giant yarn web across the family room or backyard.
- Search Engine Scavenger Hunt. Have guests ask neighbors or search the house for old computer programs, floppy disks, computer text books, a keyboard, the oldest looking mouse pad, funniest e-mail address, the signature of a person who still uses an Apple, a 5 1/4-inch floppy disk, and two pieces of tractor-fed computer paper that are still connected.
- BTW, I'm ROTFL! (For the chat room novice this is By the Way, I'm Rolling on the Floor Laughing.) Have a contest to see which team can define the most chat room abbreviations and symbols in five minutes. Award bonus points if a team comes up with another abbreviation the opposing team doesn't know. (See sidebar.)
- Mouse Byte. Hot potato using a toy mouse as the potato.
- Forward Mail "Madlibs." Write a chain-mail type letter, leaving out selected nouns, verbs, or adjectives for guests to fill in.

BTW, What Does ROTFL Mean?

IMHO	in my humble opinion
TIA	thanks in advance
:)	smile, laugh, that's a joke
:(	too bad, frown
BBIAF	be back in a flash
J/K	just kidding
LOL	laughing out loud
TTFN	ta-ta for now
:'(	crying
{{{you}}}	hugs for you
***	kisses
BTY	back to you
LTNS	long time no see
WTG!	Way to go!
ALL CAPS	shouting

Plan for a Change in Weather

Hosting a birthday party in the backyard or other outdoor location greatly increases activity options, but what if the weather forces the party back indoors? Have an alternative plan in mind when scheduling outdoor activities. Some activities can be moved inside with a few easy modifications, but others will have to be discarded. A giant piece of paper for making a mural, a new video, or a selection of board games may save the day when the weather doesn't cooperate.

Logistics of Large Groups

Involving large groups of children in the same activity can be a challenge. Children grow bored when they have to wait too long for a turn, it's difficult to provide assistance to a large group of children during a craft project, and children may have difficulty understanding directions when part of a large group. When hosting a party with ten or more guests, divide the children into two or three prearranged groups. Assign a helper to lead each group through the arranged activities on a rotating schedule. Another alternative is to assign one helper for each activity and having the groups change activities at a prearranged time. Provide a second activity to fill the extra time if one activity is significantly shorter than the others. Young children could sing songs; older children could play guessing games like Pictionary or charades. Give the children in each group the same color name tag or colored plastic visor so it's easy to discern which guest belongs in a particular group. A name tag also makes it easier for helpers to remember children's names.

Hiring Entertainment

Hired entertainment can add an element of fun to a birthday celebration. Providing outside entertainment can also alleviate the pressure of having to fill every moment of a party with creative activities. One of the easiest parties I ever threw included a rented bounce house. The children spent more than half of the party literally bouncing off the walls. And, yes, grown-ups can bounce too! High school and college students are also possible resources for party entertainment. During one daughter's third birthday party, my fifteen-year-old neighbor enthusiastically shared her love of ballet with the guests. She was prepared, patient, and the little girls adored her.

Consult friends and family for recommendations on hired entertainment, or check out the local yellow pages or ads. Prices, provided services, and quality vary. Consult the sidebars for hired entertainment suggestions and tips on selecting and hiring entertainment. Pay close

Tips for Hiring Entertainment

- *Ask the birthday child for suggestions.*
- *Ask for and call at least two references.*
- *If possible, view the entertainment at another party.*
- *Ask to see a performance videotape or brochure.*
- *What is included in the entertainment package?*
- *How long will the entertainment last?*
- *What is the recommended age range?*
- *What experience has the entertainer had with the age group you've invited?*
- *What time will the entertainment arrive?*
- *How long will set-up take?*
- *What is the total cost?*
- *What method of payment is required?*
- *When is payment rendered?*
- *What does the hostess need to provide?*

attention to the entertainment's suggested appropriate age range. Small children may be intimidated by large, noisy, or unexpected entertainment. Be sure to get a reference for an event performed for children the same age as your birthday child.

Have an alternative activity planned in case the hired entertainment doesn't show up. One mother I know had to fill the party time because the pony she hired fell into the swimming pool at the party scheduled immediately before hers. This resourceful mom filled the time with backyard toys and an impromptu hunt, then served the cake and opened gifts. By that time, the conscientious pony owner had rounded up two other ponies and arrived at the party.

Crafts

Craft activities are delightful additions to most birthday parties. Children have the opportunity to create something they are proud of, all guests are able to participate at the same time, and they provide special take-home mementos of the party. Several days before the party, help your child make the party craft. This will show about how much time to allocate for the craft, what supplies need to be prepared, and ensure the craft is within the ability level of the invited guests. It's also an opportunity to work out any "kinks" in the instructions or supplies. (One craft I purchased from a reputable company contained glue that would not dry. Since I discovered this before the party, I was able to provide the guests with a different type of glue that dried within minutes.) Organize all craft supplies in one box or bin before the party, or separate supplies into individual kits for each guest. Provide at least one finished sample so guests can see the finished product. Have extra supplies on hand in case a guest needs to start over. Provide "parent and me" craft projects for children under three. Here are a variety of craft projects suitable to birthday parties:

Entertainment Suggestions

- *Artist*
- *Clown*
- *Costumed characters*
- *Dancer*
- *Disc jockey*
- *Fire fighter*
- *Karate expert*
- *Magician*
- *Musician*
- *Naturalist (with animal friends)*
- *Police officer*
- *Scientist*
- *Sports figure*
- *Storyteller*
- *Bounce house*
- *Climbing wall*
- *Dunk tank*
- *Model train*
- *Pony rides*
- *Popcorn cart*
- *Petting zoo*
- *Puppeteer*
- *Reptile show*

Hat or Visor Decorating. Decorate a baseball hat, helmet, or plastic visor with paint pens, stickers, or buttons. Decorate a straw hat with ribbon and flowers.

Create a Party Hat. Create a construction paper hat to fit the theme.

Photo Frames. Decorate an inexpensive wooden or plastic frame with paint, paint pens, stickers, buttons, puzzle pieces, or dyed pasta. Consider taking a group photo early in the party and sending a helper to have it developed. A digital camera allows you to shoot, download, and print pictures while guests work on the frames. Place photo in frame before guests depart.

Decorate a pet rock, flowerpot, light switch plate, pumpkin, bug box, jewelry box, balloon, ball, pillowcase, tennis shoes, or toothbrush holder.

Paper Plate Crafts. Use a paper plate as the foundation for a ladybug, butterfly, monster mask, animal puppet, or something related to the party theme.

Painting. Provide finger paints, tempera paints, watercolors, or spatter paints so guests can create an original work of art or participate in a group mural.

Box Crafts. Provide a box for each child, cut and glued to be a car, doghouse, boat, or something tied to the theme of the party. Provide supplies to decorate. See chapter 6 for more ideas.

No-Cook Play Dough

4 1/2 cups flour
1 1/2 cups salt
6 tablespoons vegetable oil
Food coloring
Water

1. Using hands, mix first three ingredients in a large bowl until well blended.
2. Mix food coloring with 2 cups water; add colored water, a little at a time, to flour mixture until desired consistency. Add more water as needed.
3. Divide into 12 equal portions. Place each portion in a Ziploc bag, squeezing air out of bag before sealing.

Edible Play Dough

3 1/2 cups creamy peanut butter
4 cups powdered sugar
3 1/2 cups honey
4 cups dry milk powder

1. In a large bowl, cream together peanut butter and powdered sugar.
2. Slowly add honey and beat well.
3. Slowly fold in dry milk powder.
4. Divide into 12 equal portions. Place each portion in Ziploc bag. Refrigerate until use.

Note: Some children are allergic to peanut products.

Edible Necklaces. Let children string cereal or candy onto licorice whips. Older children can use wrapped hard candy and tie the cellophane wrapper ends together with ribbon.

Edible Dough Creations. Provide each guest with pretzel dough (see chapter 5 for recipe), thawed frozen bread dough, or edible play dough to make a creation that can be eaten.

Play Dough or Modeling Clay. Sculpt themed creations.

Puppets. Create puppets out of tube socks, paper bags, paper plates, felt, or tongue depressors and poster board.

Paper Art. Provide paper for origami, to make greeting cards, bookmarks, paper dolls and doll wardrobe, or for older children, try papermaking.

Collages. Provide a piece of white poster board and glue, along with Sunday comic strips, themed pictures, or objects from nature (leaves, seeds, flower petals) to create an original collage.

T-shirts. Place T-shirt around a T-shirt board (a piece of cardboard cut to size of T-shirt, with waxed paper placed between cardboard and section to be painted). Use masking tape or safety pins at back to stretch T-shirt tight. Provide puffy paints, sponges, fabric markers, or fabric stamps and ink. Older children might enjoy learning tie-dye or batik techniques.

Jewelry. Provide beads, ribbon, flowers, rhinestones, buttons, glitter, leather, or plastic lacing to create necklaces, bracelets, barrettes, or belts.

Games and Group Activities

Finger Plays and Sing-Alongs. See the appendix for suggested books.

Bubbles. Provide bubble solution and various bubble makers.

Mystery Dramas. See the appendix for a source.

Piñata. Purchase a piñata along with candy or small toys for filling. Provide each guest with a paper bag, labeled with guest's name, for goodie collection. Hang the piñata with a sturdy rope (a jump rope works well) in an open area. Line up children from youngest to oldest. Make sure the line is well out of striking range. Instruct all guests to sit down. Allow children to take three turns hitting the piñata with a bat or stick. Children five years and older should wear a blindfold, younger children can close eyes. To make the activity more challenging for older children, pull the piñata up and down or swing from side to side. After the piñata breaks open and the stick is safely removed, allow children to collect the piñata prizes. Challenge older guests to make certain everyone has the same exact number of prizes! Note: Preschoolers may be reluctant to hit a favorite character or animal piñata. Some will even cry at the scene. For this age I recommend an object piñata, such as a star, a baseball bat, a watermelon slice, or a decorated shape.

Hunts. Hide objects within a designated area. When guests are young, at least part of the object should be visible. Have each guest search for a certain number or color, or work as teams to allow each child the opportunity to find something. See sidebar for tips on organizing a treasure hunt and a scavenger hunt.

Classic Party Games

There are countless games and activities that can provide party fun. The following is a list of party classics. These games are proven winners and most are easily adapted to fit a specific party theme. The games are listed alphabetically. Discuss party games with the birthday child and play only those games your child enthusiastically endorses. Games best suited to younger children (3–5 years) are labeled (Y); games best suited to children 6–9 years are labeled (M); games best suited to older children (9–12 years) are labeled (O).

Balloon Bust. (M) Tie a balloon to one end of a string, then tie the other end around the player's ankle. Players try to pop other player's balloons by stomping on them. Player must also work to protect his own balloon from being stomped.

Organizing a Treasure Hunt

- *Relate clues, treasure container, and treasure to the party theme.*
- *Explore hunt area, noting potential hiding places for clues and treasure.*
- *Work backwards to plan sites. Choose the site to hide the treasure first. Write a clue to this area, then look around the hunt area to find a place to hide the clue. Go to that location, then compose a clue that describes the new spot. Continue until you have enough sites for a challenging hunt.*
- *Clues can be riddles, pictures, coded messages, or written instructions.*
- *Make a list of each clue and site in case you forget or one can't be found.*
- *Challenge guests to divide the loot so each player receives the exact same amount.*

Organizing a Scavenger Hunt

- *Try to relate items to be found to the party theme, or include some unusual or funny items on the list.*
- *Include some items that are easy to find and some that are more difficult to find.*
- *Define boundaries of the hunt. Make sure included items can be found within a given area. Make the boundaries clear to guests. Give a substantial penalty for going out-of-bounds. Boundary areas might be: within a stack of magazines, inside a set of rooms, within a designated park area, inside the back yard, on a given street or streets.*
- *If guests will be outside a visible area, include one chaperone with each group. The group must stay with the chaperone or forfeit. Declare busy streets and gated areas out-of-bounds. Guests should never go into another residence.*
- *Set a time limit. For younger children, set a kitchen timer.*
- *Consider giving each item a different point value.*
- *Divide guests into teams of three or more. Equip each team with a list, pencil, and bag to hold found items. If guests are going very far, make sure someone in the group has a watch so the group can return within the given time limit.*
- *For a different twist on a scavenger hunt, make a list of actions or items to be photographed. Provide each team with a Polaroid or digital camera and instruct guests to take pictures of listed items. (When using a digital camera, be prepared to print the pictures on inexpensive paper as soon as they are taken.)*

Beanbag Toss. (YM) Have guests take turns tossing beanbags into a bucket, hula-hoop, or box with large holes cut into front. Give each guest three turns at a time. Variations: Make a design on the box to fit the party theme. If outdoors, use wet sponges instead of beanbags.

Bingo. (MO) Purchase a commercial birthday bingo game or make your own. Create bingo cards by drawing a grid of squares five across and five down. Above each horizontal square write one letter from the word "BINGO." Randomly write numbers from one to fifty in each square. The middle square is "FREE." Write each grid combination, I-25, N-16, etc., on a caller card. All combinations used on a grid must be placed on a caller card. To play, give each player a set of twenty-five tokens. Pick one caller card at a time and say the combination. Players put a token on top of each matched combination. The first player to get five combinations in a row says, "Bingo!" Variation: Use themed stickers instead of numbers. For instance, a combination might be B-horse or C-fish.

B	I	N	G	O
4	10	3	8	5
7	5	9	6	7
1	2	FREE	10	9
3	4	6	2	3
8	9	1	4	6

Blind Man's Bluff. (M) Choose one player to be the first blind man, and then blindfold this player. The other players stand in a circle, join hands, and move in one direction around the blind man until he claps three times. The blind man then points to one player (if finger points between two players, player on the right is selected) and has one try to guess who it is. If the guess is correct, that player becomes the blind man. If the guess is incorrect, the player steps into the middle of the circle and the blind man has to identify the player by touching clothes, hair, or face. The identified player becomes the next blind man.

Charades. (MO) Before the party, write song titles, books, movies, television shows, and names of famous people on slips of paper. For younger children, use animal stickers or pictures of objects. Fold the papers and place in a bowl. At the party, divide into two teams (younger children may want to play without teams and without a timer) and take turns having a member of each team pick a paper and act it out without using words. The actor's teammates have three minutes to guess what's on the paper. Award a point for each correct guess. Commonly accepted charades signs are: open hands touching each other (book), stretching hand out from mouth (song), hand making cranking motion (movie), hands over head in a V (television show), hands moving from head to hips (famous person), hand to ear (sounds like), holding up one finger (first word), one finger on elbow (first syllable). You may want to write the charade signs on a piece of poster board for reference.

Costume Relays. (YMO) Prepare two piles of clothes that are as similar as possible. Each pile might include a hat, shirt, tie, pants, socks, shoes, and gloves. Divide guests into two teams. Each team member must run to the pile, put on all the clothes, run back to the team, and give them to the second player to put on. The second player runs back to the pile, takes off the clothes, then runs back and tags the third player. The third player proceeds like the first player. The game continues until every team member has put on and taken off the clothes. Be sure clothes are large enough to fit every player with ease. Variations: For a cowboy party, use cowboy clothes such as a vest, cowboy hat, chaps, boots, and a bandanna; for a fire fighter party, use a fireman coat, hat, boots, and shirt; for a sleepover, use nightclothes. Or, instead of clothes, have guests take off their shoes, race to the pile, find their shoes, put them on, then race back and tag the next player.

Doggie, Doggie, Where's Your Bone? (YM) Have the guests sit in a circle. Choose one person to be "it" and sit in the middle of the circle with eyes closed. Give one child in the circle a bone to hide behind his or her back. When the bone is hidden, the children in the circle sing, "Doggie, doggie, where's your bone? Somebody stole it from your home. Guess who, maybe you!" The child who is "it" can then open his eyes and has three guesses to find the bone. If "it" guesses correctly, he may choose the next "it." If "it" doesn't choose correctly, the player with the bone becomes "it." Variations: Change the chant and hidden object to suit the party theme; for instance, "Clown, clown, where's your nose?"

Duck, Duck, Goose! (Y) Seat the children in a circle. Choose one child to be "it." "It" walks around the circle, tapping each guest on the head, saying "duck." "It" taps one child on the head and says, "goose." The "goose" gets up and runs around the circle. If "it" makes it around the circle and into "goose's" spot first, "goose" becomes "it"; if not, "it" continues the game. Variations: Change the words used to fit the party theme; for instance, "Car, car, truck!"

Follow the Leader. (YM) Have the guests line up from oldest to youngest. The first player begins to walk, run, or skip and the other players must follow. Change leaders once every minute. For younger children, have an adult or teen helper serve as leader. Variations: Call the leader something to fit the party theme; for a construction party, call it Follow the Foreman or for a musical party call it Follow the Band Major.

93

Hide and Seek. (MO) One guest stands at home base, closes his eyes, and counts while the others hide within a designated area. When the counter arrives at the designated number (ten, fifty, or one hundred, depending on age), he yells, "Ready or not, here I come!" The counter then searches for hidden friends and tags them. To keep every guest involved, have the found friends assist the counter in finding the other players. The last person found gets to be the next counter.

Hot Potato. (YMO) Choose one player to be "it." Players sit in a circle, with "it" in the center. "It" tosses a potato to a player in the circle, and then closes her eyes. Players in the circle must toss the potato around the circle until "it" yells out, "Hot potato!" The player holding the potato at that moment joins "it" in the middle of the circle. "It" throws the potato out again, and closes her eyes while the remaining players toss the potato around the circle. When "it" yells, "Hot potato," the player holding the potato again comes to the middle. Play continues until there is only one player left outside the circle. If you wish to play another round, that player becomes "it." Variations: Use a tennis ball, stuffed animal, water balloon, or old sock. Rename the object to fit the party theme. For older children, eliminate the center player. When a player ends up with the potato, they must do something silly or tell a joke.

Limbo. (MO) Have two guests hold either end of a rope or stick, standing four to six feet apart. Play some upbeat music and have other players take turns going under the barrier without bending their knees or touching their hands or bottom to the ground. The stick starts out at shoulder height and moves down a few inches after each round. The winner is the player who is able to limbo the lowest. Variation: For flashlight limbo, use the beams from two strong flashlights in a darkened room instead of rope or a stick.

Memory. (MO) Place a group of objects on a tray. Bring the tray into the room and allow guests three minutes to observe. Remove tray. Give each player or team a piece of paper and pencil to write down all objects remembered. Bring the tray back and determine the winner. Variations: Use objects that relate to your theme. An unusual twist for older children is to have the birthday child carry in the tray of objects. Tell guests they have three minutes to observe. Send the birthday child and the tray out of the room. Then ask guests to write down everything they can remember about the birthday *child*—clothes, shoes, hair, eyes, or jewelry—instead of the contents of the tray.

Musical Chairs. (YM) Place chairs back to back, one for each player, minus one. Have the players form a circle around the chairs. While music plays, players walk around chairs. When the music stops, each player must find a chair. Player without a chair is out. Remove one chair. Repeat play until one player remains. Variations: Replace chairs with cushions, poster board dinosaur feet, or hats. For a noncompetitive version, remove chairs, but not players. Players who can't find an empty chair sit on the laps of seated players. Play continues until all players are piled together on one chair. Be sure to use a sturdy old chair!

Obstacle Course. (YMO) Set up an obstacle course. A course might include crawling through a big box, running to a designated area, jumping over a small stack of bricks, walking across a board (balance beam), jumping through some tires, riding a scooter a short distance, and digging in a sand box to find a small toy. Be sure the birthday child is able to accomplish each element. Help guests as necessary. Award a big sticker ribbon as each guest completes the course.

Pictionary. (MO) Before the party, write down several objects or actions pertaining to the party theme on 3" x 5" cards. Provide a dry erase board or large tablet of paper and pens. Divide guests into two teams. The teams take turns sending a player to pick a card, and then draw a picture that causes his team to say the word or words on the card within three minutes. The artist may not use letters, numbers, or say anything. The winning team is the first one to earn ten points.

Pin the Tail on the Donkey. (YM) Purchase or draw a large picture of a donkey and enough paper tails for every guest. Label paper tails with guests' names and put a piece of double backed tape on each one. Tape the donkey up on a wall. Have players stand six to ten feet away from the donkey. Blindfold children or let younger children close their eyes. Spin the player around three times, and then have her walk to the donkey and stick the labeled tail where she thinks it belongs. Repeat with remaining players. The winner is the player whose tail is most realistically placed. Variations: Change the picture and object to be "pinned" to fit the party theme; for instance, "Pin the nose on the clown," "Pin the fin on the fish," or "Pin the tooth on the dinosaur."

Races. (YMO) In its simplest form, this game involves lining all the players up at a designated starting point and having them run to a designated finish line. The winner is the player who arrives first. Variations are endless with this one. A "Go fetch" race would involve the children holding a dog bone in their mouth and crawling on all fours to the finish line. Other variations include a two-legged race, wheelbarrow race, gunny-sack (a strong trash bag works well for this, just don't allow children to put their heads in the bag), racing with an object perched on the head, and racing while carrying an egg on a spoon.

Relay Races. (YMO) In its simplest form, this game involves dividing the guests into two or more teams. Line teams up separately behind the starting point. Team members take turns running to a designated spot and then returning to tag the second player. The game is over when the last player on each team runs to the designated spot, then returns and tags the first player. There are countless variations to this one, including the orange relay (having each player run and pick up an orange, then return carrying it under the neck, passing it from player to player using only the neck), the bucket brigade (having each team member run and scoop a handful of water from a bucket and then pass the water from player to player and into a second bucket), or a balloon relay (children jump with balloon between the knees to the designated spot, pop the balloon, then run back and tag the next player).

Red Light, Green Light. (YM) Use a rope or cones to mark parallel lines some distance apart. Select one player to be the police officer and stand behind one of the lines. All the other players stand behind the opposite line. The police officer turns her back to the other players and yells "green light," then counts to five as quickly as she can. The other players walk quickly towards the police officer while she counts. When the police officer has counted to five, she turns around and yells, "red light." All players must immediately freeze, or they go back to the starting line. Play continues until one player has crossed the police officer's line. That player then becomes the police officer and all other players return to the starting line.

Red Rover. (M) Divide players into two teams and line them up across parallel lines some distance away. Players tightly hold the hand of the teammate on either side. One team calls out, "Red Rover, Red Rover, send (a child's name from the opposing team) right over." The opponent runs over to the team and tries to break through the line. If the opponent successfully breaks through, she "captures" a player from the calling team, and both players return to her team who then get to call "Red Rover." If she cannot break through, she joins the opposing line as a new team member and that team gets to call for another player.

Simon Says. (YM) Have players line up youngest to oldest, except the birthday child, who is "Simon." Simon stands opposite the other players and gives a command. If Simon begins the command with "Simon says," the players must follow the command. If Simon doesn't say, "Simon says," the players must stand still. Anyone who follows a command without a "Simon says" must go to the end of the line. After ten commands, the player at the front of the line becomes "Simon" and the previous "Simon" joins the end of the line. Variations: Use the birthday child's name in place of Simon or use a name that fits the party theme.

Spoons. (MO) Gather the guests around a table or in a circle on the floor. In the center of the circle, set out one fewer spoon than there are players. Set the spoons in a starburst pattern for easy access. Shuffle a deck of playing cards and deal each player four cards. Give the remaining cards to the leader. The leader draws a card and sees if she needs it to make a set of four. The leader must decide whether to keep the new card or pass it to the player on her left. If she keeps the card, she must pass one of her original cards to the player on her left. The second player receives the card, looks to see if she needs it to make a set of four, and then must pass one of her cards to the person on her left. This is repeated around the circle with the leader continuously picking new cards off the top of the deck. The player to the left of the leader places discarded cards into a discard pile used by the leader as soon as the original pile is depleted. When a player notices she has four of one card, she quickly and quietly grabs a spoon. All other players must then immediately pick up a spoon too. The player who doesn't get a spoon must do something silly (selected by the player with four-of-a-kind) and then becomes the new leader. Variations: Put candy or small objects to fit the party theme in the center of the table instead of spoons.

Tag. (MO) Set boundaries for the tag game. Assign a "safe" location where players cannot be tagged for up to five seconds. Choose a player to be "it." The other players must try to prevent "it" from tagging them. When a player is tagged by "it," that player becomes the new "it." Variations: Instead of becoming "it," a tagged player joins hands with "it" and they both try and tag the other players. This continues until only one player has not been tagged. That player then becomes the next "it."

Tail Tag. (MO) Set boundaries for the game. Assign a "safe" location where players cannot be tagged for up to five seconds. Divide the players into two teams and give each member of one team a cloth "tail" to tuck into the waistband of their pants. The opposing team must try to capture the tail of every player on the tail team. Once a tail is captured, that player must go to the sidelines (pound, zoo, jail) until the round is over. After a team captures all the tails, that team wears the tails, and the other team must capture them.

Water Balloon Toss. (MO) Divide guests into pairs. Fill enough water balloons for each pair to have one. (Extra balloons are a good idea.) Have each pair stand about four feet away from each other and toss the water balloon. Each pair with an intact water balloon then takes one giant step backward (monitor to make sure pairs are equal distance apart) and tosses again. When a water balloon breaks, that pair is out. Keep tossing and stepping backward until only one pair has an intact water balloon.

Wink. (O) Have all the players sit around a table or on the floor in a circle. From a deck of cards, draw enough cards for every player, all of them black except for one red card. Each player takes a card and looks at it, but does not show anyone else. The person with the red card is the "winker." While everyone talks, the "winker" winks at another player without being noticed by anyone else. The player winked at must call out, "I'm dead," and dramatically play dead. The game continues until the last player is "killed" or someone catches the "winker" in the act. Shuffle the cards, distribute them, and start again.

Fun When You're One

Twelve months have flown past,
So let's have some fun.
Come celebrate,
Our baby's now one!

I fastened a bib inscribed with the words "I'm one today!" around her chubby little neck, checking one last time to be sure she was securely buckled in. My daughter's tiny hands reached to pull down the pink balloons floating from ribbons on the sides of her high chair. Eagerly, my father settled into a chair directly in front of her. In his hands I placed a bowl of ice cream. Danielle looked expectantly at her grandpa, knowing from his expression this was going to be something good. As the spoon touched her tongue, her expression initially registered her surprise at the cold, creamy substance. Her surprise quickly changed to delight. My dad and my daughter exchanged matching smiles as she devoured each bite of her very first sweet treat.

FIRST ICE CREAM, first step, first word, first trip, first tooth, first bath. A baby's life is made up of firsts. Some days it seemed like you would always measure the age of your child in months, but suddenly the months have turned into a full year and your tiny newborn has turned into a sturdy toddler. You realize it's time for yet another first—baby's first birthday.

The first birthday is a significant milestone for both baby and Mommy. As you have diligently endeavored to understand and meet your little one's needs throughout the first year of life, a mother-child bond has been created which forms the foundation for all of your child's future relationships. Under your tender care, your baby has grown from helpless newborn to sturdy toddler, newly mobile and communicating more effectively each day. The first birthday is an opportunity to celebrate both the growth and maturity of your child and your growth and maturity as a parent. It is a chance to express your gratitude to God both for the life he has entrusted into your care and for the wisdom and strength he gives which allows you to understand and care for your child.

Like many of baby's firsts, a child's first birthday is both exciting and a bit intimidating. A trip on-line for research into first birthdays provided query after query about what to do on this special birthday. To my dismay, many times the single reply to these desperate queries was from a professional party planner, offering to coordinate the party for a small (?) fee. Planning for a first birthday doesn't have to be intimidating. With a few helpful hints and some thoughtful planning, you can create a wonderful celebration for this exciting milestone in your child's life.

Choose How to Celebrate

Although your child's brain has made huge developmental strides in the first year, he cannot yet understand the significance of the occasion. Baby's only memories of his birthday will come from looking at the pictures and hearing the stories from others who were there. As a matter of fact, besides the birthday child, a camera and film are perhaps the most important components of a first birthday celebration. By the time your child turns two, he will enjoy looking back at his baby birthday pictures and hearing the story about how he smeared chocolate cake all over his face. These pictures and stories will provide your child with a sense of belonging and affirm his importance in the family.

First birthday celebrations run the gamut from simple family affairs to premiere social events with dozens of family members and friends in attendance. Use the following guidelines to help you decide what will best meet the needs of your family.

- *What are your family's first birthday traditions?* Check with your mother and mother-in-law to see if there are any special family traditions you might want to carry on. Some cultures consider the first birthday a time for significant festivities.
- *How does your baby react to people and noise?* Some babies find large groups of people and loud noise very stressful; other babies thrive on being the center of attention. Match the size of the celebration to your baby's temperament.
- *What size group are you comfortable hosting?* A house crowded with guests and a tired, stressed-out mommy is a recipe for a cranky, anxious baby. Take a look at your schedule and decide how much time you can commit to planning and preparing for baby's first birthday. Plan a celebration you can pull off within those time limitations. If your party plans seem to exceed your allotted time and energy, either simplify your plans or enlist the help of other family members and close friends.
- *When is your baby's best time of day?* Usually a party starting about one half hour after baby wakes up from her nap works best. Of course, babies don't always follow the same schedule every day. Plan to wake your baby about one half hour before the guests arrive. This will give her time to wake up, eat, and be dressed in a relatively calm atmosphere. Keep the party short, less than two hours if possible. That way baby won't be as likely to run out of energy while your guests are still present.

Consider Safety Concerns

If your guest list includes other babies and small children, you need to give close attention to party safety. Here are some safety precautions that can prevent your party from turning from festive to fiasco.

- Make sure an adult is supervising each child at all times. This includes your own child. Resist the idea that you will be able to do this yourself. I guarantee your attention will be divided throughout the entire party. Ask another adult your child knows well (grandma, favorite baby-sitter, uncle) to ensure the well-being of your child. If the birthday child has siblings under the age of four, they will also need adult supervision.
- Limit your party to a carefully selected area. Enclose this area with gates and play fences so the children cannot wander off.
- Crawl around the party area and carefully childproof. Remember other babies may be in a different developmental stage than yours is. Think about crawlers, walkers, and climbers! Cover sharp edges and electrical outlets. Secure cords for electrical appliances and window coverings. Make sure breakables and houseplants are stored in another room during the party.
- Provide your pet a comfortable spot away from the party. Even the gentlest pet may become anxious or overly excited when so many people invade its territory.
- Balloons add a festive touch to a party, but they are a choking hazard for small children. If you choose to use balloons, make sure they are out of baby's reach. If a balloon breaks, immediately pick it up and dispose of all pieces. Consider using only Mylar balloons.
- If using stuffed animals for games or activities, be sure all facial features and clothing are firmly attached.
- Avoid serving nuts, popcorn, small pieces of candy, baby carrots, and hot dogs, which are all common choking hazards for children under three.
- Either ask each infant guest to bring his own highchair or provide a low table and chairs for small children to eat at.

Decide on Refreshments

The most important food at a first birthday is, of course, a cake with one big candle on top. Some hostesses also provide unfrosted cupcakes or muffins for the littlest guests. If you want to provide more than cake and ice cream, consider finger food served buffet style. Parents can munch on finger foods as they keep close watch on their child. Sandwiches, hamburgers, pizza, vegetables or chips and dip, and pieces of fresh fruit are easy to handle when holding a baby. Babies might enjoy banana slices, teething cookies, cheese cubes, raisins, Cheerios, or graham crackers. A personalized sipper cup will make it easier for baby to quench his thirst without destroying your floor and can also serve as a party favor. Provide diluted juices and bottled water for your small guests.

Tips for a Successful First Birthday Party

- *Provide a diaper-changing station for your little guests. Stock the changing station with extra diapers, wipes, antibacterial hand gel, disposable changing pads, plastic bags for soiled diapers or clothes, and a trash can.*
- *Provide a quiet place for nursing mothers and napping babies. If you have a playpen or portable crib, set it up ahead of time in case one of your little guests needs to rest.*
- *Put together a list of gifts your child would enjoy. Often guests will ask for ideas when they RSVP and it is good to be prepared with a few specific suggestions.*
- *Take pictures right away. When babies are overstimulated, they tend to tire quickly. It's nice to have at least some pictures of a smiling face.*

Provide Age-Appropriate Games and Activities

Many entertainers refuse to perform at first birthday parties because they know flamboyant, unfamiliar characters can frighten little ones. A one-year-old has a very short attention span, making it difficult for an entertainer to keep the group's attention for more than five minutes at a time. If you really think you need to provide hired entertainment, consider having a petting zoo or renting a little merry-go-round. Little ones seem to find these enjoyable. When you ask for references, be sure they include at least one from a first birthday party to ensure the entertainer has experience with very young children.

Although adult guests are usually content to talk and watch the babies play, a planned activity can make the celebration more enjoyable and meaningful. Adult guests can participate in a baby book quiz or try to put a series of the birthday child's baby pictures in chronological order. Creating a time capsule for the birthday child is another great activity for adult guests. Ask each guest to write a note to your baby, expressing their hopes, dreams, and prayers for his or her future. Save these notes to be opened on the child's twenty-first birthday. Some families cover a serving table with an inexpensive white tablecloth and ask guests to sign the cloth with fabric pens or leave their handprints using washable fabric paint. (If you want to capture the handprints of young guests, review the hints in chapter 2.) The birthday child will treasure his personalized tablecloth or time capsule for years to come.

Three First Birthday Party Plans

As mentioned in chapter 4, selecting a theme brings focus to your party planning and makes it a unique celebration designed with your child's interests in mind. Often simply "first birthday" is the only theme necessary for this celebration. However, even at the age of one, there are probably things that especially appeal to your child (puppies, Winnie the Pooh, trains, farm animals, etc.) that can provide a personalized party theme. Many times baby's favorite book, such as *Pat the Bunny*, *The Big Hungry Caterpillar*, or *Goodnight, Moon* can be developed into an interesting party theme. On the following pages are plans for carrying out three different parties appropriate for a first birthday celebration. These party plans can be used as they are, simplified by just choosing the parts you like best, or modified to fit the theme you have chosen.

Pat the Bunny Party

Based on the book *Pat the Bunny* by Dorothy Kunhardt.

5 1/2"

4"

Length of party: 1 1/2 hours

Invitations: You can either purchase *Pat the Bunny* invitations or cut an 8 1/2" x 11" piece of white cardstock in half lengthwise. Fold half sheet across the short width. Trace bunny face as shown, putting tips of ears at top fold. Cut out bunny face, leaving tips of ears connected. Cut pink felt and glue on ears. Glue a small pink pompom in place for nose. With a black marker, draw eyes and mouth as shown. Print party information on computer and glue inside of bunny invitation.

Decorations: Mylar bunny and baby's first birthday balloons; aqua, peach, and yellow streamers; stuffed bunnies; bunches of carrots tied together with twine.

Paper goods: You can purchase *Pat the Bunny* table covers, plates, and napkins, or purchase aqua paper table covers, peach luncheon and cake plates, and peach cups for adults. Purchase sipper cups for children.

Food: Finger sandwiches, vegetables and dip (rabbit food), pretzel sticks (bunny whiskers), beverages, Bunny Cake, and ice cream.

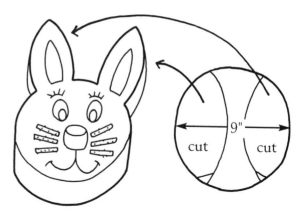

Some vegetables, such as carrot sticks, can be a choking hazard for children under three years of age. Serve these to adults only.

Activities for children:

- Paint a pink bunny nose and black whiskers on each child.
- Sit in a circle with babies on laps and play patty-cake.
- Read *Pat the Bunny* and/or have a sing-along to a *Pat the Bunny* cassette.
- Hide stuffed bunnies around the room and let babies find them.
- Play "Touchy-feely." Collect a group of items with varied textures. Pass these around for babies to feel. Items to include: sandpaper,

---

Bunny Cake

1. *Bake your favorite carrot cake recipe in two 9-inch round cake pans. Cool in pans.*
2. *Remove from pans. Place one cake at the bottom of a cake or cutting board. Cut two ears from other cake as shown and place them on top of round cake.*
3. *Frost with white icing. Place a large marshmallow on round cake for nose. Form the mouth using thin black licorice (or use tube of chocolate icing with decorating tip). Use 2 pink Necco wafers for eyes. Make eyelashes out of pretzel stick pieces and whiskers out of whole pretzel sticks or black licorice. Sprinkle middle of ears with pink sugar.**

Decorating time: 45 minutes. Serves 16.

*Colored sugar is available in the baking aisle of most supermarkets, at craft stores, and at cake decorating supply shops.

cotton ball, keys, cooked pasta, ice cube, fake fur, big pretzels, and beach ball.

Activities for adults: Write "honey bunny" notes for the birthday child. Set out pastel colored note cards and bunny stickers. Ask each adult to write a sweet note to the birthday child. Place these in a memory book with pictures of each guest.

Party favors: *Pat the Bunny* book or cassette tape; sipper cups with child's name; Polaroid photo of baby and guest; carrots made of orange cellophane filled with Cheerios and tied with green raffia; small stuffed bunny.

Barnyard Babies Party

Length of party: 1 1/2 hours

Invitations: Purchase Barnyard Friends invitations or cut an 8 1/2" x 11" piece of red cardstock in half across the short side. Enlarge and trace barn pattern onto half sheet as shown. Cut. With a black pen draw in the barn doors, window, and silo roof. Draw a heavy black outline along top of barn roof. With an X-Acto knife, cut the window and barn doors so they open. Cut a piece of white cardstock the same size as the barn. Glue it to the back of the barn. Put a farm animal sticker in the window and print the party information inside the barn doors.

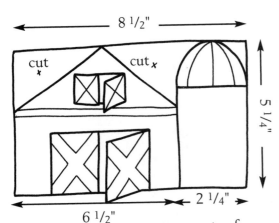

8 1/2"

cut x

cut x

5 1/4"

2 1/4"

6 1/2"

Decorations: Barnyard Friends and "Baby's 1st Birthday" balloons; red, white, and black streamers; toy farm animals, barns, or tractors; a scarecrow; corn stalks or hay (if outside or in garage); bandannas; barn made out of a large packing box.

Paper goods: Purchase Barnyard Friends table cover, plates, napkins, and cups, or use red-and-white checked table covers, disposable pie pans as luncheon plates, red cake plates, red cups for adults, and bandannas for napkins. Purchase sipper cups with farm animals on them for children.

Food for adults: Barbecued chicken, corn on the cob, potato salad, deviled eggs, haystacks (potato sticks), produce (vegetable plate), Barnyard Cake, and ice cream.

Food for children under three: Slivers of chicken meat, corn off the cob, potato salad, deviled eggs, small pieces of vegetables, Barnyard

Barnyard Cake

1. *Bake two 9" x 13" cakes. Cool and remove from pans.*
2. *Place one cake on a cake or cutting board and frost with chocolate icing. Cut the other cake as shown. Be sure C-F are triangles cut from a 4 1/2" square. Stack pieces A and B on top of whole cake. Place C, D, E, and F on top to form roof. Frost entire barn with a thin layer of white icing to glue together. Let dry.*
3. *Frost the door and window areas in white. Use graham cracker sections to form an open barn door, and smaller pieces to form an open window. Use a black tube of icing to make an X on each window shutter and doors. Frost the barn walls red and the roof with brown icing. Cover the roof with Life cereal "shingles."*
4. *For silo, cut a paper towel tube to size. Cover with red cellophane. Place a foil cupcake holder on top for silo roof. Press silo into frosting on one side of barn. Add several small plastic farm animals around barn and place a rooster on the barn roof.*

Decorating time: 1 1/2 hours. Serves 24–30.

Note: This is the most difficult cake included in this book. An easier alternative would be to arrange the fence and plastic animals from a child's farm play set on top of a chocolate frosted sheet cake.

Cake, and ice cream. Remember, some hard vegetables like carrots can be a choking hazard for children under three years.

Activities for children:

- Paint children's faces to look like animals (some babies may not like this idea).
- Play in box painted to resemble a barn (see invitation) and filled with stuffed animals.
- Hide stuffed animals around the room and have a stuffed animal hunt.
- Finger plays: "Itsy Bitsy Spider" and "This Little Piggy."
- Sing "Old McDonald Had a Farm."
- Hire a petting zoo or pony.
- Look at picture books about farm animals.

Activities for adults: Create a memory book. Purchase memory album pages, farm stickers, and paper. Ask guests to write a note or prayer for baby on a page, then decorate it.

Favors: Small stuffed animals; red sipper cups; bandannas; a small copy of *Old McDonald Had a Farm*; animal crackers; piggy banks.

It's a "One"-derful Life Party

Length of party: 1 1/2 hours

Invitations: Purchase "Baby's 1st Birthday" invitations or make *Life* magazine invitations. On a piece of white cardstock, print the phrase "It's a 'One'-derful Life" and the party information twice on right half of paper. Cut paper in half and fold so party information is on inside.

On outside, glue a picture of the birthday child. At top left, print the word "LIFE" in red, and underneath this write baby's birth date. (You can also make the cover by scanning the photo and adding computer lettering for the word "LIFE.")

Decorations: "Baby's 1st Birthday" balloons; enlarged poster size photos of baby; several number ones cut out of poster board and hanging from the ceiling; a poster board of baby pictures; streamers; *Life* magazines.

Paper goods: Purchase "Baby's 1st Birthday" paper goods or paper goods in favorite color.

Food: One long submarine sandwich, single serve bags of chips, single serve fruit cups, Jell-O jigglers cut into number ones, single cans of soda, and junior-size water bottles. Serve cupcakes with one candle on top and a single scoop of ice cream. As an alternative to decorating a cake, have the party invitation copied onto the top of a sheet cake.

Activities for children:

- Baby Can. For this simplified lap game version of Simon Says, the leader calls out "Baby can" and then gives a simple instruction like "Touch your nose" or "Find your belly button."
- Play peek-a-boo.
- Put out favorite baby toys like blocks, stacking cups, baby gyms, beach balls, or mirrors.

Activities for adults: Create a time capsule. Take a Polaroid picture of baby with each adult. Ask each adult to write a note to the child on the back of the photo. Place this inside a plastic box along with baby's hand- and footprints, a party napkin, and any other special mementos of the day. Bury the time capsule in a designated spot in the backyard or store in an out-of-the-way closet until baby turns ten or twenty-one.

Favors: A photo of guest and baby; a board book about babies; Play doh; bubbles; "number one" hands (used at sporting events); single serve pudding cups; candy bar wrapped in a computer-generated label printed with baby's name and photo.

Terrific Times for Twos and Threes

**My two pudgy fingers
Proudly displayed,
Let everyone know
I'm two today!**

His freckled nose close to the table, Dillon carefully glued the lion's eyes and nose onto the brown paper bag. With much assistance from his dad, he attached five sticky pieces of yellow yarn along the top of the bag until a kingly mane appeared. Impatiently insisting his "wion" didn't need any more "whiskers," Dillon plunged his tiny hand into the brown bag. Now intent on the brightly painted puppet theater, he darted across the room, growling at the other excited guests along the way. For one or two minutes Dillon stood behind the theater, totally absorbed in entertaining anyone interested with his lion puppet; then on he moved to the circle of friends, performing finger plays with his mommy.

IF YOU'RE PLANNING A PARTY for a two- or three-year-old, it's likely you're well-acquainted with a curious, energetic, self-absorbed little person like Dillon. In some ways, twos and threes are the easiest children for whom to plan a birthday party, but in other ways they are the most challenging. Twos and threes have a refreshing fascination for just about anything, but that fascination rarely lasts long. Children this age are usually curious and interested in playing with other children, but are not very far along in their journey away from self-absorption. These precious little ones desire to assert their independence, but often need the security and guidance of a familiar person. And while tiny tots move energetically from task to task without the aid of caffeine, they do tire quickly, becoming increasingly irritable and difficult to engage. In order to host a successful party for two- or three-year-old children, one needs to cater to their strengths and allow for their immaturity.

Plan a Low Child-to-Adult Ratio

When developing the guest list, think like Noah, and invite by twos: one child plus one parent. It is wise to team any unaccompanied child with an adult or teen helper. At a minimum, have at least one adult helper for every two children. This strategy insures there is always someone available to assist, redirect, cuddle, and console the guests.

Limit the Guest List

Ever noticed how preschool classes are kept very small? Early childhood educators know that very young children function best in a small group. As mentioned in the chapter on party planning, most party planners suggest inviting one guest for every year of the birthday child's life, plus one. This means a guest list of three children for a two-year-old and four children for a three-year-old. While this may not seem like much of a party to an adult, to a child this age it is a huge event! Sometimes it is necessary to expand the guest list, but do your best to keep the party small.

Think about your child's ability to deal with people. At this age, some children are involved in playgroups, preschool, or church children's groups and have had experience dealing with bigger groups of people, but others have spent most of their lives nurtured in a quieter home environment. Parties are not much fun if the birthday child (or his mommy) is overwhelmed. Also, keep in mind that most children will be accompanied by at least one parent, and sometimes a sibling or two. A guest list of three can quickly turn into a group of eight to ten people!

Keep the Party Short

Between the ages of two and three, human beings experience their highest levels of energy. As toddlers focus this high level of energy into enjoying a birthday party, they make tremendous demands on their body—and yours! This very normal aspect of their development means twos and threes will tire easily, and entertaining them will cause you to tire easily as well. Therefore, it's best to plan a short party for these little dynamos, about one to two hours long. When asked to party longer, charming cherubs quickly transform into "terrible twos and threes." Tears, tantrums, and tiffs can be expected if a party lasts too long.

Provide Parallel Play Activities

While twos and threes are fascinated by other children, they are still extremely egocentric. Plan games and activities that allow them to explore, create, and play side by side. As few children this age are able to patiently take turns, make sure activities move quickly or allow several children to be active participants at the same time.

Children this age do not need or enjoy competition. For example, twos and threes might enjoy a bear hunt if there were enough bears for everyone to find one, the bears were obviously hidden, and an adult was on hand to play with the "bear" once a bear was found. The same bear hunt could be a disaster if the children had to work as a team, the bears were hard to find, and tots had to share the found bear with teammates!

Easy art activities, sing-alongs, finger plays, and simple games like Simon Says are fun at this age. Threes may enjoy one or two group games, such as Musical Chairs or Pin the Tail on the Donkey. Set up a book corner, art area, or toy zone for children who need time away from the entire group. Make sure parents know this is an acceptable alternative to any organized party activity. Siblings who attend the party might enjoy these alternative play stations as well.

Set Clear Boundaries

Two- and three-year-olds are curious little explorers with a decided independent streak. To keep them safe—and your home in good repair—determine boundaries before the party begins. Close the door to rooms that are off-limits, put a toddler gate across the stairway, and put away any breakables, slippery rugs, and potted plants. (See the appendix for a party safety checklist.) If the party is outside, make sure gates close securely, fences are in good repair, pools are completely secure, and tools and equipment are put away. Pets can either be fascinating or frightening to small children. Provide a comfortable, secure area for your pet, well away from little guests. As twos and threes have trouble remembering where their boundaries are, and are inclined to explore beyond those boundaries, it is important that the parents of your guests understand the boundaries you have set. As guests arrive, explain which areas you have childproofed for the party, and which are out-of-bounds. Ask each parent to assist you in keeping the children as safe as possible.

Plan with Your Child in Mind

A birthday party is an opportunity to create a fun-filled atmosphere with the activities and people your child enjoys most. Some three-year-olds are verbal enough to express specific likes and dislikes, but for most twos and many threes, it is necessary for the parent to do the talking. After thinking about the things your child enjoys most of all, present ideas to him. Encourage him to share his likes and dislikes, and then begin planning the party around this information. Parties centered on animals, storybook characters, children's media characters, favorite toys, colors, and forms of transportation (bus, plane, car, train, fire truck, etc.) are often big hits at this age. Include the birthday child in some of the party preparations. Twos and threes enjoy putting stickers and stamps on envelopes, putting envelopes in the mailbox, mixing birthday cake batter, and setting cups, plates, and napkins on the party table. If possible, take the birthday child to the store when purchasing party supplies.

Serve Age-Appropriate Refreshments

Little party guests have little appetites. Their parent partners, however, may well have big appetites. Remember, they'll have been the low energy half of a dynamic duo! Cake or cupcakes and ice cream is sufficient for parties held between traditional mealtimes. Cut the cake into small pieces for children and larger pieces for adults. Consider using bowls instead of cake plates to accommodate the still-developing fine motor skills of little guests. Have a container of wet wipes available for sticky fingers and faces.

When planning a party during a mealtime, stick to the simple foods your child enjoys eating. Again, think small. Cut sandwiches into quarters, or cut them out with small cookie cutters. Serve very small portions of a familiar main course: pasta in fun shapes, hamburgers quartered, pizza slices halved. Small pieces of soft fruit, cubes of cheese, mini bagels, raisins, and little cookies and crackers are all popular food choices. Set out bigger portions for parents or allow them to nibble on kid-sized portions. Twos and threes enjoy juice boxes or brightly colored cups with sipper lids or straws. Fill regular cups only one-third full, then refill as needed. Parents, busily helping their own child, will appreciate individual servings of drinks; cans of soda and bottled water work well.

Choking is still a danger for twos and threes. Avoid hot dogs, big chunks of apples, whole grapes, popcorn, nuts, hard candy, and baby carrots.

Tips for a Successful Twos or Threes Party

- *Even if your child is potty trained, it's likely some of the guests won't be. Provide a diaper-changing station as mentioned in chapter 8. Have one or two changes of clothes (labeled so that you get them back) ready in case of potty-training accidents.*
- *Provide a quiet corner for guests who tire or become cranky. A rocking chair or glider and some soothing music can calm a tired little guest or a frazzled parent.*
- *Put together a list of gifts your child would enjoy and you would appreciate receiving in case guests inquire. If there is a type of plaything you choose to avoid, politely let other parents know this information.*
- *Give guests something to play with (blocks, Legos, favor bags) while the birthday child opens gifts. Immediately remove gifts to another area so the birthday child doesn't have to cope with sharing all her new toys. Another alternative is to have the birthday child open gifts after guests leave.*

Party Plans for Twos and Threes

The following pages include plans for carrying out three different parties suitable for two- and three-year-olds. You may want to add a game or activity from chapter 7 for three-year-olds. These

5 1/2"

4 1/4"

party plans can be used as they are, simplified by choosing the parts you like best, or modified to fit your chosen theme.

Little Ballerinas Party

Length of party: 1 1/2 hours

Invitations: Purchase ballerina invitations or cut a piece of shiny pink cardstock into four 4 1/4" x 5 1/2" pieces. By hand or on the computer, print party information on a 3" x 4 1/2" paper. Cut with decorative scissors and glue to pink cardstock. Tie a pink tulle ribbon into a bow and glue at top center. Put ballet shoe stickers in bottom corners.

Decorations: Think pink! Use pink balloons and pink and white streamers. Hang old ballet shoes, recital costumes (check out thrift stores and friends with older girls), and dance posters around the room. Place a pink tutu in the center of table with a bowl of pink roses inside. Utilize any ballerina articles available.

Paper goods: Pink or white table covers, ballerina plates, and napkins. Purchase pink sipper cups for children.

Food: Strawberry jam finger sandwiches, strawberries and whipped cream (or strawberry Jell-O jigglers with whipped cream), pretzel sticks (ballet barré), pink lemonade, or berry juice boxes. Serve strawberry ice cream and Ballerina Music Box Cake (see recipe on p. 117).

Costumes: Ask guests to wear tights and leotard (a tank top or big T-shirt works too), and their favorite dancing shoes. Make a ballet headpiece for each guest by twisting pink and silver metallic garland in a circle to fit head; then tie pink and white curling ribbon to back. For a ballet wand, cut 1/4" wooden dowels into 12" lengths. Tie eight 24" lengths of curling ribbon to the end of each dowel and glue to secure. Paint a Styrofoam star or heart with tacky glue and sprinkle with pink glitter. When dry, push the Styrofoam shape onto the dowel, over the ribbon knots, and then glue with tacky glue. Curl ends of ribbon.

Activities:

- Show children two or three simple ballet steps: twirl, leap, plié, curtsy, spin. (If ballet is not your thing, consider hiring a teenage ballet student. Make sure she knows exactly what you want her to

5-6"
round

9"
round

Ballerina Music Box Cake

1. *Bake two 9-inch round layer cakes and one 5–6-inch round cake. (I used a small round glass casserole dish.)*
2. *Stack the three layers, using a thin layer of frosting between each layer as "glue."*
3. *Frost the entire cake in white, and sprinkle with pink sugar. Place a ballerina figurine on top. Around the edges, alternate 4 miniature marshmallows and 1 pink frosting flower (made or purchased from bakery). Arrange more miniature marshmallows in a zigzag pattern around the sides of the cake. (I used 12 large and 21 miniature roses.)*

Decorating time: 1 1/2 hours. Serves 18.

do.) If you have a large mirror in your house, let the guests practice in front of it. Play ballet music.
- Play Ballerina Says, using ballerina steps they have learned above.
- Perform "Ballerina at Play" (see sidebar).

Ballerina at Play

Little ballerina
Leap across the stage.
Do a little curtsy,
And a grand plié.
Skip around the circle,
Spin yourself around.
Give your fans a happy wave,
Fall gracefully to the ground.

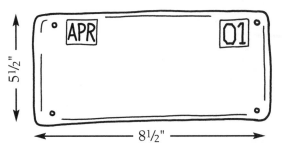

- Ballet "slipper" relay. Place pairs of Ped-style socks (1 per guest) in a pile. Ask guests to put on a pair and "dance" back to you. Award stickers as they arrive.
- Video tape guests dancing; play video at close of party.
- Read *Angelina Ballerina* by Helen Craig.

Party favors: Ballet stickers; headpiece and wand; ballerina figurine or color book.

Transportation Party

Length of party: 1 1/2 hours

Invitations: Purchase transportation (train, plane, racecars) invitations or hand-make license plate invitations. Cut cardstock (the color of your state's license plates) in half, forming two 8 1/2" x 5 1/2" rectangles. Round corners. Use a stencil or letter-shaped stickers to spell your child's name on front. Cut two 1" x 2" white rectangles. Glue in the top corners. Write child's birth month on left rectangle, his birth year on right rectangle. Write name of your state at the bottom. Put party information on back.

Decorations: Black and white streamers; red, green, and yellow balloons; poster board stop sign, street signs, and maps; cardboard box racecars. Place a train or racecar set at center of food table. Hang airplanes from the ceiling. On a white paper table cover, draw a road around each guest's table space. Write names on the top of a little toy car as a place card.

Paper goods: White paper table cover, train or racecar plates and napkins. If desired, purchase red, yellow, and green lidded cups for children.

Food: Car-shaped sandwiches (use cookie cutter), Fruit Rocketz (applesauce in tubes), Ritz crackers (steering wheels), apple juice (fuel), water bottles, Choo-Choo Cake (see p. 120), and ice cream.

Activities:

- Red Light, Green Light (see chapter 7).
- Choo-Choo Express. Have children form line, putting hands on waist of child in front of them. With an adult "engine" and "caboose", wander around the party area saying, "Chug-a-chug, choo-choo!"

10"

20"

15"

Cardboard Box Cars

Use a box approximately 15" x 20" x 10". Cut flaps off the bottom. Trim one top flap in half and fold the other to form front windshield. Cut door out of driver's side. Tape edges of box to secure. Spray paint entire box. Cut four 6" diameter wheels out of black cardstock; glue on box. Glue on a pie tin steering wheel, yellow cup lights, and foil bumpers. Add a personalized license plate.

- Sing "The Wheels on the Bus."
- Allow guests to play in cardboard cars and/or your collection of transportation toys. (We used our remote-controlled cars for my son's third birthday).
- Have guests bring their own transportation (trike, push car) to play with.
- Read *The Little Engine That Could* by Watty Piper.

Favors: Small toy cars, planes; train engineer cap; wooden train whistle; license frames.

Under the Big Top Party

Length of party: 1 ¹/₂ hours

Invitations: Purchase clown invitations or make ticket invitations. Cut light blue cardstock in four 4 ¹/₄" x 5 ¹/₂" pieces. Cut short sides

119

Choo-Choo Cake

1. *Make or buy 5 or more loaf cakes* (one for each car, plus one). On large cake board, line up all but one cake to resemble train. Leave 3 inches between each cake.*
2. *Cut unused cake in half; place one half on top of first cake to form engine. Frost in blue. Use 4 Oreos and black licorice for wheels, a wrapped Hershey's kiss for a smoke stack, and a vanilla wafer for an engineer.*
3. *Frost other cars in different colors and add wheels as described. Outline top of each car with licorice. Put mini M&Ms on top of first two cars. Put candles on last car. Connect cars with licorice.*

Decorating time: 1–1 ½ hours. Serves 20.

*Small frozen pound cakes, available in the frozen dessert section at the grocery store, are great for this.

with pinking shears. In large black letters write ADMIT ONE on center front, at top write birthday child's name, and at bottom write the words "Big Top." Print party information on back. Decorate with small balloon stickers.

Decorations: Red, blue, yellow, and green streamer canopy with matching helium balloons along ceiling; circus posters; paper plate clown faces; and cardboard boxes cut to resemble cages and filled with stuffed animals.

Food: Circus Pizzas (see chapter 5), Monkey on a Stick (see chapter 5), Giant Soft Pretzels (see

Clown Face Cake

1. *Make two 9-inch round cakes. Cool and remove from pans.*
2. *Layer and frost white. Place round orange fruit gels for hair along top edge and sides. Cut blue fruit roll-up into 2 triangle eyes. Cut clown mouth from a red fruit roll-up. (Before cutting, spray scissors with nonstick spray. Remember to remove paper backing after cutting.) Add a candy lifesaver or a Hershey's kiss to each corner of mouth for dimples. Use a red gumball for nose.*
3. *Form a clown hat from a piece of construction paper (or use a party hat) and angle it into top of clown head. Make a large construction paper bow and angle into bottom of clown face for collar. Write the words "Happy Birthday" on bow or hat.*

chapter 5), animal cookies, circus (fruit) punch, Ice Cream Clowns (see chapter 5), or Clown Face Cake (see p. 121) and ice cream.

Activities:

- Bean bag or sponge toss. Draw a clown face on the front of a large box. Cut out holes for the eyes, nose, and mouth. Cut one of the top flaps into a hat.
- Pin the Nose on the Clown. Don't use blindfolds, just let children place a clown nose where they like it on the clown's face!

- Face painting. Paint a clown face on each guest as he or she arrives.
- Organize a clown parade. Give each little guest an instrument (or any noise maker) and parade around like circus clowns.
- Shape plate clowns. Have children glue precut shapes onto a paper plate to form a clown face. Glue a tongue depressor to bottom to form a handle.
- Acrobats. Follow the leader by leaping between hula hoops, turning a somersault, walking a tightrope (on ground), sliding down a slide, etc.
- Copy the Clown (Simon Says)
- Tin Pin. Stack up six clean, empty soda cans. Toss beanbags at cans for prize.
- Read *Spot Goes to the Circus* by Eric Hill.

Favors: Face paints; clown hats; box of animal crackers; clown face plates; clown squeeze horn; clown nose.

Chapter Ten

Fun Festivities for Fours and Fives

**After waiting one whole year,
My birthday's finally drawing near;
I just don't know if I can wait
Until that all-important date!**

"Mommy, how many days left 'til my birthday?"

"Five."

"Has Sam's mommy called to say he could come?"

"Yes, Sam, Madelyn, Zach, and Pham are all coming."

"Can we bake my birthday cake today?"

"Not yet, Tyrone. We'll bake it on Friday, okay?"

"Can I cut out some more smiley faces for the wall?"

"Sure, more smiley faces would be great. Get some paper out of the drawer."

"Mommy, *how* many days left 'til my birthday?"

"Your birthday's on Saturday, Tyrone. See on the calendar—one, two three, four, five more days."

"Five, that's how old I'm going to be, huh, Mom?"

"That's right, Tyrone, a whole handful!"

WHEN YOU'RE FOUR OR FIVE, anticipating a birthday party is almost as much fun as the party itself! Most fours and fives relish the idea of a birthday party. In the days preceding the big event, you'll be peppered with questions, suggestions, and requests. The birthday child will want to be involved in all aspects of party planning, preparation, and implementation. (Notice I didn't mention cleanup!) She will have definite ideas about the type of party she wants, who she'd like to invite, and what food will be served. This is my favorite age for birthday parties. I loved discovering who my child considered her favorite friends, how she wanted to decorate the room, which kind of food she thought her friends would like best, and which party theme made her eyes sparkle and her mind start clicking with ideas. During the party, it was fascinating to watch how she interacted with her friends, to catch a peek at young relationships unfolding. Helping her decide which ideas fit within the boundaries of the party location, budget, and time constraints, while at the same time providing her guests with a wonderful party experience, was a great way to help build sound decision-making skills. Plus, planning the party together offered plenty of time for mother-child interaction and fun.

Put Together the Guest List

Putting together a guest list for this age can be challenging. By now, a child's circle of friends has started to expand. They may have friends in playgroup or at school, friends in the neighborhood, friends at church, friends from swimming lessons . . . more friends than your space and budget can accommodate. Complicating guest list decisions, some parents of fours and fives are comfortable dropping a child off at a party and returning at the designated pick-up time, while others choose to remain at the party. Then there are siblings to be considered. Will Josh's two-year-old sister be staying as well? Keeping all this in mind, decide how many guests you can reasonably accommodate before discussing the guest list with your child. Will you limit the guest list to just one or two groups of your child's friends, to one or two special friends from each group, or will you open up the backyard and invite everyone? Working within established boundaries, allow your child as much control over the guest list as possible. Many parents find six to eight children an ideal number of guests for this age. If you choose to invite more, be sure to have plenty of adult help. A four to one child-to-adult ratio is a good goal for the party. Ask parents if they plan to drop off or stay when you receive the RSVP. Parents who stay for the party are usually happy to help out.

Should you choose to invite only certain children from a group, be sensitive to the feelings of uninvited children. Mail the invitations, or quietly hand them to a parent instead of having the birthday child pass them out personally or sticking them in cubbies. Share with your child the importance of not discussing the party in front of children he couldn't invite. Consider sending cupcakes or some other treat to the entire group.

Choose a Theme

Some fours and fives have definite ideas about a party theme, some want a party just like the last one they attended, and some have no idea what they want to do. Do your best to accommodate a child with definite ideas. If your child needs some ideas, share some of the theme ideas in this chapter or from the list in the appendix. Should a child choose an inappropriate party theme, carefully explain why you consider the theme inappropriate and suggest alternatives. For instance, if you consider Barbie an inappropriate party theme for your little girl, explain to her why and suggest a dress-up party or a doll tea party as an alternative.

Once a theme is chosen, talk about the other party elements. With your party planning guide in hand, assist your child in making decisions about decorating, food, activities, and favors. Jot down all ideas and notes on the planning guide so you don't forget them. Not only is this a great opportunity to spend time one-on-one with the birthday child, you will be modeling good organizational skills and the thoughtful use of available resources.

Factor in Fun

Fours and fives have built quite an arsenal of life skills, allowing them to participate in a wide variety of activities. Most of the time, these children enjoy cooperative play and a few competitive games.

They are able to cut, paint, color, and glue with occasional adult assistance. Although skill levels vary, fours and fives can usually run smoothly, jump, hop on one foot, skip, and throw with increasing accuracy. Their attention span and ability to comprehend directions has improved and they are able to participate in more complicated games and activities. In addition, most have attended a birthday party before and know what to expect.

This is the age where children begin to enjoy traditional party games. Chapter 7 provides a myriad of games and activities fours and fives enjoy. Read through them, make some suggestions to your child, and decide together what to plan for party fun. Be sure to pick games in which the birthday child can experience success.

Be Creative with Food Choices

Fours and fives have small appetites, but they are attracted to whimsical food. Whether you decide to serve cake and ice cream or a light meal, present the food in a creative way. Look for ways to connect the food with the party theme. Make a cake in the shape of a castle, serve a snake-shaped pizza, or float ice cube stars in the punch.

Fours and fives like to participate in preparing party food. Allow them to put the toppings on mini pizzas or decorate their own cupcakes. Have them spread the peanut butter on their own celery stick and add raisins to create their own Bugs on a Log. Chapter 5 provides more festive food ideas fours and fives will appreciate.

Plan for Good Behavior

Children tend to arrive at birthday parties eager to celebrate and with a fresh parental reminder to be on their best behavior. As party "parent," you can assist guests in staying on their best behavior by planning plenty of fun activities, preparing for quick transitions between activities, providing ample adult supervision, and keeping the party under three hours in length. There were only a handful of times I had to deal with behavior problems at a birthday party, and these were most often with my own children! The behavior problems I did experience were with children who arrived at the party overly tired or upset, children frustrated by their inability to succeed at a party activity, and children unoccupied during an activity or between activities.

Should a child's behavior disrupt the birthday fun, first take a moment to explain your behavior expectations and how these allow all guests to experience a good time. If disruptive behavior continues, ask an adult helper to focus on the child, gently guiding her to appropriate behavior. The adult helper might need to take the child aside for a quiet "thinking period." If all else fails, call the child's parent to come and accompany her for the remainder of the party. Explain that the child is not herself today, and needs some special attention. Refrain from criticizing the child, and emphasize that you want the child to remain—you simply need assistance in helping the child participate successfully.

Party Plans for Fours and Fives

A birthday child of four or five can appreciate a wide variety of party plans and activities. On the following pages are three parties planned with these children in mind. If your child is interested in one of these, share the ideas with her. Add, subtract, or adjust the party to her specifications. If your birthday child is interested in a different party theme, consider how to modify or rename the activities to fit your theme.

Dinosaur Safari Party

Length of party: 2–2 $1/2$ hours

Invitations: Purchase dinosaur invitations or cut a piece of black cardstock in half. Fold the 8 $1/2$" x 5 $1/2$" cardstock in half to form a 5 $1/2$" x 4 $1/4$" card. Enlarge the pattern shown or use a dinosaur cookie cutter and trace the shape onto a piece of gray textured paper (or use textured paper of your choice). Cut a 4 $1/2$" x 3 $1/2$" piece of green or red paper (green jungle print paper looks great too). Trim with pinking scissors. Glue the pinked square onto the top of the black cardstock. Cut out the

dinosaur and glue it onto the pinked square. Print up the party information and glue this into the inside of the invitation. Add a dinosaur graphic or a dinosaur sticker.

Decorations: Collect as many dinosaurs as possible and group them around the room. Color pictures of dinosaurs and pin to the walls. Trace a dinosaur on a child-size piece of cardboard and paint the dinosaur green. There are also some great dinosaur inflatables available on-line (see the appendix). Hang or place these around the party area, then use as favors. Dangle green and brown streamers or use hanging plants and palms around the room to serve as a jungle. Use Volcano Cake as the centerpiece for the food table.

Volcano Cake

1. *Purchase or make 2 angel food cakes and a jumbo muffin. Cut off the bottom half of one angel food cake and stack it on top of the other cake, trimming edges with a serrated knife as needed to form volcano. Glue the 2 layers together with a thin layer of frosting.*
2. *Cut the rounded end from the jumbo muffin and place it upside down on top of angel cakes. (Secure it to the top angel food cake layer with a thin layer of frosting.) Frost entire cake with brown icing.*
3. *For lava, use paste food coloring to create vibrant red, yellow, and orange frosting. (Paste food coloring is available at cake decorating supply stores or order at wilton.com). Surround volcano with dinosaurs and palm trees. Stick appropriate number of sparkler candles out of the top of the volcano.*

Decorating time: 1 hour. Serves 12.

Paper goods: Purchase dinosaur table covers, plates, and napkins. For another approach, buy a white paper tablecloth, crayons, and a set of dinosaur stencils or rubber stamps, and let the children decorate the tablecloth. Use green paper plates and dinosaur napkins.

Food: Dinosaur eggs and dip (mini–corn dogs or chicken nuggets with ranch dressing), dinosaur-shaped Jell-O jigglers, celery stalks (with the leaves attached), Volcano Cake, ice cream, and Jungle Juice (combine lemon lime soda and lime sherbet).

Activities:

- Dinosaur safari hats. Give each child a purchased white safari hat and dinosaur stickers. Write each child's name on the hats with a paint pen.
- Dino Stomp. Like musical chairs but use giant dinosaur footprints and play the theme from the *Flintstones*. At the end of each round, take out a footprint but keep all kids in. Keep taking out footprints until everyone is stomping the same print.
- Dino Dig. Use a sandbox (or wading pool filled with sand) and let guests dig for dinosaur bones (dog biscuits).
- Dino Safari. Hide dinosaur eggs (see the appendix) around party area or yard. Allow each guest to find a certain number.
- Hot Lava. Lay an 8' x 6" board on two bricks. Surround the board with small red balloons. Have the kids walk the board in increasingly difficult ways (skipping, on one foot, etc.).
- Dino Tail Tag. Instructions for Tail Tag can be found in chapter 7.

Favors: Safari hats; inflatable dinosaurs; dinosaur eggs; homemade dinosaur cookies; small toy dinosaurs.

Under the Sea Party

Length of party: 2–2 ½ hours

Invitations: Purchase ocean theme invitations or write party details on a 6" x 10" sea-blue piece of cardstock or construction paper. Cut the top and bottom (6") edges to resemble waves. Fold so party information is on inside. With waves at the top, write "Under the Sea Party" in the middle. Put one tablespoon of sand, some glitter, and fish confetti into a sandwich-size Ziploc bag, add invitation, and seal. Mail in an envelope decorated with fish stickers. (Be sure to have each invitation individually weighed before mailing to see if extra postage is needed.)

Decorations: Cut multicolored fish and starfish out of construction paper. Hang fish, dangling light and dark green crepe paper, and strips of cellophane or tinsel (seaweed) from ceiling. Attach small silver balloons to string and hang as bubbles. Cover the floor with blue balloons (water). Decorate food table with sand, seashells, goldfish, and Goldfish Jell-O Bowl.

Paper goods: Purchase *Rainbow Fish* or *Little Mermaid* themed table covers, plates, and napkins, or use a blue table cover and green, blue, and silver plates and napkins.

Food: Macaroni and cheese made from shell-shaped pasta, goldfish crackers, Goldfish Jell-O Bowl, Fish Cake, and ice cream.

Activities:

- Seashore visors. Provide each child with an inexpensive plastic visor and a selection of paint pens. Have children draw their favorite ocean scene on the visor.
- Bobbing for bubbles. Hang miniature donuts from the ceiling with string so donuts are at child's mouth level. Divide into two teams and have

Goldfish Jell-O Bowl

Goldfish bowl
Rock candy
1 package blueberry Jell-O
10 Gummi fish
6 green licorice whips

1. *Wash and dry a new goldfish bowl. Distribute candy rocks along the bottom of the bowl.*
2. *In a large bowl, make blueberry Jell-O according to the quickset directions on the package. Add gummy fish and short pieces of green licorice whips.*
3. *Carefully pour Jell-O mixture into the goldfish bowl. Refrigerate at least two hours before serving.*

Serves 8.

Fish Cake

1. Bake a 9" x 13" cake. Cool and remove from pan.
2. Cut cake, then attach fin as shown.
3. Make 6 cups blue frosting and frost fish blue. Use a Lifesaver candy for eye and a gummy fish for mouth. With a two-liter pop bottle cap, cut circles from 6 fruit roll-ups in different colors. Use these as scales, overlapping them on fish as needed.*

Decorating time: 1 1/2 hours. Serves 16.

*The fruit roll-up makes terrific looking scales, but it is time-consuming to cut all those little circles. A quicker alternative is to use pastel-colored Necco wafers or other flat, round candy.

children run up to the donut, eat it off the string (no hands, of course), and then run back and tag the next team member.

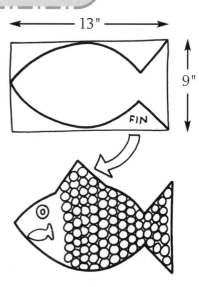

- Wet sponge/bean bag toss. Cut a large shark or octopus out of poster board and paint it. Cut a hole where the head would be. Have children try to get the wet sponge or beanbag through the hole. If possible, have an adult helper stick her head in the hole for added excitement.
- Pin the Fin on the Shark. Draw shark on a large piece of poster board. Cut enough shark fins for each child to have one. Play like "Pin the Tail on the Donkey."
- Sharks and minnows (or mermaids). Pick one child to be the shark. Place her in the middle of the party area. Have the other guests (minnows) line up on one side. When you call out "Shark attack!" the children must run to the other side of the game area. Whenever the shark tags a minnow, the minnow becomes a shark for the rest of the game. Keep playing until only one or two minnows are left.
- Sand castles. Mix 4 cups of clean sand, 2 cups cornstarch, 1 tablespoon plus 1 teaspoon cream of tartar, and 3 cups hot water into large saucepan. Cook over medium heat until stiff and water is absorbed. Cool. Kids can form castles with their hands or use small sand molds coated with vegetable spray.
- Make "Mermaid Munchies" (see recipe on p. 132).

- Goldfish guess. Fill a jar with goldfish crackers and have guests guess how many are in the jar.

Favors: Gummy fish; Shark Bites (fruit flavored candy available at grocery stores); mermaid and fish stickers; shells; bubbles; Mermaid Munchies.

Mermaid Munchies

10 ounce bag of pretzel sticks (fishing poles)
1 box goldfish crackers
1 pound M&M candies (bubbles)
1 jar salted peanuts (rocks)*
10 ounces of raisins (jelly fish)

Mix all ingredients together in a large bowl. Divide mix into twelve sandwich bags. Print recipe and glue to front of bag with fish or mermaid sticker to decorate. Serves 12.

*Some guests may be allergic to peanuts.

Western Roundup

Length of party: 2 1/2 hours

Invitations: Purchase Western theme invitations or make "Wanted" poster invitations. Cut tan cardstock in half to form 5 1/2" x 8 1/2" rectangles. Print "WANTED" across the top in bold, red letters. Then print "Guests for Jesse's Western Birthday Roundup" on the next line. Copy a picture of birthday child and glue it below the words in the upper half of invitation. In the bottom half, print party information. Using a lighter, carefully burn the edges of the invitation. Fold in half to mail.

← 5 1/4" →

8 1/2"

Decorations: Wanted posters; cowboy hats and boots; horses and cows (plastic, hobby, or real!); bales of hay; rope; OK Corral signs; green cactus cut out of poster board; bandannas.

Paper goods: Purchase Western theme plates and napkins or cover the table with a red-checkered table cover, use old pie tins for plates, pint Mason jars for cups, and red bandanna napkins.

Food: Roast hot dogs over a grill or serve chili and corn bread, corn on the cob, Cactus Coolers or root beer, Corral Cake, and ice cream.

Corral Cake

1. *Bake a two-layer 9" x 13" cake. Frost with chocolate icing.*
2. *Allow the birthday child to create a Western scene on the cake top using small plastic horses and cowboys, a toy covered wagon, and a plastic fence. (If needed, most toy stores carry inexpensive plastic cowboy playsets.)*

Costumes: Ask guests to come dressed in jeans and T-shirts. Provide a cowboy hat, bandanna, and sheriff's badge for each guest. As guests arrive, have each create a cowboy vest. (For vest: Before party, cut straight up the center of a grocery bag. Make a round opening at top and two openings at sides for neck and arms. Cut so the vest ends at child's waist. At party, have guests cut fringe around the bottom and armholes of vest and decorate with brown crayons.) If desired, use an eyebrow pencil to make a mustache on each guest.

133

Activities:

- Horseshoes. Borrow or purchase a horseshoe game. Put both the stakes at one end of the game area. Divide into two teams and see which team gets the most ringers in five minutes. (Stop after every three players to collect horseshoes.) Have birthday child test game ahead of time to determine how close to place guests for success!
- Broom Pony Relay. Use two brooms for ponies. Divide into two teams and have guests ride ponies to a designated spot and back. Set up an easy obstacle course, if desired.
- Lasso the Pony. Set up a rocking horse at one end of the play area. Have the children take turns trying to lasso the horse with a hula hoop. Use two hula hoops to keep game moving.
- Rattlesnake. Played like Hot Potato. With markers, decorate a tube sock to look like a snake. Tie a small baby rattle at one end. Stuff the tube sock with newspaper and tie off the other end. Toss the rattlesnake to your favorite cowboy music.
- Gold Rush. Hide gold foil-wrapped chocolates (gold nuggets) throughout party area. Have children hunt for "gold."
- Sharpshooter. Hang balloons covered with shaving cream and let little cowpokes shoot off the shaving cream with squirt bottles or water guns. (Fill water guns or bottles with water before game.)

Favors: Gold nuggets (foil-wrapped chocolates); bandannas; cowboy hats and vests; jump ropes; harmonicas; plastic horses.

Stupendous Fun for School-Age Kids

**Crazy games and yummy snacks,
Stuff to find and laugh attacks.
On my birthday one thing's clear—
To celebrate, my friends are here!**

As the song ended, the dee-jay announced, "We're celebrating a special occasion at Holiday Rink tonight. It's Natalie's birthday! Natalie, bring your friends and skate on out to center rink."

Laughing and pointing at Natalie, the girls skated out to center rink. Smiling wide, braces sparkling, Natalie listened as her friends joined the dee-jay in an upbeat rendition of the birthday song.

Loudly singing the final refrain, the girls hugged Natalie, then skated off en masse—talking, giggling, and enjoying each other as they celebrated Natalie's twelfth birthday.

THE SCENE ABOVE OCCURRED during the period of time I spent writing this chapter. While Natalie and I planned the final birthday celebration of her childhood, I couldn't help but think back on past birthday parties. During my girls' elementary school years we've celebrated with mermaids, hula dancers, teapots, arts and crafts, Christmas activities (Natalie means "Christmas child"), ceramic painting, roller skating, water sliding, a sock hop, and more sleepless sleep-over parties than I care to count! During the early elementary birthday parties, I busily organized activities and games, providing constant, close supervision with no empty moments for boredom to set in. In the later elementary years, the girls began planning more of their birthday parties and required less close adult supervision. Over the years, there's been a healthy move from mom-generated activity to child-generated activity. More and more, I find myself a sounding board for party plans. My role as party shopper, however, remains unchallenged!

Elementary-age children love parties. They enjoy the traditions of past years, the planning, the shopping, and especially providing a fun-filled time for friends. Elementary children can be exuberant at parties, immersing themselves in the festivities. During the early elementary years children are fairly unself-conscious, willing to try a wide variety of activities. By fourth or fifth grade, however, children become increasingly self-conscious, unwilling to embarrass themselves in front of peers. The early elementary years are also the time when children begin seeing "cooties" in the opposite sex and start wanting to invite only guests of the same gender to parties. Let your child make the decision on this.

Plan Alongside Your Child

Elementary children usually have definite ideas about their birthday parties. Take the time to listen to your child's wishes. For younger elementary children, jot down their ideas on your party planning sheet. As your child matures, make a conscious effort to give him more and more party planning responsibilities. Start by allowing him to fill out the planning sheet. Before you sit down with your child to plan the party, know the boundaries that need to be honored. Be open with your child about the party budget and how much different components of the party may cost. Know how many children you can reasonably accommodate, and have a specific date and time in mind. Together, you and your child can make decisions regarding a theme, decorating and food options, activities, and favors. Check the family calendar and set aside time to purchase supplies, make decorations and food, and put together birthday favors. Make the most of these unique opportunities to work together.

Decide on a Guest List

Earlier in the chapter, I mentioned how in the elementary years, many boys and girls prefer to celebrate exclusively with friends of the same gender. It is wise to follow your child's lead on this issue. Many times a child will have one or two special friends of the opposite sex. If you've decided to host a single gender party, but your child is reluctant to leave a friend of the opposite gender out, decide together whether it would be better to go ahead and invite the friend to the party or to enjoy an alternative activity together.

As children often have a wide circle of friends during the elementary school years, keeping the guest list manageable can be a challenge. A few options for your child to consider include:

- Invite all the children in one group.
- Invite all the same gender children in one group.
- Invite the closest one or two friends from each group.

Remind your child to refrain from discussing the party in front of children he or she could not invite.

Some children may want to invite all friends from all groups! Plan carefully and recruit plenty of help if you decide to invite a big group. Most families do set limits on the number of guests, and party planners strongly recommend following the number of years old plus one rule when deciding how many guests to invite. If guests come from several different groups, you may want to provide name tags.

Provide Fun Activities

When planning activities for the early elementary age group, plan more than enough to fill the party hours and keep the party moving! Have an opening activity ready to engage guests as soon as they arrive at the party. I've found craft activities, hunting for a small object, or an open-ended sports activity (soccer kick, free-throw contest) works well. Ask an adult or teen helper to supervise this activity so you and your child are available to greet guests. Elementary-age children enjoy working together on cooperative activities like creating a sidewalk chalk mural, but they also like a little friendly competition. Provide a mixture of both types of activities for guests. Select teams for competitive games before the party starts in order to alleviate any hurt feelings, to keep teams in balance, and to keep the party moving.

Upper-elementary children may enjoy a less structured party. Plan some organized games and activities, but also give older children open-ended time to fill as they wish (within limits, of course!). Have card games, board games, sports equipment, and art supplies ready for guests to utilize. Guests enjoy videotaping themselves, later watching the festivities on television. Polaroid and digital cameras are fun too.

Elementary children delight in parties away from home. Roller rinks, hockey rinks, bowling alleys, amusement parks, art studios, or a local children's museum provide plenty of party fun (see chapter 4 for a list of ideas). Pick an activity location the birthday child likes.

Host a Successful Sleep-Over

Sometime during his or her elementary school years, your child is likely to campaign for a sleep-over party. These are most popular with girls, but boys enjoy them as well. All-nighters might be a better title for these parties. My recollections, both as host mother and host birthday girl, do not include too many slumbering moments! Invite guests to arrive around 7 P.M., earlier if serving a meal. Plan the first third of the party like a traditional birthday party, with games, activities, food, gifts, and favors. The first segment of the party should last until 10 or 11 P.M.

The second segment of the party, the overnight part, should begin with guests donning pajamas, packing dirty clothes, rolling out sleeping bags, and preparing for the night. Plan a few quiet activities or videos for the next hour or so. Storytelling (discourage scary ones unless you want to deal with frightened guests), videos, card games, Wink, or Telephone are fun options. Set firm parameters for the wee hours of the night and explain them clearly to the guests. Some suggestions are:

- Lights out at 1 A.M. (or time you designate).
- Remain in the house or tent.
- Watch only approved videos.
- Keep voices quiet.

- Treat each other with kindness.
- Stay out of siblings' rooms, home office, et cetera.
- Allow adults to sleep until 7 A.M.

Occasionally guests are unable to remain all night. If a guest becomes fearful or tearful, encourage her to remain at the party, but call her parents if she is insistent. Parents often know ahead of time whether a child can make it the entire night or not and will likely share this information before the party. Make sure a child leaving early knows how much everyone enjoyed having her at the party. Encourage the other guests to say good-bye with big, friendly hugs.

The third segment of the party begins as the guests wake up and ends around 10 A.M. or whenever you have designated as pick-up time. In the morning, guests may enjoy repeating some of the previous night's activities (I once woke up to the sounds of "Bingo!"), gabbing, or helping with breakfast. Plan breakfast about one-and-a-half hours before pick up. About forty-five minutes before pick up, help guests roll up sleeping bags, gather belongings, and pack overnight bags. Check party rooms and bathrooms for stray items. Provide open-ended activities for the final half hour. As guests depart, do a quick check to make sure they have all their belongings: sleeping bags, pillows, toothbrushes, retainers, stuffed animals, and favors. Make sure the birthday child thanks each guest for coming. If possible, plan a quiet rest of the day for the family. Everyone, especially the birthday child, is likely to be extremely tired.

> ## Party Videos
>
> *Families have varying opinions on what is acceptable viewing for children. Decide ahead of time which videos will be offered and ask parents if these choices are acceptable. This saves a child the embarrassment of telling the host she can't watch a video and the host from finding a last-minute alternative.*

Figure on Plenty of Food

Munch, munch, munch! School-age children have varying appetites, but most like to munch during a party. Provide a snack station near the activity area where guests can grab a quick drink or snack. Consider offering a variety of nutritious and not-so-nutritious snacks. The birthday child will be happy to let you know his favorite not-so-nutritious snack foods! In addition, offer vegetables and dip, apple or melon slices, fresh berries, cheese and crackers, or popcorn. Set out water bottles, juice boxes, and, if you desire, sodas. Place several Sharpie markers near the drinks for marking cups or beverage containers.

When a party falls during a traditional mealtime, provide a simple meal your child enjoys. Like younger children, school-age children get a kick out of themed food and are enthusiastic about participating in food preparation (see chapter 5 for several menu suggestions). Eating away from the table can be challenging for guests. Provide a table or covered floor space for picnic-style eating.

Be Prepared for the Unexpected

Parents of school-age children usually drop off their children, returning at the designated pick-up time. As guests participate in a variety of activities, accidents do occasionally occur. Be sure to ask each parent where he or she can be contacted in case of emergency. I find it handy to have a small pad of paper or clipboard and pencil near the entrance to the party to jot down this information. Ask parents if their child has any allergies or special medical needs. Most likely you will never need this information, but having easy access to it will prove invaluable in an emergency situation.

I've mentioned before how important it is to have another adult or older teenager on hand during birthday parties. As children mature, the temptation to go it alone may occur. Resist this inclination. In an emergency, two responsible adults are absolutely necessary, one to handle the emergency and the other to supervise the remaining guests.

At just about every party I've organized for my children there has been at least one child who is not picked up on time. Parents can be delayed for a variety of reasons (I've been late a time or two myself). If necessary, use the contact information to call the missing parent. Knowing a parent's arrival time reassures the child and assists you in knowing how to handle the situation.

Party Plans for School-Age Children

On the following pages are four party plans for school-age children. The Pirate Party and Teddy Bear Tea are most suitable for younger elementary children, while the Pajama Party and Birthday Olympics are geared towards older elementary children. In calculating the time for each party, I've allowed twenty minutes for eating and twenty minutes for opening gifts. Except for the Pajama Party, there are enough activities included to last about 2 1/2 hours. Consider including a piñata or some of the games from chapter 7 if you'd like to plan a longer party. Modify the games to fit your child's chosen theme.

Pirate Party

Length of party: 2 ½ hours

Invitations: Purchase pirate theme invitations. Another alternative: Draw a map to the party location on an 11" x 13" piece of brown grocery bag. Mark the location with an X. At the top print "Yer Invited ta Hunt fer Treasure" and at the bottom corner print the party information, asking guests to wear old, dark pants and a T-shirt. Crinkle the invitation and burn edges with a lighter.

Decorations: Red, gold, and black balloons and streamers; handmade maps (like invitation); coconuts; fake

---

Pirate Island Cake

1. Bake a 9" x 13" sheet cake. Let cool and remove from pan.
2. Frost all but one corner with blue gel icing (available at cake decorating supply stores or wilton.com.) Frost last corner with chocolate frosting and sprinkle with graham cracker crumbs. Add chocolate-covered honeycomb or chocolate-covered peanut clusters for rocks.
3. Decorate cake with a Lego pirate set or plastic cake decorations such as a pirate ship, palm trees, treasure chests, and pirates.

Decorating time: 1 hour. Serves 12–16.

5"

3"

4 ¹/₂"

Pirate Hooks

Cut a hole in the bottom of a large black, plastic cup. Cut a hook out of cardboard (shape it like a question mark). Cover hook with foil and push into cup hole. Guests hold the end of the hook with their hand.

Spyglasses

Cover the ends of a paper towel tube with colored cellophane. Hold cellophane in place with a rubber band. Wrap a black sheet of construction paper around the tube and glue in place. Add skull and crossbones or parrot stickers.

11"

9"

gold coins; skull and crossbones pennants; parrots (toy or real!); ship in a bottle or other old sailing ships. Cover table with blue plastic cover, sprinkle sand and rocks down the middle, and add gold coins and two or three colored bottles with maps inside.

Paper goods: Purchase pirate theme plates, napkins, and cups, or buy black paper goods and decorate with skull and crossbones stickers.

Food: Buried treasure (a mound of spaghetti with a meatball buried in the middle), sea biscuits (rolls), celery boats (see chapter 5), Pirate Island Cake, and ice cream.

Costumes: Bandannas, pirate hats, black felt eye patches, and black face paint for mustache and beard. Make hooks and spyglasses (see sidebars) ahead or as an opening activity.

Activities:

- Make and don pirate costumes. Make pirate hooks and spyglasses. Tie a bandanna and felt eye patch on each guest. Use face paints to paint a mustache and beard on each guest.
- Find the Crocodile. Give one guest the "croc" (an egg timer that ticks) set for two minutes. Have the guest hide the timer, and let others search. Finder gets to hide the "croc" next.
- Hook relay. Divide into two teams. Have players each wear a pirate's hook. Each player runs to a designated location, hooks a

ring or small plastic cup, runs back, and hooks it on the next player's hook. This player runs back to the designated location, drops the ring, then picks it up again and runs to the third player. The game ends after every player has had a turn.

- One-legged race. Line up pirates at one end of the party area. Have them hop on one foot to the finish line. Play several times. Let the winner be the referee of next game.
- Pirate Snatch. Have guests sit at a table with several "treasures." For example: A bag of gold candy coins, a $100,000 candy bar, a small box covered in foil, faux jewels, a dollar bill, a pirate map, a spyglass, a small sword, a compass. One player (the Captain) turns his back to the table, and the birthday child points to another player (pirate), who snatches a treasure off the table and puts it in his lap. The Captain tries to guess the missing treasure and pirate in three tries. Let the pirate be Captain for the next round.
- Pieces of Eight. See description of Spoons in chapter 7; use candy coins instead of spoons. Guests are allowed to eat the candy they grab. Put out new candy coins for each round.
- Treasure hunt. Follow hunt directions in chapter 7.

Favors: Pirate costumes; treasure chest loot; saltwater taffy; candy gold coins; compass.

Teddy Bear Tea

Length of party: 2 1/2 hours

Invitations: Purchase tea party theme invitations or enlarge the teapot shown, trace it onto white cardstock, and cut. Decorate teapot with pink glitter paint. Place a teddy bear stamp or sticker in the middle. Print the party information on the back. Tie a piece of pink ribbon on the handle of the teapot.

Decorations: Pink and white balloons and streamers; enough card tables to seat each guest around the room; white paper or cloth table covers; a small vase of fresh carnations and a teddy bear on each table; tea cups, plates, saucers, and folded napkins at each spot; pictures of teddy bears (utilize old calendars); teddy bears, large and small, set around the room. Make a sign for the door that says "Brittany's Tea Room."

Paper goods: Purchase teddy bear theme paper plates and napkins or use real china and white tablecloths.

Food: Finger sandwiches cut in the shape of teddy bears, heart-shaped scones and honey, chocolate-covered strawberries, Teddy Bear Cupcakes, and ice cream. Serve weak tea, apple juice, cream, and sugar cubes.

Costumes: Have guests wear their best dress or wear one of their mothers'. Ask each guest to bring a favorite teddy bear.

Activities:

- Teddy bear hats. Purchase 4–6" straw hats at a craft store. Provide a variety of ribbons and silk flowers and low-temperature glue guns. Let guests decorate a hat for their teddy bear.
- Teddy bear fashion show. Have guests introduce their bears and describe their bear's hat. Give prize for each hat (prettiest, best colors, best use of flowers, craziest, most bear-like).
- Teddy bear bookmarks. Provide 2 1/2" x 5" pieces of cardstock with a hole at one short end. Have guests use teddy bear and teapot stickers and stamps to decorate. Tie ribbon at one end.
- Teddy Bear Cupcakes. Bake teddy bear cupcakes before the party (see the appendix for information on ordering a teddy bear cupcake pan from Wilton). Give each guest a teddy bear cupcake on a paper plate with her name written at the top. Provide guests with a plastic knife, chocolate and vanilla icing, and a variety of sprinkles, mini–chocolate chips, minimarshmallows, and red licorice whips to decorate cupcakes.
- Pin the Heart on Teddy. Outline and paint a teddy bear on poster board. Cut out. Cut out a heart for each guest and label with her name. Play like Pin the Tail on the Donkey.
- Pictures with Teddy. Borrow or purchase a very large teddy bear. Take a picture of each guest with the teddy bear and the birthday child. Use as thank-you notes.
- Teaspoons. See description of Spoons in chapter 7.
- Teddy's Quest. Start a story about a teddy bear. Have guests take turns continuing the story.
- Tea. Seat guests at tables. Ask Daddy, uncles, and big brothers to serve as butlers. Each butler should wear a white dress shirt and a tie, and hold a white towel over his arm. Encourage butlers to use a British accent! Butlers serve guests from real teapots, asking "one lump or two?" If possible, use silver trays or pretty serving plates.

Favors: Hats; bookmarks; teapot cookies; thrift store teacup; a small teddy bear; costume jewelry.

Birthday Olympics

Length of party: 2 ¹/₂ hours

Invitations: Purchase Olympic or sports theme invitations or make torch invitations. Cut a shiny piece of black cardstock into four 5 ¹/₂" x 4 ¹/₄" pieces. For each torch, fold one of the 5 ¹/₂" x 4 ¹/₄" pieces in half. Cut two 2-inch circles out of yellow cellophane. Holding the center of the circles, gather up the cellophane and tape it in between the folded piece of black paper for a flame. Glue all but the top of the torch handle. On front of handle print, "Carry the torch to Ethan's Birthday Olympics." On back, print party information.

Decorations: Drape red, white, blue, yellow, and green balloons and streamers; place sports-related items or posters and flags of different countries around the room; hang tennis shoes from ceiling.

Paper goods: Purchase sports or Olympic theme paper plates and napkins, or buy red, white, and blue. Give each guest a sports bottle to drink from.

Food: All-American hot dogs, chips, popcorn, soda, water to fill sports bottles, cakes from cake-decorating contest or Soccer Cake, and ice cream.

Costumes: Purchase enough baseball caps, visors, or T-shirts in three colors so that they can be split evenly. Assign one color to each team. Purchase or create award medals for closing award ceremonies.

Activities:

- Before party begins, assign guests to one of three teams. For each game, award points for first, second, and third place. Award huge numbers, like 20,000 for first place, 15,000 for second place, and 10,000 for third place. At the end of the party, tally points, play the Olympic theme song, and award purchased medals.
- Pennants. Provide a large piece of butcher paper, markers, and a 24" dowel to each team. Have each team pick a name and create a pennant.

145

- Frisbee throw. Hang a hula hoop from a tree or roof overhang. Each player who throws the Frisbee through the hoop receives 1,000 points for his team.
- Shoe kick. Line up guests and have them kick off their shoes. Guests may unlace shoes, if necessary. Award first, second, and third place points for farthest kicks.
- Torch relay. Make three torches (use paper towel rolls and yellow paper), one for each team. In teams, have students run to designated spot and back, passing the torch to the next player.
- Nerf Basketball. Set up three Nerf basketball hoops. Each player who makes a basket receives 1,000 points for his team. Allow each player five tries (or more for small teams).
- Balloon Broom Hockey Race: Provide each team with a broom and a team-colored balloon. First player of each team knocks his team's balloon down the field and back with broom. Continue until all team members have played.
- Cake-decorating contest. Give each team a 9" x 13" sheet cake, assorted frosting, sprinkles, candles, and candies. Allow teams ten minutes to decorate cake. Award 10,000 points each to the team whose cake is the funniest, shows the most team spirit, and has the most decorations on it!
- Balloon Bodybuilder. Have one member of each team put on adult-sized sweat suit. Give the teams three minutes to see how many balloons can be stuffed into their team member's sweat suit.
- Olympic events. Give each team paper and pencils. Give them five minutes to come up with as many real life Olympic events as possible. Variation: Have guests come up with as many silly Olympic events as possible.

Favors: Team hat or shirt; medals; sports bottle; trading cards; sports poster; ball.

Pajama Party

Length of party: 4–5 hours before lights out, 2–3 hours in the morning.

Invitations: Purchase pajama party theme invitations or cut a piece of shiny colored cardstock in half to form an 8 1/2" x 5 1/2" sheet. Fold in thirds to form a sleeping bag. The top edge should be 1/8" from side fold. Round bottom corners. Glue folded edge and bottom shut. Use a silver paint pen to zigzag along the front cut edge, creating a zipper.

Paint a pull-tab at the top. Cut a 5 ¹/₂" x 2" strip from tan or pink cardstock. Round out the top to form a head and shoulders. Color the face and hair. Print the party information on a computer and glue to the "body" of the child. Slide child into sleeping bag, allowing the head to peak out just a little bit. Decorate the sleeping bag with sticker stars or balloons.

Decorations: Use balloons and streamers in blue and silver or white. Hang pajamas, the funkier the better, from the corners of the room. Cut out stars and sprinkle with glitter; hang from ceiling using fishing line. Fill a small overnight case with balloons or overnight gear and use as centerpiece for the food table.

Paper goods: Purchase pajama party theme paper goods or use blue and silver. Cover food table with a dark blue table cover and sprinkle confetti stars across it.

Food: Serve make-your-own minipizzas or pigs-in-a-blanket along with vegetables and dip. Provide a variety of munchies for guests to snack on throughout the evening. Serve Starlight Cake (see p. 148) and make-your-own sundaes for dessert or a bedtime treat. For breakfast, serve pancakes or French toast, cantaloupes cut into moons (wedges) and strawberries cut into stars (use cookie cutter).

Activities:

- Paint a pillowcase. Provide each guest with a new, washed white twin pillowcase. Provide an assortment of paint pens or fabric paint and sponge shapes or stamps. Place wax paper in the center of each pillowcase and have guests decorate.

- Overnight Bag Memory. Fill an overnight bag with a variety of overnight necessities. Have birthday child show it to guests and then leave room. Guests then write down what was in the bag.

- Sleeping bag relay. You will need two old sleeping bags. Divide guests into two teams and give each team a sleeping bag. Have guests take turns stepping into their team's sleeping bag and hopping down to the end of the room and back. Continue until all team members have had a turn (like a Potato Sack Race).

- Flashlight tag. Play in a large open room or outside in the dark. A player is "caught" when tagged by the flashlight beam.

Starlight Cake

1. *Bake two 9-inch round cakes. Cut five triangles out of each cake as shown to form two stars. Arrange stars on a cutting or cake board as shown.*
2. *Frost with a thin layer of white frosting to keep crumbs on cut edges in place. Frost again in yellow or white and scatter edible star confetti all over cake. Decorate with sparkler candles.*

Decorating time: 1 hour. Serves 12–16.

- Wink. See directions in chapter 7.
- Pajama fashion relay. Fill two suitcases with zany oversized pajamas, slippers, nightcap, cold cream, toothpaste, sponge curlers (girls), and shaving cream (boys). Divide guests into two teams and give each team a suitcase. Each player must run to the suitcase, put on or use all items, take them off, and then run back and tag the next player.
- Charades or Pictionary.
- Pillow fights. Clear an area and let guests go at it.

    Favors: Pillowcase; penlight; toothbrush/paste; mini–cereal boxes; stickers.

Chapter Twelve

Totally Teens

**i'm taller than you,
But not too big to hug.
My world may be expanding,
But i still need your love!**

They tumbled into Connor's house, each group of four teens anxious to beat the deadline looming only seconds away. To miss the deadline was to lose 100,000 points!

Battle cries of, "We got the best stuff!" "Yeah, well we found everything on the list!" and "There's *no* way you can beat us!" echoed down the hall and into the family room as the kids assembled to determine a winner.

The teams presented their booty, mentally tabulating points in the hundreds of thousands, then millions. Finally, it came down to the last line on the scavenger hunt list. "Okay, for 500,000 points, who found the biggest item?"

One team shouted out, "We brought back this eight-foot ficus. Bet you can't top that!" "We can," another team hollered as they revealed an electric pump and a rapidly expanding inflatable life raft.

"Hold it guys, I'll trust you on the size. I don't really think there's room for that thing in here," stammered Connor's mom. "Anybody top that one?"

Connor's team laughed gleefully, "We can, but you have to come out to the driveway." The teens trooped outside as Connor and his teammates triumphantly unveiled . . . a real big-rig truck!

"Oh man, you guys totally win this one!"

Before following his friends back into the party, Connor called out, "Thanks for helping me out, Mr. Sampson."

"Happy birthday, Connor," his neighbor replied. "You're worth the effort."

IF YOU'RE READING this chapter as the mother of a one-year-old, you're probably thinking that hosting a birthday party for teens is a scary thought. If you're reading this chapter as the mother of a teen, however, you may be absolutely numb with fear! They're big, they're boisterous, they're thrill-seeking, they're asserting their independence, and they're way too cool to please! Ah, but they're also struggling to fit inside those changing bodies, they're vulnerable, they're anxious to fit in with the group, they still need some boundaries, and they really like to just hang out and have fun together. A birthday party for your teenager may seem like too much effort, but at this age possibly more than any other, your child needs to know that he or she is, without a doubt, a unique creation, truly special, and dearly loved.

Does it take a birthday party with a zillion friends, a mountain of junk food, and a high-decibel sound system to say "I love you" to a teen on his birthday? Of course not! Some teenagers may not even want a big birthday party. Definitely respect that choice, but do plan another way to celebrate. Some teenagers will benefit most from some focused family time or special one-on-one attention from mom or dad. Still others will cherish (albeit secretly) the security of a family birthday tradition.

But there are times that a party is what a teen really wants, and there are some definite benefits to hosting a birthday party for your teenager. Hosting a birthday party will provide opportunities to work side-by-side with your teen formulating a budget, hammering out appropriate activities, selecting the yummiest food, and discovering just whom your child now wants to hang out with. A teen birthday party will also give you the oft-desired privilege of seeing your teen's group in action. Most important, it's an opportunity to show your love in a big, splashy way. To say, like Mr. Sampson in the vignette that started this chapter, "You're worth the effort!"

When I first started thinking about writing this chapter on birthday parties for teens, I had two thoughts. The first one was, *There's not too much to tell, really, just three simple rules:*

- Lay in a year's supply of party food. Even those cute little teenage girls can consume massive amounts at a party!
- Figure out a way to see without being seen!
- Provide your neighbors with fresh-baked cookies and high-quality earplugs!

My second thought was, *Wait a minute, I've only hosted three teenage birthday parties, and they were all for a girl. Do I really know what I'm talking about?* I decided I'd better go to the experts—mothers in my community and others all across the country who had hosted parties for their teenagers. Armed with this expert information, my own experiences, and a few bits of wisdom I acquired during my own years as a junior high school activities director, I think I've put together some realistic information on this subject. As it turns out, those original three guidelines are a great place to start when planning.

Lay in a Year's Supply of Party Food

It won't actually be an entire year's supply, but it may feel like one while you're carting the party food from the local grocery warehouse store, then squeezing it into the backseat of your car (if you're the mother of a teen, your trunk will already be full of sports equipment, a couple of portable chairs, and one or two gigantic textbooks). Just like in the elementary school years, let the birthday child pick the food, then add some fruits or vegetables to round out the menu.

Unless the party plan calls for a formal sit-down meal, serve the food, either a meal or an assortment of snacks, buffet style. Prepare a spot for serving soft drinks in a nearby location. Many moms simply fill a big ice chest with ice, soda cans in a variety of flavors, and water bottles. Plan on two to three drinks per guest with some extras thrown in for good measure. Unless your child specifies differently, this is not the time to buy generic soda. Whether you like it or not, teens are very label conscious and typically shun bargain-brand soda. Teens do still appreciate a birthday cake in a favorite flavor and color, with the traditional side of ice cream. A sheet cake, simply decorated and adorned with the right amount of candles, is a popular choice. The birthday song is still considered de rigueur, but you may be surprised to hear it sung in new and amusing ways.

Figure Out a Way to See without Being Seen

One of the trickiest parts to hosting a teen birthday party may be providing adequate supervision to your adolescent guests without acting like the "party police." Your teen may ask, "Mom, please don't hang out in the room (replace this with backyard, bowling alley, etc., to fit the party venue) all the time. We're not little kids anymore!" You, of course, are thinking, "I know, that's why I need to be watching at all times!" Here are a few tips on how to see without being seen.

My daughter's fifteenth birthday party included the use of our pool. In order to monitor the pool without sitting at the edge like a couple of middle-aged lifeguards, my husband and I took advantage of the Ping-Pong table placed in a strategic location right next to the pool. While the guests swam, we played Ping-Pong for close to an hour and a half! Those teens probably think we are crazy about Ping-Pong!

- Greet guests as they arrive. Introduce yourself. Let each guest know you're glad he's come, take jackets and gifts, then escort the guest to the party area. This lets the guest know that a friendly adult is present and supervising the party.
- Make it clear to your teen before the party what areas are out-of-bounds during the party.
- For the duration of the party settle in a location near enough to the fun that you can hear what is going on.
- Walk through the party area every half hour or so to replenish food, drinks, and pick up trash. Mentally count to make sure all guests are accounted for and engaged in appropriate activities.
- Take a casual walk around the house or party venue about every half hour as well. Pay close attention to dark rooms and secluded spaces. If guests have moved into these areas, ask them to return to the party area.

Enjoy your teenager's party, but never forget you are responsible for the well-being of each of those young lives for the duration of the party.

Provide Your Neighbors with Cookies and Earplugs before the Party

Large groups of teenagers are, by their very nature, loud. They laugh, they joke around, they yell, they enjoy loud music. Neighbors, by their very nature, like peace and quiet. When hosting a party in your home, consider informing the nextdoor neighbors (and the ones directly behind you) about the party a day or two in advance. Explain the occasion, when the party will start and end, what is planned for the event, and how many guests are expected. Give them a card with your phone number on it and ask them to call if they are disturbed after a certain hour or if a teenager parks illegally in front of their driveway.

Plan the Party with Your Teen

Every mother I asked for input from on teen birthday parties shared that the best way to host a party teens will love is to plan the party with the birthday teen. One very experienced mother suggested, "Ask her what she wants and then scale it down a notch or two!" Teens who want a party tend to have very grandiose plans. If your teen asks to invite thirty guests, offer to host twenty. If your teen wants a live band, offer a karaoke machine or a set of new CDs to be played on the family sound system.

Two or three weeks before the party, sit down with your teen and ask her what she would like to do at her party. Share with her the amount of money budgeted for the party and the maximum number of guests you're willing to accommodate. Decide together where to host the party, what time the party should start and end, who to invite, what food and drink to serve, and what activities guests would enjoy most. Use the party planning sheet in the appendix to jot down ideas and plans. Determine which of you will be in charge of each party detail. Make a list of party responsibilities, writing down who will fulfill each responsibility, and giving suggested completion dates. Teenagers are notorious for waiting until the last minute. Even a small thing like a short list on the front of the refrigerator can help keep party plans on track.

Rose's Party To-Do List

Make guest list and find addresses	Rose	By May 1
Purchase invitations, stamps	Mom	By May 1
Design and print invitations	Rose	By May 5
Address, stamp, and mail invitations	Mom	By May 5
Select food, decorations, supplies	Rose	By May 14
Shop for party supplies	Mom	By May 20
Clean party area, bathrooms	Rose	May 21, by 2 P.M.
Decorate, set up tables	Rose/Dad	May 21, 2–4 P.M.
Make food	Mom/Rose	May 21, 4–6 P.M.
Clean up after party	Rose/Mom/Dad	

When to Have a Party

The number of major birthday parties a teen hosts varies from family to family, sometimes even within individual families. Some families prefer to host one or two close friends for a birthday celebration and never host a large party, while other families enjoy hosting the whole gang every year. Another popular choice is to host a major birthday party for the thirteenth, sixteenth, and eighteenth years and then celebrate on a smaller scale the other years.

Teens Just Want to Have Fun

For parties, most teens enjoy being someplace where they can be boisterous and active, play loud music, drink soda and eat finger foods, and stay out late. Successful parties can be held at home in the family room, finished basement, garage, or backyard, or at a variety of locations away from home.

Let your teen take the lead in choosing activities for the occasion. My daughter is a swimmer and we have a pool, so swimming is an obvious choice for her parties. Modified versions of basketball, volleyball, soccer, or flag football are fun as well. Dance contests, karaoke, team charades, scavenger hunts, or a good, old-fashioned snowball fight might be just the ticket for success. Teens like to push the envelope, so "est" activities are popular. Challenge teens to perform the zaniest lip sync, build the oddest snowman, find the tiniest car, share the hardest dance step, or be the lowest limbo dancer. When planning a contest, use outrageously big point totals. Playing Pictionary? Award 100,000 points for identification in fifteen seconds or less; 50,000 points for less than thirty seconds, and 10,000 points for identification in less than one minute.

Games, the quirkier the better, are another way to entertain teen guests, especially younger teens. Plan two or three, but don't be too upset if the group finds something else to do. Teen guests may get so involved in talking, eating, or an intense Ping-Pong tournament that they don't want to stop what they are doing. Some of the games in chapter 7 can be adapted for teens. Here are a few additional ideas.

Chubby Bunny. Divide into two or three teams. Give each team a bag of large marshmallows. Instruct the teams to experiment and find out who on their team can get the most marshmallows in his mouth and still say the words "chubby bunny." When each team has chosen a representative, give each contestant one marshmallow to put into his mouth, then ask him to say, "chubby bunny." Contestants do not swallow this marshmallow. Continue to give each contestant marshmallows, requiring them to say "chubby bunny" after each additional marshmallow. The winner is the contestant who can say "chubby bunny" with the most marshmallows in his mouth. An inflatable bunny or a fresh bunch of carrots is a fitting prize!

Suggested Party Locations

- *Amusement park*
- *Arcade*
- *Beach or shore*
- *Boardwalk*
- *Bowling alley*
- *Campground*
- *Carnival*
- *Community center*
- *Hair or nail salon*
- *Laser tag arena*
- *Local shopping mall*
- *Miniature golf*
- *Movie theater*
- *Park*
- *Performing arts center*
- *Paint ball arena*
- *Public pool*
- *Recreation center*
- *Restaurant (consider breakfast or lunch if dinner's too expensive)*
- *Skating rink*
- *Sporting event (pro, college, or high school)*
- *Water park*

Crunch and Whistle. Have guests sit in a circle. Distribute one cracker to each guest. Guests must chew the cracker, then try to whistle. Eliminate any guest who is unable to whistle. Continue distributing crackers and eliminating nonwhistlers until a winner is found. Award the winner a colorful whistle on a string and a box of animal crackers.

Ducky, Ducky? Seat guests in a circle surrounding a single sturdy chair. Blindfold one guest and have her sit in the chair. Another guest will quietly sit in her lap. The player in the blindfold asks, "Ducky, ducky?" The other player replies, "Quack, quack." The blindfolded player gets two tries to guess the identity of the duck. If she guesses correctly, the "duck" takes her place in the chair. If she is incorrect, the "duck" returns to the circle and another guest becomes the "duck." Variations:

Activity Ideas for Teen Parties

'40s or '50s dance contest	Make a video
Bonfire	Manicure/pedicure
Bounce house	Mystery dinner (see the appendix
Broomball	for some on-line resources)
Car rally	Paddle boat or surrey bike rentals
Charades	Roller hockey
Flashlight tag	Rollerblading
Glamour shots (teens dress up and	Scavenger hunt
take each others' pictures	Square or line dancing
with a digital camera)	Watch a video (with parent
Hayride	approval!)
Karaoke/Lip sync	Water balloon fight
Limbo contest	

Yes, teens like bounce houses too. One mom even arranged to keep the bounce house overnight and the teens slept inside. She reports it was very exciting, especially when the automatic sprinklers doused the house in the wee hours of the morning!

Have the guests remaining in the circle make other animal sounds to make it more difficult to figure out the duck's identity, or, instead of changing ducks when the blindfolded player guesses incorrectly, have another duck sit on top of the first one. Then they both quack!

Food Sculptures. Provide each team with an assortment of food items, a paring knife, and some toothpicks and ask them to create a food sculpture. Set a ten- or fifteen-minute time limit. It's amazing how fruits and vegetables and several fruit rollups can provide a fun medium for creative expression.

Frisbee Bowling. In a large open area arrange two sets of soda bottle bowling pins. (In case you haven't bowled in a while, that's ten pins: a single in the first row, then two, then three, then four in the last row.) Divide guests into two teams. Station one player from each team behind the "pins," with remaining players lined up at the other end of the "alley." Provide each team with two Frisbees. Each player will have two shots at knocking down the pins. If a "bowler" has a strike, the player behind the pins sets them up again for the second shot. Keep a tally of "pin falls" for each team. After a player "bowls," he takes the place of the player behind the pins. That player retrieves the Frisbees, hands them to the next person in line, and then goes to the end of the line. After every team member has "bowled," award Frisbees to everyone on the team that has the highest "pin fall."

Honey, If You Love Me, Smile! Have players sit in a circle. Choose one player to be "it." That player faces another player and says, "Honey, if you love me, smile!" "It" tries to get the other player to smile. "It" may try just about anything short of tickling to earn the smile. If the other player hasn't smiled within thirty seconds, "it" must try someone else. If the other player smiles or laughs, he becomes "it" and the original "it" takes his seat. Variation: Have "it" draw out of a hat for the name of the player he must make smile.

I Have Never . . . Seat players in a circle and provide each player with something to use as tokens (pennies, toothpicks, uncooked pasta, etc.). If you have ten players, give each player ten tokens; if you have fifteen players, give each player fifteen tokens; and so on. Go around the circle and have each player tell something he has never done. Any player who *has* done the thing mentioned must give him a token. The winner is the person with the most tokens after all the players have shared. Some examples: "I have never been outside this state." "I have never played an instrument." "I have never ridden on a train."

Mummies. Divide guests into teams of three. Give each team two rolls of toilet paper. Ask each team to select a person on their team who will be the "mummy." The winner is the team that best covers their "mummy" in three minutes. Variation: Fashion designer. Give each team a roll of paper towels or wallpaper and twelve safety pins. The winner is the team that can design the best formal outfit in five minutes.

Water Tag. Before the party, ask guests to wear an old T-shirt, or provide a thrift store find for each player. Cut an eight-inch diameter circle out of poster board for each player. Using a *watercolor* marker, color half the circles red and the other half blue. At the party, divide the guests into two teams. Use masking tape to affix a colored circle in the team color onto each player's *back*. (You don't want this to turn into a wet T-shirt contest.) State the boundaries of the playing area. Enforce a five-squirt penalty for any player who shoots another player in the face. Give each player a small squirt gun or bottle and provide a water supply for refills. (Fill plastic drink containers with water if there is no accessible water source.) After ten minutes, the team with the driest circles wins. Consider having another set of circles on hand. Teens often want to play this one again!

157

What If My Teen Wants To . . .

Invite Guests of the Opposite Sex?

Sometime during the teen years, if not before, your child will discover that the opposite sex no longer has cooties. That milestone occurs at different times in the life of each teenager and there is a wide range of opinions on how to handle this question. Some parents allow mixed parties whenever asked, and others say never! Many parents have chosen a policy that falls somewhere in between, such as only same-gender parties until fifteen, then mixed-gender parties for ages fifteen through eighteen. Often parents discourage "couples parties" until the junior or senior year of high school. Talk with other teen parents in the community, consider your teen and his friends, and then set a policy for your family.

Party into the Wee Hours?

Of course your teen would like to party into the wee hours! Unfortunately this often does not sit well with the neighbors. Many communities also have teen curfews that need to be enforced. Here are some guidelines to consider.

7th and 8th grade: 10 P.M.
9th and 10th grade: 11 P.M.
11th and 12th grade: Midnight–1 A.M.

Host a Coed Sleep-Over?

Would you lock a chocoholic in a small room for the night with an open box of Godiva chocolates and expect all the chocolates to be there the next morning? I don't think so! The combination of raging hormones, our sex-saturated society, clothing that leaves little to the imagination, a natural curiosity in the opposite sex, and a tendency to stretch the limits makes it difficult for today's teenagers to maintain their sexual purity. Let's not make this more difficult by having them spend an entire night snuggled together in the dark. Every mother I asked about hosting a coed sleep-over replied with something along the lines of, "Not on my watch!" If your teen lays the "but all the other parents let their teens do it" line on you, feel free to tell them that Mrs. Radic and the parents she asked do *not* let their teens "do it"!

Go Toilet Papering?

In some communities, decorating a friend's front yard with yards and yards of toilet paper is considered vandalism; in others, it's a harmless teenage prank. If toilet papering is safe and considered acceptable in your community, consider allowing it under the following conditions:

- The victim's parents are asked ahead of time.
- An adult is available to chaperone (this will not be popular!)
- The teens agree to arrive with coffee and bagels the next morning and help clean up the mess.

Host a Flier Party?

Your teen is not asking to go on a helicopter or hot air balloon ride. A flier party consists of printing hundreds of fliers and sliding one into every locker at the local high school. Any leftovers are stapled on signposts all over the city. If you enjoy supervising two hundred largely unknown teenagers or like the idea of the police making an appearance at your teen's party, go ahead and say yes! Just remember that while a teen is at your teen's party you are responsible for him and can be held liable for any injuries, possibly even incidents that occur after a guest leaves the party. Ask your teen for a guest list with addresses and phone numbers to insure you know who will be attending and how to contact a parent in case of emergency.

Provide Alcoholic Beverages?

In most states, providing alcohol to a minor is against the law. Studies show that teenagers have a much lower tolerance for alcohol than adults. Alcohol impairs a teen's critical thinking abilities and response times, and can reduce inhibitions. Alcohol poisoning and drunk driving fatalities are much too common among teens. To keep your party alcohol free, implement the following strategies:

- Discuss the dangers of alcohol consumption with your teenager.
- Discuss what will happen if you discover alcohol at the party.
- Make sure any alcoholic beverages (and medications) are inaccessible to teens.
- Serve drinks in cans. Do not use a punch bowl.
- Allow only beverages you purchased into the party. Teens still try the old trick of pouring an alcoholic beverage into a soft drink container.
- Be present and proactive.

Teenagers are, for the most part, respectful, responsible, and fun to have around, but unfortunately, just one or two rebellious adolescents can infiltrate a party with dangerous things like sex, drugs, and alcohol. Your presence and willingness to set and enforce boundaries will help your teen and his guests enjoy a safe, entertaining birthday party. A parent's presence and protection are valuable birthday gifts for any teenager.

Party Plans for Teens

With so many great ideas for teen parties, it was difficult to narrow it down to four. As in the other chapters, these parties can be modified to meet the needs of your teen. The first, a beach bonfire, could be held at a lake, river, campground, or possibly in the backyard. Some large parks even have fire rings and allow bonfires. The second, a car rally, takes quite a bit of advanced planning, but is a favorite with teens. Volunteerism is a growing trend among teens, and the third party provides an opportunity for a teenager to practice the Golden Rule while sharing his favorite charity with friends. Within our culture there seems to be a growing interest in celebrating the coming of age of a child. This concept truly celebrates the life of a child and deserves consideration in today's family. Similar to the Jewish bar/bat mitzvah or the Latin Quincenera (a Sweet Fifteen party for girls), the fourth party is designed to celebrate a child's crossing from childhood into adulthood and includes a strong spiritual component. Guests might include a combination of the teen's friends, adult mentors, family friends, and the extended family. However you choose to celebrate, cherish the opportunity to spend time with your teen. Soon he or she will be stepping out into the great big world of adulthood.

When Your Teen's the Guest

- *Require party information before giving permission to attend. This should include teen and parent hosts' names and phone number, exact location of the party, and the starting and ending times.*
- *If you are not acquainted with the host family, call and talk to the host parent to make sure he or she will be present. Ask what is planned for the event.*
- *Discuss transportation to and from the party.*
- *Remind your teen about the dangers of alcohol and drugs. Offer a "no questions asked" pick-up policy: If your teen finds himself in a bad situation, he can phone home and you will come and pick him up, no questions asked.*
- *Request that your teen inform you when she arrives home, even if you are sleeping.*
- *Talk about the party with your child. This should be a gentle conversation expressing interest in his activities, not a police interrogation!*

Beach Bonfire

Length of party: 3 hours (Check for beach curfew, usually 10 P.M.)

Invitations: Purchase beach scene paper and print at home on a computer. An alternative: Purchase several pair of inexpensive plastic flip-flops. Using a permanent marker, write out party information on the top. Hand-deliver or mail in large manila envelopes along with just a sprinkle of sand.

Decorations: A canopy of stars and the steady crashing of ocean waves.

Paper goods: Sturdy paper plates, plastic ware, and beach-themed napkins. New plastic sand pails make cute serving containers for food. If you are using a table, be sure to bring something to weight the tablecloth. Reshape wire coat hangers to serve as roasting skewers for hot dogs and marshmallows.

Food: Hot dogs and buns with all the trimmings, several varieties of potato chips, pasta salad made with shell-shaped pasta, baked beans, chocolate sheet cake, ice cream in individual cups, s'mores, and an ice chest of canned soda and bottled water.

BEACH PARTY

Friday July 17 6-10pm at 32nd in Newport Beach RSVP 871-2233 by July 15

Activities:

- Frisbee football. This is played like touch football except a Frisbee replaces the football. If desired, use a piece of wood or a sand shovel to mark off the playing field.

- Sky castle contest. This is a contest to see which team can build the tallest sand structure in ten minutes. Divide guests into two or more teams. Give each team a sand bucket, plastic shovels or cups, and a designated building area.

- Seashore Scavenger Hunt. (Note: play this one while it is still light outside.) Divide guests into groups of three or four. Give each group fifteen minutes to come up with the following: a plastic bottle top, the longest piece of seaweed, as many unbroken shells as possible, a sand crab (provide a small sand pail for this), the smoothest piece of driftwood, a feather, an empty chip bag, a left-behind beach shoe, and a child's sand toy.

- Fashion designer. Divide into groups of three or four. Give each group twelve safety pins. The object is to design and model the best beach ensemble using only beach towels and the safety pins. Allow ten minutes to create the ensembles, and then ask the designated person from each team to model the creation. Give prizes for best use of towels and pins, most realistic ensemble, most unusual ensemble, most wearable ensemble, and best presentation.

- Chubby Bunny. See instructions earlier in this chapter.
- Fractured Fairy Tales. This is a good one for sitting around the campfire. Ask one guest to begin telling a traditional fairy tale. Moving around the circle, each guest retells a part of the fairy tale, making it as outlandish as possible.
- Campfire songs. Ask a guitar-playing teen to bring her guitar and sing favorite songs around the campfire. Be sure to include some silly ones!

If you do not live near a beach, try this in a family room with a fireplace. Hang stars from the ceiling and play a CD with beach sounds. Ask guests to come wearing beach attire. Roast hot dogs and marshmallows in the fireplace. Hide the scavenger hunt items around the house. Instead of creating sky castles out of sand, use marshmallows and toothpicks. Replace Frisbee football with an indoor game such as "Honey, if you love me, smile."

Around the Town

Length of party: 3–4 hours

Invitations: Purchase cityscape paper and print at home on computer. An alternative: Go to an internet site that provides maps. Create a map from each guest's house to your house. Cut and paste the map on the front of a half sheet of cardstock. On the opposite side of the cardstock, print party information. (Print party information

---

Stop Sign Cake

1. *Bake a giant sugar cookie in a round pizza pan lined with wax paper. Cool cookie for 10 minutes and then slide onto a cake board.*
2. *Cut the circle into an octagon and frost the entire cookie bright red. (Use high-quality paste food coloring to get the best red color.) Using a tube of white icing, write the word "STOP."*

on the cardstock before gluing on the map or it might jam the printer.) Use tiny car stickers to decorate.

Decorations: Maps; purchased road signs or road signs made from cardstock; any type of car or car equipment.

Paper goods: Serve pizza straight from the box, vegetables and dip, snack foods, beverages, ice cream, and Stop Sign Cake.

Activity:

Car Rally. Before the party, plan a car rally route that will take guests to ten of the birthday teens favorite things. Write clues to each location and decide on a fun way each team can prove they arrived at the location. (Answer a question about a nearby store, purchase a bag of French fries, request and bring back a logo napkin, take a Polaroid/digital picture, etc.) Copy enough sets of clues for each team. Put the clue for each location in a separate, numbered envelope. The last envelope should lead the guests back to your home. Divide guests into teams of three to five. Assign each group to a car and driver. (Drivers should be *very* responsible older teens or adult friends. If possible, provide each driver with a cell phone.) For the rally, give each team a set of numbered clue envelopes. Envelopes must be opened in order. Teams must follow the rally route and obey all traffic laws, including maximum speed limit. (Recording the odometer reading and the time when teams depart and return will allow a comparison with how long it took you to make a trial trip.) Have teams depart five minutes apart. Award points for successfully finding each location and bringing back the required proof. Also award points for the team closest to your odometer reading and route time.

> ### Sample clue for car rally:
>
> *Head South on the street where new ships would dock (Newport Ave.). Where the light changes color for the third time (third stop light) turn toward the hand Terrell writes with (right). When you come to the place of the living trees (Live Oaks strip mall), turn counterclockwise (left) and park right outside the place that serves good fortune (Chinese takeout place). Write down the price of a double order of number four and bring back a set of eating utensils (chopsticks).*

The Midas Touch

Length of party: 3 hours

Invitations: Purchase invitations with gold foil border (found with fiftieth anniversary supplies) or print party information on glossy white cardstock. Punch two holes at

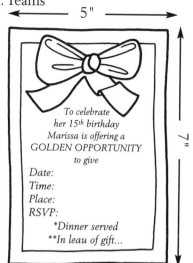

5"

7"

To celebrate
her 15th birthday
Marissa is offering a
GOLDEN OPPORTUNITY
to give

Date:
Time:
Place:
RSVP:
    *Dinner served
    **In leau of gift...

the top and tie a gold ribbon into holes. Introduce the party information with, "To celebrate her fifteenth birthday, Martina is providing a golden opportunity to give." If possible, include a pamphlet from the birthday teen's favorite charitable organization.

Decorations: Gold and white streamers and balloons; foil-wrapped gold chocolate coins. (Look for gold decorations with fiftieth anniversary supplies.) Wrap a stack of bricks with gold foil wrapping paper, tie with glossy white ribbon, and use as a centerpiece for the food table.

Paper goods: Gold plates and white napkins. White tablecloth sprinkled with gold confetti, curling ribbon, and candy coins.

Food: Golden nuggets (chicken nuggets) with dipping sauces, golden delicious apples with caramel dip (see chapter 5), Fritos, beverages, Golden Vanilla Cake, and ice cream.

Midas Projects:

In lieu of a gift, ask each guest to bring a donation for the charity of choice. If the charity is local and they are open to the idea, arrange for the guests to serve there together. If this is not possible, consult the charitable organization to discern a task the teens might do together at the party that would benefit the organization (e.g., put together art supply bags for the oncology ward at a children's hospital, make chocolate chip cookies to serve at a soup kitchen, fold brochures for an upcoming charitable event, decorate quilt squares to create a quilt for an abused child).

Sample idea 1:

Teen's favorite charity: Operation Christmas Child (see the appendix for contact information)

Project: Use collected donations along with any funds you or your teen want to contribute to fill shoe boxes for children in an impoverished country. Give guests the money and a list of needed items, take them to a discount store, and allow them to shop for an hour. Back at home, have guests wrap each shoe box in Christmas paper, fill the box, and write a group letter to the recipients. If possible, include a picture of the group.

Sample idea 2:

Teen's favorite charity: A downtown soup kitchen

Project: In lieu of a birthday gift, ask guests to bring ten of a specific toiletry or snack item (small tubes of toothpaste, toothbrushes, travel-size deodorant and shampoo, plastic comb, wrapped bar of soap, individually wrapped candy bars, gum, hard candy). Have the teens fill Ziploc bags with one of each item to create a personal care kit for a homeless individual. Deliver the bags to the soup kitchen together.

Activities:

- Golden Oldies Dance. Provide a selection of golden oldies (check your local library) and encourage teens to dance the night away.
- Silence is Golden Charades. Just a "golden" name for the party classic game of Charades. See chapter 7 for instructions
- Monopoly with a golden twist. Play like regular Monopoly, except that if another player lands on your property, you pay them to stay. The object of the game is to be the first player to *give away* all your money.

Crossing the Threshold

Length of party: 3–4 hours

Invitations: Purchase birthday theme paper and print at home or, using a computer and scanner, create a picture collage using your favorite pictures of the birthday child. Copy the collage on the front of a half sheet of cardstock. On the back, introduce the party information with "Come join our family as we celebrate Carter's crossing the threshold into adulthood," and then give party information. Ask guests to bring a copy of their favorite picture of the birthday teen or a cartoon or picture representing the teen, as well as a piece of advice for the teen.

Decorations: Balloons and streamers in the teen's favorite colors, happy birthday banners, pictures of the birthday teen, baby shoes, and childhood mementos. Use items that represent your teen's interests as decorations (hockey sticks, a flute, Bible or other favorite book, magnifying glass, boom box, skate board, theatrical costume, etc.).

Food: Serve quartered peanut butter and jelly sandwiches alongside a six-foot submarine sandwich, jars of baby food carrots (just for effect) alongside a vegetable and dip tray, teething biscuits alongside potato chips, and Jell-O jigglers alongside a favorite salad. In an ice chest, mix a few sipper cups and baby bottles in with the cans of soda and bottled water. Serve ice cream and a sheet cake inscribed with "Welcome to adulthood, Carter."

Ceremony of passage: Ask a few family members, mentors, and friends to participate in a short ceremony celebrating the teen's passage from childhood to adulthood. Use the sample program as a guide.

Crossing the Threshold Ceremony

Welcome and prayer ....Art Matthews, Carter's father
Song
of celebration............Dave Martin and Mike Shu,Carter's friends
Reminiscing
with thanks ....Esther Matthews, Carter's grandmother
................................Paul Taylor, Carter's friend since first grade
Message of inspiration ....Jose Gonzales, Carter's Youth Leader
Words of appreciation..............Nanci Matthews, Carter's mother
Challenge for the future.................Art Matthews, Carter's father
Accepting the challenge ....Carter Matthews
Song of commitment................Christa Matthews, Carter's sister
Blessing ....Art and Nanci Matthews, Carter's parents

---

Activities:

- Make a memory album. Provide a long banquet table with blank scrapbook pages, stickers, and markers. Ask each guest to create a scrapbook page using the picture he brought and including the piece of advice. Make sure each guest signs his or her page. Have guests place each page in a scrapbook.

- "I appreciate you because . . ." Give one guest a lined piece of paper with the words "Carter, I appreciate you because . . ." on the top. Ask the guest to write down something he appreciates about the birthday teen and then pass the paper on to someone else. (Check periodically to be sure the paper is circulating.) Read these words of appreciation during the ceremony. After the party, make a copy of this list. Put the original in the scrapbook for safekeeping, but have the birthday teen place the copy in a wallet, purse, or journal for quick reference whenever he or she is feeling discouraged.

- Are You the Person Who? Come up with questions pertaining to the guests at the party and their relationship to your teen. Photocopy and distribute the lists to the guests. Have each guest write down the name of the person who can answer the question positively. You may only use each guest two times.

  For example:
  Are you the person who . . .

  Coached Carter's first soccer team?
  Knocked the wind out of Carter while playing touch football?

Purchased Carter's first guitar?

Plays with Carter in the band?

Gave Carter his favorite poster?

Knitted Carter's blue baby blanket?

Taught Carter to tie his shoes?

Drove Carter to the emergency room when he broke his arm?

Works with Carter at Burger Barn?

Has gone to the same school as Carter since first grade?

Developed the recipe for Carter's favorite cookie?

Found Carter's lost tooth in the sandbox?

Can beat Carter in a bubblegum-blowing contest?

Traveled with Carter to India last summer?

Taught Carter to play chess?

Doused Carter with water balloons and shaving cream at camp?

Joins Carter Saturday morning in tutoring at the homework club?

Learned from Carter how to access the internet?

Resources for Busy Moms

So much to do,
So little time,
i'll find the things i need on-line.

Gwenna finally settled her two-month-old into the crib for the night, then sat down at her little kitchen desk to think. *What can I do to make Adam's third birthday special for him? With a new baby sister, and his big sister, Lindsey, starting kindergarten last month, he really needs some special attention. I'd like to give him a party, but I sure don't have the time or energy to traipse through a bunch of stores looking for supplies.*

Thumbing through her birthday book, Gwenna's eyes fell on a page in the last chapter. *Here are some great party themes Adam would just love,* she thought. *Oh, wow, look at this. I can order almost everything*

I need on-line! I'm going to check out these websites right now. Tomorrow morning, Adam and I can spend some couch time together and plan a little party for his four best buddies. This I think I can handle!

"SO MUCH TO DO, so little time" is a common lament among mothers. As you've thumbed through the pages of this book, I pray that you've become excited about using birthdays as an opportunity to celebrate the life of the child God has entrusted into your care. As a mother of four of those precious gifts, I know how challenging it can be to find enough time to do more than meet the current day's demands. Consider the list of resources in this chapter as a gift of time from one busy mom to another. While I cannot guarantee the products and services these resources represent, they are the most helpful ones I found in researching this book. Websites and resources tend to come and go, so I endeavored to share only those that have a well-established reputation. I spent hours and hours browsing through books and surfing the web for useful birthday information, and share the results with the hope that this will save you time as you plan and prepare for your child's celebration. Use the time you save to savor a few extra moments with your birthday child.

Chapter One: Why Celebrate?

Elisa Morgan and Carol Kuykendall, *What Every Child Needs* (Grand Rapids: Zondervan, 1997). Order this resource through the MOPShop at mopshop@MOPS.org, or 888-545-4040.

Chapter Two: Ways to Celebrate

The "Preparing for Adolescence" audiotape series by Dr. James Dobson is available at family.org or by calling 800-A-FAMILY.

Chapter Three: Let's Plan a Family Party

Party Planning Timeline

1–2 Weeks before the Party

- Choose a date and time. Write this on your planning sheet (p. 174), the family calendar, and Daddy's calendar.
- With your child (if he is old enough) decide on a theme, menu, and activities. This might be a good time to ask for any gift suggestions.

- Fill out the party planning sheet and shopping list. Add to these as you plan over the next few days.
- Call and invite any extended family members.

1 Week before the Party

- Order the cake, if necessary.
- Gather all birthday supplies (decorations, project supplies, paper goods, photo and video equipment).
- Purchase all nonperishables, including birthday gifts (see shopping list on p. 177).
- Set aside specific times in the coming week to work on any special birthday traditions and activities. Delegate tasks if possible.

2–3 Days before the Party

- Wrap gifts.
- Bake and freeze cake for decorating later.
- Finish making decorations.

1 Day before the Party

- Call and confirm the cake order.
- Check cameras and video equipment for batteries and film.
- Shop for perishables and last-minute supplies.

Early on the Day of the Party (or the night before)

- Frost and decorate the cake (if necessary).
- Put up decorations and set the table.
- Organize supplies for any traditions or activities.
- Pick up cake, helium balloons, and any other last-minute items.
- Remind family members of the party time and of anything they need to bring to the celebration.

2 Hours before the Party

- Prepare the meal.
- Finish any last-minute decorating or activity details.

Half Hour before the Party

- Help birthday child and siblings dress for party.
- If you desire, change clothes for the party.
- Take a few minutes to sit down and go over your planning sheet one last time.

After the Party

- Cuddle with your child. Find out what she enjoyed most about her birthday celebration.
- Make a thank-you note list (if needed).
- Enlist family members to help clean up meal and decorations or do cleanup yourself as you pray for the birthday child.
- Store reusable decorations or birthday-related items in storage boxes for future use. Be sure to label boxes clearly.
- Make notes or comments on your planning sheets of things you would like to remember for the next birthday party. Store planning sheets with the birthday supplies or in a designated birthday file.
- Grab a cup of tea and a favorite book or magazine and take some mommy time. You've earned it!

Within 1 Week after the Party

- Help your child write and send any needed thank-you notes.

Party Supply Sources

Amazingmoms.com. Provides many theme ideas, party-planning ideas, and supplies.

The American Girl Store, 800-845-0005 or americangirlstore.com. Provides books for school-age girls on party planning.

Birthday Direct, birthdaydirect.com. Birthday supplies.

Birthday Express, 800-424-7843 or birthdayexpress.com. Provides a wide variety of party supplies and ideas for party planning.

Birthday in a Box, 800-989-5506 or birthdayinabox.com. Provides a wide variety of party supplies and ideas for party planning.

Birthday USA, 240-453-0111 or birthdayusa.com. Provides a wide variety of party supplies.

Boardman's Birthday Party Ideas, boardmanweb.com/party. Provides detailed party ideas, birthday supplies, a myriad of cake-decorating items, edible craft ideas, and more.

Oriental Trading Company, Inc., 800-526-9300 or orientaltrading.com. Provides a large selection of inexpensive party favors, bulk candy, piñatas, decorations, hats, and a treasure chest.

Simplifun.com. Provides a variety of downloadable party goods like invitations, favors, and coloring sheets, some for free. This site has several plans for mystery parties.

ThePlunge.com. Provides party-planning organization, build a birthday website, and on-line invitations and thank-you notes you can send.

U.S. Toy, 800-255-6124 or ustoy.com. Provides a large selection of inexpensive party favors, bulk candy, piñatas, decorations, hats, and a treasure chest.

Worksheets

The following pages contain worksheets for planning a family celebration, planning a party, the guest list, and a party shopping list. These sheets may be reproduced for the buyer's personal use. All other reproductions are by permission only.

Family Celebration Planning Sheet

BIRTHDAY CHILD: _____ AGE: _____

DATE: _____ TIME:____ to _____ BUDGET: $_____

LOCATION: _____ PHONE: _____

ADDRESS: _____

EXTENDED FAMILY:

Name:	Ph #
Name:	Ph #
Name:	Ph #
Name:	Ph #

CHILD'S FAVORITES:

Theme/Colors: _____

Decorations: _____

        (cost $_____)

Food: (cost $_____)

Drink: (cost $_____)

Cake/Ice Cream/Candles: _____

Bakery Ph #_____ (cost $_____)

TRADITIONS:

A.

B.

ACTIVITIES:

A.

B.

SUPPLIES

(cost $_____)

MULTIMEDIA:		GIFT SUGGESTIONS:
Camera	Tape Recorder	Budget: $
Film	Cassette	
Video	Batteries	
(cost $____)		

174

Party Planning List

BIRTHDAY CHILD: _____ AGE: _____

Theme: _____ Budget: $_____

DATE: _____ TIME:___TO — # GUESTS: _____

LOCATION: _____ PHONE: _____

ADDRESS: _____

HELPERS: _____

Invitations/Thank-Yous/Stamps	Cake/Candles/Ice Cream Size/shape Ingredients/Decorations Bakery Ph #
Total $	Pickup Cost $

PAPER GOODS: Cups Plates Napkins Plastic ware Tablecloth Other Total $	FOOD AND BEVERAGES Total $

DECORATIONS Total $	GAMES/PRIZES Total $

OTHER ACTIVITIES Supply Total $ Bakery Ph # Fee: $	PARTY FAVORS: Cost Per Child $ Total $

Guest List

BIRTHDAY CHILD: AGE:

DATE: TIME: TO   # GUESTS:

LOCATION: PHONE:

ADDRESS:

SPECIAL INSTRUCTIONS:

GUEST	ADDRESS	PHONE	INVITE	RSVP	THANK-YOU
1					
2					
3					
4					
5					
6					
7					
8					
9					
10					
11					
12					
13					
14					
15					
16					
17					
18					
19					
20					
21					
22					
23					
24					
25					
26					
27					
28					
29					
30					
31					

Party Shopping List

BIRTHDAY CHILD: _____ AGE: _____

FOOD (MEAL AND SNACKS):	DECORATIONS:
	Streamers
	Banners
Cake and ice cream	Centerpiece
	Flowers
	Balloons #
	Helium
Frosting	Pump
	Balloon Clips
	Weights
	Ribbons
Cake decorations	Balloons ordered at
	Ph #
	Pick-up date & time _____
# Candles	Cost/Form of payment _____
	Other
_____ Matches	

PAPER GOODS:	GAME/ACTIVITY SUPPLIES:
Cups	
Plates (cake)	
Plates (luncheon)	
Napkins	
Plastic ware	
Tablecloth	
Invitations	
Thank-You Notes	

CAKE ORDER:

Bakery   Ph #_____

Pickup date and time_____

Cost/Form of payment _____

PARTY FAVORS AND PRIZES:

\#_____

FOOD ORDER:

Caterer   Ph # _____

Pickup date & time_____

Cost/form of payment _____

MISC:

Film	Trash bags
Batteries	Stamps
Cassette	Scotch Tape
CD Player	Masking Tape

Chapter Four: Let's Plan a Birthday Party

85 Additional Party Themes

Alice in Wonderland (or "One"-derland)
Alphabet
Army
Around the World
Arts and Crafts
Baby-doll Shower
Back-to-the-Future (Science Fiction)
Backwards
Beach
Beading
Bookworm
Bubbles
Bugs
Butterfly
Campout
Candid Camera
Candyland
Cheerleading
Christmas in (birthday month)
Cinderella
Computers/Cyberspace
Construction
Dalmatians ("Who Let the Dogs Out?")
David and Goliath (Big and Small)
Disco Dance
Dress-Up Party
Extreme Sports
Firefighters
Flower Power
Game Show
Garden
Glow-in-the-Dark
Goldilocks and the Three Bears
Groovy Sixties
Gymnastics
Half Birthday

Hats
Ice Cream
Jack in Giant Land
Junior Chefs
Karaoke
Knights and Ladies
Ladybugs
Lights, Camera, Action!
Luau
Mad Scientist
Makeover
Masquerade/Mardi Gras
Mickey/Minnie Mouse
Mother Goose
Motocross/Bicycles
Music Makers
Mystery
Nifty Fifties
Noah's Ark
Peter Pan
Pet Show
Playground
Pioneer Days
Princess
Prom Night
Puppet
Racecar
Raggedy Ann and Andy
Rainbow
Robin Hood
Rubber Ducky
Safari
Sesame Street
Shop 'Til You Drop
Snakes and Reptiles
Snow

Space

Sports

Superheroes

Supersleuth/Detective

Talent Show

This Is Your Life

Three Little Kittens

Tiny Tea Party

Trains

Veggie Tales

Wet-and-Wild

Winnie the Pooh

Wizard of Oz

Zoofari

Party Safety Checklist

General

_____ Have you planned plenty of activities to keep guests occupied?

_____ Have you enlisted adequate help?

_____ Are balloons, confetti, and other small decorations out of reach of small children and pets?

_____ Do any of your guests have known allergies or medical conditions for which you need to make accommodations?

_____ Do you have a basic first-aid kit and emergency numbers readily available?

_____ Do you have contact information for every child dropped off at the party?

Indoors

_____ Have you removed slippery rugs, breakable items, or fragile furniture?

_____ Have you created a large, safe play area by moving or removing furniture?

_____ Are there any dangling cords or wires that should be secured?

_____ Have you blocked home areas that are "off limits" with streamers? (Be sure to leave access to bathroom and exits.)

_____ Are there any sharp objects or items that could be used as swords? (Little boys can be especially imaginative!)

Outdoors

_____ Are there any poisonous plants (i.e., oleanders, lily of the valley, poinsettia, azalea, mushrooms)? Keep small children away from these.

_____ Are sprinkler spigots adjusted so children won't trip? If not, place a small flag to identify any hazards.

_____ Is your yard secure so that children cannot wander out into the street?

_____ If you have a pool, jacuzzi, pond, or fountain, is it inaccessible to children?

_____ Is all play equipment free of loose screws or broken parts that could catch on clothes or harm children?

Chapter Five: Fun Fixin's for Festivities

Sources for Birthday Cake Ideas

Bake and Make Amazing Cakes by Elizabeth Macleod (available at amazon.com). This book contains several wonderful cakes, many for the novice decorator.

Birthdayexpress.com. (See Party Supply Sources in the resources for chapter 3.) Offers several fun cake ideas.

Boardmanweb.com/parties. (See Party Supply Sources in the resources for chapter 3.) Offers several fun cake ideas.

Cakes-online.com. An on-line order desk for cakes. An affiliated local bakery bakes, decorates, and delivers the cake.

Children's Party Cakes by Sue Aldridge (available at amazon.com). This book contains several wonderful cakes designed for parent and child to create together.

Family.go.com/parties. This is the website of "Family Fun Magazine." Check out the A to Z list of birthday cakes.

Kidsdomain.com/crafts. Offers several fun cake ideas for parent and child to create together.

Special Effects Cookbook by Michael E. Samonek. Order at special-effectscookbook.com. These cakes and other edibles entertain as well. The volcano cake actually erupts!

Wilton Industries, 800-794-5866 or wilton.com. Wilton cake baking and decorating products are available at most party supply and craft stores. The website offers many cake ideas and supplies. Cookie- and candy-making supplies are also available. There are a few free cake-decorating lessons, and links to local cake-decorating classes.

Wireacake.com. An on-line order desk for cakes. An affiliated local bakery bakes, decorates, and delivers the cake.

Chapter Six: Creating a Festive Environment

See Party Supply Sources in the resources for chapter 3. Many of these same suppliers sell decorating supplies as well as offer tips for creating a festive environment.

Chapter Seven: Great Games and Activities

Sources for Finger Plays and Children's Songs

All of the following books are available at amazon.com.

Eentsy, Weentsy Spider: Fingerplays and Action Rhymes, Joanna Cole

Pat-a-Cake and Other Play Rhymes, Joanna Cole

Wee Sing Children's Songs and Fingerplays, Pamela Conn Beal and Susan Hagen Nipp

Chapter Ten: Fun Festivities for Fours and Fives

Dinosaur Products

All the Right Stuff, 800-799-8697 or alltherightstuff.com. Sells dinosaurs, space, and ocean-themed goods and more. The fossilized dinosaur food is intriguing.

The Dinosaur Farm, 888-658-2388 or dinofarm.com. Sells dinosaur inflatables, party goods, favors, mobiles, and more.

See the *Special Effects Cookbook* in resources for chapter 5 for a volcano cake that really erupts.

Chapter Twelve: Totally Teens

Operation Christmas Child: www.samaritanspurse.org.

index

How moms can break down phony barriers and find self-acceptance and intimacy with God and others

Real Moms
Exploding the Myths of Motherhood
Elisa Morgan and
Carol Kuykendall

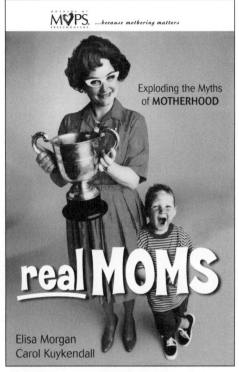

How many moms think they are the only mothers in their circle of friends who blow it with their kids? Or live in a not-so-clean house? Or long to go back to work? Or don't have a perfect marriage or perfect children? Confessing these weaknesses can make a woman feel guilty, so she hides behind the barrier of a "Good Mommy Mask." She wants greater self-acceptance and more intimate relationships with others and with God, but she doesn't realize that being real will bring her what she desires most.

Real Moms unmasks the myths of the American culture and affirms the real struggles of real moms. Each chapter helps moms recognize and break down one of the barriers to real mothering. Chapters include: PermaGuilt Mom, Judge Not Mom, Monster Mom, Party Mom, and Viagra Mom. Written by MOPS authors and columnists Elisa Morgan and Carol Kuykendall, this book is good for personal reading but also as a tool for small group discussions.

Softcover: 0-310-24703-9

ZONDERVAN™

GRAND RAPIDS, MICHIGAN 49530 USA

WWW.ZONDERVAN.COM

Little Books for Busy Moms Series

Softcover 0-310-23997-4

Softcover 0-310-23515-4

Softcover 0-310-23514-6

Softcover 0-310-24178-2

Softcover 0-310-23511-1

Softcover 0-310-23999-0

Softcover 0-310-23513-8

The MOPS Story

MOPS stands for Mothers of Preschoolers, a program designed to encourage mothers with children under school age through relationships and resources. These women come from different backgrounds and lifestyles, yet have similar needs and a shared desire to be the best mothers they can be!

A MOPS group provides a caring, accepting atmosphere for today's mother of preschoolers. Here she has an opportunity to share concerns, explore areas of creativity, and hear instruction that equips her for the responsibilities of family and community. The MOPS group also includes MOPPETS, a loving, learning experience for children.

Approximately 2,700 groups meet in churches throughout the United States, Canada, and 19 other countries, to meet the needs of more than 100,000 women. Many more mothers are encouraged by MOPS resources, including *MOMSense* radio and magazine, MOPS' web site, and publications such as this book.

Find out how MOPS International can help you become part of the MOPS♥to♥Mom Connection.

MOPS International
P.O. Box 102200
Denver, CO 80250-2200
Phone 1-800-929-1287 or 303-733-5353
E-mail: Info@MOPS.org
Web site: http://www.MOPS.org

To learn how to start a MOPS group,
call 1-888-910-MOPS.
For MOPS products call The MOPShop
1-888-545-4040.

We want to hear from you. Please send your comments about this
book to us in care of the address below. Thank you.

GRAND RAPIDS, MICHIGAN 49530 USA

WWW.ZONDERVAN.COM